S0-AGY-617

Perspectives in European History

No. 5

LAZARE CARNOT: REPUBLICAN PATRIOT

Lazare Carnot

LAZARE CARNOT
Republican Patriot

BY

HUNTLEY DUPRE

PORCUPINE PRESS

Philadelphia 1975

First edition 1940
(Oxford, Ohio: The Mississippi Valley Press, 1940)

Reprinted 1975 by
PORCUPINE PRESS, INC.
Philadelphia, Pennsylvania 19107

Library of Congress Cataloging in Publication Data

Dupre, Huntley, 1892-
Lazare Carnot.

(Perspective in European history ; no. 5)
Reprint of the 1940 ed. published by Mississippi Valley Press, Oxford, Ohio, which was issued as v. 1 of Foundation studies in culture.
Bibliography: p.
Includes index.
1. Carnot, Lazare Nicolas Marguerite, comte, 1753-1823. 2. France--History--Revolution, 1789-1799. 3. France--History--1789-1815. I. Series: Foundation studies in culture ; v. 1.
DC146.C15D8 1975 944.04'092'4 [B] 75-29217
ISBN 0-87991-612-5

Manufactured in the United States of America

PREFACE

For several years now I have been exploring about in the French Revolution. There are characters and forces in that germinal period yet to be reconstructed and interpreted. In this study I have attempted to depict the life and significance of an important figure fortunate enough to live through the Revolutionary and Napoleonic eras and even into the Restoration, though then in exile from his beloved native land. Lazare Carnot is universally known as the "Organizer of Victory," but beyond that most persons know little of him. He has a great deal to offer to the person interested in the period, not because he was an extraordinary Revolutionary figure, which he was not, but because he was a real son of his times, and a truly great Frenchman. I have striven to reveal Carnot as a man, as thinker, as public servant, and as patriot. In doing so, I have left the telling wherever I could to Carnot himself.

Friends too numerous to mention have contributed, in one way or another, to the preparation of this volume. The services of some were so valuable as to call for specific acknowledgment. My debt is great to the late Dean Walter J. Shepard for his unflagging interest in this and every one of my modest endeavors. The memory of my association with him remains the inspiration for my professional life and more. My debt is deep to Professor Edgar H. McNeal for his scholarly stimulation and friendly encouragement; to Professor Carl Wittke for his helpful criticism of the chapters he read in manuscript, and for his sound counsel throughout; to Professor Carlton J. H. Hayes for his graciousness in reading and commenting upon the manuscript, and for the suggestiveness of his scholarship in the field of French nationalism; to Mr. John Weller Brown for the friendship and generosity that contributed materially to my final research in France; to President Frank L. McVey for his friendly interest in the work; to my colleague Professor Thomas D. Clark for his critical reading of the manuscript; to Professor Don L. Demorest, with whom I first came to know France, for helpfulness both here and abroad; to Lieut.-Col. Sadi Carnot, himself a devoted and competent authority on the life and times of his great-grandfather, for his fraternal hospitality in opening the family archives to me, for his graciousness in welcoming me to the ancestral homestead in old Burgundy, for his sincere interest in the progress of the work, and for the understanding of France that he has given me, in conversation and in correspondence; to the Administration of the University of Kentucky for material assistance in getting the manuscript finally in shape; to the authorities of the Archives Nationales, of the Bibliothèque Nationale, of the Archives Historiques du Ministère de la Guerre, of the Bibliothèque de l'Arsenal, in Paris, of the Andrew D. White Collection in the Library of Cornell University, and of the Widener Library of Harvard University, for their many professional courtesies; to the editors, Professor Philip D. Jordan and Charles M. Thomas for a very cordial fellowship and for a very helpful relationship; to Miss Margaret Smith for her faithful and accurate help in the original typing; to Miss Mary Johnston for her efficient stenographic assistance in the final draft; to Miss Roeml Henry for valuable help in proof-reading and in checking bibliography; to my wife for her enduring inspiration, for her criticism of chapter after chapter, and for her very substantial help in proof-reading; to my two sons for their affectionate interest and for their patience.

Huntley Dupre

Lexington, Kentucky.
April 1, 1940.

CONTENTS

Chapter I

THE FASHIONING

LAZARE NICOLAS Marguerite Carnot, "Organizer of Victory" and "republican impenitent"[1] was born in the village of Nolay in the old Duchy of Burgundy, on May 13, 1753.

Burgundy had been rigorously fashioning her children for long centuries before the time of Louis XVI and the French Revolution. North, and west and south from her crest of land flowed the Seine, the Loire and the Saone, through the valleys they served, on their way to the Atlantic and the Mediterranean. Slightly farther to the north, the Meuse, the Marne and the Moselle stemmed from the Langres plateau. These rugged hills, these table lands, and these vineyarded plains had long been the permanent stage for the successive episodes in man's historic drama.

In ancient times, as the Roman power relentlessly pushed northward, Alesia, peopled by a Celtic tribe, the Mandubiens, emerged from its obscurity to become "the last citadel, the supreme refuge"[2] of Gallic independence. Its capitulation in 52 B. C. to the Roman Legions is considered to be Caesar's decisive victory over Vercingterix, and thus of Rome over Gaul, bringing the Graeco-Roman civilization into the north. This Burgundy country was early strategic in the highways of Europe, keeping it ever an important political quantity. The Autun basin, in particular, was a center of Roman roads, and Autun was famed, with Treves, for the making of the weapons used by the Roman forces. Autun was also renowned as an academic center in the time of the Roman dominion. Throughout the Middle Ages and the early centuries of Modern Europe Burgundian political fortunes were significant in the history of France.

The village of Nolay is almost at the tip end of the limestone hills that stretch in a southwesterly direction from Dijon for thirty or thirty-five miles, with fertile plain, and rolling country, and distant hills to the eastward towards the Saone. These slopes, with their open southeasterly exposure to the morning and midday sun, have long and admirably nurtured the vine culture that has been the consistent wealth of the Burgundy country. In October 1763 Tobias Smollett wrote that he "Was very much struck with the sight of large ripe clusters of grapes, entwined with the briars and thorns of common hedges on the wayside. The mountains of Burgundy are covered with vines from the bottom to the top, and seem to be raised by nature on purpose, to extend the surface, and to expose it the more advantageously to the rays of the sun."[3]

On the present road from Dijon to Nolay, through Nuits and Beaune the slopes of the Côte d'Or change again and again from gentleness to perpendicular ruggedness, with naked rock rising starkly beyond verdure and timber in some of the sharp escarpments. The panorama is startlingly beautiful on a clear day. Seven or eight miles before reaching Nolay on the Dijon road the hills close in and are more tangibly rugged. The village nestles among slopes that rise to more than fifteen hundred feet. The country due westward for the twenty miles to Autun flattens out and the valley broadens, until decided hills again prevail around Autun. In the eighteenth century a post road ran from Paris through Sens to Dijon, and thence to Lyons, with fifty-nine posts en route, according to Tobias Smollett. Another post road to Lyons ran through Autun, with an east-west post road from Autun to the Dijon road that must have skirted Nolay, if it did not traverse it.

English travelers in the province of Burgundy in the eighteenth century had mixed impressions of the country. Smollett found the wine weak and thin, but he surmised that the best was reserved for the *noblesse,* or for the foreign market. He remarked on the excellent Burgundy he tasted in Brussels. Smollett was struck by the "three pleasant pastoral rivers, the Seine, the Yonne, and the Saone." He also commented on the "many convents, sweetly situated." "In Burgundy," he writes, "I saw a peasant ploughing the ground with a jack-ass, a lean cow, and a he-goat, yoked together. . . . The peasants in France are so wretchedly poor."[4] "My personal adventures," he went on, "on the road were such as will not bear a recital. They consisted of petty disputes with landladies, post-masters and postillions. The highways seem to be perfectly safe."[5] On his trip north in 1765 he passed through Beaune, where he found nothing good but the wine. He stopped in Dijon, which he called "a venerable old city," only long enough to change horses.

Mrs. Piozzi, in 1784, found the ordinary wine of Burgundy "cool and sharp" and "the country really beautiful," but, "the Inns detestable much beyond what I had any idea of."After rhapsodizing over details of the landscape, she concludes: "Every Town one sees scattered about these lovely Hills and Plains however, shews on a nearer approach misery the more mortifying as less expected by a spectator, who pays at night by lodging in Wretchedness and Dirt, for the Pleasures he has enjoyed in the Day Time, derived from an appearance."[6]

That gentleman farmer, Arthur Young, accustomed to a more advanced agriculture, in early August, 1789, was not much impressed by the country from Dijon to Autun, when he must have at least passed within a few miles of Nolay, if not actually traversing it. He called Nuits a "little insignificant town," and the country from Chagny "a disagreeable country, singular in its features."[7] As he continued his journey, his abbreviated traveler's notes read: "By a miserable country most of the way, and through hideous roads to Autun. The first seven or eight miles the agriculture quite contemptible. From thence to Autun all, or nearly all, enclosed, and the first so for many miles. From the hill before Autun an immense view down on that town, and the flat country of the Bourbonnois for a great extent."[8] But things picked up from Autun westward towards the Loire country. "To Maison de Bourgogne, I thought myself in a new world; the road is not only excellent, of gravel, but the country is enclosed and wooded. There are many gentle inequalities, and several ponds that decorate them."[9]

The discerning Abbé Barthélémy, on a trip to Italy in 1755, remarked: "Some of our journeys have been very tiresome. The one from Auxerre to Dijon, which is two and thirty leagues, was most intolerable. The road passes through a very fine country, but itself is the worst I have ever seen."[10]

This was the countryside that first bred in the boy Lazare Carnot his deep, almost passionate, love of France.

Burgundy was a *pays d'état* in the eighteenth century, with Dijon the capital of the province and the meeting place for the Estates. This city of twenty-one thousand was also the seat of one of the fourteen judicial Parlements of France. Dijon was a great center for religious orders with a score located in the city. Those historic capitals of Christendom, the monasteries of Cluny and Citeaux, were Burgundian foundations, that contributed materially to give a religious tone to the life and thought of the region. The clergy owned about fifteen per cent of the land of Burgundy, the nobility thirty-five per cent, and the peasants possessed about one-third of the soil. Henri Sée has written that the manorial system was oppressive in the vicinity of Autun late in the century.

Evidently a prevalent consciousness in Burgundy of much of all that was anachronistic in the *Ancien Régime,* and a general diffusion of enlightened ideas throughout this relatively prosperous and advanced province combined later to make the subsequent Côte d'Or, known as a "good Jacobin" department.[11]

Legend has it that there were Carnots in the Burgundy country in ancient times. There is some real evidence for direct ancestors of the family in the thirteenth century, and there was a Perrenot Carnot serving as the chatelain of the Duke of Burgundy, in Nolay in 1380. The family tree of the Nolay branch that hangs in the ancestral home in Nolay dates from 1526. The family became a solid, substantial, intelligent bourgeois one. The men ran particularly to the law. Lazare's father was the twentieth "homme de robe" in the family since the sixteenth century. On the paternal side, of seventy-four ancestors since the end of the sixteenth century there were twenty lawyers, notaries or judicial functionaries, four ecclesiastics, five public or private administrators, one officer, three doctors and surgeons, and one painter.

Lazare's great-grandfather Lazare, an *avocat en Parlement,* took for his second wife, Antoinette Durand, sister of Abraham d'Aubigny, plenipotentiary to Holland under Louis XV. By his two wives he had thirteen children. One of the second crop was

Jean, royal notary at Nolay, who sired fourteen children to Anne Moreau. One of these was Claude, father of Lazare-Marguerite.

Claude Carnot was a leading and respected citizen of Nolay. He was an *avocat en Parlement,* royal notary, and local judge. In 1756 he became the trusted and esteemed bailiff of the Duke d'Aumont, Marquis of Nolay, who had an ancestral patrimony adjacent to Nolay, dating back for three hundred years.

The Carnot home in Nolay was the first house on a street running off the square into the country. This comfortable, commodious house was built in 1515. The adjoining house facing the square belonged to the bourgeois Pothier family. When Claude Carnot espoused Marguerite Pothier the two houses were physically united by the building of a door to connect them. In this expanded home were born the eighteen children of this worthy and fecund couple. Fourteen were sons and four were daughters. The mother was twenty years of age when her first and forty-one when her last child was born. The father was six years older than she. Marguerite Carnot died in 1788 at sixty-two, and her husband in 1797, at seventy-eight ripe years. Both lived out their lives in Nolay. Ten of their children died under six years of age, and seven of these within the first year. The two oldest children to live were daughters, the elder becoming a local Sister of the Poor, and the younger the Mother Superior of the Hospital in Nolay. The oldest son to live, Joseph-François, was born in 1752, to become a Counsellor at the Court of Cassation. He had been preceded by six brothers who died in infancy.

In his well-kept Family Book Claude Carnot entered the following record "On Sunday, May 13, 1753, at the close of vespers, at four o'clock, my wife brought a son into the world, who was baptised on that same day by M. Boussey, priest-vicar at Nolay; for godfather he had Nicolas Clement, son of Marie Carnot, my sister, and for godmother, Mademoiselle Marguerite Pothier, daughter of M. Pothier, living at Nolay, uncle of my wife. He was named Lazare-Nicolas-Marguerite. This infant was born in a time of calamity when sudden and frequent deaths afflicted the region, as well as in the whole province. May God thus manifest his anger to him throughout his life, so that he may conduct it with fear, and merit His mercy." The boy was named after a grand uncle who was a learned doctor of the Sorbonne and a vicar general of the diocese of Chalon. Lazare was born in a crimson-canopied bed in the salon on the ground floor, across the hall from the study and office of his father. Shortly after birth he was moved—bed and all—into a spacious bedroom on the second floor.

The period beginning with the year 1752 was decisive for the revolution—already so far advanced in many ways—which was to be visibly precipitated in 1789.[12] In the month between January 20 and February 20 of that year, eight-hundred unfortunates died of hunger in the Faubourg Saint-Antoine. At Rennes, at Bordeaux, in Languedoc, in Guyenne, in Auvergne, in Normandy, there were riots. Troops were dispatched to these centers and the disturbances were soon quelled. The Jacquerie (peasant rebellion) came to life again in the provinces. The monarchy was already decayed to the core. In most respects conditions were worse in 1753 than they were to be in 1789 but the *philosophes* had not yet had time to transform the spirit of the nation. "For well nigh forty years," writes Roustan, "the *philosophes* were to be educating the nation; they were to teach it that it was made up of men, they were to teach it how to reason things out. The moment was to come when it would no longer be possible to quell a riot. Logically, fatally, the riot was to become a revolution."[13]

True, the period of the Enlightenment was well under way, utilizing the intellectual heritage of Montaigne, Descartes, Hobbes, Bayle, Locke, Newton, the Abbe de Saint-Pierre, and others, as well as the social sensibility of men like Vauban. For years before 1753 Voltaire had been expressing "the views and arguments of the average educated man in the most felicitous language, with the most marvelous lucidity, and with the most brilliant wit."[14] But his *Candide* had only appeared in 1751, and his *Siècle de Louis* XIV, in the following year. In 1753 this man who, by his transcendant influence, gave his name to the age, was lingering in Berlin, just before establishing himself in Ferney. Montesquieu's life was running to its end two years later, but his disturbing *magnum opus,* the *Esprit des Lois,* into which had gone twenty years of careful work, had only appeared in 1748, to run through twenty-one editions in eighteen months. Diderot, the versatile and indefatigable editor of the *Encyclopédie,* brought out the first volume of that great solvent in 1751, to have the first volumes suppressed in the following year by the Government as containing maxims hostile to royal authority and to the church. This was soon revoked and the work, contributed to by most of the able minds of the period, went on relentlessly. In 1749 DuPin had published his *Mémoire Sur les Bleds,* the first plea for free trade in grain in France. Cantillon's *Essai sur la Nature du Commerce*, was to appear in 1755, followed in the next year by the Marquis de Mirabeau's *L'Ami des Hommes*, and by Quesnay's important *Tableau Économique,* printed at Versailles at the royal press in 1758. The Abbe Morelly's *Code de la Nature* was to come in 1756. In this significant year, 1753, Rousseau revealed the germs of his thought in his *Discourse on the Origin of Inequality*, which were to be modified and elaborated in his *Contrat Social*, seven years later.

When Lazare Carnot was born, Condorcet was a child of ten, Tom Paine was a youth of seventeen, and Roland was nineteen. Louis XVI, Talleyrand, and the future Madame Roland were born in the year after Carnot, and Barras in the following year. Robespierre saw the light of day in 1758 and Danton in 1759. Babeuf, the future Madame de Staël, Saint Just and Bonaparte were still nestling in the womb of time, to make their appearances in 1764, 1766, 1767 and 1769. Thus the actors gradually assembled.

Claude Carnot, father of Lazare, read widely in the critical literature of the day. The well-stocked shelves in his office-library attest to the breadth and quality of his intellectual and public interests. He also seems to have known men and affairs well. No doubt the ideas generally current among the literate in the "Enlightenment" were the intellectual stock in trade in this respected bourgeois family living in its tiny Burgundian village.

There was a fine, but restrained and well-regulated affection in the Carnot household. The father was severe with his children but it is evident that he instructed them wisely in the home. His wife thought him to be the most perfect of husbands, but she was inclined to be jealous of him. She worshipped her family, and her eldest son once said that her family was a second cult for her. Lazare's intimate in the family was the brother two years younger than he, later called Carnot Feulins. These two brothers became inseparables. Both were military engineers and both pursued somewhat parallel political careers. When they married, they united with sisters. A brother, Claude-Marguerite, between these two, became *Procureur-Imperial* at Chalon. Jean-François-Reine, 1760-1829, succeeded his father as royal notary, and became the mayor of Nolay. The youngest brother to live, Gabriel-Bernard-Jean, 1767-1826, became an Inspecteur des Domaines. This well-knit provincial family grew up in mutual respect and affection. One can recapture something of the character and intimacy of that life in viewing the children's toys that were so lovingly laid by by the parents, and so pridefully preserved by their descendants. The shoes of the members of the family—some wooden—and for all the members and at all ages—that repose now so mutely in an anteroom still speak vividly of running feet, laughing voices and parental solicitude.

Following the instruction which he received at home from his father, the young Carnot studied with the local masters, Masson and Boisson, successively the regents of the tiny *collège* of Nolay. These two were excellent Latin scholars, and took Carnot as far as the second class in Latin rhetoric. The boy was known in the village as "studious and reflective." He had a deep love of nature and spent much time exploring the rugged countryside. At the age of ten his mother rewarded him for his "thoughtful docility" by taking him with her on a trip to Dijon. While there they attended a spectacle, which included a review of troops, during which the boy, rapt in attention and unselfconscious, rose to audibly criticize the placement of the artillery in a military manoeuvre. His mother was embarrassed at the confusion and amusement raised in the hall by her son's remarks.[15]

At the age of fourteen, Lazare, with his older brother, was lodged with a Madame Gondier, in Autun, and enrolled in the Collège d'Autun for the study of the classics. The Oratoriens had recently succeeded the Jesuits in the governance of this excellent *Collège*. At the time, of course, elementary and secondary education in France was almost exclusively in the hands of the various orders of the church. After the suppression and expulsion of the Jesuits in 1762, the Oratoriens took the lead in the instruction offered in the thirty *collèges* scattered throughout France.[16] It is quite evident that the Oratoriens were liberal innovators in education in the eighteenth century. They took the lead in introducing the study of the French language and literature and in the simplification of the study of Latin. In addition to the improved study of the classics, this order introduced and emphasized the teaching of geography, history, mathematics, and science. The Oratoriens also warmly supported the philosophy of Descartes. Many of the Fathers of this order were versifiers and they stimulated the poetical aptitudes of their pupils. It is possible that Carnot's tastes in this direction were cultivated in the Collège d'Autun under the inspiration of some one of the teaching Fathers.

Despite the attacks levelled against the teaching of the classics and the classical languages during the century, the Oratoriens continued to emphasize these. However, this order did not exclusively teach the classics, as was true in many quarters, but it supplemented them by a much broader curriculum than had hitherto existed. A perusal of the plan of studies of the Oratoriens for 1745[17] reveals how central was the place of Cicero, Cato, Ovid, Virgil, Caesar, Terence, St. Chrysostome, Sallust, Livy, Tacitus, Suetonius, Horace, Seneca, Juvenal, Demosthenes, Homer, Pindar, Sophocles, Euripides, and other literary and history-writing figures of ancient Greece and Rome. Erasmus and Comenius were also given an important place.

Carnot was thoroughly absorbed in the study of classical antiquity. This was common for his class in the period.[18] There is no doubt that this discipline and this taste date from the years which he spent in the Collège d'Autun. It was particularly easy to become absorbed in the classics in Autun because of the Roman history of the town and the presence of so many relics of Roman civilization. Later on in life Carnot translated a great deal from the Latin for his own pleasure and profit. His political speeches and writings are replete with classical references and allusions that reveal a thorough familiarity with the history of Greece and Rome.[19]

His feelings for a common humanity, his leanings towards a universal principle of justice and right, and his theory of natural rights bear testimony to his close study of the Stoic philosophy. The natural tendency of the period to idealize and glorify ancient Greece and Rome was characteristic of Carnot. Dissatisfied with their own society, the educated of the period looked back to the model of an earlier one, in order to sketch a new order for themselves.

After leaving the school of the Oratoriens at the age of fifteen Carnot studied philosophy under the Sulpiciens at the Seminary in Autun. Here he studied logic under the Abbé Bisson, who also taught mathematics and the elements of theology. An attack of small-pox at this time was short-lived due to the care of his landlady and of a certain doctor, Lhomme. In 1768 he passed a brilliant public examination conducted in Latin, declining the usual assistance of his masters in the defense of his thesis, and in the face of learned objections presented by a public auditor, Madame Lhomme, the wife of his physician. At this time the boy was so devout that certain of his relatives suggested holy orders for him.

At this moment, however, the Duke d'Aumont, Marquis de Nolay, intervened and recommended a military career for the young Carnot, offering to intercede with the Ministry of War so that the recent ordinance limiting admissions to the engineering corps to the nobility could be waived. The Duke was informed that in lieu of noble blood in the family, relatives or ancestors who were or had been officers would suffice. Six such, starting in the year 1576, were offered. Finally, in December, 1769, the authorization for the examination arrived in Nolay. It was first necessary to repair to Paris for the preparation, in one of the two schools there, that prepared for the entrance examinations for the schools in engineering, artillery and the marine.

Claude Carnot accompanied his son to La Rochepot, where he would catch the post from Lyon to Auxerre and Paris. On separating he gave his son a letter for the Duke d'Aumont, in whose pretentious establishment Lazare was to stop temporarily, and another containing certain paternal injunctions. These reveal both father and son. "On all occasions, towards all persons and towards yourself, maintain yourself properly, decently and honestly. Speak as little as possible. . . . Speak well of everyone. . . . Work unceasingly and without vanity or pride. Observe those who have the best demeanor and imitate them. Do not listen to flatteries, no matter from what source. . . . An honest modesty wins respect for one. . . . Direct the conversation, promptly and adroitly, to whatever good there is to say. . . . Be gracious to domestics; they are the ones who best characterize the ones they serve. . . . Guard very carefully against leaning back in your chair at the table. This reveals the poorest kind of bringing up."[20]

Carnot first stopped in the residence of the Duke d'Aumont, in the rue de Beaune, Faubourg Saint-Germain, where the Duke's excellent housekeeper, Madame Delorme, who had managed the household since the death of the Duchess in 1753, treated him like a son. The Duke's intendant, M. Ogé occupied himself with the boy's affairs. This agent of the boy's benefactor was frequently writing to Claude Carnot concerning the boy's progress. It was he who arranged for Carnot to be one of the current eleven boys in M. de Longpré's pension-school. The price for a year's instruction was thirteen hundred livres for room, lodging, and instruction in mathematics. In addition the pupil had to furnish wood and light, pay the drawing master twelve francs a month, and pay the barber and the laundress. In the letter announcing these "dear" expenses, M. Ogé commented: "Your son hopes that the sacrifice that you must make will not be too onerous; this reflection reflects his honesty."[21] The father's decision was in the affirmative and on February 21, 1770, Lazare entered the school of M. de Longpré. The father had instructed M. Ogé to let the boy himself have the custody of a certain sum for incidental expenses. In the first elimination examinations for the military schools, given that spring, Carnot ranked but in the twelfth grouping, with this notation: "Shows a great deal of intelligence; only knows his course superficially. He is very young. Design: the figure of a hermit, very badly executed in every respect."

During his first eighteen months in this private school the

youth systematically studied theology largely under his own direction and under the compulsion of his own conscience and doubts. He suffered the ridicule of his classmates because of his piety. He ended this period of search by discarding theological works forever and by adopting the prevalent ideas of deism. He retained, however, a deep respect for the holy books of Christianity. His son noted much later that "as to his religious principles, these were based upon a deism freed of all mythology, and upon a considered confidence in immortality."[22] The boy kept up his reading in the critical literature of the day.

Jean Jacques Rousseau was stopping at the time in Paris in the Rue Platrière with M. Venant. The young Carnot, with an equally enamoured comrade, sought out the temperamental sage on the first day of their first holiday. Just exactly when, where and how Carnot became acquainted with the writings of Rousseau is not known. No doubt the acquaintance was naturally made in the home at Nolay where the *philosophes* were well known. Rousseau, on the day the boys presented themselvs, was found to be in such a state of moroseness and ill-humour that he sent them scampering. This rebuff which the two lads received at the hands of the sage was evidently not enough to prejudice the mind of the somewhat stubborn Carnot, for the influence of the Savoyard Vicar is clearly marked in the matured ideas of the man, Carnot, although he followed an independent line, and was skeptical concerning the religious ideas of the Genevan.[23] Near the end of his life, while in exile in Magdebourg, Carnot, among other recorded reflections, made some sympathetic, though critical, "Notes on the Works of J. J. Rousseau."[24] Another of the *philosophes* was more sympathetic to the impressionable pupils of the school. D'Alembert, an intimate of M. de Longpré, frequented the school of his friend, and in his contacts with the youths he delighted in drawing out the responsive Carnot. Undoubtedly the thinker, with his flair for mathematics, was attracted by the like interests and talents of the boy.

In August, 1770 M. Ogé reported to the father that Lazare had been working too hard but that recently he had lightened up and was enjoying himself more with his comrades. He added that he had prescribed milk in the spring, "for his chest which is delicate." In September he reported that the boy looked well, although he had lost some weight. In December he reported excellent progress in the boy's studies. In February, 1771, after having been the third highest among the twelve chosen in a class of one hundred and fifteen taking the examination, Carnot was appointed as a second lieutenant to the engineering school at Mézières. He was then eighteen years of age. The examiners said of him: "An excellent prospect, very intelligent, knows his course excellently. . . . Design: head of Jason, very well executed." On the thirteenth of February he left for Mézières, a fact which M. Ogé reported to the father as follows: "He wanted to arrive among the first in order to prove his zeal and in order to secure a better lodging. . . . He was very modest in his personal belongings, and only asked for those things that were indispensable. . . . He does not want to be a further charge upon you. . . . I congratulate you on having a son so reasonable and so promising."

In the engineering school Carnot studied assiduously and well and, incidentally, became fascinated by Caesar's *Commentaries*. The students were assumed to have had enough arithmetic, geometry and mechanics in the preparatory school. At Mézières the first year was devoted to hydraulics, to the preparation of stone and wood, to the resistance of materials, to geometrical designing, and to geography. During the second year the entire time was spent on fortifications in all of their details. On January 1, 1773, Carnot left the school as a first lieutenant, bound on a round of garrison duty. In the following year, his younger brother Carnot Feulins, was admitted to the engineering school at Mézières.

Chapter II

APPRENTICESHIP

CARNOT'S FIRST station in a long round of garrison duty was at Calais, where the Prince de Croy had his headquarters as the governor-general of Picardy. Here and subsequently Carnot was considered by his fellow officers to be "an original fellow, or a philosopher,"[1] because he diligently read Thucydides, Polybius and Caesar. Napoleon, much later, directly attested to this estimate.[2] This characterization was perhaps more of a commentary on his lazy and class-minded fellows than upon any profound philosophical tendencies of his own. Of the latter there is little evidence. That he was a genuine student of classical antiquity and a sensitive observer of the contemporary scene there can be no doubt. It is interesting to record that this somewhat lonely figure began his writing of poetry in this first garrison at Calais.

Carnot's younger brother, later dubbed Carnot Feulins to distinguish the two, joined him at Calais for the purpose of being prepared for the engineering school at Mézières. This was, no doubt, a pleasant experience for the congenial brothers. That the instruction was successful in the willing and talented subject was demonstrated by the brilliant way in which the younger Carnot passed the competitive entrance examinations in 1774.

Robespierre and Carnot first met in Arras. After rounds of duty in Havre, Béthune and Aire, Carnot was assigned for military duty to Arras. In 1780 he became a member of the local literary and singing "Société des Rosati," a group dedicated to Chapelle, La Fontaine and Chanlieu, where one sang of "the Rose, Wine and Love."[3] This society had been founded in 1778 by the *aimable* advocate, Le Gay. Two years after Carnot's installation, Robespierre, on his return from his legal studies in Paris, became a member. Carnot's apologist, his son, reports that the two were but casual acquaintances and that the "Incorruptible" failed to make a significant impression upon the young officer.[3] There is evidence, however, that the two members were friends and met frequently in the home of a mutual friend.[4] The last couplet of one of the original creations which Robespierre sang at the society speaks of "friend Carnot."[5] Political matters were not discussed in this congenial and convivial society. The member Le Gay, after soliciting the friendly but unsuccessful help of Carnot for a publisher in 1784, published a volume two years later containing a section entitled "Selections read or sung under the rose arbor," and headed by a motto written by Carnot. Several of Carnot's songs appeared in contemporary collections, particularly in the *Almanach des Muses.* At a later date his fellow-Burgundian and fellow-officer, Prieur, composed the music for his elegies and verses.

In 1783, the year he was named captain, Carnot published his first work anonymously. This was an *Essay on Machines in General,* by an engineering officer, in which appeared a new theory on the loss of force. In the following year, immediately after the title page of his *Eulogy of Vauban,* appeared an advertisement acknowledging authorship as follows: "One can procure at the same publisher, a book by the same author, entitled: *An Essay on Machines in General,* a work which has merited the praise of the Academy of Sciences in Paris." The treatise was republished over Carnot's name in 1787, and was amplified and published in 1803 under the title *Equilibrium and Movement.*

Robespierre preceded his colleague into the Academy of Arras, being elected to it on November 15, 1783, and publicly inducted into it on April 21, 1784. Three years later, on May 25, 1787, Carnot was welcomed into the academy. At his reception he read a discourse upon "The Power of Habit," which was applauded by the young lawyer.[6]

The young engineer's first outstanding public effort in writing was a professional essay on Vauban which won the first prize from the Academy of Dijon in its contest of 1784. The Academy of Sciences, Arts and Belles-Lettres of Dijon owed its existence to a legacy of Hector-Bernard Pouffier, dean of the Parlement of Burgundy, who died in 1736, the letters patent for the foundation being granted in 1740, and the formal opening of the academy occurring in 1741. Contests were to be held in successive years for essays in the fields of the physical sciences, medicine, and literature and public morality. The prize in each instance was a gold medal. Rousseau won the prize in 1750 when the problem presented was "Whether the progress of the sciences and the arts has contributed to refine customs and morals?" In that year, devoted to the literary contest, there were thirteen competitors. In 1781 two prizes were announcd for the literary contest, for eulogies on Vauban and Saumaise. No one of the five submitted on Vauban was deemed worthy of the prize. The Academicians decided at the time to announce that subject again for the prize of 1784, which would accordingly be doubled in value. Five essays were presented in 1784 and on July 1 a commission of eight recommended that the prize be awarded to the essay then discovered to have been written by Carnot, on the condition that he make certain minor corrections and combine the first two of the three parts into which the essay was divided. The commission reported that the author's style was "noble, precise, vigorous."[7] "One discerns," the commission's recommendation continued, "in his treatment many eloquent passages, and particularly a considerable number of new and profound ideas, forcefully expressed." It was also noted that "this eulogy is followed by notes which do honor to the knowledge and to the patriotism of the author."

This prize-winning essay was read before the Academy by Carnot, who happened to be in Nolay on leave, on August 2, 1784, in the presence of Prince Henry of Prussia. The Prince of Condé, governor-general of the province, awarded the prize to Carnot. Second prize went to Maret, later the Duc de Bassano. The two gold medals, which had a value of three-hundred livres were immediately loaned to a financially-embarrassed distant relative, the Chevalier de Gaigne, who used them as security. When they came back to Carnot he preserved them faithfully through the storms of the Revolution and carried them into exile as souvenirs of his youth.

Prince Henry presided at the session of the Academy on August 14 and complimented the prize-winner. In fact he was so impressed by Carnot that he, unsuccessfully, offered him a higher rank in the Prussian army.

Carnot's *Eulogy* stands as a point of departure for his career in politics and in engineering. Sebastien Le Prestre De Vauban (1633-1707) was of a type to challenge the attention of Carnot. The two had kindred minds. Vauban, too, was a native of the ancient Duchy of Burgundy. His father was "one of the poorest gentlemen of France."[8] Vauban, left an orphan at the age of ten, developed and retained a profound sympathy for the oppressed and unprivileged masses.[9] By sheer ability he rose to be director-general of fortifications and Marshal of France in the armies of Louis XIV. It has been said that "it was by the constant practice of the highest virtues that he achieved the very summit in the official hierarchy."[10] He revolutionized the art of fortifications and instituted modern methods of mining fortified places. His technical treatises and achievements established the modern bases of defense. The current phrase of his day was "town besieged by Vauban, town taken; town defended by Vauban, town impregnable." The engineering corps in the royal army was his creation. He also founded the order of Saint-Louis which brought its wearers a pension. Carnot earned this distinction on the eve of the Revolution. Vauban had a reformer's cast of mind.[11] The last twenty years of his life were devoted largely to his economic and political researches. He spent a considerable amount of money in this work, and employed a considerable staff to collect data. Almost alone among prominent persons he vigorously opposed the Revocation of the Edict of Nantes and in a letter to Louvois enumerated the evil consequences to France of the persecution and emigration of the Hoguenots. He favored the practice of religious toleration. He favored internal free trade on canals, a codification of the laws, the standardization of weights and measures, and proposed that the noble class be open to merit as well as to birth. In his economic thinking he was influenced by Boisguillebert, intendant of the diocese of Rouen, who had written on taxation in a reforming spirit in *Le Détail de la France*. In 1698 Vauban began his *Projet d'une Dixième royale* which proposed the equalization of taxation upon all classes, by the imposition of a single tax, the so-called *dîme royale*, levied both upon the land and upon commerce and industry. This critical, almost revolutionary, work was not published until 1707. Its appearance brought its author into disfavor with the King, and the treatise was immediately suppressed by royal order. This blow evidently hastened the death of the patriot, loyal alike to nation and to King. Saint-Simon called Vauban "perhaps the most honest and the most virtuous man of his century . . . the simplest, the truest, the most modest."

Through his depiction of Vauban, his hero, one catches revelations of Carnot, himself, in his prize-winning essay. His opening words strike the note for the general treatment: "At the very name of Vauban patriotism awakens, the soul is aroused to noble thoughts, the sensitive heart is moved, at one and the same time, to heroism and to the tender emotion which embraces humanity."[12] The younger patriot speaking of the older wrote that "the love of the Fatherland captivated and subjugated him."[13] Near the conclusion he wrote: "Our hearts are the Temple where the sacred fire of patriotism is never extinguished."[14] Their temperamental likeness as public figures was sympathetically foreshadowed in these words, "Vauban could never succeed in the art of intrigue or of adulation."[15] The mathematician shines forth when Carnot eulogizes Mathematics, particularly geometry, of which he writes: "It is a science—simple, exact, luminous, profound, sublime."[16] In almost poetical terms he described the mission of the engineer-inventor. Carnot proceeded to develop the metaphysical aspects of higher Mathematics, indicating their debt to imagination more than to study. He ended by glorifying the rôle of the imaginative genius who conceives new geometrical combinations in a multitude of forms. In Vauban he found a man willing to criticize the errors of the past and fearless enough to hazard innovations. The young engineer elaborated the technical reforms that emanated from the mind of his illustrious model. With complete accord Carnot wrote of Vauban: "He recognized this fundamental truth that, no matter from what point of view one considers fortresses, they are always in the last analysis, uniquely destined to reduce the *consommation* of men, and wherever they do not fulfill this purpose, they are superfluous."[17] He also commends Vauban for not adhering to any fixed absolutes for the art of fortification for "good sense suffices for knowing the true principles, which the engineers are to apply with intelligence."[18]

Having treated Vauban as a military figure, Carnot turned to eulogize him as a citizen, as a philanthropic man of the state, who lived before his time and prepared for it. He quoted Vauban as having said in his youth: "I have received much from nature, I owe a great deal to society, and I can have no rest so long as I can serve the state."[19] Work, he called "a contribution which it is not permitted man to get rid of."[20] Carnot revealed the sensitivity and the social thought of Vauban, as follows: "Vauban intimately saw the extreme misery of the country; he loved the people. Then what! Is misfortune inseparable with virtue? Ah! let us banish this oppressive idea! Misfortune is not exclusively associated with poverty; it is often the effect of the pride and of the passions that wealth carries along with it."[21] Vauban's treatise on the *Dîme royale,* Carnot called, "a simple and pathetic exposé of the facts."[22] "Vauban," he wrote, "sought for the source of disorder, and he found it in the excessive inequality of fortunes, in a disturbing multitude of employments without function, in the barbarous division of taxation and in the even more barbarous manner of their collection."[23] "But the number of citizens," he proceeded, "is proportional to the sum of their united useful labors. What then is the object of Government if not to oblige all individuals in the state to work? And how determine this, if not by transferring riches from those where they are superfluous to those where they are necessary, by giving to the ones the means of working, and by depriving the others of the means of remaining idle?"[24] . . . "Thus thought the Marshal Vauban; . . . that the Government ought establish a kind of equilibrium between the citizens, or at least prevent the frightful misery of some, and the excessive opulence of others, and the odious multiplicity of privileges which condemns the class made up of the most precious persons to indigence and contempt."[25] Carnot added that Vauban "thought that the morality of nations should be the same as that of individuals."[26] Vauban, Carnot wrote, "lived too long; he saw the beginning of the abuses that afflicted the country. . . . Vauban saw the people dismayed, the finances exhausted, the Government without force or resolution."[27] Carnot's sympathetic estimate of Vauban was that "This century is not yet philosophical enough for his dreams to be realized. Oh! How rare it is that the sage can harvest the fruit of his efforts! He outruns his century, and his language is only understood by posterity."[28] The maturing convictions of this young engineer are evident in these sincere and glowing pages that trace the career and the ideas of this precursor of the Revolution. When, in recognition, the heart of Vauban was transferred to the church of the Invalides on May 26, 1808, Carnot delivered a Eulogy.

Carnot's *Éloge* had a wide enough audience to call for felicitation and criticism. Buffon wrote to encourage the young engineer. Choderlos de Laclos, the author of the well-known romance, *Les Liaisons dangereuses*, vigorously attacked Carnot's favorable estimate of Vauban, in a memorial that took the form of a "Lettre à messieurs de l'Académie française." In his reply Carnot launched out with a polemical verve that evidenced another literary means at his disposal. In it he paid tribute incidentally to Montesquieu in a way that indicated a natural enough familiarity with this early political scientist and sociologist. A more serious attack by the Marquis de Montalembert in a critical edition of the *Éloge,* published anonymously in 1786, created far-reaching and unsuspected complications for the young engineer. In the meantime Carnot, ever receptive to new scientific ideas, had gotten into the current discussion on aerostatics by addressing a *Mémoire détaillé sur les ballons* to the Académie des Sciences, on January 17, 1784, in which he revealed a sympathetic and optimistic interest in air navigation. The Académie referred this Mémoire to one of its most illustrious members, Meunier, with whom Carnot thereafter had the most cordial relations.

Military tactics and strategy were increasingly debated in professional circles in France after the defeats suffered by French arms in the Seven Years War. Some substantial reforms were made in the years just before the Revolution.[29] On its very eve a vigorous battle raged between the various branches of the army, centering around the number and kind of fortifications essential for the defense of France. A separate engineering corps was relatively new in the military system of France and its prestige was slight. Its leading officers therefore were jealous for the corps and proud of the achievements of their greatest figures, Vauban and M. de Cormontaigne, who they believed had said the last word on the art of fortfications. The Comte de Guibert, *rapporteur* of the Council of War at the moment, took the lead in the attack upon the necessity of fortifications. He was an admirer and advocate of the Prussian tactics, and had a great disdain for fortifications. In his *Essai général de tactique* he had treated the engineering corps in a cavalier fashion. Under his influence, in 1788, a *Collection of Memoirs on the excessive quantity of Strongholds existing in France* was officially published. These were erroneously announced as extracts of the manuscripts of Marshall Vauban, thus attributing to the great constructor of fortresses, the origin of the scheme for their reduction. The real purpose of the publication was, under the pretext of economizing men and money, to increase the regular army by dismantling a number of fortresses. This proposal naturally aroused many of the engineering officers. D'-Arçon, friend of M. de Fourcroy, chief of the engineering Corps, was one of these, having already opposed M. de Guibert's championship of Prussian tactics. D'Arçon was aggressive and resorted to personalities in his polemical writing.

Carnot soon entered the lists against M. de Guibert, taking a more objective and moderate line than d'Arçon. As early as January 3, 1788, he proposed a special concourse to the Academy of Dijon, of which he had become a non-resident associate on August 19, 1784, on the subject: "Is it necessary that there be fortresses on the frontiers of the kingdom of France?" He stated that this was a most timely theme because of the agitation to demolish many fortresses as being too expensive. In his proposal Carnot said that, on the other hand, there were many persons "who regarded fortresses as the safety of the state, and as a powerful means of economy."[30] The academy agreed to the suggestion, changing the word "necessary" to "advantageous," in the title. Two *Mémoires* were presented between January 29 and April 2, 1789, and the one with the epigraph "Strongholds of War are the anchors of security, which in times of distress preserve states," was declared the winner. The author had not signed his name and efforts to discover him through publicity were unavailing.

In August 1788 Carnot addressed to the Minister of War, Comte de Brienne, a "Memoire presented to the Council of War on the subject of the fortresses that ought to be destroyed or abandoned, or an examination of this question: Is it advantageous to the King of France to have strongholds on the frontiers of his Kingdom?" Carnot and d'Arçon were agreed that the French were better qualified temperamentally for attack than for defense. The eternal question with Carnot was how to "transform defense in such a way as to utilize best the military qualities of a soldier essentially apt for attack." In this *Mémoire*[31] Carnot pled that all national efforts be directed to the security of the frontiers. He spoke of the active and the passive forces to be utilized in defense against an enemy. The first consisted of men, the second of inanimate objects such as natural and artificial fortifications, that men can use for protection. Wherever possible, he said, passive forces should be used because this is to "use machines in order to economize human strength, to replace force by industry, and to compel the enemy to oppose walls and earthworks with men. . . . United to the active forces, these forces multiply the effect of the former; they serve as the support that doubles their energy and releases their resources into activity." He called fortresses "monuments of peace," since they permitted a considerable reduction in the regular army, thus restoring a great many young men to peacetime productive labor. From an even larger point of view he wrote: "But the principle in the name of humanity is that when a fortress is lost it is merely the work of men that is gone, while when a battle is lost the men themselves are gone."

Carnot also proposed a fundamental reorganization of the army. He suggested that of the three hundred thousand men composing it but one-third should be on duty at any one time, for a period of twelve to eighteen months, rotating with the other thirds, during their common term of service. He also proposed the abolition of the militia and that the parishes be made responsible for the replacement of recruits in the army.

In this *Mémoire* Carnot combined general political discussion with the technical treatment. His general position was revealed when he wrote "War is the art of conserving; the art of destruction is its abuse. . . . Every just war, every war which merits the name, is essentially defensive." He criticised rulers for invoking divine sanction for their wars of aggression, and in no uncertain terms he protested against wars of conquest. "If there is a country in Europe," he wrote, "whose particular interest is in accord on this point (the laws of equity and natural religion) with the principles of this universal morality, of this great political philosophy which considers all nations as parts of the same humanity, it is undoubtedly France." Thus this military engineer reveals his absorption in the ideas of the *philosophes* which were the current stock in trade of the literate, sensitive bourgeoisie. His ideas also attest his familiarity with the central theses of the Stoics in Ancient Greece and Rome.

Carnot proceeded to remark "Into what horrible desolation this kingdom is plunged every time it succumbs to ambition and to the mania for conquest." He became more explicit: "What trouble in all of Europe and what misfortunes in France the haughtiness and ambition of Louis XIV caused! The provinces that he conquered cost four times what they would have had he bought them outright." He concluded the document with a stirring appeal to Louis XVI to take the lead in the military reforms he had suggested, and in maintaining the tranquillity of Europe, so that "sweet peace descend from the skies; that it repose over France; that it cover the nations with its wings." Twenty years later, in his *Défense des Places*, commissioned by Napoleon, Carnot was repeating the same general principles.

The Marquis de Montalembert, after a distinguished active career in the army in the wars of the century, had turned to writing on the art of fortification, in which task he revealed himself as a reformer. When Carnot's *Éloge de Vauban* appeared, this seasoned warrior was already in the ripe age of three score years and ten. As it became apparent that he was departing from the principles of Vauban, the caste-spirit of the engineering corps was roused to defend the master, and although Montalembert was permitted to conduct some experiments in fortifications.

he was forbidden to publish his system. After fifteen years of secrecy he published in 1776-1778 the first volumes of *La Fortification perpendiculaire*. Eleven volumes ultimately appeared over a twenty year period, concluded in 1796. The seventh volume was published in 1788 as his answer to M. de Fourcroy. According to his system fortresses were to be made impregnable by a series of casemates, one over the other, each of which would contain powerful batteries. In fact, his fortress has been aptly described as an "immense battery." Montalembert abandoned the intricacies of trace developed by Vauban and Cormontaigne designed to minimize the power of attack, in favor of a simple tenaille plan arranged so that the defenders could bring an overwhelming fire to bear on the works of the besieger. The "polygonal" method of fortification is thus the direct outcome of Montalembert's system. As he developed his method it was vigorously attacked by the engineering corps. He secured permission, however, from the Minister of War, the Prince de Montbarry, to erect a model fort, constructed of wood, on the island d'Aix. The demonstration there, in the presence of a great number of French and foreign officers, was very successful. The hue and cry increased.

M. de Fourcroy, the chief of the engineering corps, was in his seventy-first year. He was a zealous traditionalist whose professional cult included the tenet "the science of fortifications is infallible." To him Vauban was the law and the prophets. Fourcroy took the lead in the battle against the proposed reforms. In 1786 the adversaries of Montalembert, who was not an engineer, issued a *Mémoire sur la fortification perpendiculaire*, addressed to the Academy of Science, and "written by several officers of engineering." The prime spirits in the publication were M. de Fourcroy, the Major Grenier, long in retirement, and a much younger officer, M. de Frescheville.

The aroused Montalembert took this occasion to publish anonymously in the same year an edition of the *Éloge de Vauban*, with critical notes attacking Carnot's treatment of Vauban's principles of military engineering. He evidently believed that Carnot was one of the authors of the engineers' attack upon his system, and resorted to this means of retaliation. In 1787 Montalembert specifically singled Carnot out as implicated in his vehement direct reply to the *Mémoire*.

Carnot, in the meantime, had informed himself thoroughly on the ideas of Montalembert. Despotic control was such in the various branches of the army that an officer could not publish anything professional without it going through the hands of his superiors. Carnot made himself liable to discipline on this score by addressing a letter to Montalembert with the request that it be published. The latter used it as the preface to his *Réponse au Mémoire sur la Fortification perpendiculaire*. In this letter,[32] Carnot after disclaiming any connections with the attacks on the system of Montalembert announced that he found the method "so estimable, so full of genius, that I have given it due justice whenever the occasion has arisen . . . having no other purpose in mind than to recognize the truth and to see light prevail, no matter from what quarter it shines forth. . . . Now that your casemates are known and proven, fortification will take on a new aspect and become a new art. It will no longer be permitted to fortify without them, nor to employ the revenues of the state to construct the mediocre when one can build the good; to you alone belongs the honor. . . . It is certain that you have resolved the problem so long and so fruitlessly sought for, that of securing a protected fire, in great quantity and easy to execute." Carnot went on to caution against a closed mind on the finality of details in the new system, while recognizing that its fundamental principles would have henceforth to serve as the base of the defensive system of France. He assured Montalembert that there were many in the engineering corps who recognized as their "colleague, chief and benefactor," whoever "extends our knowledge, and whoever presents new means of being useful to our country." In reply Montalembert withdrew his criticisms of the *Éloge de Vauban*.[33] Carnot's superiors, however, were furious at these direct and friendly communications between Carnot and the detested Montalembert, and looked about for some adequate means of revenge for his breach of regulations and for his disloyalty to the service. The most that could be secured was a *lettre de cachet*, on the pretext of an "absent without leave" and the challenge to a duel on the part of Carnot occasioned by a rivals' quarrel over the hand of a young lady of Dijon. Carnot was *embastillé* for a time in the chateau de Béthune.

The young lady in question was Ursule de Bouillet, the younger daughter of the Chevalier Bouillet, a prominent citizen of Dijon, whose relations with the Carnot family were cordial and longstanding. Among her intimates this daughter was known as Nanette. Her father was favorably disposed to a marriage between Nanette and Carnot. The latter frequently dined with the Bouillets where he was considered as one of the family. He would stop with his brother, Joseph, then an advocate before the Parlement of Dijon. The Chevalier corresponded with Carnot in a friendly, even playful, fashion, with frequent references to Carnot's beloved. Nanette carried on a regular correspondence with Carnot and wore his picture in a locket.

Affairs dragged on for three years without the marriage being consummated. M. de Bouillet was evidently not satisfied with the terms of the negotiations between the heads of the two families. In any case, while Carnot was in garrison in Artois, Bouillet, suddenly and without notice, published a notice of the forthcoming marriage eight days later of his daughter, Nanette, with a fairly wealthy young infantry officer, Bichot-Morel de Duesme. Joseph Carnot sent word immediately to his brother, who left his garrison post haste, without delaying to secure a leave of absence, arriving in Dijon on the very day of the marriage, at five o'clock in the morning. He informed his fiancée of his arrival and for reply received word that "affairs were too far advanced" for reconsideration. Without reflection, Carnot then rushed off to his rival's lodging, finding him still in bed. He was unwilling to retire in Carnot's favor, and the latter immediately challenged him to a duel. M. Bichot-Morel then seemed willing to reconsider if Carnot could prove the intimacy of his relations with Mlle. Bouillet. Carnot produced letters from her for this purpose. His rival requested these in order to show them to his uncle, M. Pasquier, a local magistrate. Carnot consented on his rival's word of honor that no one else would see them. The uncle, however, broadcast the contents of the letters, causing a considerable tempest throughout the town. Carnot immediately wrote to Bouillet, offering to repair the harm he had unwittingly done to his daughter, fully explaining the circumstances. M. Bouillet did not reply but laid a complaint before M. de La Tour du Pin, commandant of the province. The latter had Carnot appear before him, and secured all of the letters from Nanette to Carnot. His efforts to get Bouillet to terminate the affair were unavailing. The latter got his brother-in-law Calon, who had a position in Paris at Court, to use his influence for a *lettre de cachet*, which was forthcoming. Ursule Bouillet was married subsequently, but not to the young infantry officer.

The Minister of War, M. de Puységur, only discovered the imprisonment when he wanted to designate Carnot as the guide for Prince Henry of Prussia, who had returned to France and desired to visit the fortresses in the Nord that had been constructed by Vauban. The Minister had Carnot released immediately, directing severe castigations at Calon. Carnot's release was the occasion for official rejoicing in the town of Béthune, where he was stationed at the time and where he was well liked. The town was illuminated and the commandant gave a dinner in his honor. On June 5, 1789, Carnot wrote to the Minister to thank him for his intervention on his behalf. In his "Protest against the oppressive régime under which the engineering corps is governed," addressed to the National Assembly from garrison at Béthune, on September 28, 1789, he attributed his imprisonment to the jealously and rancour of his superiors in the engineering corps, because of his partisanship for the principles of Montalembert.

On September 28, 1789, still smarting from his imprisonment but moved likewise by larger considerations, Carnot addressed a "Protest against the oppressive régime under which the engineering corps is governed," to the National Assembly from Béthune. In this he appealed for a self-elected committee of officers which would be empowered to discuss freely the current theories relative to fortifications. He reiterated his own adherence to the system of Montalembert. In this position nearly all of his colleagues disagreed with him, including D'Arçon. In October of the same year he wrote on the same subject to M. de la Tour du Pin, Minister of War, in no uncertain terms.[34]

He called for a committee to investigate the validity of the new theories on the art of fortification. "You will make yourself culpable of a crime," he warned the Minister, "if you neglect the proper means for the defense of the Kingdom." Naturally, he announced his own belief in the system of Montalembert, stating that he stood alone among his fellow-officers in championing these novel ideas. Little came of his efforts, excepting increasing official unfriendliness to him in the engineering corps. In a letter to Montalembert on May 1, 1791, from Saint-Omer, he remarked that "it is easier to reform drastically the constitution of a kingdom, than to conquer the sectarian spirit of a handful of individuals.[35]

By this time the Revolution was well under way. As the means of last resort in preventing national bankruptcy, the King and his ministers had decided on December 27, 1788, on an appeal to the nation for help by calling a meeting of the Estates-General, an institution that had fallen out of use for one hundred and seventy-five years. On January 24 regulations concerning the elections and the memorials, or *cahiers*, were announced. The *cahiers* give a vivid picture of the structure, the inequalities, the privileges, and the abuses of the Old Régime, of the conscious grievances of the unprivileged, and of the proposals for reorganization and reform.

The Estates were to assemble on May 1. They actually met on May 5, after three days of preliminary ceremonies, to listen to the King and Necker appeal to them to devise means to bring order into the distracted finances, but with no word said concerning reforms, or a constitution. By now much of France wanted a constitution, wanted to constitutionalize the Monarchy. The King and his Third Estate became deadlocked over the vital problem of the meeting and voting of the Estates, whether separately by orders, or united. The well-intentioned, but irresolute and class-loyal, King and the unstatesman-like and unprepared Necker were unable to cope with the will of the members of the Third Estate, who wanted to combine with the other two orders, and proceed to the business of making a constitution.

Events moved rapidly. On June 17 the Third Estate declared

itself the National Assembly. On the 20th, with certain additions from the clergy, the National Assembly took the "Tennis Court" oath not to separate until a constitution was made for the Kingdom. The royal sitting on the 23rd was fruitless for the Third Estate refused to obey the King's orders to sit and deliberate separately. Certain members of the nobility joined the National Assembly, and on the 27th the unwilling King capitulated, and ordered the clergy and nobility to join with the Third Estate as a single assembly. France now had a Constituent Assembly to draft a constitution.

The King, under court pressure, dismissed the popular Necker on July 11. A suspicion grew that certain troops were being assembled in and around Paris and Versailles for misuse against the Constituent Assembly. A popular rising resulted in Paris, and on July 14th the Bastille, symbol of despotism, fell. The populace of Paris became a force in the Revolution, and the revolutionary Commune of Paris was set up. Confusion and anarchy reigned in the provinces, the "Great Fear" terrified the country, and land-hungry and tax-ridden peasants burned feudal records throughout France. On August 4, in an orgy of renunciation, feudal privileges were abolished in principle in the Constituent Assembly. On the 27th, the pregnant Declaration of the Rights of Man, worked on since July, was adopted and became the foreword to the Constitution. As a result of the popular rising of October 5th and 6th, the Court moved permanently to Paris, to be followed at once by the Constituent Assembly. The rôle of Paris was thus again enlarged. The Constituent Assembly gave itself during the following months to the piecemeal adoption of a constitution for France.

The rank and file of the army was favorably disposed to the Revolution and aimed immediately at the democratization of the army, where privilege remained strongly entrenched.

Early in August, 1790, the soldiers in garrison at Nancy, suspecting the administration of their affairs, demanded a rendering of account by their officers. After an unfavorable response, they sent a protest to the National Assembly by a deputation. Their petition was intercepted and their delegates were imprisoned by order of the Minister of War. What was considered by the authorities to be a mutinous insubordination was put down with violence and bloodshed by the royalist general Bouillé, sent to Nancy explicitly for the purpose. All of France was aroused. Generally speaking, the people sided with the insurgent soldiers. A lively controversy ensued on the conduct of the government and on the civic rights of the troops. Carnot took this occasion to plead publicly for the civil rights of the soldiers.

On April 2, 1790, Carnot addressed a memorandum to the National Assembly proposing the restoration of the national finances by paying the debts of the state with the goods of the clergy.[36] This was a most significant document. The Law of November 2, 1789, had put the property of the Church at the "disposal" of the state. On December 19 it was voted to use this property as security for state debts. Large amounts were to be sold and assignats were to be issued on the strength of these projected sales. These first assignats of the Revolution were thus to be treasury bonds redeemable in land instead of in cash. The matter of church property was still unsettled when Carnot presented his scheme on April 2. He proposed that the state pay the national debts with the property of the Church *en nature* and not by sale and the subsequent liquidation of the debts by cash payments. He gave the advantages of his plan as follows: the state will meet the financial crisis at once; the national debt will be reduced, bankruptcy will be prevented, and confidence will be restored; the clergy will be dispossessed without hope of return of property; the charges of administration would be easily met; the assignat, contracts and other paper money, by being convertible into real property, would recover value and credit until the time when they could be totally abolished; and the excessive and sudden fall in the value of property, which would be bound to happen if the state put a great quantity of property on sale at one time, would be avoided.

The National Assembly, however, decided otherwise and by various decrees passed on April 14-17 voted to nationalize the property of the Church and declared the assignats to be legal tender. The evils happened that Carnot had sought to avert in his plan. Land values declined and property was bought at a song, on long term credit, with rapidly depreciating assignats.

Carnot's ideas in this matter were original and unusual. Under the circumstances of the time they seem to have been eminently sound.

It was in this period that Carnot wrote some charming and wistful verses under the title: "Adieu to My Springtime." In 1791 he was stationed at Aire. By a regulation of January 1, 1791, the engineering corps was composed of 310 officers, including twenty colonel directors, forty lieutenant-colonels, 180 captains, fifty lieutenants and ten student under-lieutenants. The six top-ranking colonel directors received seven thousand livres, the twenty ranking captains received 2800 livres and the sixty at the bottom received 1600. Carnot was fifty-seventh on the list of captains and received an annual salary of 2400 livres. His brother was seventieth on the same list.[37]

This younger brother, Carnot Feulins,[38] was garrisoned in nearby Saint-Omer, where he became acquainted with the DuPont family. Jacques-Antoine-Léonard DuPont was an influential landed citizen of the town. He had been formerly the director of the military establishments in Friesland during the Seven Years' War, was a secretary of the King, a state pensioner, and seigneur of Moringhem, Canteleu, of the Mairie of Burques, and of other properties. In 1790 he was director of supplies for the troops at Saint-Omer. He had three daughters, "distinguished by their beauty and by their intelligence." In 1790 Carnot Feulins married the second daughter, with his brother in attendance. Some months thereafter Lazare Carnot injured himself in a fall and his brother solicitously transported him to his apartment in the home of his father-in-law. The eldest daughter devoted herself to the care of the patient. They played the game tric-trac together. She was an excellent pianist and played to distract him. As he improved he versified and she put the verses to music. On May 1, 1791, he served by proxy as godfather for his father at the birth of his brother's first child. When the cure was effected, another wedding in the family was arranged. On May 17, 1791 Marie-Jacqueline-Sophie DuPont and Carnot were married. Carnot was then thirty-eight and his wife was twenty-six.

While at Aire Carnot had become the president of the Society of Friends of the Constitution, the local affiliate of the Jacobin Club. Carnot Feulins, who was quite an orator, became, in turn, the president of the popular society of Saint-Omer, elector, then president of the new departmental assembly. Finally, he was the first deputy elected by the Pas-de-Calais to the Legislative Assembly. The elder Carnot followed his brother in filling the local offices and on August 31, 1791, was elected with him, as ninth on the list, to the Legislative Assembly. The *Almanach historique et critique des députés* disposed of them in these words: "Same profession, same rank, same talent, same genius; they have every resemblance, and, if they differ at all, it is only in age and in appearance."

Carnot was now on the threshold of his long active public career in the Revolution. He had studied and reflected deeply and independently on the affairs of the nation, far beyond the confines of his profession, and he had expressed publicly his opinions and convictions fearlessly and stubbornly. This had at least won him no little notoriety. His character was steadily defining itself.

Chapter III

CARNOT—LEGISLATOR AND ON MISSION

THE NATIONAL Constituent Assembly laid down its monumental tasks of destruction and construction on September 30, 1791. On the following day, due to the self-denying ordinance of the makers of the constitution, seven hundred and forty-five inexperienced property-owning deputies, indirectly elected by a suffrage of tax-paying active citizens, assembled in a unicameral legislature to fulfill the constitution and to govern France under the newly-limited monarchy, in collaboration with a reluctant king who had unsuccessfully fled the capital on June 20 with the intent of joining the counter-revolutionaries beyond the frontiers. The bourgeoisie were convinced that their revolution was consummated.

The brothers Carnot were earnest members of the new Government. They lodged together in Paris, first in the Place du Carrousel, then in the rue Saint-Florentin, at the corner of the rue Saint-Honoré. Probably prompted by their admiration for Rousseau, and because of their provincial affiliation, they immediately inscribed themselves at the Jacobin Club, and attended a meeting.[1] At that particular session the President, Stanislas Girardin, spoke to the effect that the only good citizens and patriots were to be found in the Jacobin Club. Carnot Feulins replied heatedly to this limitation and evidently neither brother reappeared at the Club nor did they seem to attach themselves to any other.[2] In the new Assembly one hundred and thirty-six deputies were members of the Jacobins, and two hundred and forty-six were numbered among the Constitutional Feuillants, while the remaining three hundred and forty-five were independent adherents of the Revolution. Carnot's particular friends at the time were Jean-François Ducos, Condorcet, and Prieur (de la Côte-d'Or). The first of these was an imaginative young merchant and man of letters from Bordeaux, who had a great admiration for the republican heroes of antiquity. He did not achieve prominence in either the Legislative Assembly or Convention. Condorcet and Carnot had a deep common interest in mathematics, and both had had D'Alembert for a friend. Both were greatly interested in education. Prieur[3] and Carnot were to become close collaborators in military affairs as members of the Committee of Public Safety. They were both Burgundians, were engineering officers, had similar scientific interests, and had a taste in common for poetry and music.[4]

In the Legislative Assembly Carnot was a member of the diplomatic and military committees, and of the committee on public instruction. His maiden speech in the assembly was made on November 8, 1791,[5] in the general debate on the legislation proposed against the *emigré* princes. He called attention to the fact that a legislature did not need legal proofs to sustain an accusation, as did a tribunal of justice, but that a "moral conviction" of wrongdoing would suffice. He questioned whether any of the deputies doubted but that the princes who headed the revolt beyond the frontiers were guilty. He proposed the replacement of the emigrant officers by under-officers and sergeants. He concluded by proposing a motion of accusation against the emigrant princes without exception, against certain groups of persons in general, and against Mirabeau Cadet, Calonne, and the Cardinal de Rohan in particular. An earlier motion to outlaw and penalize those *emigrés* remaining out of the country on January 1, 1792, with a subsequent amendment by Couthon, was finally adopted on November 9, only to be vetoed unwisely though very naturally by the King on November 12, 1791.

A proposal by Carnot on January 3, 1792 that the citadel of Perpignan be destroyed was poorly received and nothing came of it. Carnot considered this stronghold, which had been used on occasion as a bastille, to be useless for defense, and he feared it as a possible menace to the inhabitants of the town under officers faithless to the Revolution, since the citadel dominated the heart of the town. In his brief speech he concluded by saying: "If I have brought any sentiment into this Assembly, it is above all else the love of liberty, the hatred of tyrants. I demand therefore the destruction of all the bastilles in the Kingdom (mur-

muring). Do not the French of 1792 resemble those of 1789?"[6] It is reported, beyond the official record, that he also said on this occasion: "I am a military person, I speak little, and I do not care to be attached to any party."[7]

On April 19, 1792, on the very eve of the declaration of war on Austria, Carnot severely criticized an army regulation decreed by the royalist ex-minister of war, Narbonne, who had been dismissed on March 10, after three months and three days in office. This regulation was intended to restore discipline in the army by the imposition of old-fashioned rules and regulations which were out of harmony with the new republican spirit abroad in the land and in the army. The indiscipline and insubordination in the army was due to the increasing desertion of officers to the ranks of the *emigrés,* to the promotion of non-commissioned officers, to the spirit of democracy abroad among the troops evidenced by the autonomous election of officers in certain regiments, to the division of military counsels within the army, within the Court, and within the Legislative Assembly, and to confusion and conflict between the three.

In his speech[8] on this regulation Carnot developed his "famous"[9] attack on the principle of passive obedience, revealing ideas which must have been germinating in his mind in the years preparatory to the Revolution, and which would have sat strangely on a military officer who was not also profoundly devoted to republican ideas. Carnot inquired first whether the minister of war had any right to so regulate the soldiery without the action of the Legislative Assembly, and whether the regulation was in conformity with the Constitution. If, said Carnot, the regulation is a law, then the executive has violated the Constitution in decreeing it, since the executive can only issue proclamations which conform to the laws. If it was not a law, then the Constitution was still infringed upon because it specifies that what is not prohibited by law cannot be prohibited. If, then, this regulation does have the character of a law, it is an arbitrary act. No one can be bound by its execution. The soldiers were right in refusing to obey it, and the minister was wrong to complain of their disobedience. The regulation was plainly an usurpation of power which could not be tolerated.

Adherence to the principle of passive obedience, Carnot said, might result, through blind obedience to command, in the turning of arms against the citizens, in the surrender of a fortress, or in assistance to the King in flight. In other words, the soldier would be obliged to betray his country in obedience to the voice of his commander. Carnot insisted, on the contrary, that the soldier had only the obligation to obey when commanded in the name of the law and by virtue of the law. Otherwise "passive obedience would be unconstitutional; and in every case, resistance to oppression is a natural right." In former times, he pointed out, despotism had always been established through reliance on this principle of passive obedience.

Carnot denied that the soldiers had alienated their liberty by becoming soldiers and that they could not be assimilated into the citizenry. The Constitution, he said, states that liberty is inalienable and imprescriptible. This constitutional principle ought to be observed rigorously in the army, because a single arbitrary order, executed by the armed force, could destroy liberty and dissolve the state. This principle would not lead to indiscipline. It is obedience through reason that results in the victory of troops over an army mechanically motivated, because a free soldier is always better than a slave.

After revealing the absurdities in the regulation under discussion, such as how the hair and mustaches should be cut, Carnot went on to say that provisionally the regulation, with modifications, would have to be enforced, in the face of an enemy army threatening the frontiers. He suggested the equalizing of conditions under which the men and officers lived and he urged that the officers be subjected to the same regulations as the troops, or those even more severe, with the hope that thus they might be the more reluctant to impose what they themselves resented. The officer who cannot undergo the hardships of the soldiers, he said, has no right to lead the troops, and he cited the hardihood of Alexander to illustrate his point.

Carnot concluded by proposing that the Minister of War be forbidden to publish any regulation without having submitted it to the Legislative Assembly a month in advance, and that a sub-committee of the Military Committee revise the existing regulations in order to invalidate those that are contrary to the laws and to the Constitution. The official report states that a part of the Assembly applauded and demanded the printing of the speech, while other members vehemently opposed this proposition. It has been remarked that this question of military discipline "was treated by Carnot with that superiority of civic and military genius which alone could assure the triumph of the improvised armies of the Republic."[10]

On May 15, 1792 Carnot made a motion in the Legislative Assembly to strengthen two police decrees proposed by Bigot for the purpose of quelling the disorders in Paris and of preserving the public tranquillity by police regulation.[11] Carnot's proposal provided that all voyagers and foreigners who had not inhabited Paris from at least March 1 were to be vouched for to the police by two active citizens within twenty-four hours on pain of imprisonment for the duration of the war; that citizens so attesting were to be held accountable; and that citizens not having had an habitual residence in Paris before March 1 were to be denied the right to carry arms. The motion was applauded, particularly in the tribunes. It was proposed, however, to adjourn and to postpone the vote on the motion until two days later. Carnot supported this by saying: "If my project is good today it will be good tomorrow, or the day after tomorrow." Larivière, however, opposed adjournment and called for a vote on Carnot's motion, to the cries of "Oui, Oui, Bravo!" from the tribunes. The proposed decrees of Bigot, and the motion of Carnot were then adopted. On the following day Carnot received the Cross of Knight of Saint-Louis, which was his of right after twenty years of service.

Speaking for the committee on public instruction and the extraordinary finance committee on June 9, Carnot proposed that the state pay indemnities to the families of Théobald Dillon and Pierre-François Berthois, officers massacred at Lille by their soldiers on April 29.[12] Dillon had been a Maréchal-de-camp, and Berthois, Colonel-director of fortifications, was his chief of staff. Dillon was caught between the counter plans of Rochambeau and Dumouriez, and became a victim of the friction between the generals and the indiscipline of the troops. While advancing on Tournai, according to orders, he was suddenly faced by the enemy, and presumably fearing insurrection because of the prevalent insubordination in the army, gave the order to retreat. This was misunderstood as treachery by the suspicious troops, and the two officers were killed by their own men. They were, Carnot contended, "the victims of plots against the public interest and the success of our armies." Dillon left a "natural" wife and three children, and Berthois, a wife and four children. Carnot proposed a pension of fifteen hundred livres for each widow, and of eight hundred livres to each child until he reached the age of twenty-one, in order to provide for his education. This decree was adopted, but the Legislative Assembly did not approve Carnot's motion for a monument to Dillon.

The tide of Monarchy was rapidly beginning to run out in the early summer of 1792. There were divided and partisan counsels in the Legislative Assembly, and in the rapidly-changing ministries. The struggle between the Girondins in the Legislative Assembly and the Jacobins in Paris was tightening. The King was playing an equivocal, but an increasingly courageous, game. His stubborn refusal to approve recent decrees was alienating greater numbers, and strengthening the opposition. Military fortunes were at a low ebb, and the country was seriously menaced by the enemy armies. On the occasion of the anniversary of the Tennis Court oath and of the flight to Varennes, on June 20, the Girondins staged a none-too-successful popular demonstration that included a harmless invasion of the Tuileries. Carnot was named as one of the legislative commissioners to go to the Tuileries to protect the menaced royal family.

On July 11 the Legislative Assembly issued a proclamation to the effect that the country was in danger. Three days later the Federation of July 14 was held, participated in by great numbers of radical *fédérés* from the provinces. On July 25 Carnot proposed in the Legislative Assembly that it distribute pikes to the unarmed citizens.[13] This was sent to the military committee, and was adopted by the Legislative Assembly on August 1.

Carnot's first important mission came on July 31, when he was named on a commission with two other deputies, Lacombe Saint-Michel and Thomas Augustin de Gasparin, to visit Soissons to investigate reports of maladministration affecting eight-thousand *fédérés.* The King and his Minister of War were suspected in connection with the charges at Soissons. These rumours were proved to be groundless. The three legislators were on this mission from August 1-5. Its mandate from the Legislative Assembly was a very broad one.[14] The letters and the report of the Commission reveal the care with which it went into all aspects of the civil and military situation at Soissons and in its vicinity.[15]

In its first letter to the president of the Legislative Assembly from Soissons on August 2 the Commission stated that there had been "great negligence" in the administration of military affairs, but not a "meditated crime."[16] Their second letter on the following day called particular attention to "the devotion of the brave inhabitants of the countryside, their willingness to pay their impositions, their confidence in the Assembly of the representatives of the people, and their feeling of security in the face of the enemy."[17] In another letter on the same day they called attention to the former Abbey of Notre Dame, occupied by forty-eight members who could be easily placed elsewhere, in order to transform the abbey into a "magnificent" hospital or into a caserne for two thousand men, and thus "correct the most pestilential aristocracy."[18]

The *compe rendu* of the Commission was given to the Legislative Assembly on August 6, Lacombe Saint-Michel reading the first part, and Carnot the second. The report was most thorough, comprehensive, and detailed.[19] The Commissioners remarked that among the recruits from Paris were a great number whose height and strength in no way corresponded with their courage and their *civisme.* Carnot's first words were: "Gentlemen, you have listened to our observations: the facts are in these four words of the *fédérés*: 'We lack everything.' Nothing is more true than this absolute destitution; the majority have no hose, no shoes, no shirts; but their courage and their patience is a substitute for everything; in a word, these are real sans-cullottes. A great number of them, just out of their childhood, present themselves naively, almost naked, for arms, which they can barely carry."

Faith in the ability of the soldiers to think and to act intelligently was affirmed in the report, in which the commissioners praised the exercise of equality and the responsible use of the elective suffrage by the troops, poorly equipped and fed as they were. They said: "It is the equality of rights that made the elections successful in the battalions. We observed these elections and we can say that if we had made them ourselves, in following our consciences, they would not have been better made. Those who were the best instructed, were chosen." In commenting upon the spirit of the population the Commission reported: "It was impossible not to notice, in traversing the countryside, that the people is enlightened daily as to its own interests; it recognizes its true friends; its opinion crystallizes and its love for liberty and equality grows day by day through reflection. No longer is it a vague desire of some sentiment, such as tormented it before the Revolution; it is now the desire to enjoy the happiness which it actually does enjoy." The report commented on the Society of the Friends of the Constitution at Soissons: "We found there an ardent patriotism, but none of those furors for which the popular societies are so often criticized. This society adores liberty and submits to the law." This behavior must have pleased Carnot who does not seem to have been particularly friendly to the political clubs of the day.

In the meantime, in Paris, the forty-eight sections had begun sitting night and day, and had established a central committee. The popular movement was led by the Jacobin and Cordelier leaders, particularly by Robespierre, and was directed against the Girondins in the Legislative Assembly. The moment for successful action was ready when the revolutionary commune captured the leadership of the National Guard. The insurrection of August 10 was not only directed against the throne but also against the Legislative Assembly, which meant that "the legal power was face to face with a revolutionary power." The monarchy was finally overthrown by a group of politicians in Paris working through the peculiar local machinery of government in the capital.

"That extraordinary session,"[20] of the Legislative Assembly beginning at two o'clock in the morning of August 10, when the King and his family fled to it for refuge, carried on business with its entire Right, and much of its Center absent. It immediately established a Provisional Executive Committee of six members, with Danton the principal figure as Minister of Justice. The other members were Girondins. But in the troubled seven weeks from August 10 to September 22, the real power lay, if anywhere, with the new revolutionary Commune of Paris.

On August 10 Carnot was a member of the commission of twenty appointed to reassure the Paris populace. The mob got out of hand and the mission failed. On the same day, a decree moved by Carnot Feulins in the name of the joint military commission and committee, authorized the sending of commissioners with extraordinary powers to the armies. In the elections on that day to these important commissions, Carnot was among the first three chosen, the others being Coustard and Prieur (de la Côte-d'Or). This group of three was sent to the Army of the Rhine (August 11-September 5, 1792). Carnot was thus out of Paris during most of the September Massacres.

The *procès-verbal* of the Legislative Assembly on August 10 charged the commissioners to the armies to spread the news of the events of August 10, of the sudden changes in the political order of the government, of the decrees of the Assembly, and of the oath that it had taken to maintain liberty and equality or to die in the attempt. The decree of that date empowered the commissioners to dismiss generals, officers of all grades, civil or military officials, and to make provisional appointments, on the condition of informing the Legislative Assembly. On the following day the Assembly gave specific directions to the commissioners to the Army of the Rhine, commanded at the time by General Biron.[21]

The commissioners to the Army of the Rhine worked indefatigably at their mission. Most of their letters[22] to the Legislative Assembly were written by Carnot,[23] though signed by the three commissioners. The Assembly relayed the letters to the eighty-three departments as models and as objects of emulation. In a letter from Wissembourg on August 17 the Commissioners remarked the dangerous intrigues prevalent in the army, whose seduction was only prevented by the integrity, courage and fidelity of General Biron. They spoke in the same sense of General Kellermann. The letter of August 21 reported the general plaint of officers and men that they had no adequate means of ascertaining the laws that concerned them, which prevented them from knowing whether they were treated justly, or in an arbitrary fashion by their superior officers. The newspapers that came their way rarely met these desires. The commissioners suggested to the Assembly the establishment of a military journal to be sent gratis to each army corps for the purpose of informing the troops on the laws concerning them and instructing them in the moral principles that would prevent them from being led astray and from becoming disunited. In its letter of August 27 from the general headquarters at Delémont, the Commission for the first time added "Year one of equality" to its customary dating "Year four of Liberty."[24] In this same letter the commissioners reported that , on August 25 in the "patriotic town" of Huningue, they were "obliged to suspend . . . M. Rouget de Lisle, engineering officer, who did not care to submit to the laws of the Assembly," after Carnot had vainly pled with him not to force them to dismiss the author of the"Marseillaise" for want of patriotism. Carnot had had a band outside play the stirring revolutionary song, but to no avail.[25]

The letter of the following day recounted the negotiations of the commissioners with the representatives of the Swiss Republic concerning the pass of one Pierre-Pertius. "We did not hesitate," wrote the commissioners, "to assure them that France will always observe her treaties religiously . . . that she has never had any other purpose than to provide for her own safety."[26] The *compte rendu* of this important mission was given to the Legislative Assembly on September 5, 1792, by Prieur (de la Côte-d'Or).[27] It was comprehensive and complete. In it the commissioners spoke particularly of the "marked patriotism" of the Generals Biron, Kellermann, Custine and Ferrier. They spoke of the scarcity of food supplies and of equipages for the army, which they attributed to the lack of ready money, to the delay in payments, to bureaucratic formalities, and to the ill will of agents. The majority of the war commissaries, they said, were unpatriotic. On this mission, the commissioners provisionally dismissed twenty-five military officers, and thirty-three civil officers. In addition to reporting the condition and needs of the troops and recapitulating the acts of suspension and promotion of civil and military authorities which the commission exercised, it devoted time to an interpretation of the spirit of the people. It reported that everywhere "a form of government absolutely new, absolutely popular, is desired. The slightest distinctions are abhorred. . . . The National Convention cannot choose between forms of government; it is essential that a Republic be organized; this form must be adapted to the vast empire of France."[28]

On the very day that this report was read to the Legislative Assembly Carnot was elected deputy to the Convention from Pas-de-Calais, as the second to Robespierre, on the list of eleven elected.[29] Carnot received 677 votes out of 753 cast. On the same day he was named, along with Prieur (de la Côte d'Or) and Nicolas de Beaupuy, to supervise and accelerate the organization of the army at Chalons. Carnot, however, was ill and declined membership on the Commission. Within less than a month he was bound on another important mission, this time to the Army of the Pyrenees, on mandate from the Convention.

Conditions were bad in the nation in the late summer and early autumn. Enemy armies occupied French territory. French arms were suffering a series of reverses. Lafayette deserted on August 19. The capitulation of Verdun to the enemy took place on September 2, although the news was not generally known in Paris until the Fourth. The food crisis was becoming steadily more acute. The assignats fell forty-one per cent in Paris during August, and almost as much in other sections of the country. Luxury trades were at a standstill. Wages in general had not increased fast enough to make up for the rise in the price of commodities. Although the year's harvest was a good one, the markets were but poorly supplied. Grain was being hoarded, and bread was very scarce. At the end of September, Rouen, for instance, had flour enough for only three days and the city was forced to commandeer grain from the army storehouses. Food speculation was rife. The silk factories had been closed down at Tours, and at Lyons thirty-thousand silk-weavers were out of work. The conviction spread at Lyons that it was necessary to adopt terrorist measures against food-speculators, and use the guillotine to solve economic difficulties. Rioting was widespread in France, and in some departments the National Guards, when summoned to preserve order, made common cause with the rioters. Many were clamoring for food-rationing and price-fixing decrees, and some tentative steps were taken in this direction. There were revolutionaries, mostly obscure, here and there, who wanted a further social revolution, and, in order to put an end to the economic crisis, were proposing measures of a somewhat communistic nature, with real restrictions on the rights of property. The agrarian law was agitated in certain quarters by a limited few, to the alarm particularly of the Girondins. The lot of the masses was one of great insecurity and misery.

Shortly after August 10, despairing of the Legislative Assembly establishing an effective tribunal to try counter-revolutionaries, the Paris Commune set up its own Committees of Surveillance and Police. Marat and Deforgues were leading members of the first of these committees. Even the activities of these bodies were not vigorous and thorough-going enough to satisfy the Parisian populace and on September 2-6 a series of jail deliveries and lynchings took place, embracing not only priests and aristocrats but also innocent proletarians. The invaders of the prisons constituted themselves into impromptu courts. The Mayor at the time was Pétion, a Girondin, and Roland was Minister of the Interior. They did little to stem the fury of the revolutionaries. Nor was Danton, as Jacobin Minister of Justice, any more effective, although he could not have been ignorant of the popular plans.

The troublous weeks in Paris from August 10 to September 22, were characterized by the violent struggle between the Legislative Assembly and the Commune, with the leadership of the latter generally victorious in the determination of the course of events. On September 18, however, the Assembly suppressed the Revolutionary Commune, ordered its reconstitution, and reinstated Pétion to his full authority as Mayor of Paris. The Assembly thus had the last word in the conflict. Two days later it held its last meeting. On the same day Dumouriez, commanding the Army of the North, stopped the invading armies at Valmy and compelled them to retreat. This was considered at the time to be the decisive turn in the military tide. Two days later the Convention met and took over the governance of France.

The Democratic Republic was ushered in by the elections to the Convention on what was virtually universal manhood suffrage. A determined minority of convinced republicans alone voted for members of the new Assembly. Most of them belonged to the middle class whose interests were caught up with those of the Revolution. The chief concern of these electors was to choose men capable of defending the Revolution against its internal and foreign enemies. The monarchy found no defenders in the elections. Of the 783 members of the Convention, seventy-five had sat in the National Constituent Assembly, and 183 in the Legislative Assembly. The Girondins, who were masters of the Convention in its early days, counted 165 members, while the Montagnards had a few members less. The majority of over four-hundred sat in the Plain. The Gironde, the radical party in the Legislative Assembly, had now become the conservative party, with the Mountain taking the radical position.

The Girondins concluded early in the Convention that the Revolution had gone far enough, and that the attempt to level off all social differences must cease. As early as September 10 Brissot had represented the Massacres as a Montagnard plot, the ultimate object of which was an agrarian law, calling for the division of land and fortunes among the people. The signal was thus given to property-owners to rally against the Mountain. Henceforward the Gironde posed as the party of order and social stability. The Girondins lost contact with and control of the Jacobins, which became almost wholly identified thereafter with the Mountain. The Girondins were recruited from the upper bourgeoisie and seemed to be defenders of the sacredness of private property, committed to a laissez-faire philosophy in economic life. They had constituted the war party in the Legislative Assembly, while the Mountain had been the peace party.

The Mountain, too, was bourgeois in membership, but its policy was directed by its reliance on the common people, and its social politics were primarily the work of circumstance. It stood for a strongly centralized government that would be able to curb the unduly rich, that could establish food-rationing and price-fixing, and that could confiscate property and levy progressive taxation, in recognition of the right of the individual to the means of subsistence.[30] Generally speaking, the Montagnards, with some exceptions, of whom Carnot was one, were Jacobins. The Jacobins never quite constituted a party in the modern sense, but worked usually as a voluntary organization for influencing public opinion and for using pressure politics for particular measures. They were definitely upper middle class in character and the "statistics confirm their respectability." Their leaders were men of the middle class and men of a certain education. Lawyers were certainly not in the majority. In the period 1789-92 their membership was sixty-six per cent bourgeois, twenty-six per cent working class, and eight per cent peasant.[31] Out of the confusion concerning what their aims consistently were it has been suggested that "Our mythical 'average' Jacobin would have accepted as a statement of his aims something like this: an independent nation-state, a republican form of government, universal manhood suffrage, separation of church and state; equal civil rights for all, and the abolition of hereditary distinctions and social privileges; a competitive industrial and agricultural society, with private ownership of property, but without great fortunes and without dire poverty; a virtuous, hard-working society, without luxuries and without vices, where the individual freely conforms to standards of middle-class decency."[32]

The Plain represented the group of moderation, made up of persons ideally unwilling to commit themselves to either extreme and prepared to vote upon each measure according to its merits or in accord with popular pressure. Actually, it was a neutral, irresponsible group susceptible to conviction by the more aggressive minority.

On September 22, 1792, the Convention assembled for the first time. On the following day a report was made in the Convention concerning the suspected breach of neutrality by Spain and the disaffection of the nobles, the priests and the members of the Parlements in the departments adjacent to the Pyrenees and Spain. The need for strengthened defenses and a reorganization of the military command was stressed. On a motion of Barère it was voted to send a commission of six members to the Pyrenees. On the 24th the Convention delegated large powers to this commission, authorizing it to "prepare means of assuring defense, and to re-establish public order wherever it has been disturbed."[33] The commission was deputized to suspend military and civil officials, to arrest suspected persons, and to replace those suspended or arrested. The local military and civil forces were called upon to obey the behests of the commission. The latter was appointed in two groups, one to proceed in its investigations with Bayonne as its center, the other to use Perpignan as its base. The three appointed for Bayonne were Carnot, Pierre-Anselme Garrau, and François Lamarque. Lamarque and Garrau were both lawyers.[34] At the same time the Ministry of War appointed the Adjutant-General Jean-Gérard Lacuée as commissioner of the Executive Council to put Bayonne in a proper state of defense.

In the elections in the Convention for the first committee on war, held on September 26, Carnot headed the elected list of twenty-four members and eight substitutes, with 110 votes. It is interesting to note that his later colleagues in the Directory, Letourneur and Reubell, were also elected, farther down the list. This committee organized itself on the 28th but Carnot was already en route for Bordeaux. On December 22, he was one of the twelve who automatically left the committee.

The three commissioners to the Pyrenees arrived in Bordeaux on October 2. From then until early in January the movements of the three members covered a great deal of territory and were full of fruitful activity. Despite the arduous duties of the commissioners Carnot found time to discuss scientific matters with the Constitutional Bishop Sermet at Toulouse and with the botanist Picot de la Peirouse. During this period the correspondence of the commission was voluminous, both with civil and military authorities, and with the Convention.[35] Carnot was in reality the chief of this important mission, and seems to have written most of the letters of the group. He prepared and read the final report to the Convention.[36] Professor Aulard has written that these letters and this report "are among the most important documents for the history of the Revolution, and for the biography of Carnot, himself,"[37] whose political program and thought in 1793 they reveal.

The three colleagues were fêted everywhere beginning with the civic fête in Bordeaux on October 5 which had been proposed by the Society of the Friends of Liberty and Equality. On October 12 the Club of the Friends of the Constitution (local Jacobins) at Bayonne formally received the Commissioners and laid various problems of the department before them. On November 1, Carnot, for himself and his colleagues, bade farewell to this Society in a special session. The Society of the Friends of the Constitution of Toulouse welcomed the Commissioners on November 21 and reported that "the Commissioner Carnot spoke and manifested the purest kind of patriotism in his discourse, which called forth lively applause."[38] On December 13, Carnot was present at a theatrical presentation at Toulouse and took the ovation of the audience with a bow. Evidently Carnot, as a Commissioner, was not unwilling to utilize the political clubs. In the final report to the Convention he spoke in laudatory terms of the rôle of the clubs, and stated that in those towns where none had existed, the Commissioners organized them.[39]

The Commission occupied itself with a multitude of investigations and orders. It prohibited the export of beeves to Spain. It corresponded with local officials. It carried on a lively correspondence with Lacuée, with the Minister of War, Jean-Nicolas Pache, with the Minister of Interior, Roland, with the Committee of Correspondence of the Convention, and with Jean-François, baron de Bourgoing, Minister Plenipotentiary to Spain. It reported frequently to the Convention, and its letter on October 16 from Bayonne[40] outlined much that appeared in the final report to the Convention. The Commission took time to regulate certain petty local abuses. At Bayonne, on October 13, it authorized passports for four former Carmelite sisters who desired to go to Spain because of their religious opinions.[41] Two days later, in a requisition regarding these four women, the Commission stated that "because of the principle of humanity and of tolerance for their religious opinions, we have found it impossible to refuse them passports."[42]

The Commission levied, organized and regulated the disposition of the troops in the region. This was usually done through orders issued to Lacuée. It requisitioned materials and empowered Lacuée to purchase supplies and munitions. Friction developed between the Commission and the Minister of War,[43] particularly after the Convention decreed on November 15 that Commissioners could no longer authorize expenditures or order supplies. This so irritated the Commission that it wrote from Toulouse on November 22 that the members considered themselves recalled and that they would leave for Paris on December 12. The relations between Lacuée and the Commissioners seem to have remained cordial and intimate, and the detailed and comprehensive report of Lacuée to Carnot, from Toulouse on December 12, concerning the disposition and condition of the troops,[44] was printed with the report of the Commission by order of the Convention. Evidently Lacuée, too, was critical of the Minister of War.[45] The cordial relations between Lacuée and Carnot continued after the latter returned to Paris.[46]

Carnot returned to Paris around January 9, 1793. On January 12 the official Report of the Commission was deposited in the Convention. It was read before the members in the session of January 29 by Carnot.[47] The applause of the Convention frequently interrupted the reading of the Report and it was ordered to be printed and distributed. Throughout, the Report was a most thorough, practical, sane, concrete document of grievances and of suggested remedies.[48] It spoke particularly in terms of specific abuses rather than in terms of principles, and asked for their redress by the responsible government. The report breathed the spirit of Turgot. It is truly a masterly document in practical politics. It gives the "highest idea of Carnot, as thinker and as writer."[49] An analysis of this document reveals the ideas of Carnot early in the period of the experiment with the democratic republic. It also indicates the thought of many other patriotic republicans, since Carnot's ideas at the time were not entirely original with him.

Some of the demagogical phraseology of the republicans appears in the introduction: "The irresistible voice of reason, in proclaiming the rights of the people and in opening their eyes, taught them that they had no other sovereigns than themselves, no other enemies than the stupid idols worshipped under the name of Kings, and that in the whole world there should no longer be any but equals, friends and brothers."[50] The Report went on to state that the league of princes formed to preserve their own tyranny would be dissolved by the general love of equality and by the courage of free men.

This introduction is followed by a precise description of the physical situation in the Pyrenees region from the point of view of defense, with concrete suggestions as to the strategic places to be fortified and those to serve as depots of supply. The Report called attention to the fact that these military preparations must continue unabated even in the face of Spain's desire to keep the peace, for war was inevitable unless a new treaty superseded the one made between the two Bourbon houses. A new treaty would need to establish absolute free trade between the two nations and to revise the boundary line. The Report elaborated the military arrangements made by the Commission and referred the Convention to the appended report by Lacuée.

The Report then went into the question of the civil administration and local conditions. This section of the Report occupied over half of the total and evidenced the scientific attitude and approach which the Commission took towards the problems of reorganizing and republicanizing the country. The Commission expressed the hope that the knowledge of the data collected "might lead to the reform of abuses in civil administration, and to the promotion of public prosperity."[51] It called attention to the fact that such information was especially important in these departments because they had been neglected for so long by the former regime that drastic measures would be necessary to incorporate them into the unity of the Republic. The Report went on to indicate the disproportion existing between the districts in the departments, the difficulty of some communities in finding responsible officers, and the general illiteracy prevalent in others. It pointed out financial, judicial, and religious abuses existing in the region. It counseled against the harsh and sudden violation by the state of the religious practices of the people. In speaking of the burdens of taxation the Commission said:

> One truth stands out particularly regarding the matter of tax levies and that is that contributions ought to be proportional, not to the income and fortune of the citizens, but to their superfluity.
>
> Never will there be either justice or the semblance of equality

on earth, so long as it is necessary in paying taxes for one citizen to give a quarter part of the very bread that is essential to subsistence, while another has only to give up a personal servant to pay his.

Be convinced, Citizens, that the agitations of the people, whatever their immediate or apparent causes may be, have but a single foundation—that of being freed from the burden of taxation.[52]

The Report proceeded to state that the principle to be used in the new constitution ought to be: "that the contributions ought to be taken only from that portion of the income that exceeds a specified sum judged to be indispensable to the primary needs of man."[53]

In the report the Commission went on to outline policies regarding commerce and industry, roads and canals. On the latter it said:

The need for communication includes, from our point of view all the other needs, because, where it is easy to travel, education spreads, industry expands, and there is naturally developed every degree of movement of which the locality is capable.[54]
. . . The lack of communication results in adjoining districts being strangers to each other; language, customs, costumes, everything is different; these separations preserve ignorance, particularism, and indifference to the general affairs of the republic.[55]

These regions, the Report stated, had long been bled by taxes which had not gone back into them for improvements, and now it was the obligation of the national treasury to furnish the funds essential to local public works, for "otherwise the region would never find the means of enriching itself."[56] This point was aptly supported by a homely and somewhat humorous statement: "As a great man has said, the first ten thousand francs are more difficult to amass than the second million." The principle behind this general recommendation the Commission stated in no uncertain terms:

"The Republic will never be one, indivisible and prosperous until all come to the aid of each. It is odious and contrary to all principles, that among the regions of the state, some are rich and others are poor; that one has immense patrimonial wealth and the other nothing but debts. . . . If men are to be equal among themselves, the first thing to do is to see that the parts are equal, that is, that they have means proportional to their needs; if there are local privileges then there will develop privileges for individuals."[57]

The Commission stated that a comprehensive program of public works would absorb the labor of demobilized soldiers to whom the state would owe the means to a livelihood when the war was over. It indicated, too, that the state was under the compulsion to provide the possibility of work to the families of the soldiers under arms. This could be done by encouraging new industries, such as the new cotton industry at Toulouse, which would put the indigent to work, would make it possible to compete with the cotton industry of England, and would keep the profits of the industry within the country.

This part of the Report reveals sound economic reasoning and it manifests the advanced social thinking of Carnot, combined with an ability to foresee and forestall the inevitable readjustments associated with the conclusion of war and the demobilization of great numbers of men. Carnot's liberal social ideas were not generally common early in the Revolution. He evidenced them as early as his *Eulogy of Vauban* and they reappear in his proposal for a Declaration of Rights. Although these ideas were radical, and seem to the modern to be socialistic in character, Carnot never sympathized with the social radicals nor with their doctrines as these developed in the Revolution. Nonetheless Carnot honestly and sincerely believed in the necessity of social reform for the successful republic.

The Report went on to emphasize the need of reorganizing the private hospitals which were still being managed by the old foundations. These hospitals were centers of fanaticism and counter revolution. The poor condition of the military hospitals was expressed in these words: "These establishments are not compatible with the grandeur of a republic in which humanity is the first principle."[58] The Report summarized succinctly the major general abuses existing in these departments and stated that of all the evils visited upon these peoples the greatest was the denial of justice. This statement was documented by citing specific instances.

Education was thoroughly treated by the Commission. This was always a central theme with Carnot. The significance of this matter for the republican state was stressed in these words:

> Citizens, we have rarely written you without speaking of the need for public education. . . . A generation is growing up in which education has been abandoned for three years; the longer this continues, the less will it know how to enjoy the gift of liberty. Already new prejudices have replaced those destroyed; one sees citizens of good faith who have come to consider intolerance and harshness as the distinctive characteristic of the true republican. . . .[59]
>
> National education alone can destroy these sad impressions which, otherwise, will soon make of France a horde of savages; it alone can develop in the hearts of youth the principles of their own happiness: the ardent, yet enlightened love of country, filial piety, the taste for simplicity, the sentiment of benevolence, and the respect for customs and traditions. These principles are those of natural equality.[60]

These are strong words but they reflect the convictions of the republican patriots who were nurtured in the "philosophy" of the century. Education was the *sine qua non* if man was to perfect himself and his society. Such a passion must lie at the heart of society if it believed in the possibility of progress. The Eighteenth Century crystallized and popularized this idea of progress which is a distinctly modern dogma.[61]

The Commission proceeded to make a most interesting proposal.[62] This was that every year a body of savants and artists was to tour throughout France and make a *tableau* of the general conditions existing, as a basis for a definite program to promote national prosperity. It is said that "these pictures . . . ought to be presented to the legislative body every year at a stated time and in them should be found the mathematical basis without which it is impossible to arrive at an intelligent system of general administration." This is, indeed, a scientific, objective approach to the problems of government. Implicit in the plan is the idea of a "planned economy." The Commission went on to plead for the continued use of commissions to be sent out frequently into the departments, both to collect grievances and hear complaints, and to support the local authorities. To be most effective, it is said, these commissions should be changed frequently. The Commission then took the occasion to criticize the organization of the central government and suggested that the committees of the Convention might well replace the Executive Council and thus reduce the bureaucratic hierarchy of government and destroy the cabals that existed within it. This suggestion was finally realized in the Convention when it adopted a report made by Carnot in the name of the Committee of Public Safety, on April 1, 1794.

The concluding words of the Report were these:

"If the great vice of the abolished constitution was the independence and rivalry of powers, and if this vice will inevitably produce a new revolution because its principle is to divide and to separate, perhaps we shall find that the new constitution should make every effort to unify everything; for it is indeed less in limiting the power of the authorities in their extent, than in abridging their duration that one avoids despotism. The rotation of officers, the election of magistrates, the assemblage of several of these for the emission of every judgment, the publicity of decisions: herein are found, in all times, the safeguard of liberty and the true guarantees of the Safety of the Republic."[63]

This truly is a remarkable practical document for such an early stage in the democratic republic. It is remarkable, too, as the product of the reflections and convictions of men as yet untrained in self-government, but eager to make a success of the republican state. It presents an interesting synthesis of political speculation imbued with the thought of the century, and the practical wisdom and observation of an engineer and a mathematician, who also happened to be a devoted republican patriot. This document is full of social compassion and some of the ideas implicit in the social proposals mentioned are more revolutionary than the majority of revolutionaries were ready for. Carnot was probably not fully aware of all the implications inherent in these proposals. His sincerity and honesty in enunciating them cannot be impugned. He held to them consistently and, on the contrary, he was usually silent or quiet brief in speaking of the rights of property. Very few of the thinkers in the period had gone on to think in terms of social democracy and most of those who had, did so in a vague sort of way. The emphasis on public education is conventional in the republican thinking of the day. The insistence upon the development of a strongly centralized government that would consolidate and unify the whole fabric of France was not universally shared by the Conventionals. It became, however, the object of the faction that gained control through the purging of the Girondins by the Convention. It is interesting to note that the conclusions of the commission in this regard came in a report covering a region in which the federalists were numerous.

With the completion of this important mission Carnot was ready for participation in the deliberations of the Convention. In three months, however, he was bound on another significant mission, this time to the Army of the North. These assignments were preparing him admirably for the special functions he was to assume in August as a member of the Committee of Public Safety.

Chapter IV

THE REVOLUTION TIGHTENS

THE QUESTION of what to do with the King in a Republic was on the agenda from August 10. Few doubted that Louis was guilty of treason. The problem was the penalty. The Girondins generally favored leniency. Most of them inclined to life imprisonment. They were, however, hopelessly divided on the issue. The Jacobins, on the other hand, never deviated from their original insistence upon the death penalty. The trial of Louis was well advanced before Carnot returned to Paris. On January 15, 1793, he voted yes on the question of Louis' guilt of conspiracy against the public liberty and the general security.[1] Louis was overwhelmingly adjudged guilty of treason and perjury and the only question remaining was the one of punishment, a political question. The death penalty was voted by a narrow margin. Carnot voted for the extreme penalty in these words:

"In my opinion, justice wills that Louis die, and politics wills it equally. Never, I vow, has a duty weighed more heavily on my heart than this that is laid upon me; but I believe that, to prove your attachment to the laws of equality, and to prove that the ambitious do not frighten you, you must execute the tyrant. I vote for death."[2]

The subsequent attempt of the Girondins to have final decision referred to a popular plebiscite failed. As a last resort the Girondins proposed that the penalty be postponed until a more expedient time, but the Convention voted for its immediate execution. Carnot voted against the postponement.[3] In private notes Carnot recorded his ideas regarding the nation and the King. "The oath of fidelity to the King," he wrote, "is conditional: it assumes that the King himself will remain faithful to the nation. In case of conflict, the nation comes before the King. Circumstances developed to the point where it was necessary that the King perish, or the Convention and France. The real regicides were the *émigrés*, who deserted him who had loaded them with favors and who had summoned them to come to his aid, after they had ruined him by their faulty advice. In the eyes of republicans, the King was no other than a perjurer and a criminal, and so they punished him."[4]

By retroaction, as of January 4, 1793, Carnot was entered on the Committee of General Defense. On January 29 he presented a report to the Convention proposing the levy of a legion for the army of the Pyrenees. This was adopted on the same day and the military committee was authorized to work out the details. Adjutant-General Lacuée, in a letter to Carnot from Toulouse on February 9, wrote: "Do not forget, my dear Carnot, that this army [of the Pyrenees] is yours."[5]

Revolutionary France was gravitating gradually, under the Convention, from waging a war of defense, to a war of propaganda and finally to a war of conquest. On November 19, 1792, the Convention enunciated its ringing proclamation to the effect that "it would accord fraternity and aid to all peoples who should wish to recover their liberty." Savoy, which was largely French-speaking, had been occupied in September. On October 22 its people expressed their desire for union with France, and on November 27 the Convention decreed the annexation of Savoy. Bishop Grégoire justified this, in an eloquent speech, not only by the imprescriptible right of a people to choose its nationality freely, but also by the consideration of French national interest. The Convention decreed on December 15 that the wealth and welfare of occupied territories were to be put at the disposal of the French generals, as the price of the "liberty" conquered for them. These territories were to be "democratized" by the establishment of revolutionary institutions. In January Danton announced that the limits of the Republic were "marked by nature." Nice was annexed to France by decree of the Convention on January 31, although there was no great popular enthusiasm locally for this.

The war went well for France for a time after Valmy. Custine had captured Mainz, and Dumouriez had overrun Belgium after the victory of Jemappes on November 6. He entered Brussels on November 14. By November 28 the Austrians had evacuated

Belgium. The Convention at once opened the Scheldt and Antwerp to international commerce. This was a direct challenge to the commercial and naval interests of England. In 1793 the Belgian troops were incorporated into the French army, and after January 31, the only government in the country was that of the French generals. The Second Partition of Poland on January 23, 1793, created an international diversion helpful to French plans. England was being steadily alienated by the developments in France. On the day of Louis' execution Chauvelin, the French ambassador, was given eight days in which to leave England. On February 1, 1793, the Convention declared war on England and on Holland. Spain joined with the allies on March 7. Austria, Prussia, Sardinia, England, Holland, and Spain thus opposed republican France.

Carnot was a member of the Diplomatic Committee in the Convention. On February 13, 1793, he presented to the Committee a Report on the incorporation of Monaco and other states into the territory of the Republic. The Committee approved the Report and on the following day Carnot presented it to the Convention, which adopted it and ordered it printed.[6] This report is the public statement of the theory of the Convention regarding the incorporation of territories into the French Republic. It can also be taken to represent the current thinking of Carnot on international problems. It is important, too, as a revelation of the "altruistic and messianic character of the new nationalism,"[7] although, as Sorel points out, the report "marked the triumph of politics: politics, in this report, decided everything."[8]

Carnot, after remarking that the law of December 15 engaged "the honor of the French nation to protect liberty among all peoples who wanted to conquer it," very candidly stated that in every political matter there are two points to consider and all else is reducible to these—interest and the fatherland.

> It is absurd that a nation act against its own interests; it is odious that it have the intention of harming others except under an indispensable necessity for itself.
>
> These truths, written by nature in the heart of all men, constitute the rights of men and are the foundation of private as well as of public morality.

In effect, nations are in a political system, just as individuals are in a social order. Nations, like individuals, have their respective rights; these rights are: independence, security from without, unity within, and the national honor. . . . Natural law prescribes that these rights be respected . . . and mutually defended so that one avoids compromising one's own interests. . . . Beyond a doubt, this innate justice, which is nothing more than conformity to natural law, obliges no one to sacrifice his own interest to that of his neighbor. . . . Such is the justice that preserves the harmony of societies and the equilibrium of states.

Carnot proceeded to state the two general maxims in politics which establish the difference between just and unjust action: Every political act is legitimate when it is commanded by the safety of the state; every act which harms the interests of another without indispensable necessity for oneself is unjust.

Without registering a final opinion on the question of the possibilities of a universal republic, Carnot said that the best way for France to realize this end would be, not by precipitate and direct action, but by remaining within her natural frontiers and achieving such national prosperity that her neighbors would want to imitate her. To admit that sovereignty resides in the universality of the human race, he said, would deprive France of her right to make laws in her own interest as she saw fit. On the contrary he emphasized the principle that every people is its own master. This led him to conclude: "Since sovereignty belongs to all peoples there can be no reunion among them except by virtue of a formal and free transaction. . . . This consent, once given, cannot deprive them of the right to return to their original independence, because liberty and sovereignty are inalienable." Carnot warned, however, that within the single state itself, indivisibility is essential. The parts within the state cannot become independent. Otherwise, federalism, even anarchy, would result. Carnot held consistently to the idea of the unity of the state.

The principle of democratic self-determination of nationhood was clearly stated by Carnot. "The invariable right of every nation," he said, "is to live independently, if it so pleases, or to unite with others, if they so desire, for the common interest. We French people only recognize the peoples themselves as sovereign; our system is not that of domination, it is that of fraternity." He concluded by recommending that Monaco and the other territories involved be incorporated into the French state since their reunion fulfilled the specifications laid down in his report. He did recommend that the Prince of Monaco be protected and safeguarded in all that belonged to him as a private citizen.

This document demonstrated that Jacobin nationalism had not yet completely superseded humanitarian nationalism in the thinking and policies of some of the republican partiots, for it was infused with elements of both kinds. The immediate course of events was to consolidate the narrower, more intense form of nationalism.

French propaganda in Belgium for union with France had been particularly active since January. There was some local sentiment for this, particularly in the popular societies. On March 1, 1793, Carnot, in the name of the Diplomatic Committee, recommended to the Convention that Brussels be incorporated into the Republic.[9] Carnot, of course, justified the reunion on the expressed will of the inhabitants of Brussels. Groups of citizens had so expressed themselves and an assembly of citizens had voted for reunion, but these expressions were not completely representative, and there was vigorous and widespread opposition to union with France.

In this brief report Carnot evidently depended upon the logic and the principles of his earlier report, without taking the occasion to repeat them. In the style of the demagogues, he began by stating: "Belgium, born for liberty, has tried to break her chains a thousand times and each effort has only plunged her more profoundly into the abyss. Every blow at her chains has prompted her tyrants to render her slavery more adject and cruel." He concluded by a statement in which there was some equivocation: "I shall not attempt to examine the respective interests of the two peoples for the desired union. At this moment a single one ought to decide us—the national glory, the engagement which we have taken to aid and defend all peoples who wish to achieve their liberty. Brussels cannot preserve hers without us; that is enough; from this moment Brussels is French." Several other incorporations, supported by the same reasoning, were made in the month of March on the recommendation of the Diplomatic

Committee through Carnot, as its reporter.[10] These included Hainault, Franchimont, Stavelot, Logne, the principality of Salm, Florennes and the thirty-six villages in its arrondisement, Tournay, Louvain, Ostende, Namur, and some other Belgian towns.

Within a month after these separate incorporations of some of the principal Belgian towns and communities, Belgium was evacuated by the French, as a result of a series of reverses, and of the developing defection of Dumouriez. After his defeat at Maestricht, Dumouriez had retreated from Holland into Belgium, where he suffered a severe defeat at Neerwinden on March 18-19. Dumouriez had been playing a double game for some time and seems to have been planning for the erection of an Orleanist dynasty, with Louis-Philippe as King, and himself as major-domo. The growing suspicion concerning Dumouriez in Paris and in the Convention only aggravated the tension in the government, and contributed to restleness and dissatisfaction in the sections.

On March 8, on the motion of Danton, the Convention voted to send two commissioners to each of the forty-eight sections of Paris to inform their populations of the situation of the Army of Belgium, and to recruit all the citizens capable of bearing arms. Carnot was one of these commissioners. On the day after his selection he reported his satisfaction with the spirit and condition of the men in section "1792," to which he had been sent. On the same day Carnot, in the name of the Committees of the General Defense and War, presented in the Convention a project which provided for the sending of eighty-two commissioners into the departments. These were to go in pairs, into the forty-one regions into which the departments were arranged for the purpose. This important proposal was accordingly decreed.[11] These commissions were to inform the citizens of the new dangers menacing the nation and were given wide powers to levy troops and to take other measures essential to the national defense, in accord with the enabling act of February 24, 1793. They were granted authority superior to that of local military and civil officials. In the proclamation[12] accompanying the projected decree, Carnot concluded with the flaming words: "Citizens, the people suffer from this prolonged struggle between liberty and despotism, between armies and a nation. The destiny of despotism is sealed; it perishes. Hasten its last hour. Make peace only with peoples freed of kings and thus prepare the universal peace." Carnot was elected a member of one of these commissions, and, with Lesage-Senault, went into the Departments of the North and of the Pas-de-Calais.

Before leaving on this important mission which, with extensions, was to occupy him until early August, Carnot presented a Declaration of Rights to the Convention on March 10, which he proposed to have serve as a basis for a new constitution.[13] The Convention had been convened, of course, to draft a republican constitution for France. On September 29, 1792, on the suggestion of Cambon, the Committee on the Constitution had been constituted. With the exception of Danton, the nine members were Girondins. They were Siéyès, Thomas Paine, Brissot (soon replaced by Barbaroux), Pétion, Vergniaud, Gensonne, Barère and Condorcet. Barère was soon to become a leader of the Plain, and finally go over to the Mountain after the Paris insurrection of June 2, 1793. On October 19 the Convention adoped Barère's motion that the Committee invite the friends of liberty and equality, no matter of what nationality, to present their views concerning the French Constitution, which might indeed turn out to be "the political code of all peoples," in the language of Rabaut-Pommier. In response to this general invitation the Committee received more than three hundred *Mémoires,* of which several were in English. Finally, on February 15, Condorcet, in the name of the Committee, laid before the Convention a proposed Constitution, and a "Declaration of the natural, civil and political rights of man," in thirty-three articles. The proposed Constitution was lengthy, abstruse, and theoretical. It was not, however, fundamentally different from the Constitution hastily completed by the Montagnards on June 24, 1793. Condorcet's proposals were coldly received, discussion was postponed, and the Constitution was laid aside. The exigencies of the moment forced the responsibilities of government on the Convention and it had little time for constitution-making. Rapidly developing partisan politics, too, prevented the Montagnards from supporting any important proposal of the Girondins. The Mountain preferred to stall for time on the Constitution. The military and foreign crisis was also coming to a head in March. On February 16 the Convention decided to print and distribute to its members whatevery proposed constitutions were offered by any of them. It was in response to this that Carnot presented his Declaration of Rights. On April 4 the Convention named a committee of six to study the various projects that had been presented. Only one of the six was a Montagnard.

In the lengthy foreword to his Declaration of Rights, Carnot developed some general principles of the state. He began by pleading for simplicity in the enunciation of principles and in the emission of laws. Few and simple basic principles and laws, he said, made instruction in them easy, and enforcement of them effective. He went on to say that in the state of nature men's rights are undefined. Men unite with one another in order that their primitive rights may be better guaranteed and be more surely directed. This is possible, he said, through the concordance of the wills and by individual efforts. In the state of nature the rights of men are not only undefined but often they are illusory because one is often contradicted by another, or they are rendered useless by the feeble means of each isolated individual to struggle against the elements and other obstacles. In this natural state everything belongs to the strongest, and everything is subjugated by him. There then exists neither liberty, equality, property nor the right of resistance to oppression. Men unite to prevent such despotism by making the general will and the public force supreme. Man organized in the state does not lose rights, but, rather, he increases them. He particularly gains the right of benevolence, or social protection, which is the aid that every other member of society can bring him, without working harm to himself.

The tacit convention, or natural pact, that unites men who leave the state of nature is that "each one ought to aid his fellows as much as he can without harming his own proper interests, and no one ought to hurt the interests of others excepting under necessity for himself." This is the very core and essence of every social body. Its development forms the social pact, or the Declaration of Rights. In a note to his Declaration, Carnot commented on the currently accepted maxim: "Do not do unto others what you would not have them do unto you," that became incorporated in the Declaration of Rights adopted by the Convention on June 24, 1793. Carnot called this maxim superb, but false, impractical, and obscure. He said: "It is in the nature of every person to put his own interest above all other interests. The first incentive to human action is the love of one's self and the desire for happiness. This instinct can be directed into public usefulness but this egoism must be recognized and reckoned with." Much later in life he reflected that "We are on earth both to be happy ourselves and to be generators of happiness for others; nature has given us both the egoism that relates everything to ourselves, and the instinct of reciprocity, or natural equity, that reveals to us the necessary tie between our own interest and those of our fellows."[14]

The social pact and every legislative act, Carnot continued, assures advantages to and imposes obligations upon the contracting parties. The advantages are called the rights of the citizens and the obligations, or duties, form what are known as the universal morality. The declaration of rights, and of duties, are the same because the rights of each are the duties of all, and reciprocally, the rights of all are the duties of each.

The principal and significant articles in Carnot's proposed Declaration can be summarized as follows: the rights of the state are above those of the citizens; the safety of the people is the supreme law; every people has the right to remain isolated and independent of every state and of every individual; the individual has this same right but the society which he leaves owes him no further protection and the citizens no further benevolence; sovereignty belongs exclusively to the entire people; law is the expression of the general will; a delegated body has only the right to make alterable rules; the state has the right to decree that each of its members contribute, as much as lies within his power, to the public prosperity, so that there will be no exemption or privilege; every citizen has the right of life and death over himself, that of speaking, writing, printing and publishing his thoughts, that of adopting the cult that pleases him, of doing what he considers appropriate, so long as he does not disturb the social order; every citizen is born a soldier: society has the right to demand that each of its members unite with the others to repel the force that attacks the sovereignty that belongs to all or that harms in any way the common interests.

The state has the right to demand that every citizen be instructed in a useful profession, so that he can contribute to the strength of the whole, and be prepared for its defense; the state has the right to establish a system of national education adequate to prevent the faults that ignorance and the corruption of traditions and customs cause; every citizen, reciprocally, has the right to secure from society the means of acquiring the knowledge and instruction that can contribute to his happiness in his particular profession, and to the public service in the employments which he may be called to fill by the will of his follow-citizens; the state ought to distribute happiness and enjoyment as uniformly as possible among the members who compose it; every government should attempt to establish, as much as is possible, the perfect equality of its citizens; the state ought so to organize itself and so delegate its powers as to secure, as far as is possible, the convergence and accord of the wills of its members that the general interest derives from the individual interest; the state should reserve to itself the certain means of changing its organization and of revoking, when it pleases, the powers which it has delegated.

The state should provide for those who serve the state, and should care for those who suffer because of indigent old age or infirmities; taxation should be levied only against the superfluity of the income of each citizen; the state has the right to demand that every public agent be held accountable for the public trust vested in him; publicity and responsibility are the safeguards of the general and individual rights; the rights of one state in respect to another are the same as those between members of the same society; the citizens have the right to peaceable assembly, to confer together on their own interests, and to present petitions to the constituted authorities; every citizen has the right to arm himself in his own defense, and, in the case of danger to himself or to the public, he has the right to repulse force with force.

Whence did Carnot derive the ideas, explicit and implict, in his Declaration of Rights? There is no single, simple answer to this question. The debt must be variously apportioned. The Declaration of Rights of the American Colonies,[15] and the Declaration of Independence wielded a wide and profound influence in France.[16] On a later occasion than this Carnot lauded the experience and example of the United States and indicated his own debt to their models.[17] The similarities between the articles of the declarations of the individual states, particularly of Virginia, and of the Declaration of Rights in 1789 in the Constitution of 1791, and of 1793, are striking. Carnot's Declaration of Rights and Condorcet's rejected Declaration of some days earlier run parallel courses with these others. Carnot's statements are, in general, much shorter, much more terse and less idealistic in expression than are Condorcet's. The Declaration of Rights of 1789 had seventeen articles, Carnot's had twenty-two, Condorcet's had thirty-three, and the one incorporated in the Constitution of 1793 had thirty-five. The Constitution of 1795 contained twenty-two articles of rights, and nine of duties.

Condorcet's Declaration differed from that of Carnot in that it defined liberty, expanded legal protection more fully, and treated property and property rights much more fully. The Declaration of Rights of 1789 was silent on education. Carnot was quite detailed in this and surpassed Condorcet in it. The Declaration of 1793 had but one short article on education. Carnot's proposal differs from all these other Declarations in that he put the rights of the whole community before those of the citizens, and he named the safety of the people as the supreme law and end of the state. The other declarations speak of the conservation of the natural rights of men as the object of society. They list these rights as liberty, property, security and resistance to oppression. The Declaration of Rights of 1793 announced "the common happiness" as the end of society. In general, the similarities characterize these various Declarations, and the differences are the exceptions.[18]

In general, Carnot's ideas are in accord with those of Rousseau.[19] Carnot, however, had very little to say about the original contract and his general view of man in his "natural" or "unorganized" state was that it was not as agreeable as Rousseau would lead us to believe. In Carnot's thinking political society is a good that wholesomely serves man and it is not a necessary evil that only brings him some slight surcease from the sorry state into which he has gotten as he has traveled away from his primitive state. In his writings Rousseau moved away from his position of enthroning the rights of the individual to the position that the whole prevails over the individual.[20] Carnot made the general will supreme but he posited the ideal as the coincidence of the collective and particular interests. Rousseau believed a republic to be possible only in a small state, or through federalism in the larger one. Carnot believed in the possibility of a unified, unitary republic in a large state and therefore was much more agreeable to representative democracy than was Rousseau. The latter had difficulty in accepting the idea of representation of the sovereign people. Rousseau, too, thought that the maxim "do unto others as you would be done by," was beautiful and sublime, but "subject to a thousand exceptions." He challenged it, however, on other grounds than the practical Carnot did. Rousseau emphasized property much more than did Carnot. Rousseau incorporated supernatural religion in his political system. Carnot pled only for religious toleration, which Rousseau also would guarantee. Rousseau gave the objective of political association to be: "the conservation and the prosperity of its members." In his *Project of a Constitution for Corsica* (1765), Rousseau favored a wide diffusion of goods rather than the undue enrichment of certain individuals. He also spoke of the love of the fatherland as the essential emotion of the state. In his *Considerations on the Government of Poland* (1771-1772), Rousseau was most explicit on the need of educating the children in the virtues of patriotism. He wrote that "the true republican suckles with the milk of his mother the love of his fatherland."[21] Carnot thoroughly agreed with this. In this both were thinking in accord with the thought forms of the century. Turgot had urged "civic education" upon the King in order to form a people "informed and virtuous."[22] Turgot, like Carnot, detested the spirit of faction. In the field of practical politics, Turgot championed the principle of the equalization of taxation and the destruction of privilege. Carnot adhered to these principles, but they were not peculiar to him. The enlightened self-interest which Carnot accepted as the motive for proper personal and social conduct was in accord with the ideas of Adam Smith and D'Alembert.[23] The latter held the idea in common with Carnot that the state owed to the citizen the right of earning a livelihood.[24] Carnot did not include this, however, in his Declaration of Rights. Carnot did not have the passionate faith in the perfectibility of man that Turgot and Condorcet had. Carnot's evolving political ideas had no single source, but represented a synthesis, tempered and fused by his own temperament, his wide reading, his status, his experiences, and the force of circumstance.

The six months following the submission of Condorcet's proposal for a Constitution were decisive in the politics of the Convention, for the leadership of the Revolution, and for the policies of the government. During this period the Committee of Public Safety was established, the law of the maximum was decreed, the Convention was purged of the Girondins, the Montagnard Constitution of 1793 was adopted, and then approved by a popular plebiscite, Marat was assassinated, and French arms suffered a series of defeats. For nearly five of these months Carnot was out of Paris and absent from the deliberations of the Convention. He was representing the Convention, however, in the Departments of the North and the Pas-de-Calais, and with the Army of the North, from March 12 to August 6, as one of the eighty-two Commissioners appointed on his motion of March 9 to help in the levy of 300,000 troops. To April 8 his colleague was a former merchant, Lesage-Senault, an elderly deputy of sixty-three from the North. After that date the lawyer Ernest Duquesnoy, a middle-aged deputy from the Pas-de-Calais, was associated with him.

The law of February 24, 1793, had provided for the amalgamation of the regular and the volunteer troops, had ordered the levy of 300,000 men, and had fixed the contingent to be raised by each department. When Carnot and Lesage arrived in Baupaume they discovered that there was confusion among the authorities because of a conflict between this law and an order of March 5 from the Commissioners of the Convention to Belgium, inspired by Danton. The officers of the municipality soon discovered that the two Commissioners agreeed with their point of view that the decree of the Convention prevailed over the order of the Representatives. The report, however, became current that Carnot and Lesage had been assassinated during disorders growing out of this controversy in Baupaume. On March 19 Duhem read a letter to the Convention reporting that the two commissioners had been insulted in Baupaume. The two denied these reports in a letter to the Committee of General Defense on March 24.

After helping put Douai and Lille in a proper state of defense, Carnot and Lesage went on into Maritime Flanders, stopping in succession at Dunkirk, Bergues and Cassel. They were constantly traveling about, inspecting fortifications, participating in the assemblies of the departments, districts and communes, and attending, as often as possible, the plenary sessions of all the Commissioners in the north of France. These meetings were held each week, first at Douai, then at Arras. The division of the Army of the North operating in Maritime Flanders was commanded by the aged and infirm General O'Moran.

In their first report to the Convention on March 15, the two Commissioners reported that the counter-revolutionaries were actively opposing the levy of the troops and announced that they had ordered the arrest of certain ringleaders in these movements against the state.[25] Carnot and Lesage early sensed the insidious influence of English propaganda in this region and forbade all communication with England, pending an order from the Convention.

Dumouriez arrived in Brussels on March 10, to find the troops disorganized, and the Belgians in revolt against the French. Dumouriez severely censured the French national commissioners, invited the city magistrates to lay their complaints before him, and dissolved the Jacobin clubs. He wrote his famous letter to the Convention on March 12 in which he justified his conduct by pointing out that the situation in Belgium was due to the avarice and injustice of the national commissioners. He began restoring discipline in the army, which he took steps to reorganize. He was eager to assume the offensive, but Coburg and the Austrians anticipated him in this, and the French troops were severely defeated at Neerwinden, March 18-19. Coburg let a golden opportunity pass by not following up the victory by pursuit of the French troops. Coburg and Dumouriez, and then Mack and Dumouriez concluded an agreement for the evacuation of Belgium on the part of the French, by March 30. By the 31st the French were all on the French side of the frontier.

On March 29, Carnot and Lesage, meeting at Lille with the Commissioners to Belgium, ordered General Dumouriez to appear before them to answer the charge of treason which had been laid against him.[26] Dumouriez replied on the same day from Tournai that it was impossible for him to appear because of the military crisis which compelled his continued presence with the army. The Commissioners decided to wait upon him at his headquarters, but on the following day they concluded to wait until he had effected the retreat which he had planned. On that same day the Convention issued an order to Dumouriez to appear before it. It ordered the minister of war to the Army of the North, and called the Commissioners to Belgium back to report. It then appointed a new commission of five to the Army of the North.[27] One of these was Carnot, who thereby had his powers enlarged.

Dumouriez ordered the arrest of these five Commissioners on April 2. The four who were already at Lille, Camus, Quinette, Lamarque and Bancal, were arrested and sent into Austrian prison camps. Carnot was at Douai and escaped. Dumouriez then announced that he would march on Paris and "stop the bloody anarchy which reigned there,"[28] but his army would not follow him. Carnot and Lesage issued a resounding decree and put a price upon Dumouriez, dead or alive.[29] Carnot wrote to the Convention on April 3 to recommend the appointment of Dampierre to succeed Dumouriez. The two Commissioners took vigorous measures to counteract the treason of Dumouriez.[30] The Convention outlawed him on April 3. Dampierre issued a patriotic proclamation to his troops on the following day. On the same day the Provisional Executive Council named him to be Commander-in-chief of the Army of the North, and the Convention approved the appointment. Dumouriez deserted the army and France on April 5 and went over to the enemy, taking a handful of hussars, and his own staff comprising three lieutenant-generals, eight major-generals, and two commissioners of war. On April 8 Carnot and Lesage reported to the Convention that order had been restored in the army and that Dampierre had begun the necessary reorganization.

The Convention appointed eight commissioners to the Army of the North and the Ardennes on April 4. Carnot and Duquesnoy were among these. The others were commissioners for the first time. The Committee of Public Safety, in its session of April 7, decided to correspond directly with the commissioners to the armies and to the departments, and on the 9th it sent its first despatch to Carnot and Lesage. April 13 was the date of the first correspondence from Carnot and his colleagues to the Committee. The Convention had extended Carnot's membership on the departmental commission on the preceding day. On the 13th Carnot and his associates authorized General La Marliere to make Colonel Macdonald (the future Marshal of Napoleon) his adjutant-general. Carnot and Duquesnoy reported to the Convention from Dunkirk on April 16. Their lengthy report dealt with the command, the disposition of the troops, and the spirit of the people and the troops. They called particular attention to the numerous women camp-followers who were demoralizing the troops, and recommended legislation to regulate this.[31] They mentioned the same matter to the Committee of Public Safety on April 22. In a report on April 29 to the Committee of Public Safety Carnot and Duquesnoy commented that the breach in commercial relations between England and France was harmful to England but advantageous to France. The same report included a severe criticism of the ministry of war for the delays involved in the provisioning and the payment of the troops. It also bewailed the lack of small change in commercial circulation and suggested an ingenious remedy. It called attention to the fact that the army was infested with spies.

Carnot's commission to the Army of the North was again renewed on April 30. The twelve members who constituted this commission were invested with "unlimited powers." They were required to report daily to the Committee of Public Safety, and weekly to the Convention. The Committee of Public Safety was required to present a resumé of the various commissions' work to the Convention each week. The Committee on Finance also had to make a weekly report on the sums expended by the commissions to the eleven armies. One-half of the representatives to the armies were replaced each month. Thus the system of government and administration in the Convention was gradually taking form through the trial and error method.

Carnot and Duquesnoy had the unpleasant duty of reporting to the Convention on May 1 that the citizens of Saint-Omer were complaining about and protesting the recruitment in their town, claiming that their quota was proportionally in excess of that of other towns in the department, particularly of Arras.[32] They questioned the impartiality of the Commissioners. These admitted to the Convention that the quota levied on Saint-Omer was disproportionate but stated that the original fault lay with the municipality for giving incomplete statistics on its men already serving in the army. The Commissioners reported that it was too late and too inexpedient for a complete revision of the levy in the department, for the benefit of Saint-Omer. Carnot remarked, in the report, that Saint-Omer was a place of residence for him that "he loved infinitely," and that, if "he was accessible at all to partiality, he would certainly favor this town above all others." It took some time to liquidate the grievances of the citizens of Saint-Omer and the Commissioners devoted considerable correspondence to the matter. On May 15, Carnot and Duquesnoy began sending fifty-four men from each battalion to the Vendée, under the provisions of the order of May 4 in the Committee of Public Safety.[33]

The Convention named Custine to be Commander-in-chief of the Army of the North on May 13, on the recommendation of the Executive Council. He succeeded Dampierre who had just been killed in battle. On the 6th Bouchotte, minister of war, had named Carnot-Feulins, then chief of battalion in the engineering corps and serving in Paris, to act as Special Commissioner of the Executive Council to the Army of the North. The Committee of Public Safety, in a decree of May 28 to the Representatives of the People with the Army of the North, outlined the respective authorities of the general and the commissioners.[34] It named the general as the "responsible agent" for military operations. The Commissioners were to serve as a "council of state" to the army.

The Commissioners were, however, granted powers superior to those of the civil and military administration.

In a despatch to the Convention on May 30, Carnot and Duquesnoy announced the attack planned for that night on Furnes, a town important because it was strategic in the penetration to Nieuport and Ostende. It was a strongly-entrenched place, defended by 1200 infantrymen, sixty dragoons and forty hussars. Two French columns of 2500 and 1500 men each were to converge on Furnes, one debouching from Bergues under General Stettenhoffen, the other from the camp of Ghyvelde under General Ricardot. The general attack was under the direction of General O'Moran. The despatch stated that the two Commissioners intended to march at the head of the first-named column.[35] The following day the two colleagues announced the capture of Furnes.[36] Nine prisoners, eleven horses, and considerable stores were taken. The two Commissioners also mentioned the consequent pillaging. The troops could easily have followed up their advantage by pushing on to Nieuport. They had already started, under orders, when the lassitude, drunkenness, and disorderliness of the troops, loaded as they were with plunder, compelled the order to retreat. This behavior called forth the ringing proclamation and appeal to the troops from the two Commissioners on June 1 from Bergues.[37] In it they said:

> The entire world will know that these soldiers, these Frenchmen, these republicans have forgotten their laws, their principles, that they have forgotten their honor, have outraged nature and have violated the rights of man. What a triumph for our enemies! What a pretext for calumniating our revolution! . . .
>
> Remember, Soldiers, that the first of your titles is that of citizen: do not become a scourge more terrible to our fatherland than that of our enemies; they know that the Republic cannot exist without virtue, and they want, by intrigues and by spying, to stifle its germ among us. Put aside this spirit of rapine and cupidity; let us honor the civil virtues more than the military; let the feeble and the oppressed be sure to find in you a protecting force. The aged, the women, the children, the cultivators of the soil, peaceful men of all countries, are our brothers; we ought to protect them against tyranny; we ought to defend their persons and their property as we would our own. Such have been the sentiments, even in the centuries of despotism, of

French soldiers; such ought to be, even more, the sentiments of the soldiers of the Republic, one and indivisible.

The Commissioners saw to it that as much of the stolen goods as possible was restored. Carnot recommended that the Convention indemnify the inhabitants for that which could not be restored.

The Committee of Public Safety sent General O'Moran a copy of the new Constitution on July 4, with a letter in which the Committee said: "Never has a constitution so well consecrated the principles of national sovereignty, the rights of the man and citizen, the security of persons and property, the national recognition of those who serve the fatherland, the influence of traditions and the public instruction. The Convention congratulates itself in having fixed the epoch of French regeneration."[38] Bouchotte addressed a proclamation to the troops on the subject of this Constitution on the 7th of July. In an interesting report by Carnot, Desacy and Delbrel to the Committee of Public Safety on July 13 from Arras, attention was urgently called to the growing practice of men buying their way out of the army by purchasing replacements.[39]

Early in August the Committee of Public Safety called Carnot to Paris to present detailed information to it. On the 11th it ordered him to present himself to Houchard, the new Commander-in-chief of the Army of the North, and to confer with him relative to the "important views" which Carnot had presented to the Committee.[40] Carnot left Houchard's headquarters on August 14 for Paris. Le Tourneur, writing from Arras on August 16 stated that if Carnot's plans as presented to Houchard were followed, the French would soon be in Belgium.[41] Carnot had just been added to the Committee of Public Safety.

Carnot's life as a Representative of the People with the Army of the North and in the departments of the North and the Pas-de-Calais had been full of activity. His numerous reports to Paris reveal a wide grasp of economic and political, as well as military facts. There is little of the oratorical or demagogical in these reports, or in the orders of Carnot. Nearly everything is practical and matter of fact. His local orders were almost countless and covered nearly every conceivable subject, from intervention on behalf of a destitute woman, widowed by the war, to the ordering of great quantities of supplies, suspension of officers and officials, and the nomination of local councils. He counselled capably with the military commanders as to the movements of the troops. The relations between the Representatives and the armies were intimate. The Government was closely controlling the army. Carnot was becoming increasingly critical of the ministry of war and of the Executive Council. These criticisms had been acquiring steady momentum from the time of his mission to the Pyrenees. He was gravitating toward the conviction that a strongly centralized government was essential to the successful conduct of the war. His correspondence with the Committee of Public Safety was formal but cordial. Mutual respect was apparent.

Carnot served a hard apprenticeship in the military aspect of the Revolution in thus helping organize the defense in the North, in helping levy the troops, in helping find provisions, in facing the problems incident with new recruits and a changing command, and in combatting treason, particularly in high places, and the activities of spies and counter-revolutionaries. Throughout this experience and service Carnot continued to emphasize the pre-eminence of the civic virtues, even for the soldier at war. He resumed his duties in the Convention fully aware of the gravity of the nation's internal and external situation. For him there was no turning back, or compromise. He had a critical confidence in the future. He would try to maintain a balanced judgment in the turbulent times that beset France.

The Revolution moved on relentlessly and changefully in Paris during Carnot's absence in the North. In March and April the Convention took rigorous action against the enemies of the state. The Committee of Public Safety was established by the Convention on April 6 with nine members. This was a victory for the Mountain. There were no Girondins elected to the Committee. Danton and Delacroix were Montagnards and the other seven were from the Plain. Barère, Cambon and Robert Lindet were leading members. This Committee was vested with authority to supervise the ministers, to deliberate in secret, and, under urgent circumstances, to assume responsibility for the general defense, both domestic and external. It was granted a special fund of 100,000 francs for which there was to be no accounting. On March 13 an extraordinary revolutionary tribunal was established. On the 30th the deputies on mission in the departments to raise the new army were given extraordinary and almost arbitrary powers. This enrollment of 300,000 recruits was the beginning of the huge scheme of national conscription that was to be perfected during the Convention. The law of the *Maximum* was decreed by the Convention on May 3. This was a uniform price for grain, although the table of prices varied according to local conditions.

In mid-spring the Girondins still controlled the Convention, but popular petitions against them were increasing steadily. Danton had been striving consistently to effect a compromise between the groups. The Commission of Twelve, which had been established to investigate and quell the disorders in Paris, was suppressed on May 27, after which Danton definitely aligned himself with the Jacobins. Through the strenuous, almost desperate, efforts, of the Girondins the Commission was re-established on May 28, and, in reply, the sections began preparing for insurrection. The Central Insurrectionary Committee declared itself *en permanence* on May 30, and when the Convention assembled on the 31st it was surrounded by 30,000 Parisians. The Convention proceeded to abolish the Commission of Twelve and the mob dispersed. On June 1 a petition against thirty-two Girondins was again introduced in the Convention and on the following day the mob again surrounded the Convention to force action on the petition. The Convention finally decreed the arrest of thirty deputies, including all of the members of the Twelve and two ministers. The Girondins were put under arrest in their own homes to await trial by the Revolutionary Tribunal. Some of the detained Girondins, refusing to abide by their arrest and joined by other Girondins, began organizing resistance to the Convention. This proved to be futile. Their course was run for the time, and "the experiment in popular government had failed. France was under the dictatorship of the Mountain, and the Mountain was under the dictatorship of the organized petty bourgeoisie and artisans of Paris."[42]

The Montagnard victors in the Convention on May 31 and

June 2 evidently demanded the adhesion of the Representatives-on-mission to this proscription of the Girondins.[43] Carnot's biographer-son states that Carnot and Duquesnoy had many live discussions concerning their response to this demand. They then decided, he says, to send in separate replies since they could not agree. Duquesnoy, according to this statement, adhered to the action of the Convention. Carnot replied that he would have to suspend judgment because he lacked knowledge of the facts. He did announce, says the biographer, that he deplored the conflict between the parties in the Convention.[44]

The Mountain busied itself upon a Constitution immediately after June 2. The one hastily completed and adopted on June 24 was intended to disarm the Federalists. It did not differ radically from the one submitted by Condorcet to the Convention on February 15. It tended however to strengthen the central government, particularly by subordinating the ministers to the representative body, whereas the Girondin Constitution had strengthened the Executive Council. The Jacobin Constitution promised popular education, guaranteed the right to a livelihood, and made the declaration of war dependent upon a previous consultation of the country. It included the Declaration of Rights proposed by Robespierre to the Convention on April 24, although it omitted four articles whereby poor citizens received tax exemptions and economic support from the fortunes of the rich. The Jacobin Constitution did effectively guarantee political democracy but it did little to organize social democracy. It recognized the right of insurrection against an unjust government, but it did not adequately recognize any fundamental obligation on the part of the government to guarantee the social rights of the poor. It contained provisions for public relief, and it stated the workers' right to subsistence, but otherwise it came out strongly for the rights of property owners. It was provided that the new Constitution was not to become effective until it was ratified by a majority of the people voting in the primary assemblies. The Constitution of 1793 was probably devised more as a weapon in the campaign against the Federalists than as a true reflection of the Montagnard social philosophy.

The true Federal movement generally collapsed after this. In

Marseilles, Lyons, and Toulon, however, it developed into a Royalist movement, and in the Vendée the movement was thoroughly royalist and completely counter-revolutionary.

Marat, the "militant professional radical," was assassinated by Charlotte Corday on July 13. By August 6 the number of Girondins proscribed had grown to fifty-five. On August 10 representatives of the primary assemblies announced the popular approval of the Constitution by a small vote of 1,801,918 to 11,610, but with about 100,000 approving only on certain conditions, including the adoption of federalist amendments, the liberation of the arrested Girondins, the convocation of a new assembly, the recall of the representatives on mission, and the suppression of the maximum. The Constitution was suspended by the Convention on October 10 by a decree that the government of France was "revolutionary until the peace." During the summer Metz, Valenciennes, and Condé fell to the Austrians and Prussians, the Vendéans were generally successful, and the citizens of Toulon welcomed the English Admiral Hood into their harbor on August 28.

The Committee of Public Safety was reorganized on July 10, with nine members. Danton was not re-elected to the Committee. Gasparin resigned on July 27 because of ill health and was replaced by Robespierre. No military man had as yet been a member of the Committee. All during August conscription was discussed, and on August 12 the Convention suggested to the Committee a *levée en masse.* Two days later, on the 14th, Carnot and Prieur (de la Côte-d'Or), both engineering officers, were added to the Committee of Public Safety, despite certain objections of Robespierre. Thuriot resigned on September 20. Billaud-Varenne and Collot d'Herbois were added on September 6 and the number of members stood at twelve. For nearly a year (until 9 Thermidor) there were really nine active members of the Committee. Herault de Sechelles was arrested on 25 Ventôse (March 15) and was executed, along with Danton, on 16 Germinal (April 15). Jean-Bon Saint-Andre and Prieur (de la Marne) were usually on mission to the armies. The other members were Barère, Couthon, Saint-Just and Robert Lindet. There were six lawyers, two army officers, two men of letters, a civil servant, and a

Protestant pastor in the Committee. Their average age was just over thirty-seven. The oldest was Robert Lindet, who was forty-seven. Carnot was forty. Saint-Just, who was the youngest, was twenty-six. Danton was thirty-four at the time.

The dictatorship of this Committee of Public Safety was to raise the "nation in arms," and save France and the Revolution from its foreign foes. It was to govern France strongly and effectively. It was to create and use the instrument of the Terror to combat the counter-revolution and to consolidate the Revolution, and then direct it to partisan purposes. It was to breed the inevitable revulsion and reaction, and was to condition the conservative, weak bourgeois republic of the Directory.

Chapter V

THE DICTATORSHIP IN COMMISSION

THE DICTATORSHIP of the great Committee of Public Safety and its organized establishment and exercise of the Terror took shape gradually in the late summer of 1793, and by December 4 the revolutionary government had been completed and codified. This took place under the pressure of events and the conflict of leaders and groups.

The national crisis had been acute in mid-summer. The Federalist insurrection had just collapsed, but by the end of August the English were in control of the local governement in Toulon, and in Lyons class war raged between the Royalists and the Jacobins. The republican government began a systematic siege of the city early in August. The stalemate in the Vendée continued. Throughout France, but particularly in Paris, the financial crisis and the food shortage were severe. In Paris the spokesmen of the popular extremists, the *Enragés,* were continuing their attacks on the Convention. The militant left-wing republicans, later to be known as the Hébertists, or the ultra-revolutionists, were in the process of taking over the social program of the *Enragés.* These radicals were strongly represented in the Commune, in the Cordelier Club, in the ministry of war, and had nameless thousands behind them in the poor sections of Paris.

During the summer all remaining vestiges of feudalism were abolished, the metric system of weights and measures was adopted, the conservative old academies were discontinued, granaries were established for each district, and the Bourse, the stronghold of the speculators and stockjobbers, was closed. In August the arrest of all nationals of enemy countries was decreed, Marie Antoinette was transferred to the Conciergerie, and the tombs of the Kings of France at Saint-Denis were destroyed. August 10 was made a fête to welcome the delegates of the primary assemblies, to celebrate the ratification of the Constitution, and to honor the first year of the Republic.

The delegates from the primary assemblies brought popular demands with them, particularly that all suspects be arrested, and that a *levée en masse* be effected. The Committee of Public Safety finally yielded to the latter demand and on August 23 presented a systematic scheme for the war-time organization of the entire nation under which France was to become a huge armed camp, a "nation in arms," under the control of the Convention. During the month a serious attempt was made at financial and currency reform. The national debt was funded by converting the capital of each bond into a perpetual annuity paying five per cent interest. The old distinctions between government bonds of the Old Régime and of the Revolution were abolished. Assignats issued before the advent of the Republic were to lose all legal value after January 1, 1794. The Convention also decided to enforce the compulsory loan, decreed in principle in May, upon all citizens, proportionate to their income and progressively to a one-hundred per cent loan on sums beyond nine-thousand livres.

The outlook was indeed dark as September came in. The food supply in Paris was very low. A long drought in the summer had materially reduced the harvests. Despite popular pressure the deputies refused to vote governmental regulation of food prices. The exasperated Paris populace threatened violence. They criticized particularly the revolutionary tribunal for its slowness, and the Committee of Public Safety for retaining generals of noble birth at the front. The departments were reluctant to execute the *levée en masse*. The last straw in the popular unrest was the official receipt on September 4 of the news of the surrender of Toulon, the chief naval base on the Mediterranean, which had opened its doors to Admiral Hood on August 28. The popular excitement came to a head and the extremists organized their new offensive against the Convention. Hébert and Billaud-Varenne joined them, the Jacobins fell into line, and the Commune added its blessing. On September 5 a mob of petitioners under the leadership of Chaumette, the procurator of the Commune, invaded the Convention, and demanded bread and the establishment of a revolutionary army of the interior.

The Committee of Public Safety yielded and made Terror the order of the day. Billaud-Varenne and Collot-d'Herbois, "sincere republicans and fanatical terrorists," were added to the Committee on the following day. The revolutionary army of the interior was organized under Rousin, a staunch Hébertist. Pay of forty sous a day was decreed for attendance at meetings of the sections so that the poor could attend. The Revolutionary Tribunal was reorganized and divided into four sections, in two groups working alternately. The number of judges was increased from ten to sixteen, the jury to sixty, and the public prosecutor, Fouquier-Tinville, was given five assistants, and the entire personnel was to be closely supervised by the Committees of Public Safety and General Security. This Tribunal became the supreme court of the system of revolutionary justice, and death was the exclusive penalty. There were similar courts in the departments. These revolutionary tribunals became an integral part of the revolutionary machinery, and the Terror which had been spasmodic up until then, became regular and permanent.

The first comprehensive law of suspects was voted by the Convention on September 17, but the current personnel of the Committee of General Security was not particularly well qualified to execute the new decrees through the committees of surveillance throughout France. The Committee of Public Safety secured the right, therefore, to name the members of the Committee of General Security, as well as of all other governmental committees. The Committee of Public Safety immediately eliminated four members of the Committee of General Security who had been implicated in financial and jobbing scandals and intrigues. In the reorganized Committee the "fierce terrorists" were in the majority. The Committee of General Security formed the central administration of the revolutionary police. It supervised the police throughout all of France, issued warrants of arrest unhampered by *habeas corpus*, had charge of prisons, and administered "revolutionary justice" through the committees of surveillance in the departments. Its twelve members lacked the personal distinction and prestige of the members of the Committee of Public Safety. The two Committees were supposed to be coordinate. At first they cooperated well with each other, even meeting together occasionally as one body, but dissension devoloped and grew between them as time went on.

The Jacobin Clubs were incorporated into the governmental system by decree on September 13. They were empowered to denounce all suspects and unworthy officials, and to express the voice of the sovereign people. These clubs were distributed throughout France. In 1794 there were 6800 clubs with about 500,000 members, held together by correspondence, by the exchange of club journals, and by the visits of "missionary" delegates.

Some disgruntled Montagnards in the Convention attacked the Committee of Public Safety on September 24-25 because of its "purification" of the army staffs and the arrest of Houchard, the commander-in-chief of the Army of the North. Thuriot, a friend of Danton, had just resigned from the Committee and was vigorous in his criticisms of its activity. This general attack coincided with the agitation in the streets of Paris, where the masses clamored for the trial of Marie Antoinette and the imprisoned Girondins, as well as for the governmental regulation of prices. The Committee called for a show-down in the Convention and won a vote of confidence. The opposition scattered and Danton withdrew to his country home near Paris. The Committee then strengthened itself by granting the demands of the Parisians. The law of the *Maximum*, fixing maximum prices on commodities of prime necessity, was finally decreed on September 29. Commodity prices were to be determined in each department on the basis of the prices of 1790 plus one-third. By the provisions of the same decree, the wages of workers were also regulated, on the basis of the 1790 level plus one-half. The "economic dictatorship" of the Terror as finally completed included government requisitioning for military purposes at the official maximum, municipal or district requisitioning to feed civilians, with the necessary system of bread- and meat-cards, the establishment of a uniform *pain d'égalité,* the closing of the Stock Exchange, and the governmental supervision of foreign trade and foreign exchange.

The Convention, on October 3, ordered forty-one of the imprisoned Girondins, and Marie Antoinette, to be brought before the Revolutionary Tribunal for trial. On the tenth, on a motion of Saint-Just, the Convention decreed that "the provisional Government of France is revolutionary until the peace." Marie Antoinette was guillotined on the 16th, followed by twenty-one Girondin leaders on the 31st, while the seventy-three members of the Convention who had protested the events of May 31-June 2 were imprisoned.

On December 4 the numerous decrees that had decreed the government of the Terror were codified in a single document commonly called the constitution of the Terror. By this the ministers and the Executive Council were made directly responsible to the Committee of Public Safety. The ministers and the members of the ordinary committees of the Convention were reduced to the position of clerks. The Convention itself was reduced to a subordinate position and parliamentary debates during the Terror were quite perfunctory. The only stirring sessions were those in which reports of the two great committees were read by Robespierre, Barère, Amar, Billaud, Saint-Just, or another, and then faithfully accepted. Attendance in the Convention was small with oftentimes not more than one hundred constituting the quorum. At times as many as one-half the members were on mission. Others voluntarily absented themselves from a body that had largely become impotent.

The constitution of the Terror also provided that the representatives on mission, chosen by the Committee of Public Safety and approved by the Convention, were to supervise the conscription of men and horses, and to keep the armies in the field efficient and their generals faithful and loyal. They were to report every ten days to the Committee of Public Safety. Most of these representatives fulfilled their tasks conscientiously, some very ably. A few of these *proconsuls,* however, set up temporary principalities of their own. By the decrees of December 4 the departments were shorn of much of their authority. The powers of departmental assemblies were limited to taxation, and all but taxation officials in the departments were to be discharged. The central government was to work particularly through the districts and municipalities, because these had proved themselves more revolutionary than the departments. The district officials were to be known as national agents, and were permanent resident officials, appointed by the Executive Council with the approval of the Committee of Public Safety. All police in the municipalities were to be under the domination of the Committee of Public Safety.

It was the legislation of September, codified in December, that created "the octopus-like revolutionary government, focused in the Committee of Public Safety, working in Paris through the Committee of General Security and the Revolutionary Tribunal and thrusting its tentacles out into the departments through the representatives on mission, the Revolutionary army, and revolutionary committees."[1]

Excepting for the abolition of the Executive Council in the following April on motion of Carnot the machinery of the revolutionary government of the Terror was now completed. It was, essentially, a war government, not a constitutional one but one that was truly "revolutionary until the peace." It was centralized and dictatorial and it ruthlessly and consciously used the Terror, that "dictatorship of distress," against the foreign enemy and all the domestic enemies of the Republic. Robespierre said at the time, "the mainspring of popular government in a revolution is at once virtue and terror; virtue without which terror is baleful, terror without which virtue is powerless." By virtue the revolutionaries meant "love of the patrie, the sacrifice of personal interests to the state, the quasi-mystical absorption of the individual will into the general will."[2]

The dynamo of the revolutionary power house was the great Committee of Public Safety. Given complete administrative powers by the Convention it soon took over general supervision of policy. Urged on by "irresistible necessities" it became virtually the government of republican France. Although it was more informal than a modern cabinet, for the critical months in the Convention it demonstrated solidarity in important affairs of general concern. The really important measures were thoroughly discussed in the sessions of the Committee, and the decisions were made on the responsibility of the Committee as a whole.[3] For these it seems that at least three signatures were necessary, while the signature of a single member was sufficient to validate a decree of the Convention, and many of the orders and decrees of the Committee have but one or two signatures.[4] Carnot, who attended the majority of the Committee's meetings and signed most of its orders and decrees, once spoke of the necessity of giving between five and six hundred signatures a day,[5] many of which he said were given without reading and "as of confidence."[6] The members were all equal in authority and no one of them ever assumed a recognized predominance among them. The Committee had no responsible head charged with the formulation of a general policy. The members were all radical revolutionaries, well-educated and of respectable antecedents. They were experienced and competent and their sincerity and devotion were beyond question. Unlike the leaders in the Directory, they were all scrupulously honest, and remained above every consideration of personal profit.

The Committee of Public Safety gradually organized itself into specialties and within these the responsible members were pretty much their own masters, their colleagues approving as of confidence and usually without discussion those proposals that did not touch matters of general political concern.[7] Carnot, Lindet and Prieur (de la Côte-d'Or) occupied themselves with military affairs. The "cool, methodical, tireless"[8] Carnot had as his special function the personnel and the tactical direction of the armies. Prieur was charged with the manufactury of arms and munitions, and the hospital service. Lindet was responsible for subsistence, clothing, and transportation. He also did much of the work usually assumed by a minister of the interior. The work of this faithful and single-minded revolutionary was indeed colossal, as the records of the Committee of Public Safety amply demonstrate. The "indefatigable" Barère, who was a facile, conciliatory speaker and a thorough parliamentarian, usually reported to the Convention for the Committee, and served as its chief liaison officer with the Convention. Barère and Herault directed foreign affairs. Barère, Collot d'Herbois and Couthon were entrusted with the correspondence with the officials and with representatives of the government on mission. The honest and conscientious Saint-André directed the "miserable" navy, and was much of the time on mission. This was also true of Prieur (de la Marne) who hardly ever attended a meeting of the Committee because of his official absences from Paris. Couthon, of the twisted legs, the noble brow, the "bell-like voice," and the revolutionary spirit of a fanatic, gave himself to politics and the police. He was the devoted adherent of Robespierre. Saint-Just spent about half his time on mission, a work in which he was highly successful. He also devoted himself to constitutional legislation. Robespierre gave some particular attention to public instruction but he mixed freely in most matters, especially in foreign affairs, usually in a large, general fashion without attention to technical knowledge or to the practical application of details. He served as a sort of "front"[9] for the Committee, whose members used his popularity to get their measures through.

Collot and Billaud were sadists. The former, a "dissolute cutthroat,"[10] was a brutal terrorist, the latter, cold and relentless, was a gloomy fanatic. For both, the excesses of the Terror were the gratification of natural ferocity. To Robespierre, Couthon and Saint-Just, on the contrary, these excesses were the "logical reduction into practice of a political theory."[11] The very youthful Saint-Just was an ardent revolutionary, a fearless visionary, with rigid convictions and strong decisiveness of character. He was more energetic and more ruthless than Robespierre. A recent biographer has aptly characterized this flaming spirit: "He was too young to learn tolerance for others, too successful to harbour doubts of himself, and too lacking in humour to suspect that he might be clinging to a pose instead of a principle."[12]

Around Robespierre, the truly "Incorruptible," and the prophet of a new religion, the conflict between the partisans and the severe critics rages with increasing force. The debunkers and the rehabilitators wage an unceasing academic struggle for a "true" reconstruction and assessment. His greatest apologist, Mathiez, makes him the leader of the democratic party,[13] the champion of the social revolution,[14] the "unchallenged leader of the *sans-culottes*,"[15] the "just and clear sighted statesman who lived but for the good of his country,"[16] and whose religion was that of social deism. The secret of this svelt and gracious person, Mathiez says, was his sincerity. He praises unstintedly his "rare personal qualities, his coolness and courage, his acute insight, his formidable eloquence, his remarkable faculty of organization, his entire disinterestedness."[17] Others, however, call him cold, aloof, uncertain, fearful, not an organizer nor a leader, a mediocre man with a great religious passion. Louis Madelin says: "Virtue: this is the key-word to Maximilien Robespierre's character; he was a man of virtue."[18] He goes on to paint this devotee of Rousseau as an honest, upright, harsh, utterly chaste, ever-prudent man of simple, frugal tastes; a small, slender but well-built man of portentous gravity; not a man of action; very long-winded; a man of boundless vanity; a very dogmatic being, a high priest, with a perpetually frozen, pontifical expression; a man who carried idealism to the point of absurdity; and the people he loved and vaunted was an ideal, almost conventional people.[19]

Whatever he was, Robespierre personified the more radical forces waging the feud of principle, emphasis, direction and leadership, with Danton, his temperamental antithesis. Around Robespierre the Terror was to climax, and then consume him as its last great victim. Satiated, it was then to die and the Great Committee was to gradually disintegrate.

There is some evidence that the public opinion of the day classified the nine active members of the Committee of Public Safety into three groups, named by their contemporaries as the revolutionaries, the *politiques*, and the workers.[20] According to this point of view, the first group included Barère, Billaud-Varenne and Collot d'Herbois. Their reports were particularly designed to arouse the political emotions. The second group prepared the legislative program, and controlled the police and the revolutionary tribunal. It included Robespierre, Couthon and Saint-Just. The third group was composed of Carnot, Lindet and Prieur (de la Côte-d'Or). Modern authorities dispute this classification and while they admit the special functions and responsibilities of the individual members they unite them in responsibility, not necessarily equal, for public and political policy.[21] Certainly it is hardly fair not to call all of the members workers. They all worked with feverish activity.

One is astounded at the variety of problems resolved by the Committee, at the multitude of orders and decrees ground out daily in the political and administrative mill, and at the quantity of letters comprising the official correspondence of the members. These men were not trained administrators, nor were most of them of a bureaucratic type. The methods of executing the will of the Committee strike a modern as confused, cumbersome and inefficient. Much of the clerical work was done laboriously, by hand of course, by the members themselves, or was delegated to the host of persons attached to the Committee and to the ministers. The National Archives attest, however, to the tremendous amount of work contributed by each member to the conduct of government. These ardent novices threw themselves with enthusiasm and fidelity into the task of consolidating the Revolution, defending the nation, and governing France.

Carnot, in close association with Lindet and Prieur (de la Côte-d'Or), and in collaboration with Bouchotte, minister of war, who played a decidedly subordinate, but hardworking, rôle, buried himself in his bureau for fourteen to sixteen hours a day.[22] Madelin characterizes him at the time as "tenacious to the point of obstinacy, and not very easy going, being rather dictatorial; unable to bear contradiction, he was hard sometimes even harsh, and always unbending; he seldom smiled, and never flattered," he "distrusted politicians," and he was "upright, disinterested and scrupulously honest. . . .[23] "Although he seemed cold and reserved, he was really an enthusiast. 'All greatness must have a soul capable of deep feeling,' he said later. And these words embody the spirit of his own enterprise. . . . Thanks to his many solid, harmonious qualities he was the dispassionate organizer of victory amidst this effervescent nation, because, in spite of his deep passions, he had methodically arranged his work."[24] With a passion for details, he "hated fuss and worked in silence."[25]

Carnot minutely directed all operations, corresponded voluminously, by hand and by dictation, with the generals on the field and with the Representatives-on-mission, directed, changed and controlled personnel, and, on occasion, took the field to supervise and stimulate the action of the troops.[26] He was absent, however, only twice from the central office during his membership on the Committee, once from September 25 to 28, 1793, to take instructions to Jourdan, the newly-appointed general of the Army of the North, and from October 6 to 20, 1793, to see to the execution of the plans leading to the important victory of Wattignies and the lifting of the siege of Maubeuge. In the engagement at Wattignies, which Napoleon later called "the finest feat of arms of the Revolution," Carnot demonstrated great personal bravery in leading the attack and in inspiring the troops to action.

In short, Carnot, in eighteen months, staffed and directed to victory the fourteen raw armies raised by the Revolution. This was truly a colossal task. Carnot, in a report to the Convention on March 4, 1795, summarized the military achievements of the Republic for the seventeen months from the battle of Hondschoote on September 8, 1793 to February 3, 1795, as follows: "Twenty-seven victories, of which eight were in pitched battles; one hundred and twenty lesser engagements; eighty-thousand of the enemy killed; ninety-one-thousand prisoners of war taken; one hundred and sixteen fortified places or important towns captured, of which thirty-six fell after siege or blockade; two-hundred and thirty forts or redoubts taken; thirty-eight hundred cannons and seventy-thousand muskets captured; nineteen hundred *milliers* of powder; ninety flags taken."[27] In this detailed report appear the names of men well on their way to military fame: Houchard, Daoust, Kellermann, Jourdan, Dugommier, Pichegru, and Hoche as generals in chief; Lepelletier, Desjardin, and Saint-Cyr as generals; Macdonald, Masséna, Desaix, Lefevre, Moreau, Souham, Kléber, Lemoine, Moncey, Lebrun, Schérer, Augereau, Marceau, Laurent, Vandamme, and Marbot as commandants, in Carnot's phraseology. The most of these latter officers were at least generals of brigade at the time, and some were generals of division.

To discover what kind of an instrument Carnot inherited to make these achievements possible it is necessary to go back in some detail into the history of the French army in the eighteenth century.[28] The pre-revolutionary French army was effective according to the standards of the times. It was partly an army of volunteers, recruited mainly from the lowest part of the population. Unruly lads, unemployed mechanics and runaway apprentices were readily enlisted by skillful recruiting agents.[29]

Many soldiers were only twenty years of age, and boys of sixteen could be recruited. The term of service was eight years and the soldiers were likely to re-enlist so that military service became a lifelong profession.[30] There were enough mercenaries in the army to comprise twenty-three regiments. The relations between the officers and the men were more intimate and kindly than was true elsewhere in Europe. The command of a company was sometimes almost hereditary. The strength of the army lay in the non-commissioned officer, "grown gray in arms, and proud of his authority; always capable of commanding a section, usually fit to command a company. He understood his men, guided them, and enjoyed their complete confidence."[31] Discipline was good, and there was a strong feeling of *esprit de corps* in the several regiments. But the pay was poor, the food was bad, the barrack accommodations were cramped and inadequate, the hospitals were unsanitary, and the uniforms were ill adapted to military life and to campaigning. Desertions were very common. It is said that during the Seven Years' War desertions caused even greater losses than the enemy's fire. In the subsequent period of peace the army lost on an average 20,000 men a year from death or desertion.

Following the Seven Years' War reforms were attempted in the army, particularly under the influence of the great Foreign Minister Choiseul.[32] The manoeuvres of the troops became more regular, and the discipline stricter and more exacting. There was some retrogression under the Duc d'Aiguillon, and Louis XVI inherited a demoralized army and navy. The reforms attempted by Saint-Germain, appointed minister in 1775, were unpopular and unavailing.

The nobility had a virtual monopoly of the officerships in the army.[33] For many of these the positions were but sinecures granted as a part of the royal patronage, or purchased at a fancy price. In 1758 there were 364 general staff officers, from the higher nobility, of course, for an army of 300,000 men. The non-commissioned officers alone held the army together. The hope of promotion served as the incentive to these men. In 1781, however, their ambitions were stifled by the regulation that henceforth no one could receive a commission as second lieutenant who could not show four generations of nobility on the paternal side. This had been extorted from Ségur, the minister of war, against his will. Exceptions were made in favor of sons of members of the military order of Saint Louis, and some exceptions were made for the engineering and artillery corps. Discouraged by this regulation the non-commissioned officers Oudinot, Masséna and Murat left the army on the eve of the Revolution. Officialism increasingly superseded the close personal connections in the army. In 1788 it was decreed that no one should become a general officer who had not previously been a colonel. A colonel's commission was both expensive and given by favor alone. The lower officerships in the army were generally held by the poorer, lesser nobility.

In 1781 the officers "belonged to one or other of five different classes, as distinct as though they had been five different castes."[34] Three of these classes were noble, the others bourgeois. Jealousy and ill-will prevailed between the higher and lower nobility, and between the noble and the bourgeois officers. These jealousies and quarrels were "fatal to discipline, subordination and cohesion."[35]

Many of the higher officers had not attained their majority, and those still in childhood were dubbed the "colonels in bibs." The noble officers were not particularly reactionary in the period before the Revolution.[36]

At the commencement of the Revolution the Austrian army was the largest in Europe. It had a peace strength of some 270,000 regular troops, with a war footing of 400,000. The Prussian army had a peace footing of 162,658 and a war strength of 250,000, with a general reputation for rapid mobilization and hard fighting. The French army had a peace footing of 172,974 regular troops, and 55,240 militia, with a war footing of 210,948 regulars, and 76,000 milita. There were some 36,000 officers on paper, but only 13,000 were actively employed. The soldiers cost the state 44,100,000 livres, and the officers 46,400,000 livres annually.

The militia was composed of seventy-eight garrison batallions, fourteen provincial regiments, and fifteen regiments of royal grenadiers. These fulfilled garrison duty in time of war and could be called upon as reserves. In peace time they were not kept constantly together but assembled from time to time to drill. Their term of service was six years and the number of men drawn annually into the militia did not exceed fifteen thousand. Militia duty was greatly hated, however. This was partly because men did not volunteer for it but were drafted, and there were many exemptions from the draft. As a matter of fact, militia service was a form of conscription. In practice the burden fell almost exclusively on the poorer peasantry.

So far as tactics was concerned, the classical tradition prevailed generally in the seventeenth and eighteenth centuries. Gustavus Adolphus, the "greatest military pioneer"[37] of the seventeenth century, was steeped in Xenophon, and used the Roman legion and its manoeuvrable maniples, which proved their superiority to the Spanish "phalanx." His administrative reforms were probably as important as his tactical. "His was a regular army, regularly paid, endowed with a proper supply system, a medical service, and a military code that served as a model for subsequent military law.[38]

This classical tradition reached its peak in the eighteenth century. During the first half of the century the proposals of the Chevalier Folard for an attack formation in massive columns sixteen to thirty-two ranks deep, representing a crude revival of the Greek phalanx, dominated military thought. This tactics ignored the modern fact of the bullet. Mesnil-Durand went even further a generation later in championing a massive and unarticulated battalion column, thirty-two ranks deep with a front of only twenty-four men. Later, some of the best tacticians came to favor the column in a more flexible form for purposes of manoeuvre, while admitting its defects for shock. In a modified form their views prevailed and were incorporated in the French drill book in 1791, remaining the tactical regulations of the French army for over forty years.

Frederick the Great was the military innovator most imitated in the century. It was his "tactical eye" rather than his tactical forms that accounted for his successes,[39] but his military contemporaries attributed them to his celebrated "oblique order," the flank approach by which he concentrated his strength against one of the enemy's wings, while withholding one of his own. Frederick adopted the manoeuvre from classical antiquity.

In France in the second half of the century the beginnings of a military revolution were apparent, due to a "positive movement of military thought that eventually found its vehicle in new conditions of mobility."[40] Wars in the century were characterized by the rareness of battles and the indecisiveness of campaigns. Army commanders did not believe in fighting a battle without a reasonable assurance of victory. The physical conditions of warfare largely accounted for this. Battle implies tactical and strategic mobility, both in battle and in pursuit of the enemy to complete the victory. It also implies the *immobilization* of the enemy so that he may not escape nor counter your blows. Mobility, however, was greatly hampered by miserable roads, by cumbrous formations, by the difficulty of feeding the "magazine-chained" army when in movement, and because of strong fortresses blocking the pathways. These brakes on mobility, more on the strategic than the tactical, gave the supremacy to defensive tactics in the eighteenth century. Custom had fixed that an army should be drawn up in a rigid line of battle, usually with the infantry massed in the center and the cavalry on the wings. It was supposed to move, and to fight, in a solid block. Detachments were little used. In this "block system" each army was a "single piece on the chessboard of war." Conditions more than men were responsible for this system.

It was Marshal Saxe who moulded French military thought on the eve of the Revolution rather than Frederick, despite the temporary supremacy of Frederick's influence after 1763. The line of evolution runs from Saxe through Bourcet, Guibert, and the revolutionary soldiers, to Napoleon. Two theorists early in the century challenged the prevailing system of rare and decisive battles, and of heavy, unwieldy formations. Feuquières "proclaimed the sovereign efficacy of battle," and a successor, Bosroger, added a significant note, "Offensive war requires a vigorous opening to astonish the enemy and to spread alarm among his troops and in his country; one is halfway to victory when one has succeeded in inspiring terror in him. He must be given no chance to recover from it." Saxe, by his victories and by his *Reveries,* published after his death in 1757, profoundly questioned in fact and in theory the conventional system and paved the way for the new. Saxe did not believe in avoiding battle, but thought that where the issue was uncertain because of the equality of the opponents the enemy should first be weakened and disturbed "by frequent encounters," and that the attack should be declined altogether unless it could be made with advantage. He insisted that the distraction of the enemy was the necessary condition to any decision and thus he directed himself to the problem of upsetting the enemy's "mental and physical balance—of dislocating their plan and the organization of their forces." Beyond that he opposed the prudency that permitted an enemy to retreat in order, by advocating the pursuit of the defeated enemy until the retreat became a complete rout. In these maxims Saxe was introducing irregularity as a lever in an age of regularity, and was laying the foundations of mobility in an age of immobility. He recognized, of course, that "rapidity of movement, security of movement, ease of manoeuvre, and efficient supply" are the conditions essential for mobility. In this connection he clearly recognized, as Napoleon failed to recognize later, that there is a limit to what is the *economic size* of an army, that is, that the effective strength of an army ceases to increase when its numbers cause a decline in mobility. This same idea accounts for his opposition to the prevailing practice of fortifying towns and for his advocacy rather of fortifying natural barriers. He bewailed "the rage for sieges which prevails at present." To him fortification was merely a means to advantageous battle.

To secure the mobility he desired Saxe reorganized his army. He formed his infantry in legions, each of four regiments, and each regiment was composed of four "centuries" with a half-century of light infantry and a half-century of horse. In this system is the embryo of the "divisional system—the organization of the army into permanently organized divisions capable of moving and acting independently. It meant that an army grew limbs, limbs which it could use to grip the enemy at one point while it struck him elsewhere." The cavalry, in Saxe's scheme, was to operate with "irresistible impetuosity." A century ahead of his time Saxe armed all of his infantry with breech-loaders. In actual battle his highly-trained skirmishers were to prepare the attack for the assaulting troops and create the disorganization that should precede the decision. In the attack the light infantry would form an advanced and dispersed line along the front of the regiment, falling back after the opening fire into the intervals between the centuries, which would be advancing to the charge. For this charge through, Saxe made a modified use of Folard's columns. Saxe emphasized the use of surprise, based on a skillful use of the ground, as a prelude to a "swift concentration of strength against weakness, to crush some fraction of the enemy's army which he has temporarily isolated by his distracting moves." As further aids to mobility Saxe introduced cadenced marching, and proposed a system of company transport and messing in place of the magazine-system of supply.

The revolutionary armies owe a great deal to Marshal Saxe.[41] Their debt is also considerable to Bourcet and Guibert. Pierre de Bourcet, that "greatest of chiefs of staff,"[42] saw a great deal of mountain fighting, which led him to discover the true theory of concentration, which he once expressed in a concrete situation as follows: "This will make him [the enemy, Charles Emanuel and his Piedmontese] divide his forces and then we can take advantage of the geographical conditions to reunite our own at the critical point before he can unite his." His cardinal principle was that "a plan ought to have several branches. . . . And in case all these diversions, countermarches or other ruses fail of their purpose— to hide the real aim—one must be ready to profit by a second or third branch of the plan without giving one's enemy time to consider it." He also demonstrated how a wide distribution could be reconciled with security. In his plans for campaigns in Italy he based them on "an acute exploitation of the psychology of allies and the nature of the country."Napoleon was to be an apt pupil of Bourcet. In 1759-60, Broglie, the new commander-in-chief, influenced by both Saxe and Bourcet, issued regulations organizing the army, infantry and cavalry, in permanent divisions for the campaign. Each division was to form a separate column on the march, and when close to the enemy was itself formed into two or more columns, so that it took less than half an hour to deploy into line of battle. In 1762 Bourcet became lieutenant-general, and in 1764, Choiseul appointed him director of the newly-established school for staff officers at Grenoble. With twenty campaigns behind him Bourcet enunciated his principles in a manuscript book, *Principes de la guerre de Montagnes,* for the use of his students. He died at eighty in 1780, "almost blind from ceaseless study of his beloved maps."

Guibert made a frontal attack on the military conventions of the age. Born in 1743, his father, the Comte de Guibert, early conditioned him for military action and thought. At sixteen he accompanied his father, who was Broglie's chief-of-staff, throughout the German campaign. At twenty-four he won the Cross of Saint Louis in the Corsican expedition. In 1772, at twenty-nine, he produced his revolutionary work on war, *Essai général de tactique,* which ran through several editions and was widely translated.[43] Guibert belonged to a generation that was fermenting with new social ideas and he saw clearly that for the real fulfillment of his military ideas, a thorough change of spirit was necessary both in the army and in the society upon which is was based.

Guibert based his tactics on the fighting individual and unit. He advocated the simplification of drill movements, both to quicken manoeuvre and to save time for useful training. He wanted to increase the rate of step, and first increased it up from sixty to seventy a minute, and then to a hundred and twenty, which gave the French armies a great advantage. "On this simple, yet pivotal fact was based the conquering mobility of the new tactics. It suited the national character no less than the temper of the Revolution." Guibert firmly believed in the need of basing each nation's military system on its national characteristics. This led him to insist upon "reasoning with the French soldier," in order to get a quicker and fuller response from him.

Guibert advocated the training of all the infantry for scouting and skirmishing. For the infantry he believed in fire *effect* and favored deliberate fire for this, which suited "the address and vivacity of the French." He wanted to substitute a really mobile artillery for the current unwieldy artillery trains that "braked" the mobility of the army. He wanted fewer batteries with a quick concentration of fire. The Chevalier du Teil elaborated Guibert's ideas on artillery, insisting on the planned and effective use of the artillery as the preparation for the attack. Guibert emphasized the need for the mobile distribution of an army in divisions, advancing in a flexible group of columns, with rapid means of deployment. He applied the same methods to the defensive. "A general," he said, "should occupy the likely points of attack with his advanced troops and keep, behind and between them, the rest of his army in columns, so as to transfer his forces to the point where the enemy make their effort, and sometimes to the point where . . . they lay themselves open to attack." He insisted on adaptability to ground and circumstances. In his *Défense du Système de guerre moderne*, in 1779, he went beyond his idea that the army should concentrate if battle was anticipated, to suggest "extending one's forces of calculated intent." "The art," he said, "is to extend them without exposing them, to embrace the enemy without being disunited, to link up the operations or the attacks to take [the enemy] in flank without exposing one's own flank.

Guibert attacked vigorously the problem of the magazine-chained army. The current practice was to hand over supply to profiteering contractors. Guibert wanted to add the science of subsistence to that of war, by having the whole system reorganized and co-ordinated with the new army system, have officers taught the details of supply, and greatly reduce both baggage and magazines. This last could best be achieved by making a better use of the resources of the country where the army was campaigning. He advocated the principle that the army should live at the enemy's expense in the enemy's country, thus putting a premium on an offensive war. "What I want to avoid," he wrote, "is that my supplies should command me. It is in this case my movement that is the main thing; all the other combinations are accessory and I must try to make them subordinate to the movement. The enemy must see me marching when he supposes me fettered by the calculations of my supplies; this new kind of war must astonish him, must nowhere leave him time to breathe, and make him see at his own expense this constant truth that hardly any position is tenable before an army well constituted, sober, patient, and able to manoeuvre."[44]

Guibert's ideas, with their insistence upon national patriotism, upon the need for thoroughgoing reform in France, for a constitution, for a new spirit in the army and the nation, for a common and proud citizenship, for a national discipline, and for a "complete tactic," found a ready response in the intellectual world and in the *Salons*, but only suspicion and distrust among the privileged and powerful. For a time his influence was greater outside France than within it. Eventually he came into his own in France. In 1775 the Comte de Saint-Germain, a military reformer, was named minister of war. With Guibert's help, improvements were made in the army. An efficient artillery was developed, regiments of light horse and light infantry were raised, manuals were rewritten, and tactical exercises were developed. These and other reforms, particularly to regularize punishment, antagonized the privileged and Saint-Germain left the ministry in 1777. Not until ten years later did the monarchy, then in *extremis,* countenance reform. An Army Council was formed with Guibert as its secretary. Gribeauval was a member of this Council. The new artillery owed a great deal to him, particularly from the time that he was Inspector-General at the close of the Seven Years' War. His guns were the best in Europe and were not replaced in France until 1825. Significant reforms were made in the army. A permanent organization by divisions was established. The manuals were revised, to stand for over forty years. Drill movements were shortened and simplified. The pay and conditions of the soldiers were raised. The top-heavy establishment of thirty-five thousand officers was reduced to ten thousand by the elimination of those who had absentee sinecures in the army. The disciplinary code, and the promotion of officers, however, were left unreformed by the Council.

In March, 1788 the Council of War organized France and Corsica into seventeen military districts, three of which were commanded by Marshals of France, and the rest by Lieutenant-Generals, with complete powers within their districts. As a result of this reform the French army of 1789 was composed of twenty-one divisions, split up into brigades, so that in case of war the army would be ready to take the field under the same staff that had trained it in time of peace. The army equalled the renowned Prussian army in its infantry and cavalry, and excelled it in respect to the artillery and engineering corps. The French artillery was the finest in Europe in every respect, and France was the only European Power that paid proper attention to the art and science of military engineering. It would take a war to test the new organization and the efficacy of the new tactical theories. This was not far off.

The French navy was weak at the time. The naval officers were quite as aristocratic and feudal as those of the army, but even more exclusive. They held in contempt the bourgeois officers drawn from the merchant marine for the duration of a war. The education of the naval officers was faulty and too theoretical. They were ignorant of good seamanship. Bureaucracy dominated the naval administration. The system of naval conscription, the *classement,* was vicious. The current French conception of the function of the navy was that it was to conduct piratical raids on commerce, not to destroy the enemy's navy. The French navy was out of the class of the English navy.

The stage was set for the revolutionary armies and Guibert's prophecy was not long delayed in fulfillment: "A people that, to strict virtue and a national soldiery, would join a settled plan of aggrandizement, who, . . . knowing how to carry on a war with little expense, and to subsist by their conquests, could not be defeated by financial manoeuvres. As the north wind bends the tender reed, that people would be seen to subjugate their neighbours, and overthrow their feeble constitutions."

As the Revolution approached its spirit became evident in the army although the meeting of the Estates General had little effect at first on the army. Some of the *cahiers,* however, did call for an improvement in the lot of the soldier. Better barrack accommodations, better winter clothing, better food, more sanitary conditions were called for in some. Others wanted better pay. Most of them, however, demanded the abolition of all degrading forms of punishment, with special reference to flogging. The army was ready to welcome the Revolution. This was particularly true in the large regiment of the *Gardes Françaises*, a highly privileged body permanently located in Paris, and thoroughly infected with the spirit of revolt. The common soldiers were rapidly catching the spirit of insubordination that characterized their officers. In the early months of the Revolution mutiny and sedition were rife in the army culminating in the great insurrections of the troops in the Luneville and Nancy garrisons, which almost led to civil war, but which were severly put down by Bouillé. Many officers resigned and emigrated.

The Revolution, of course, would not succeed and there would be no successful transfer of power in the state, unless the army and the police became instruments in the hands of the revolutionaries. So long as both public services remained loyal to the Monarchy the Revolution would be stalemated. The army, however, excepting many of the officers, was ready for the Revolution, and the police, particularly in Paris, was soon captured by the more radical revolutionaries.

In the early days of the Revolution, the bourgeoisie organized themselves into National Guards. As a general rule, only active citizens could serve in the National Guard. These Guardsmen elected their own officers and wore the uniform prescribed by the nation. Some 16,000 regulars had deserted and had enrolled in the National Guard of Paris by September, 1789. The National Guards had a paper enrollment of more than two millions, but in reality their numbers were considerably less. They aided the regular army in putting down the swarming bands of brigands throughout France and assisted in the transportation of grain supplies. They retained their local character and opposed attempts to transform them into troops for active service. The militia had been dissolved on the creation of the National Guard.

Early in the Revolution the sale of officers in the army was abolished, the pay of soldiers was raised, and an incomplete system of promotion based on seniority was established. On February 28, 1790, the highest ranks were declared open to all candidates, but the appointment of the highest officers of the regular army was left to the King. During 1791 the regular army was reduced to sixty thousand men. On December 14, 1791 three armies were forced to defend the northeastern frontier—the Armies of the North, of the Center (which changed its name in October, 1792 to the Army of the Moselle), and of the Rhine. In the South the Army of the Midi was formed. Gradually these armies grew until by a decree of the Convention on April 30, 1793, eleven armies encircled France both on the coastal, and on the land frontiers.

The National Assembly, under the panic of the flight of the King in June, 1791, passed several decrees concerning the army. At first it hoped to recruit two hundred thousand volunteers, but on August 17 it called for one hundred and one thousand volunteers, to be organized into one hundred and sixty-nine battalions. Those who enlisted were mostly from the bourgeoisie and were patriotic men of sense and intelligence. Some former members of the militia, and many of those who had fought in America volunteered. The new battalions had the right to elect their own officers from those officers and non-commissioned officers who had served in the regulars or in the militia. They elected competent men as battalion commanders. At the time nine of the twenty-six future marshals of Napoleon were officers in the regular army. Ten others were, or had been, serving in the ranks as privates or as non-commissioned officers. Of the seven remaining six were still civilians soon to enlist, and one was to rise in the period of the Empire. Bonaparte himself was a lieutenant of Artillery of nearly six years service. The first of the future marshals to enter the army was Kellermann in 1752, and the last was to be Suchet in 1793. Of the thirty-two general officers who left for Egypt with the Army of the Orient in 1798, fourteen had served as officers before 1789, and eleven others had served as privates or as non-commissioned officers before 1789.

In January, 1792, the Comte de Narbonne, Minister of War, reported to the Legislative Assembly that the army was fifty-one thousand below strength and that it was impossible to get recruits for the regular army because of the more attractive pay and service in the volunteers. Three months before war was declared on April 20, 1792, France possessed an army composed partly of regular soldiers of the old *régime*, whose discipline had been undermined, whose officers were either under suspicion, or were competent but untried former non-commissioned officers, and partly of incompletely organized and undisciplined volunteers. The general staff was changed at every breath of suspicion. In the armies, during 1791 and to July 17, 1792 five hundred and ninety-three generals had been replaced. The noble officers were emigrating in increasing numbers, many because they could not sincerely take the oaths of allegiance that followed each other in rapid succession. One authority remarks that of the 9,500 officers in 1789, 6,600 were noblemen, and of these, by the end of 1794, 5,500 had gone.[45] There was no system of transportation and supply and the fortresses of France had been long neglected, were badly armed, and poorly provisioned. The war office lacked both method and responsibility. There were six ministers of war in as many months. The Assembly interfered increasingly in the conduct of military affairs. Fortunately for France, the armies of Austria and Prussia were infinitely below their former standard and a divided command was to further handicap them in the impending struggle.

The volunteers of 1792 were materially different in character from those of 1791. In July, twenty thousand *fédérés* were encamped near Paris, and their representatives were "federated" at the fête of July 14, 1792. In August and September the Legislative Assembly, after the Brunswick Manifesto of August 3, and after August 10, voted a new levy of forty-two battalions, when only eighty-three of the levy of 1791 had really been completed. These new recruits were not strictly volunteers since the various departments and districts were given their quotas to fill. Many who were either too young, or too infirm, were accepted. On the whole, these recruits of 1792 were "composed of fanatics of the lower orders, impregnated with all the doctrines of Jacobinism, and never took any active part in the war."[46] The levies of 1791, on the other hand, in time formed excellent troops. The Legislative Assembly had planned to oppose three hundred thousand regulars and volunteers to the enemy invaders. On August 10, however, the forces that covered the frontier from Dunkirk to Basel amounted to not more than eighty-two thousand men, divided into three commands. Lafayette commanded the left with forty-three thousand men covering the frontier from Dunkirk to Montmédy. Luckner commanded the center with seventeen thousand men, with headquarters at Metz, to watch the roads which led into France by the Moselle. Biron commanded the right, the Army of the Rhine, with the responsibility of closing the passes near Lindau and Bitsch, and the great gap between the Vosges and the Jura, known as the Gate of Burgundy. The unorganized, badly equipped and poorly supplied Army of the Reserve, composed of the volunteers of 1792, was stationed at Soissons.

Early in 1793 all Europe with the exception of Switzerland, Denmark, Sweden, and Turkey, was at war with France and during the year the first coalition against France was consummated largely due to the alliances England effected with each of the Powers and to the subsidies she granted them. Soon nearly three hundred and fifty thousand men were in the field against the revolutionaries. On February 20, 1793 the Convention decreed a new levy of 300,000 men to oppose the enemy. All physically fit, unmarried men from eighteen to forty were liable to service, but enlistment was only compulsory if volunteers did not fill the local quotas. Deputies of the Convention were sent into the departments with extraordinary powers, to supervise the enrolment. On April 30, 1793 the Convention decreed the system of Representatives-on-Mission to the eleven armies then organized, usually four Representatives to an army. This levy of 300,000 men was completed during the summer. The opposition to it contributed to the organized revolt and civil war in the Vendée and in Brittany that took on alarming proportions as the year advanced. In midsummer this struggle was in stalemate. The initial victories and subsequent reverses of French arms and the treason of Dumouriez have already been recounted. France had her back to the wall in August. It was into this situation that Carnot, Lindet, and Prieur (de la Côte-d'Or) stepped to bring order out of confusion, to complete the *levée en masse*, to give a unitary direction to the armies, to utilize the new tactics and strategy, and to turn defeat and disaster into victory.

The democratic army and the revolutionary "nation in arms," that new phenomenon of democracy and popular nationalism, were made possible by the *levée en masse,* urged by the deputies of the primary assemblies in Paris for the fête of August 10, and decreed by the Convention on August 23, 1793, on recommendation of Barère from the Committee of Public Safety. On August 14 the Convention had proclaimed the *levée en masse* in principle and had charged the delegates from the primary assemblies with the responsibility of stimulating the *levée*, in the name of patriotism.[47] In proposing this decree to the Convention Barère, reporting for the Great Committee, remarked that the French generals had hitherto disregarded the true national temperament, to which sudden, unexpected attack was far more congenial than softening in the inactivity of life in camp, awaiting the usually successful attack of an enemy. The French, he said, should assume the offensive, to strike the troops of the tyrants like lightning. The declaration itself decreed that "the French people proclaims, through its representatives, that it rises *en masse* for the defense of its independence, of its liberty, of its constitution, and in order to deliver its territory from the presence of despots and their satellities." On the sixteenth the deputies of the primary assemblies, still lingering in Paris, petitioned the Convention to proceed promptly to the execution of this proclamation. The detailed, comprehensive decree of August 23 was the result of this pressure.[48] In his speech introducing the decree, Barère declared that the Republic was a great besieged city, which compelled France to become a vast camp. Conscription was to be complete. "The contingent of France for her liberty comprises her entire population, all her industry, all her labors, all her genius." The justifying principle was that in a free country, every citizen is a soldier. All Frenchmen, of whatever age or sex, were called to defend liberty. Every physical and moral faculty, all political and industrial means were to be made available to the nation. All citizens between eighteen and fifty were to be subject to military service, but those between eighteen and twenty-five who were unmarried, or widowers without children, were to be called for active service first. No one was allowed to hire a substitute.

The decree itself contained seventeen articles.[49] The first one stated that "From this moment until the enemy is driven from the territory of the Republic, all Frenchmen are in permanent requisition for the service of the armies. Young men will go to the front; married men will forge arms and transport food-stuffs; women will make tents and clothes, and will serve in the hospitals; children will tear rags into lint; old men will get themselves carried to public places, there to stimulate the courage of the warriors, the hatred of kings, and the unity of the republic." The Committee of Public Safety was authorized to take every means to establish immediately an extraordinary manufactury for all kinds of arms required by the spirit and energy of the French, with the central headquarters of these establishments in Paris. The representatives-on-mission were to have the powers of the Committee of Public Safety, in concert with that Committee, in their respective districts. They were "invested with the unlimited powers attributed to the representatives of the people with the armies." The Minister of War was empowered to take all measures necessary for the prompt execution of this decree.

The crisis in supplies for the army was serious. Under the authorization of this decree, Carnot and the two Prieurs gave themselves unstintedly to the organization of the manufacture and distribution of everything essential to the equipment and ordnance of the troops. Since all three men were devoted to science and to its application, they turned to the patriotic scientists for assistance. They enlisted Berthollet, Chaptal, Monge, Perier, Guyton de Morveau, Vandermonde, Fourcroy and Hassenfratz, among others. Monge wrote a booklet on the *Art of Manufacturing Cannon*, and organized a great factory for guns and cannon in Paris. Vandermonde was entrusted with the manufacture of side arms. Hassenfratz became the commissary of arms factories; Fourcroy began turning bells into ordnance by discovering a process of extracting copper from them; Chaptal served in the powder and saltpeter department, and the previous dependence of France upon imports for this element essential to gunpowder was broken. Experiments with gunpowder and with military balloons[50] were conducted incessantly, and the semaphore was invented. The Chateau of Petit-Meudon was put at the disposal of the scientists with adequate grounds for an experimental station. A census of industrial workers in Paris was taken and workmen were conscripted from private industries and sent into government armories. It was not long before 258 forges were producing a thousand gun barrels a day in Paris alone. Within a few months the powder factory at Grenelle, using a new system invented there, was turning out thirty thousand pounds a day. Clouet, professor of Chemistry at Mézières, established four huge forges in the Ardennes. Wherever the private munitions industries would cooperate vigorously with the government they were permitted to continue, under threat of becoming nationalized.[51] On November 3, Carnot, in the name of the Committee of Public Safety, read a report to the Convention on the extraordinary manufactury of arms established in Paris.[52] To document the report a deputation of workers in these arms factories presented to the Convention specimens of each kind of gun being produced at the rate of a thousand guns a day.[53] The report was supplemented by a detailed treatment[54] of the organization of the new national industry, dealing both with materials and with personnel, and revealing the patriotic competition stimulated in the factories, as well as the concern of the Government for the wages and conditions of the workers. In the supplying of other necessities to the armies such as shoes and uniforms there were at first some scandals associated with shoddy materials and there was some profiteering, some slowness and inefficiency, but soon the job was being done effectively and quickly, under the pressure and scrutiny of officials and of ubiquitous patriots who were depriving themselves of food and clothing necessities and luxuries in support of the great national effort.

Carnot's energies were completely consumed in the military activities of the Committee of Public Safety. The tasks that he and his immedate associates, Lindet and Prieur (de la Côte d'Or) faced in the autumn of 1793 were colossal. Carnot, whom Albert Sorel called "the great Chief of Staff of the Revolution" gave himself with a vengeance to the multitude of tasks having to do with the personnel and movements of the armies, both then very much in confusion. It may be too much to call Carnot an "administrator of the first order,"[55] but he certainly had a passion for details, and gave himself methodically and meticulously to the understanding of the minutiae of his functions, and to the execution of the smallest details of his assignment. One critic, with a tendency to glorify Napoleon and his marshals, spoke of Carnot as the man "with the undying spirit of the war office clerk, never able to understand why the man in the field sees differently from the man in the office."[56] The National Archives of France[57] bear mute though eloquent testimony to the quantity of Carnot's endeavors, while the achievements of the Revolutionary armies in 1793 and 1794 testify to the quality of his direction.

His finger was everywhere, he was preoccupied with the minutiae of every army and his knowledge of the minutest details of the personnel of the armies is amazing. While he had a staff of secretaries much of his correspondence and many of his orders were written and signed personally. Bureau organization and management labored under the handicaps and limitations of the eighteenth century. There was no great formality in the administration of Carnot's office. There had to be a great deal of improvization, if imperative action was to take precedence over form and method. Bureaucratic red tape was at a minimum. Many of the most important orders emanating from Carnot, such as the movements of major officers from one army to another, and instructions to commanders-in-chief, were issued in the form of informal memoranda, not even on official letterheads. A great number of citations and promotions, even to humble soldiers and underofficers, as well as suspensions, throughout the armies, were written and signed by Carnot alone. Carnot early established certain specialties in his work and called experts to fulfill them. Clarke was given responsibility for the map and topographical division; Montalembert was called in for the artillery, and d'Arçon was assigned to fortifications. The historical division was added later. Carnot was probably not the easiest person to work with. He was not always "accommodating." Madelin speaks of him at this time as being, "tenacious to the point of obstinacy, and not very easy-going, being rather dictatorial; unable to bear contradiction, he was hard, sometimes harsh, and always unbending. . . . He was upright, disinterested and scrupulously honest."[58] There is no doubt but that his "republicanism was entirely sincere."[59]

Bouchotte was the Minister of War at the time. He was a devoted Jacobin who possessed some merits as an administrator, who brought untiring activity to his tasks, who was honest, and who oftentimes made happy choices of subordinates. Phipps' appellation of him as "that evil official,"[60] who "was always more engaged in spying on and denouncing the Generals than in sending them supplies and reinforcements,"[61] is not entirely supportable. Bouchotte conceived of his tasks as essentially administrative. He was responsible to the Committee of Public Safety. The work of his Ministry was well systematized, there was a divisional organization within it, and an intelligent division of labor.[62] This office, older than the newly-established functions of Carnot, had all of the paraphernalia of bureaucracy such as form letters, printed forms, and divisional letterheads. The Committee of Public Safety continued to utilize the Ministry of War for certain important administrative tasks. The Committee frequently called upon Bouchotte for detailed reports[63] and the Ministry furnished the Committee with an extract of its daily military correspondence. Friction sometimes developed between the Committee of Public Safety and Bouchotte,[64] but on the whole cooperation was good and Bouchotte was loyal and hard-working. He was naturally partial to the prerogatives of the Executive Council. In the summer of 1793 he was responsible, with the representatives-on-mission, for the substitution of the new Republican blue uniforms for the old white uniforms of the regulars. On August 10 he inspired a decree in the Convention that all remaining officers of noble birth were to be cashiered, with the result that the staffs of the armies had to be entirely reorganized.

When Carnot came into the Committee of Public Safety Beauharnais was commanding the Army of the Rhine, to be succeeded soon in quick succession by Landremont and Carlenc. The Army of the Moselle was commanded by Schauenburg, and the two armies in the West, with headquarters at Nantes and Saumur, respectively, were commanded by Canclaux, Rossignol and Ronsin, Kellermann was besieging Lyons, and Toulon was being blockaded by the Republican troops. Dagobert commanded in the Pyrenees. In the Army of the North, "the most important of all the armies of France, for the first years of the War,"[65] Custine had commanded in the early summer. He proposed to concentrate the three armies in the North and East on the task of clearing the Netherlands, but failed to get the consent of Bouchotte. He then set himself to the reorganization of his own troops, and soon had thirty-nine thousand disciplined troops, including forty-eight hundred cavalry, ready for action. His political indiscretions in criticizing the Jacobin leaders and his quarrels with Bouchotte and the Representatives of the people resulted in his downfall. He was recalled to Paris on July 10, the very day Condé fell to the enemy, and on August 28 he was guillotined. He was succeeded in July by the cavalry officer, Kilmaine. In August, Houchard, an old professional soldier of plebeian stock, replaced Kilmaine, largely on the recommendation of Carnot.

Coburg, who commanded the Allied forces in the North, was concentrating twenty-four thousand men in the siege of Valenciennes, supported by a covering force of twenty thousand and with ten thousand in reserve at his headquarters. In July he received fifteen thousand Hessians as reinforcements. On the 26th the fortress and town of Valenciennes surrendered. Austria at once claimed Condé and Valenciennes as her own possessions and announced that she would expand to the Somme and to Sedan. Kilmaine had entrenched his troops strongly in Caesar's Camp and on August 7 the French escaped the enveloping movement of the Allies and entrenched themselves at Biache, between Arras and Douai. The road to Paris was open to the Allies, while the English under the Duke of York had laid siege to Dunkirk. Kilmaine was recalled and Houchard was given the command at this critical moment. Carnot now began to develop his strategy, according to which the French armies were no longer to be frittered away in detachments, but were to be concentrated in masses to deal crushing blows upon the enemy. By September the force to relieve Dunkirk had been assembled and numbered forty-two thousand men. Carnot's plan was to have Houchard seize Furnes and cut off the enemy from their base.[66] Houchard, however, preferred to attack the Hanoverian covering force at Bergues and Hondschoote. On September 6, the French had to fall back behind the Yser, but on the 8th Houchard, under the stimulation of Delbrel and Levasseur (de la Sarthe), the representatives-on-mission, drove the enemy out of Hondschoote, but did not follow up the victory by pursuing the enemy. Dunkirk, however, was relieved. The effect of the uncompleted victory of Hondschoote on the comparative military situation was not great, but the moral significance of the victory for France was very great, for it broke the long series of defeats which had begun at Aix-la-Chapelle in March.

The hesitant, anxious Houchard failed to utilize his success, and retired to his camp at Arras. Quesnoy fell to the enemy on

September 13, after only one major attempt by Houchard to relieve it. The representatives -on-mission denounced Houchard for his dilatory tactics, and he was dismissed on September 20, to be sent before the Revolutionary Tribunal, and to the guillotine on November 16. His "bloody inheritance fell to Jourdan"[67] evidently on Carnot's recommendation,[68] on September 22, and he arrived at his headquarters on the 25th.

This appointment was a part of the radical shake-up in commands just effected by Carnot and the Committee of Public Safety, that sent Hoche as commander-in-chief, to the Army of the Moselle, and Pichegru to the Army of the Rhine. Jourdan was thirty-one at the time, Pichegru was a year younger, and Hoche was a youth of twenty-five. Wurmser, on the contrary, was an old war horse of sixty-eight, and Brunswick was ten years his junior. These young sons of the Revolution were the first products of the new democratic principle of "careers open to talent." "These young generals, who owed everything to the Revolution," writes Professor Mathiez, "espoused its cause completely and staked their whole existence on victory. . . . But for them Carnot's offensive tactics would have been impracticable. . . . By their audacity and powers of rapid adaptation they disconcerted the rigid and hide-bound generals of the coalition. A new war called for new men, a national war needed leaders whose every fibre bound them to the nation."[69] These young generals knew that failure ended on the guillotine and so they staked everything on victory. The political control of the armies and of their commanders was close, and all were fired with a common national purpose, but the military efforts had to be successful.

Jourdan had served in America but on his return he had had to give up his commission because of Ségur's decree. At the beginning of the revolutionary wars he was chosen to command a battalion of volunteers. He served in the Army of the North under Dumouriez, Dampierre and Custine, and commanded the centre at Hondschoote under Houchard. He distinguished himself in this engagement, in which he suffered a slight wound. Following that he had had less than two weeks as commander-in-chief of the Army of the Ardennes. Colonel Phipps speaks of him as "ever the same man, modest, earnest, sometimes blundering, but with a good deal of obstinacy that often helped him to achieve his purpose."[70] Jourdan demurred at his appointment, pleading a lack of experience and a lack of talents for such an important post.

Carnot was at the headquarters of the Army of the North when Jourdan arrived there. He had been sent there by the Committee of Public Safety by order of September 23, to report on the condition of the army. Jourdan found "wild confusion" in the army, aggravated by the recent arrests. He also bewailed the lack of competent officers. Carnot agreed with him in his analysis, and before he returned to Paris, they talked over the plan of operations to be pursued. Jourdan's task was to cover Paris and relieve Maubeuge, which was strongly invested with twenty thousand French. Coburg had surrounded it with twenty-five thousand troops, mostly Dutch, covered by about forty-five[71] thousand more at Wattignies and along a line of villages in front of it, stretching far to their flanks. Maubeuge was the last fortress of the French barrier in the Northeast and its loss would completely open up the way to Paris.

The Committee of Public Safety decided to strike first in the North. For this important action Carnot returned to the Army of the North on October 6 and remained with it until the 20th.[72] His former Colleague-on-Mission, Duquesnoy, was associated with him on this occasion. In their despatch to the Committee of Public Safety from Péronne on October 7, they reported the good spirits of the troops, but pled for the immediate transmission by the minister of war of shoes, uniforms, and guns for the men, and collars, harness and grain for the horses.[73] From Réunion two days later they despatched an "extraordinary" courier in order to strengthen their demands for necessities for the men.[74] Indicative of the new tactics they said, "We need at least fifteen thousand bayonets; we cannot charge the enemy *à la française*, if we do not have them." They reported that three-fourths of the men were barefoot. Fortunately, they said, the weather was still good. They called attention to the unfortunate circumstance that the new levies were better clothed than the staunch old regulars. The new soldiers, however, were useless for they had no weapons. On the 10th they deprived General of Division

Merenvue, commandant of the artillery, of his command because of neglect of duty, and had him sent to Arras under arrest, where he committed suicide on the twelfth. They immediately promoted Boubers, the second in command, to succeed him. The two representatives-on-mission suspended or dismissed other officers during their mission, as well as making certain promotions, including that of Lieutenant-colonel Soland to become general of brigade in command of the cavalry on October 13. Carnot Feulins was called to the Army for special duty.

The Committee of Public Safety reported the entry into Lyons to the Army of the North on October 11 and took the occasion to challenge the army to action: "Victory belongs to courage. It is yours. Strike, exterminate the satellites of the tyrants. . . . The nation is watching you, the Convention seconds your generous devotion. In a few days the tyrants will be no more, and the Republic will owe its happiness and its glory to you. *Vive la République*."[75]

Carnot and Duquesnoy announced the impending battle and outlined its strategy on October 14, stating that the enemy claimed to have 115,000 men, but that they comprised probably no more than their own fifty thousand effectives, exclusive of the seventeen thousand at Maubeuge. It was resolved to mass the French troops against Coburg, by calling in the soldiers from all sides, even at the risk of leaving the flanks bare. This concentration has been called "a miracle of smoothness and speed."[76]

Jourdan and Carnot led the French into battle against the Austrians at Wattignies on October 15.[77] The battle raged for two days. On the first day, following a strategy that "smacks of Carnot,"[78] both wings attacked those of the enemy while Balland's division in the center, where Bernadotte and Mortier were, was to be thrown on the enemy's center when their wings had been drawn back. Fromentin on the left, and General Duquesnoy on right, at first, made good progress and Carnot evidently proposed to throw Balland on Dourlers. It is said that Jourdan opined that it was too soon and that this advance should be delayed until the left had made more progress, but that he yielded to Carnot's insistence.[79] The fighting was furious on the right, in front of the village of Wattignies, which was taken and lost three times by the French. At nightfall the French had been checked.

It was decided in a council of war that night, probably on Jourdan's suggestion, that the decisive attack on the morrow was to be made by the right, while the center and left held the enemy in front. On the morning of the 16th Jourdan and Carnot went to the right where they gallantly led the troops into the stubborn action of the day. A thick fog covered the advance until nine o'clock. Twice the French advanced with what the enemy called "an unspeakable rage," but twice they were swept back. Carnot and Duquesnoy arrested Gratien, general of brigade, on the field of battle because he refused to execute General Duquesnoy's orders to pursue the enemy, and retreated instead. Finally all the columns were joined in the attack on the village and it was taken. A further struggle cleared the slopes beyond the village. Jourdan did not consider that he had won a decisive victory, and he prepared for the counter-stroke that he thought would come on the next day. He had lost three thousand men, while Coburg had lost three hundred and sixty-five killed, one thousand seven hundred and fifty-three wounded, and three hundred and sixty-nine prisoners or missing.

The Allies, however, under cover of a fog, withdrew during the night and the siege of Maubeuge was raised. The French lost contact so completely that it was only at two in the afternoon on the 17th that Jourdan and Carnot entered Maubeuge. The French troops in Maubeuge had remained strangely inactive. They had been expected to engage Coburg in the rear. The victory was thus not as complete as it had been planned. The Allies still held Valenciennes and Condé, but they had failed in their attempts on Dunkirk and Maubeuge.

Jourdan said that lifting the siege of Maubeuge "turned the fortunes of war in favor of France."[80] and Kerr calls this battle "the turning point in the revolutionary war," for which, he says, the credit "belongs chiefly to Carnot."[81] Phipps, on the other hand, ridicules and discards "the Carnot legend" that "it is Carnot who rides the whirlwind and directs the storm . . . and Jourdan is assigned the part of a respectable figure-head, issuing orders to be corrected by the Representative."[82] "The mistakes and achievements of the battle," he says, "were those characteristic of Jourdan and of the armies of the period. The attacks on both wings of the enemy on the first day may pass as the favorite plan of Carnot in strategy and tactics, but the interposition of a central attack points to a compromise between him and Jourdan."

Jourdan wrote to Bouchotte from Avesnes on October 17.[83] "This village," he wrote, "was taken and retaken three times; the representatives of the people, Carnot and Duquesnoy, were at the head of the troops; by their example they inspired in our soldiers the courage worthy of French Republicans. Nothing could resist them. . . . Citizen Carnot . . . rendered the highest services. It is of greatest importance to keep this brave man in the Army of the North, that is absolutely lacking in engineers." Jourdan took occasion to criticize the new officers and although Fromentin had distinguished himself in the battle, his commander-in-chief said, "Fromentin, a citizen devoted to the nation and full of courage, ignores the first elements of the art of war and firmly believes that which is repeated without cessation at the tribune of the Convention and at that of the Jacobins, namely, that the sole talent of a general consists in charging the enemy wherever he may be found. It is not surprising that he does not know how to conduct an operation that demands combinations and prudence."[84] Carnot and Duquesnoy wrote a short report to the Committee of Public Safety from Avesnes at six o'clock on the morning of October 17. "Yesterday, dear colleagues," they wrote, "we took several important posts at the bayonet. The soldiers of the Republic demonstrated the courage of lions. . . . It is impossible to behave with greater intrepidity and wisdom than did General Jourdan. General Duquesnoy also displays the highest talents. The other generals also enjoy a merited confidence."[85] Later on the same day, joined with the Representative Bar, they sent a despatch to the Convention: "The republican army has conquered that of the coalition despots. . . . The achievement of General Jourdan is to have defeated Coburg; herein lies the eulogy of his talents; that of his patriotism is on the lips of his companions in arms."[86] This was read to the Convention on the 19th by Barère, to frequent applause, and was followed by a decree congratulating the army in that it had well represented the nation.[87]

Carnot wrote to the Committee on the same day,[88] reporting that they had found the inhabitants of Maubeuge very cool and the garrison very indolent. "We are going to work to electrify this region a little and to restore the public spirit. . . . The army is worthy of the highest praise. Jourdan is worthy of the command confided in him. He is a brave and honest *sansculotte,* this Jourdan. . . . I shall determine further operations with Jourdan." Carnot and Duquesnoy issued a ringing proclamation to the troops on October 18,[89] saying that officers and soldiers alike had fulfilled their duty "with gayety and as free men. . . . The Representatives of the people were honored to share your labors and your dangers; you will see them ever at your head on the road of honor."

Jourdan wrote to Bouchotte on the 19th announcing the departure of Carnot for Paris, and stating that he had requested Carnot to have the Committee of Public Safety devise a plan of operations for him.[90] "We have had a long conference on this subject; we discussed the pros and cons of different projects so that the Committee can easily pronounce, after the report of Carnot. . . . The counsel of these two citizens [the brothers Carnot] were infinitely useful to me and I tell you frankly that, seeing myself left alone, I distrust my own capacities."

The Committee of Public Safety in the handwriting of Carnot instructed Jourdan on October 22 to advance down the Sambre on Charleroi with his right and attempt to take Namur and to relieve Quesnoy.[91] He was told to keep his troops concentrated *en masse*, but to divide the forces of the enemy as much as possible. Carnot supplemented these orders on the same day with personal cautions of his own.[92] On the following day he sent further detailed instructions of his own.[93] After stating that the enemy has no other intention than of passing the winter in France, Carnot insists that the enemy must be expelled from France. "Once master of the country of the Sambre-et-Meuse," he writes, "and particularly of Namur, if that be possible, you will menace Belgium and Liege, you can cross the Sambre without fearing for your communications, and I cannot then see how the enemy can remain in France. Any other project . . . leaves the enemy the master of the places he has taken and visibly exposes the army to total destruction. Never attack the enemy excepting with a great superiority in effectives and in reserves."

Bouchotte communicated with Jourdan on the 24th in answer to his request for a plan of campaign.[94] "I believe it to be," wrote the minister, "based on the reflections of citizen Carnot, and after conferences which you had together." Carnot instructed Jourdan on October 26 how to treat invaded territories, based upon their friendliness or hostility in preceding months to France and to republicanism.[95] Jourdan bared his doubts to Carnot on the 29th.[96] "I state frankly that my position is delicate. I can freely say that I have plenty of good will and courage, but I have need of counsel for an operation. I believe that no one can do this better than you. Come to the army. . . . I await your coming with impatience and you will render a great service to the Republic and to me." On that same day he reported to Bouchotte that the rains were impeding the advance of the troops according to plan.[97] Two days later he announced to Bouchotte that the general advance would take place on November 12 or 13, at the latest.[98] In both communications he reported the increasing desertions from the army. Duquesnoy, in a despatch to the Committee of Public Safety on October 30, requested the presence of Carnot, if at all possible.[99] Carnot's next communication with Jourdan was on the 31st.[100] "It is your responsibility, citizen general, to weigh the projects that have been proposed to you; the confidence of the Committee gives you large latitude; the only thing that it has prescribed absolutely, is to try every means to completely expel the enemy from the territory of the Republic, without laying sieges, whether by an enveloping movement, or by a powerful diversion." The Committee of Public Safety, in a letter written and signed by Carnot on November 3, authorized Jourdan to modify the plans of operation as circumstances compelled.[101] Carnot wrote to Duquesnoy on the same day to the same effect.[102]

When the necessary preparations had been completed and Jourdan was ready to cross the Sambre he found its passage opposed, rain flooded the country, the roads were impassable, and all movement seemed to be impossible. The Committee of Public Safety continued to urge an advance. Jourdan finally took the bold step of announcing to the Committee on November 4 that if it insisted on the advance he would be forced to resign. "I cannot bear," he wrote, "the heartbreaking sight of an army destroyed without fighting. I render justice to the brave soldiers who compose it: not the least murmur has escaped from them, although they are half-naked and shoeless, exposed to all the effects of the weather, as it has been impossible to move the wagons."[103] Duquesnoy wrote to the Committee from Maubeuge on November 15, "Our troops here are in the mud up to their knees. They lack shoes, shirts, and uniforms."[104] Carnot replied for the Committee requesting Jourdan to come to Paris to consult with the Committee. Jourdan evidently obeyed this summons,[105] and presented a plan for the Army of the North on November 16. He urged that the troops take up winter quarters so that they might be properly instructed, be adequately clothed and supplied, and become recuperated for a vigorous campaign in the spring. He proposed a disposition of the troops in detail. On the following day, Carnot at the session of the Committee of Public Safety was authorized to approve this plan.[106]

In the meantime, Wurmser, a "fiery Alsatian" of sixty-eight, had driven the French in the Army of the Rhine back from their advanced position on the Bienwald to the lines of Wissembourg on August 24, as a result of which the Representatives-on-Mission had replaced Beauharnais with Landremont. The French were strongly situated with thirty-five thousand troops, to which Wurmser opposed thirty thousand Austrians. The latter could not move until he received reinforcements from Prussia, and the promise of these was not forthcoming until in October. Landremont's offensive against Wurmser on September 18, 19 and 20, made no progress. The Representatives-on-Mission interpreted this as evidence of his inefficiency and the Committee of Public Safety replaced Landremont with Carlenc, "an old soldier with no faint trace of any military aptitude whatever."[107] On October 13, Wurmser penetrated the French lines while the Prussians occupied Bitsch. The French fell back in great disorder, and by late October had taken up a position under the guns of Strassbourg. The French armies in the East were now completely separated but Brunswick made no attempt to crush the Army of the Moselle, which was retreating behind the Saar. Wurmser refrained from making a bold attack on the French in front of Strassbourg, and occupied himself with preparing what he hoped would be the new Austrian régime in Alsace. This alarmed both the Alsatians and the Prussians. The latter refused to help Wurmser in his attempt to drive the French into Upper Alsace.

In this critical juncture, Saint-Just and Le Bas were despatched as Representatives-on-Mission on October 16 to Strassbourg to report on the failure of the army to hold the line of Wissembourg and to punish all abuses without pity. They found an army that was weak in leadership and that lacked discipline, and a town that was divided in its loyalties. In short order they communicated martial ardor to the officers and soldiers, imposed a forced loan of nine million livres on the rich, dismissed all of the members of the Strassbourg Council, excepting the mayor, who was a reliable patriot, arrested many offenders, and announced severe penalties for profiteering. They immediately replaced Carlenc by Pichegru. With him, they established a military tribunal to deal summarily with all cases sent before it. They organized an effective system of requisition and enforced the law of the maximum.

Pichegru was one of the first of the new crop of commanders to whom the Revolution had opened a career. He had enlisted in the artillery as a private in 1789 and by the end of 1792 he was a colonel of volunteers. Subsequently he had commanded a corps on the Upper Rhine. Pichegru had a fine power of penetration and a strong personality that inspired the soldiers. He lacked originality but he had that instinctive knowledge which could distinguish a good from a bad plan. Above all he knew how to select men and make them work for him.

The Committee of Public Safety kept in close touch with the Army of the Rhine, through Saint-Just and Le Bas. The Committee in a despatch written by Carnot on October 27 approved the plans of operation presented by Saint-Just, and announced the sending of reinforcements to the army.[108] On the 30th Carnot, for the Committee, recommended to the Representatives that the enemy be attacked, not frontally, but on the flanks and from the rear, but that these suggestions should be modified as circumstances compelled.[109] These instructions, usually written by Carnot and oftentimes signed only by him, were sent regularly to Saint-Just and Le Bas.[110] On November 2 Carnot offered to join the Representatives if they needed him.

In the Army of the Moselle the Representatives Lacoste and Baudot attempted reforms similar to those effected in the Army of the Rhine, but with little success. On November 6, the Representatives announced the arrival of the young and ardent Hoche to succeed Delauney.[111] Hoche was the son of an old soldier and had been a groom in the royal stables in his early youth. He enlisted at twenty-one in the *Gardes Françaises*, and in three years had climbed up through eight grades to command the Army of the Moselle. He had distinguished himself at Maestricht and Nieuport and had skillfully defended Dunkirk, where he had behaved with a "rare bravery and intelligence."[112] These exploits had attracted the attention of Carnot and Hoche owed his new command to him.[113] A visitor to his new headquarters in the Army of the Moselle said of Hoche, "He seemed as young as the Revolution and as strong as the people."[114]

Hoche began immediately to reorganize his army and restore discipline. By the end of November he commanded forty thousand troops and he was determined to assume the offensive. This should have been done in conjunction with Pichegru, so that the Allies would be driven back from Strassbourg by threatening their right in the direction of Wörth and Bitsch. But Hoche was jealous of Pichegru and decided to try to relieve Landau by way of Kaiserslautern. Operations opened on the 17th of November. The Prussians evacuated Wörth at once and, concentrating quickly and fighting on the way, fell back on Kaiserslautern. On November 28 the battle of Kaiserslautern began and raged for three days.[115] Hoche attacked the twenty thousand well-entrenched Prussians with thirty-five thousand men. The French were unfamiliar with the ground and a large part of the army lost its way. They fought well but on the 30th Hoche fell back after losing two thousand men to eight hundred and twenty-nine for the Prussians.

Pichegru, in the meantime, had decided to capitalize on this diversion and on November 18 moved out with thirty-three thousand men to attack Wurmser. The Austrian right had been uncovered by the withdrawal of the Prussian troops. Wurmser had to fall back on Hagenau.[116]

On December 5 Carnot, writing in the name of the Committee of Public Safety to the Representatives with the Army of the Moselle, suggested that Hoche investigate the possibilities of making a forced march to attack the flank and rear of the enemy army that held the Army of the Rhine in check.[117] Carnot admitted that the nature of the roads and of the region would have to determine operations. He concluded by saying, "We count on your firmness and on the talents of the Commander-in-chief whom we persist in believing worthy of our confidence, in spite of the setback he has recently suffered."

Spurred to action, Hoche decided to leave troops to occupy the attention of the Prussians who continued to control the three roads leading to Landau by Kaiserslautern, Amweiler and Dahme, and go to the help of Pichegru. After a week's hard fighting columns of the two armies drove the enemy out of Wörth and effected a junction on December 22.[118] Wurmser fell back at once on the lines of Wissembourg. Jealously and friction between Hoche and Pichegru prevented the fullest use of the French advantage. To resolve this Lacoste and Baudot, who were resentful to the activities of Saint-Just and Le Bas, appointed Hoche as Commander-in-chief of the united Armies of the Rhine and of the Moselle on December 24.[119] Carnot and Barère answered for the Committee, regretting this precipitate action and speaking highly of both Hoche and Pichegru. They instructed Lacoste and Baudot to act hereafter only in concert with Saint-Just and Le Bas.[120] Carnot wrote in the same vein to Saint-Just and Le Bas on December 27.[121] Lacoste and Baudot defended their action in a despatch from Strassbourg in January, praising Hoche and criticizing Pichegru for not being active enough, admitting his patriotism but calling him a "cold and inanimate patriot."[122]

Wurmser was preparing to evacuate Wissembourg on December 26 when Hoche attacked him with great fury. The result was that by the 27th the French were again masters of the lines of

Wissembourg and Hoche had actually entered Wissembourg. On the 30th Wurmser retreated across the Rhine at Phillipsburg, while Brunswick evacuated Worms and Oppenheim. Landau was relieved and by early January, 1794 the whole of the Palatinate was in the hands of the French. The Committee of Public Safety wanted the Army of the Moselle to undertake an expedition to Treves but the troops had been promised a rest, and their grumblings, and some desertions, brought the consent of the Committee to cantonments for the winter.

The two armies were separated on January 14, 1794.[123] Pichegru had been appointed to succeed Jourdan in the command of the Army of the North on January 9, and on the 14th he relinquished his command of the Army of the Rhine to General Michaud, a "respectable but not gifted commander with whom we need not concern ourselves."[124] Michaud was ordered to take Mannheim and Kehl, but refused because of the wretched state of his troops. Carnot "angrily consented"[125] to his taking up cantonments.

In the other theatres of war fortunes had fluctuated. The situation in the Vendée caused the greatest concern. In the spring of 1793 the countryside in the regions known as the Bocage, the Plaine, and the Marais in the West were seething for insurrection. This broke out in February among the peasants. At first it was a revolt for religion's sake and against compulsory military service, and was thus social and religious in nature. On the appeal of the peasants for leadership the seigneurs responded and the insurrection became tinged with Royalism. Heroic figures rose to lead the bitter struggle. Outstanding were Charette, Stofflet, Cathelineau, Henri de La Rochejaquelin, de Lescure, and Bonchamps. The rebels, opposed at first only by the raw Republican recruits, were victorious. The Bocage was cleared in April. In May Thouars, Fontenay, Parthenay, La Chataigneraie fell to the insurrectionists, and the Marais was cleared. On June 10 they compelled Saumur to surrender and this gave them access to the right bank of the Loire. The Vendéan leaders then decided to spread the revolt through Brittany, Normandy, and Maine, and then, united, to march on Paris. Nantes, a city favorable to the Republic, was their first objective. Angers and Ancenis fell without resistance and on June 29 the rebels were before unfortified Nantes. The heroic defense of the town, however, withstood the fierce onslaughts of the valorous rebels, who were handicapped by the absence of artillery. The Vendéans fell back and that crisis for the Republic was averted. Efforts of Westermann and his Republican troops in July to establish a footing in the Bocage and lay waste to the country were unavailing and the violence resorted to only produced vindictive reprisals.

The "ruffian" Rossignol was appointed to the chief command on July 27, and on August 1 the government decreed the ruthless devastation and depopulation of the revolted districts. The insurgents suffered their first serious defeat before the important town of Luçon where they are reported to have lost six thousand men. They recovered rapidly and between September 18 and 22 they won five victories in pitched battles. On October 16-18 a desperate struggle was waged at Cholet, the strongest eastern outwork of the Bocage. The Republican troops were led by Westermann, the "chivalrous" Marceau, and the "herculean Kléber, who with his rough joviality and strongly impetuous Alsatian courage, bubbled over with patriotism."[126] When Bonchamps and d'Elbée were mortally wounded the peasants fled, leaving four thousand Vendéan dead on the field of battle.

After Cholet eighty thousand Vendéans, including fifty thousand of the boldest men, crossed over to the right bank of the Loire, where they had no difficulty in repulsing the few Republican troops located there. L'Échelle had succeeded Rossignol in command. On the rebel side the dying Bonchamps had been succeeded by the able but inexperienced Henri de La Rochejaquelin, a youth of twenty-one. The insurgents moved northward and on October 23 occupied Laval. L'Échelle was replaced by Chalbos. The Representatives Prieur (de la Marne), Turreau, and Bourbotte, constantly overrode the generals and not infrequently differed among themselves. The Republican troops were repulsed on November 21 at Dol. Finally the peasants, overwhelmed by homesickness, decided to return to their homes south of the Loire. The capture of Angers was necessary to effect this and that city was attacked on December 3. Marceau now commanded the Republican forces. Lacking artillery, the Vendéans were unable to capture the strongly-fortified city. Great cruelties were practiced by both sides. The main body of rebels turned back, hoping to cross the Loire at Saumur or Tours, but were overtaken by the Republicans under Marceau, Kléber and Westermann at Le Mans on December 13. The Republicans gained a bloody victory, followed by a wanton slaughter of the Vendéans, regardless of age or sex. Over fifteen thousand are said to have perished. The fleeing remnants of the army, numbering about seven thousand, were caught in the marshes and woods of Savenay by Kléber and entirely annihilated on December 23. Savenay marked the end of the great struggle in Upper Vendée, but Charette was still at large in Lower Vendée and the main body of rebels was beating off the attacks of the Republicans. The war might have ended had a policy of leniency been adopted after Savenay. During this period Carrier was fulfilling the wholesale execution of military suspects in the infamous *Noyades* at Nantes, and the Revolutionary Tribunal was also hard at work at Angers. The Vendée was scoured systematically by the *colonnes infernales* of General Turreau and soon became a desert waste. This only aggravated the resistance. The struggle in Brittany, where no unity was ever attained, continued. The Chouans under Cadoudal, Cotterau, Boishardi, and Cormatin carried on a ceaseless guerrilla warfare. The Republican troops had made a victorious entry into Lyons on October 9.

The occupation of Toulon by the English was a thorn in the Republican side during the early autumn. Carnot, in the name of the Committee of Public Safety, sent detailed instructions for the siege of Toulon on the fourth of November.[127] Ricord, Fréron, the younger Robespierre, Saliceti and Barras were active as Representatives before Toulon. The city was finally taken on December 18, by the French under General Dugommier, with the valuable support of the battery of artillery commanded by Bonaparte.[128]

The campaign of 1793 had finally ended most successfully for the French, who now had the decided advantage of a single control under Carnot.[129]

Chapter VI

LA PATRIE IS DEFENDED

THE GREATEST victories of the Revolutionary armies came during the year 1794. By its end France and the Revolution had been saved from their external foes; Belgium, Holland and the Rhinelands had been occupied, and the amnesty offered in December to the insurrectionists in the West was to bring the rebels gradually back into the bosom of the republican nation.

The famous *amalgamation* of all units in the army, regular and volunteer, into fresh regiments, or demi-brigades, while under way in 1793, was formally decreed by the Convention on January 9, 1794, on the motion of Dubois-Crancé, for the military committee.[1] All of the new soldiers—the volunteers of '91 and '92, and the conscripts of '93 and '94—were to be absorbed into the old line army of professional soldiers. Two volunteer battalions were mixed with a veterans' battalion to form the demi-brigades that were to cover themselves with such glory. The *amalgamation* was effected according to a symbolic Republican ceremonial. One Representative reported that the *amalgamation* at Cherbourg was made into "a true civic fête."[2] The brigading was completed by March 21. At that time the French army was composed of one hundred and ninety-six demi-brigades of infantry of the line, and twenty-two demi-brigades of light infantry. The cavalry was composed of twenty-seven regiments of heavy cavalry, and fifty-nine of light cavalry, forming ninety thousand sabres in all. The artillery was composed of fifteen thousand men and retained its old regular organization. Nine new light artillery regiments, however, were added to it. The engineering corps was left unchanged and comprised fifty-three hundred men.

The total number of men under arms was 850,000. The fighting strength of the armies in the early part of 1794 was 794,333,[3] divided as follows: North, 245,822; Ardennes, 37,630; Moselle, 103,323; Rhine, 93,390; Alps 43,042; Italy, 60,551; Eastern Pyrenees, 70,508; Western Pyrenees, 50,782; West 22,519; Coast of Cherbourg, 27,388; Coast of Brest, 34,378. "Each of these armies," writes Colonel Phipps, "acquired a history, style, prejudice and reputation of its own."[4] This was due to their departmental character before the *amalgamation*, to the replacements made by the departments nearest the armies after the brigading, and to the fact that the theatres in which the different armies operated affected their style of warfare and their own character as armies.

The soldiers themselves have been characterized aptly as "at one and the same time, gross and grandiloquent, ragged yet alert, wide-awake fellows though ranters. They combined in themselves the qualities of rough plebeian warriors and the exaltation of apostles entrusted with the task of spreading abroad the doctrines of faith and even love."[5] The spirit of republicanism and patriotic devotion of Carnot, Lindet and Prieur (de la Côte-d'Or), and of some of the Representatives of the people such as Saint-Just, Prieur (de la Marne), Gillet, and Le Bas, so permeated and inflamed the susceptible revolutionary troops that Madame de Staël could say: "The fatherland no longer exists excepting in the Armies; but there at least it is still beautiful."[6] In the troublous month of April, 1794, Representative Dumas wrote from the Army of the Alps that "in the presence of the treachery that oppresses the Republic, it is a sweet consolation to acclaim the children [soldiers] who remain faithful to it."[7]

The cultivation of a republican spirit among the Revolutionary armies was not left to chance. The Representatives, of course, did a great deal to inspire and feed it. The troops were kept informed of political events. On January 19, 1794 the Committee of Public Safety ordered the Minister of War to send a sufficient number of copies of the *Journal Universel*, edited by Audoin, member and printer of the Convention, to all of the armies.[8] This journal was one of "the most revolutionary papers of the period."[9] The paper was politically partisan to the Mountain and to the Jacobins, and contained a good deal of news of the popular societies. Audoin was an ardent Robespierrist. The paper was readable and the running account of events was made vivid, personal, and even gossipy. Military news received ample attention and much was made of heroic exploits in the armies.[10]

The *Journal des hommes libres,* was also sent regularly to the troops.[11] This paper was directed by Vatar and Duval, the latter being a member of the Convention. It had been launched to combat the Girondin press and was also a very revolutionary journal.[12] This exceptionally well-printed paper was started on November 2, 1792. It gave lengthy, informal reports of the Convention, and of the Commune of Paris. It published letters to the editor, poems and hymns. The paper gave little attention to military news, concentrating on the political, despite the announcement on the first page of its prospectus: "Our Armies! Our Armies! They constitute the vital point. We will be particularly concerned to publish everything that concerns them, and we hope to be able to publish only successes."[13] Duval did not parade his own views editorially. At least on 9 thermidor and thereafter the paper was anti-Robespierrist. On July 7, 1794 the Committee of Public Safety authorized the Commission on Public Instruction to sent one-thousand copies of *Le Republican français,* to the troops free of charge."[14]

Carnot sponsored a journal *la Soirée du Camp*, that was authorized on July 8, 1794.[15] On the 17th of July, the Committee of Public Safety over the signatures of Lindet, Barère, Saint-Just, and Carnot, outlined a minute plan of organization for this journal.[16] There were to be three editors, with one serving as the director of the enterprise, and to devote his free time to the military history of the Revolution. This directing editor was Larozerie,[17] who was evidently attached to the Topographical Bureau of the Committee of Public Safety, where his relations with Carnot must have been professionally intimate. This Committee-sponsored journal ran for thirty-nine numbers, beginning on 1 thermidor (July 19, 1794).[18] There are only three numbers of this tiny, four-page paper publicly extant.[19] After a political survey of Europe in each issue, a good deal of space was given to the relating of little human interest stories of bravery and patriotism. General military and naval news also appeared. There was little on domestic politics. There is no convincing evidence for Aulard's statement that Carnot edited the journal "to create gradually among the soldiers an anti-Robespierrist state of mind.[20]

The Committee of Public Safety discontinued its subscriptions of the journals on August 18, 1794.[21]

As a part of its conscious, directed propaganda the Committee of Public Safety commissioned a number of artists to execute caricatures to ridicule the members of the Coalition, to glorify the Revolution and the troops, and to idealize the principles of the Revolution.[22] The Committee also used the popular societies as centers for molding the Republican Spirit.[23] The funds voted to these societies were taken from the fifty millions at the free disposal of the Committee. On July 9, 1794, the Committee ordered the Association of Musicians and Composers to send to the various armies twelve thousand copies of songs and patriotic hymns suitable to "propagate the republican spirit and the love of the public virtues."[24]

The new strategy and the new tactics of 1794 that had been hammered out on the anvil of necessity, practice and experience were not entirely new. They were simply a modification of the old principle of throwing superior weight on the vital spot. The new slogans were to attack boldly when possible and to surprise the enemy by sudden concentrations and rapid movements. The art of war was no longer to consist in guarding every pass, defending fortresses, and besieging towns and fortified places. The counter-stroke was to succeed a passive defense. A new tactics to accommodate the new strategy and to harmonize with the intelligence and élan of the ardent Republican soldiers was developed. The old attack in line was superseded by a return to the old system of attack in columns. These were so spaced that they could be deployed rapidly into line, and were then covered on the center and flanks by "heavy clouds of skirmishers." After these skirmishers had pushed boldly up to the enemy lines, the battalion columns supplied the superior weight which was necessary to crush the enemy at the vital spot. The objective was more often the enemy's center than his flank, so that his force might be split in two, and one-half of it be surrounded and annihilated. Carnot's strategy, however, was often to operate on one flank, or on both flanks of the enemy.[25]

The artillery was used to prepare the advance of the infantry. The cavalry was usually handled with great daring and its task was to break the enemy's cavalry, or infantry. The mobility of the armies was also increased by the fact that they moved without magazines or supplies, and became dependent upon occupied territories to sustain them.

These various changes were congenial to the character of the new troops, and to the Government that used and directed them. "The military leaders of the Republic," one scholar has written, "scornful of the science of tactics, of perpetual precautions, of timid advances and consolidations, would gather their men into masses, and march in overwhelming force straight to the point of decision, confident that republican courage and faith could not fail. In this way France inaugurated a great change in tactics, and more significant still, the revolution in wars."[26] Mathiez says that the young generals "by their audacity and powers of rapid adaptation . . . disconcerted the rigid and hidebound generals of the Coalition," who were entirely content to abide by the old tactics.

Carnot outlined the new strategy in a long report to the Committee of Public Safety on January 30, 1794, in which he developed the general plans for the spring campaign on all the fronts.[27] "All the armies of the Republic ought to act on the offensive, but not with the same vigor everywhere. The decisive blows ought to be struck on two or three points only; otherwise it would be necessary to distribute the troops uniformly on all frontiers and the campaign would be concluded on all of them with certain advantages gained but not sufficient to put the enemy *hors d'état* for the next year, while the resources of the Republic would be dissipated." Carnot proceeded to state certain general rules that the Committee had been insisting on. "These general rules are to operate always in mass and offensively; to maintain a severe but not a trifling discipline in the armies; to hold the troops ever in readiness; . . . to make frequent changes in garrisons, in headquarters and in temporary commands, in order to dissolve the webs that spin themselves by an unlimited stay in the same locality, and from which the treasons develop that deliver the defenses to the enemy; to give the greatest vigilance to the outposts; to oblige the general officers to visit them frequently; to engage the enemy in combat on every occasion by bayonet; and to pursue him to his complete destruction." Carnot listed the objectives of the three armies in the West: to finish the war in the Vendée, to guard the coasts, and to prepare the projected descent upon the shores of England. He admitted that the actual invasion was impossible during the current year but stated that the active threat of it would compel the English to keep a substantial portion of its fleet concentrated in the Channel as well as a considerable land army that might otherwise be sent to the continent.

For the spring campaign Carnot believed that the Allies would concentrate on the Sambre or Meuse, attempt to overwhelm the French resistance in the North-east, and march on Paris. Instead of waiting for the first moves of the enemy, he decided on a system of bold counter strokes. The Committee of Public Safety sent instructions to the Army of the Moselle on March 9, ordering the general-in-chief to hold his troops to continuous action, short of exhausting them, and to act ceaselessly on the offensive.[28] On March 11, Pichegru, then commanding both the Armies of the North and the Ardennes, received Carnot's rough sketch for the campaign. Pichegru was evidently in full accord with these plans.[29] The plan was to stand firmly on the defensive around Maubeuge, to feint in Flanders, and to throw the main attack against the Austrian communications in the direction of Charleroi. Pichegru had 130,000 French to oppose the 148,000 of the Allies.

Landrecies had fallen to the Allies in late winter. In April the French left under Moreau and Souham advanced against Clerfayt and defeated him at Courtrai late in the month.[30] This town was rich in supplies and resources for the French.[31] Moreau and Souham pushed on in the direction of Ghent. Mack, Coburg's chief of staff, resolved to cut off this column by a joint movement on Lille from the direction of Menin and Tournay. The French, however, took Menin on April 30.[32] On the previous day the Committee of Public Safety had ordered Saint-Just and Le Bas to the Army of the North to execute the "views of the Committee."[33] On the 30th, Carnot sent operations instructions to the two Representatives.[34] He continued to do this, although he left a considerable margin of independent action to the Representatives.[35]

According to Mack's plan, the English and Austrian columns

were scheduled to reach Lille on May 18. Souham, commanding in Pichegru's absence, heard of this scheme and by an admirable forced march from Lille brought the columns commanded by Moreau, Macdonald and Vandamme together at Turcoing on May 17. On the following day the French defeated the English and Austrians before they could effect a junction.[36] Coburg withdrew a large portion of his forces to the north, on the assumption that the French would make their principal effort in the direction of Flanders.

On April 30 the Committee of Public Safety ordered Jourdan to march secretly and immediately on Liège and Namur.[37] At the time he had forty-five thousand men in the Army of the Moselle. In May he added the Army of the Ardennes to his command, and thus had 100,000 soldiers in what came to be known later as the Army of the Sambre-et-Meuse. Jourdan now commanded an army of real veterans.

Jourdan forced his way over the Meuse and drove Beaulieu back before him in ten days of severe fighting (May 21-31).[38] He had thus penetrated the allied line of defense and threatened Namur. Carnot, in the name of the Committee, wrote to him, urging him to take Dinant and Charleroi, to guard the banks of the Meuse, and to blockade Namur.[39] In this despatch Carnot gave instructions for the treatment of occupied territories: "Spare all religious objects, protect the cottagers, the unfortunate, the women, the children, and the aged; advance as the benefactors of the people but at the same time as the plague of the aristocrats, the rich, and the special enemies of the French; impose on these the entire burden of contributions; take them as hostages. . . . We should live at the expense of the enemy."

In early June the right of the Army of the North was added to Jourdan's command, and he was to be responsible to Pichegru for their joint action in Belgium from the Meuse to the sea.[40] Jourdan immediately took steps to lay siege to Charleroi. On June 6 the Committee of Public Safety despatched Saint-Just to the frontiers of the north and east, from the sea to the Rhine, to "superintend the armies and to see to the execution of the decrees of the Convention and the orders of the Committee of Public Safety."[41] Saint-Just arrived in the camp before Charleroi on June 12.[42]

The Army of the North advanced and captured Ypres.[43] Carnot, in the name of the Committee, wrote to Choudieu and Richard on June 18 to felicitate them and Pichegru on the capture of Ypres.[44] He went on to urge them "to pursue them [the enemy] without giving them time to breathe. It is time to cut the bond which unites England and Austria by taking Ostend. . . . It is legitimate that you levy contributions in the territory you enter; however, since we should probably safeguard it for the security of our own frontiers, it is essential that you avoid excesses, that you maintain the most exact discipline among the troops, and that the local customs and religion be respected. The contributions should fall exclusively on the rich. . . . It is also necessary to disarm every one. In the meantime, let Jourdan take Charleroi, and give the enemy a decisive battle."

After Ypres, Jourdan administered a defeat to Clerfayt at Hooglide. Gillet, Saint-Just and Guyton wrote to the Committee on June 23, "Europe is in decadence and we shall flourish. The spirit of the army is triumphant."[45] Saint-Just added a postscript, "After Charleroi we shall fall upon Namur and Mons." Jourdan suffered a reversal on June 16, but on June 25[46] Charleroi was taken. Coburg appeared immediately with nearly seventy thousand troops[47] to relieve it. Jourdan had eighty thousand men at Fleurus to oppose the enemy. Coburg's force was too small, and he committed the usual Austrian fault of neglecting to concentrate his forces. The French occupied the heights of Fleurus.

The battle of Fleurus began on June 26 at three o'clock in the morning. The Allies were well supplied with artillery which was well handled during the engagement. The French were driven back thrice on their entrenchments. An observation balloon was used effectively by the French.[48] Kléber finally managed to restore order on the left and at six o'clock in the evening Jourdan gathered together all of his reserves and succeeded in completely routing the enemy.[49] The Allies lost nearly eight thousand men in the encounter. The battle of Fleurus was far-reaching in its consequences. It sounded the knell of the Reign of Terror in France. The effect on the war was immeditely felt. The Allies were each desirous of protecting their own lines of communication. The English only thought of covering Holland, the Austrians of reaching the Rhine. The French were thus able to gain easy possession of many important places and could continue their advance unhindered.

Carnot's former associate on mission, Lacombe Saint-Michel, was sent to the Army of the North by the Committee on June 26, "to follow and to superintend the operations."[50] On July 1 the Committee acknowledged the action of the Convention on June 29 forming the Army of the Sambre-et-Meuse out of the forces assembled on the Meuse.[51] The capture of Mons was announced on the same day by Laurent, with a postscript by Gillet praising the "brave" Kléber, and the "intrepid" Lefebvre.[52] The Committee ordered the transfer of sixteen thousand five hundred troops from the new Army of the Sambre-et-Meuse to Dunkirk. Gillet protested this vigorously, particularly calling attention to the fact that the cavalry requested would be almost useless in their new destination.[53] He insisted that the need was still great in the North. Carnot, for the Committee, reduced the requisition to five thousand men in a despatch to Lacombe Saint-Michel on July 4, in which he also ordered the temporary abandonment of the project on Holland, in favor of the conquest of Maritime Flanders and Zeeland.[54]

The capture of Tournai, and the blockade of Landrecies were announced on July 4. [55] Brussels was taken on July 8.[56] Richard reported to the Committee from Brussels on the tenth that the Armies of the North, and of the Sambre-et-Meuse had effected a juncture at Ath and were marching on the enemy, who seemed to be retiring to three points, Antwerp, Maëstricht and the Rhine.[57] Carnot, for the Committee, wrote to the Representatives with the army of the Sambre-et-Meuse on July 11.[58]

Here is the only rule to follow: We wish neither to excite the country or to fraternize with it; it is a conquered country that has large restitutions to make to us; and it is necessary to immediately extract all the resources that might favor a new invasion on the part of the enemy. You should not ignore the fact that the Brabant in general is greatly devoted to the Emperor. . . . It is not therefore a country to spare; but everywhere there are peoples who are good; it is necessary to win them gradually, in respecting their persons, their manners and customs, and in levelling all the blows upon the rich and the enemies of France. One cannot follow the same rule everywhere, for Liège, West-Flanders, Dutch Flanders, and even Namur, it is said, are in general favorable to us. . . . It is up to your wisdom to apply these principles in accordance with circumstances. . . . Accelerate as much as possible the siege of Namur, for one cannot leave a place of such importance in our rear."

Carnot sent an equally important despatch to the Representatives with the armies of the Rhine and of the Moselle on the same day, urging a *coup de main* on Trèves, and promising a reinforcement of fifteen thousand men from the Army of the West.[59] He wrote, however, "If you see some other better *coup* to make, indicate it to us; we shall entertain it with a lively eagerness. . . . It is necessary to attack the enemy daily. It is by the continuity of attack, by the most obstinant perseverance that will wear down the enemy and throw terror into his camp. Make useful forages, collect the subsistence, arms and supplies necessary for the consumption of the armies; snatch from the enemy all their resources, all their means of existence; the necessity to ravage is a great misfortune; but it is better to carry destruction abroad, than to suffer it in our own land."

On July 13 Carnot instructed the Representatives with the Army of the Sambre-et-Meuse not to overlook the requisition of artistic productions in Brussels that might embellish Paris.[60] Richard announced to the Committee on August 10 from Antwerp that the finest works of the Flemish artists were being sent to Paris, including the famous "Descent of the Cross," by Rubens.[61] The Committee of Public Safety, on July 14, decreed a contribution of fifty millions on Brussels, and six hundred hostages from among the wealthiest citizens; ten millions on Tournai, and thirty hostages; three thousand horses and one thousand carriages from Belgium.[62]

The Army of the Sambre-et-Meuse took Malines and Louvain on July 15,[63] at the same time that Hentz and Goujon announced the occupation of Spire and Kirweiler by the Armies of the Rhine and the Moselle.[64] Landrecies was taken on July 16 by Schérer.[65] Kaiserslautern was evacuated by the enemy on July 17.[66] Quesnoy was invested on the same day.[67] On the 18th and

19th Lacombe Saint-Michel announced the taking of Nieuport to both the Committee and Carnot from Dunkirk, which had been renamed Dunelibre.[68] General Moreau marched on Bruges immediately after the capture of Nieuport.[69] Richard begged the Committee on July 19 to send Saint-Just into Belgium to take full charge of the general administration of the country, saying that a task of such importance called for a member of the Committee of Public Safety.[70] Laurent reported from Brussels on July 19 that he had imposed a contribution of fifteen thousand livres on Malines, and one of two millions on Louvain, of which one-half was to be paid by the University.[71]

On July 20 Carnot, in the name of the Committee, ordered the demolition of Ostend, and its destruction as a port, for military and political reasons, and the transfer of its facilities to Dunkirk "to which it is time to restore its former splendor."[72] He proceeded to trace what he considered to be France's rightful northern frontier. On the next day for the Committee, he wrote to Lacombe Saint-Michel stating that the conquest of Nieuport would remove the obstacles to the invasion of Holland.[73] "All our solicitude now turns," he wrote, "to this great operation, which ought to snap the knot of the Coalition and assure the success of the campaign."

Laurent notified the Committee on July 24 that Antwerp, the "richest city in Belgium," with its citadel, had been taken.[74] On the same day Hentz and Goujon wrote from Kaiserslautern that the Armies of the Rhine and the Moselle were concerting the movement on Trèves which was scheduled to start on the following day.[75] The Representatives incidentally praised the merits of Saint-Cyr, general-of-division, recommending him for the first available command of an army. Liège was occupied on July 27.[76]

After 9 Thermidor, on July 29, the Convention decreed the renewal of the two great Committees by one-fourth every month, with the proviso that no retired member could be re-elected until after an interval of one month. As reconstituted on July 31 the Committee of Public Safety included Barère, Eschassériaux, Lindet, Thuriot, C.-A. Prieur, Tallien, Carnot, Laloy, Billaud-Varenne, Collot-d'Herbois, Bréard, and Treilhard.[77]

The new Committee on August 3 directed the Representatives

to the Armies of the North and Sambre-et-Meuse to speed up the attacks on Condé, Valenciennes, and Quesnoy.[78] On the following day a despatch from the Armies of the Rhine and Moselle announced the taking of Trèves.[79] Quesnoy capitulated on August 15. In recounting this victory, Carnot's former Colleague-on-mission, Duquesnoy, paid high tribute to the patience, the activity, and the courage of the troops.[80] "Almost continuous rains inundated the trenches," he wrote; "eh bien! it was to the cries of *Vive la République!* and to the sound of a thousand martial songs that our intrepid soldiers labored." The insatiable Carnot acknowledged this victory for the Committee, and went on to urge the actions against Valenciennes and Condé, reiterating that "the state of stagnation . . . is alien to our system. We do not believe that one should engage constantly in general action; but we have never ceased to say that it is necessary to multiply partial actions, in order to harrass and exterminate the enemy in every manner possible. These principles are invariable, no matter in what situation one finds oneself."[81]

Lacombe Saint-Michel, in announcing the capture of the fortress of Écluse, on August 26, after twenty-two days in the trenches, eulogized Moreau, who directed the siege, and praised the exploits of a humble, but brave grenadier.[82] Valenciennes fell before the assaults of the Armies of the Rhine and Moselle on the same day.[83] On the 30th Carnot, for the Committee, directed the Army of the North to follow up the capture of Écluse by a decisive combat against the enemy in Dutch Brabant so as to penetrate into Holland, demolishing all fortifications taken, notably that of Écluse.[84] On September 7 he urged the siege of Maëstricht.[85]

Lacombe Saint-Michel wrote to Carnot on September 21 announcing that he was sending Dulanloy to Paris to give his ideas, confidentially, to Carnot.[86] On September 23 Lacombe Saint-Michel repeated his earlier counsel against an immediate invasion of Holland.[87] Gillet wrote to the Committee from the Army of the Sambre-et-Meuse on September 22, advising against the expedition into Holland during the current campaign, because of the fatigue of the troops and their need for well-deserved billets after a brilliant campaign.[88] He suggested that Maëstricht be taken by the Army of the North, while the Armies of the Moselle and Sambre-et-Meuse jointly pushed on to the Rhine, covering the siege of Maëstricht by guarding the Rhine towards Dusseldorf and Cologne. These two armies might even try to take Coblenz, Trarbarch and Mont-Royal, and, in concert with the Army of the Rhine, expel the Prussians from Mayence. He stated that Jourdan thought his ideas were excellent. On the following day he announced the capture of Backheim and Reckheim, and the evacuation of Aix-la-Chapelle by the Austrians, taking the occasion to repeat his complaints at the failure of the Army of the Moselle to co-operate.[89]

Carnot, for the Committee, sent detailed instructions to the Armies of the Rhine and Moselle on September 26, in which he said: "Attack the enemy daily, morning and evening. . . . Fall successively, in mass, on each part of his formations" to prevent their union.[90] Bellegarde and Lacombe Saint-Michel announced the taking of Crèvecoeur-sur-le-Meuse on September 30,[91] which Lacombe Saint-Michel, in a despatch to Carnot, said was taken in a novel manner not found in Vauban or Coborn.[92] In his announcement of the capture of Juliers by the Army of the Sambre-et-Meuse on October 3, Gillet stated that Jourdan had commanded the center, Schérer the right, Kléber the left, and Lefebvre the advance guard.[93] Marceau, Soult, Ney and Bernadotte were also with the Sambre-et-Meuse at the time.

By lot the trio most responsible for the conduct of the war, Carnot, Lindet, and Prieur (de la Côte-d'Or) left the Committee of Public Safety on October 6, and were succeeded by Prieur (de la Marne), Guyton-Morveau and Richard.[94] Carnot continued, however, to take part in the activities of the Committee, particularly those of a military nature, for some time. He continued to draft directions for the Representatives with the armies, some of which he alone signed.[95] Robert Lindet also continued to give his expert assistance to the Committee.

Gillet announced the entry into Cologne on October 7, and in a subsequent despatch enthused over the immense resources opened up to the Republican troops by the victory.[96] Lacombe Saint-Michel wrote to Carnot on October 10, announcing the capture of Bois-le-Duc, and urging winter quarters for the troops.[97] Féraud reported that the Army of the Rhine had taken Frankenthal on October 17, and Worms on the following day.[98] On the 22nd, Carnot for the Committee, instructed the Representatives with the Armies of the Rhine and Moselle to execute a general engagement for the purpose of taking Coblenz, Mayence, Mannheim and all of Palatinate.[99] In the same capacity he sent directions to the Representatives with the Armies of the North and the Sambre-et-Meuse, on October 28, urging the immediate penetration into Holland, and the taking of Maëstricht, Vanloo, Grave and Nimègue, and outlining wherein the politics to be pursued in Holland was to differ from that followed in Belgium.[100] On the same day, Carnot wrote to the Representatives with the Armies of the Rhine and the Moselle that it was essential to clear the entire left bank of the Rhine.[101] On November 3, however, Carnot, for the Committee, wrote to the same Representatives to the effect that the safety and welfare of the army took precedence over this desire to push the enemy everywhere beyond the Rhine.[102] Vanloo had fallen a few days previously,[103] and on November 4 the Representatives with the Armies of the North and the Sambre-et-Meuse announced that Maëstricht had fallen at five o'clock in the morning after twelve days of siege.[104]

Carnot returned to the Committee of Public Safety as a member on November 5, along with Cambacérès and Pelet (de la Lozière), succeeding Laloy, Eschassériaux and Treilhard. Nimègue capitulated on November 8.[105] This prompted instructions from Carnot, in the name of the Committee, again urging the expedition into Holland in order to take advantage of the rout of the enemy and the disunion in the Coalition.[106] Carnot ordered the destruction of most of the border fortresses so that French troops could enter Holland thereafter at will without resistance. In order to guarantee the "irrevocable possession of the country," Maëstricht, Juliers, Vanloo, Bois-le-Duc, Crèvecoeur and Antwerp were to be put in a good condition of defense. The Committee of Public Safety communicated with Gillet in the same vein on the following day, but cautioned against precipitate action that might jeopardize operations where a delay might increase the chances of success, and prevent a needless sacrifice of "heroes."[107] The Committee expressed regret at the prolongation of the "bloody war" that the postponement of the invasion of Holland might cause. Gillet wrote to the Committee on November 23 advising against the invasion because of the "nakedness" of the troops, and the rigors of the season.[108]

The Committee of Public Safety bowed to the counsel of the Representatives and to the necessities of the situation, on November 25 in giving an order for the Armies of the North and the Sambre-et-Meuse to take up winter quarters after Grave, Bréda, Heusden and Bommel were taken, stating that the safety of the army was the supreme law.[109] The Representatives were directed to entertain any peace proposals made by Holland since it was not the intention of the Committee "to reply with disdain to a conquered enemy."

Carnot, in the name of the Committee, wrote to the Representatives with the armies of the Rhine and the Moselle on November 14, insisting on the capture of Mayence and Mannheim.[110] Writing of General Michaud, he said, "This general, honest and brave personally, distrusts himself, and lacks audacity. You must . . . inspire him with some of your own." He announced that Kléber was being sent to aid Michaud. More than a month later, on December 20, Carnot wrote to these Representatives suggesting that the siege of Mayence be raised and the troops be put into winter quarters so that they might be reorganized.[111] He requested that they counsel privately with the generals-in-chief and advise him. He mentioned the fact that the King of Prussia seemed to be willing to negotiate for peace and desired a temporary cessation of hostilities before Mayence as an evidence of French good faith. Mannheim fell to the French on Christmas Day.[112]

A series of minor victories in Holland by the armies of the North and the Sambre-et-Meuse were climaxed by the occupation of Amsterdam and the flight of the Stadtholder, announced by the Representatives on January 21, 1795.[113] Rotterdam, the Hague and other Dutch towns surrendered without a blow. The French cavalry under Moreau crossed the frozen River Helder to the Island of Texel and captured the Dutch fleet. By February the whole of the United Provinces had submitted to the French. Carnot sent instructions for the occupation on February 8, and ordered the invasion of Zeeland.[114] This rich province capitulated two days later.[115] On the 15th Gillet objected to the imposition of twenty-five millions on the territory between the Meuse and the Rhine, on the grounds that the country had been fought over for three years, and the rich had fled.[116] He announced that he had reduced the contribution to eight millions. Charles Cochon, as Representative in Holland, wrote to the Committee on March 3, to urge an alliance with Holland, based on mutual interests.[117] He criticized the policy of retribution and imposition which alienated the Dutch, but remarked that Carnot's instructions had somewhat mollified the citizens.

Carnot was already urging preparations for the new campaign when he wrote to Gillet on February 22, reminding him that the enemy would begin operations early in the spring to succour Luxembourg.[118] He cautioned against any action that might obstruct the peace negotiations with the King of Prussia. On March 3, the Committee of Public Safety sent Legrand, an engineering officer, to make a military survey and reconnaissance of the frontiers from Strassburg to the Meuse, Liège and Cologne.[119] On March 5, 1795, Cambacérès, Carnot, and Pelet (de la Lozière) left the Committee of Public Safety, and were succeeded by Reubell, Siéyès, and Laporte. In the reorganized Committee Dubois-Crancé and Lacombe Saint-Michel were in charge of military operations.

French arms were not as consistently successful in 1794 on the other fronts as they were in the North and North-east. In the South-east the important neutrality of Switzerland had been secured, Nice and Savoy had been violated, and Sardinia had been estranged. The French forces in the South-east were split up into two corps, known as the Armies of the Alps and of Italy. This was probably a grave mistake, as Bonaparte and other generals pointed out, since it resulted in ill-timed efforts and wasted opportunities.

On March 20 the Committee of Public Safety appointed General Petit-Guillaume to succeed Hoche in the command of the expedition on Oneille, which was important for its communications.[120] Saliceti, Representative with the Army of Italy, sent Bonaparte, general of artillery, to Nice on March 24 to perfect plans for the spring campaign. On April 18, in conformity with instructions from Paris, the Army of the Alps took Oneille.[121] In March and April this army made several unsuccessful attempts to seize the Mont Cenis Pass.[122] Robespierre, jeune, and Saliceti were able, however, on April 18, to report the taking of Ornéa, the gate to Piedmont.[123] Dumas captured the Saint Bernard Pass on April 23,[124] and on the 29th Saorgia was taken.[125] The Mont Cenis Pass fell on May 14. Bonaparte was acting as adviser to the aged Dumerbion. On his advice the Committee of Public Safety permitted Dumerbion to violate the neutrality of Genoa. Masséna seized the redoubts of the Col de Tendo on April 20. As a result of ten days of fighting the French captured four thousand prisoners and seventy guns and made contact with the Army of the Alps and were at liberty to invade Piedmont. The Sardinians and Austrians held the line of fortresses Coni, Mondava and Ceva.

Bonaparte wanted to reinforce the Army of Italy with troops from the two armies on the Spanish frontier and from the Army of the Rhine, and then to advance into Lombardy, and, moving by the Tyrolese passes, act in concert with the Army of the Rhine.[126] Carnot objected to this, preferring to keep the Armies of the Alps and of Italy on the defensive. Robespierre jeune and Ricord agreed with Bonaparte, and the younger Robespierre went to Paris on about July 3 to win over his brother to the plan.[127] Carnot continued his opposition because he thought such an offensive would expose the frontiers, would cause the abandonment of Corsica, would lose Toulon,[128] would expose the rear of the army to attack, and would paralyze the armies in the South. Nine Thermidor intervened and little came of Bonaparte's plan, which had already been launched contrary to orders from Paris. Bonaparte was severely under suspicion because of his friendliness with the younger Robespierre. Albitte, Saliceti and Laporte had written to the Committee of Public Safety from the two armies on August 6, associating Robespierre jeune, Ricord and Bonaparte in a scheme to disobey the Committee. They announced that they were arresting Ricord and Bonaparte, and sending them and their papers to Paris.[129] Albitte and Saliceti reported on August 24 that they found nothing incriminating in the papers of Bonaparte and that there was, therefore, no reason to hold him.[130] "We are convinced," they wrote, "of the utility of using the talents of this officer, who, we cannot deny, is very essential to an army of which he has a greater understanding than anyone else, and in which men of his type are extremely difficult to find." The Representatives released him, but did not restore him to his command until they had word from Paris.

In his despatch to the Representatives, for the Committee of Public Safety on August 13,[131] Carnot said: "We do not doubt that the new conspirary which has just been extirpated, had one of its most dangerous branches in the territories where the Robespierres exercised such a perfidious and active influence. The project which Robespierre jeune came to snatch from us, so to speak, through the tyranny of his brother—the project to invade Piedmont, and abandon our rightful frontiers, and let Corsica go —this project, I repeat, appears to us to be the fruit of intrigue and the product of these conspirators. . . . What astonishes us is to discover that the system of Robespierre has found some favor among you." Carnot proceeded to outline the operations proposed for the Armies of Italy and the Alps in the following year.

Carnot, in the name of the Committee of Public Safety, ordered the provisional union of the Armies of the Alps and of Italy on August 21.[132] This despatch also contained instructions to the effect that the two armies were to cease their offensive in Piedmont, and were to satisfy themselves with securely defending the places already won. Organization was to be perfected, and discipline was to be improved. Plans were to be made for the campaign in the coming year. Garrisons and officers were to be changed frequently. The greatest mobility possible was to be secured. Corsica was to be recaptured as soon as possible, by an imposing force.

On October 18, Carnot, for the Committee, wrote to Ritter, Representative with the Army of Italy, advising the continued maintenance of the neutrality of Genoa in order to safeguard the trade between France and Genoa, so essential to the provisioning of the troops.[133] Ritter and Turreau wrote to Carnot, ex-member of the Committee, on November 4,[134] giving him a copy of their proposals sent to the Committee of Public Safety,[135] in which they urged a winter campaign. The Representatives requested Carnot "to weigh this plan in your wisdom." In the first session of the Committee that Carnot attended after his re-election, an immediate expedition on Corsica and a naval engagement on the Mediterranean were decreed.[136] On November 12, Carnot wrote to Jeanbon Saint-André, Representative at Toulon, agreeing with him that it was imperative for the French to secure the ascendancy on the Mediterranean, for which, he said, the reconquest of Corsica was the first step.[137] He announced that Saliceti was being sent to direct the military and political activities concerned with this expedition, since he knew the island perfectly. In a despatch on January 1, 1795, Carnot regretted the discovery of the secret plans on Corsica, an expedition which remained central in his mind.[138] He proceeded to support the projected attack on Leghorn. This *entrepot* of English commerce with the Levant would greatly enrich Marseilles. "The real object of the Committee of Public Safety," he wrote, "is to chase the English from the Mediterranean. . . . If the English fleet takes refuge in Corsica, then Corsica must be attacked; if it goes to Leghorn, then it must be pursued there. . . . Expel the English from the Mediterranean, take Corsica, take the riches of Tuscany, seize the island of Elba —these are the results we await. It matters not to us the order in which these objectives are executed, so long as they are achieved. . . . We are certain that a decisive engagement would immortalize the French fleet and assure us the rule of the Mediterranean." Carnot wrote to the Representatives with the Army of Italy for the Committee on February 13, 1795, stating that the treaty just concluded between the Republic and the Grand Duke of Tuscany made the expedition against Leghorn unnecessary; but that the urgent necessity of fighting the enemy on the sea as soon as possible and chasing him from the Mediterranean still remained.[139]

When Spain entered the war the fortresses on both sides of the frontier were in bad disrepair and the armies there had been materially reduced. Charles IV of Spain, however, decided to conquer Roussilon and penetrate further north. There were only two practicable passes through the Pyrenees at the eastern end —the Col de Perche between the rivers Segre and Auch, and the Col de Perthes between the Têt and the Ter. At the western end lie the passes of Roncesvalles and Meyo, covered by Pampeluna.

There were four passes along the Shore road, covered by the towns of San Sebastian, Bilboa, Santander, and Oviedo.

The French troops on the Spanish frontier were divided in two armies, the Eastern (Pyrenées Orientales) and the Western (Pyrenées Occidentales). In the early part of 1793 these armies were in a complete state of demoralization and were commanded by a rapid succession of generals. By the end of the year the Eastern Army had had to abandon its first line of resistance on the Tech, and had fallen back on its second line of the Têt. The Western Army suffered serious reverses in August and September, and by the end of the year the two Armies had just managed to cover Saint-Jean-Pied-de-Port and Bayonne.

The campaign of 1794 was more successful. The Eastern Army, under the elderly Dagobert, took the initiative and, crossing the Col de Perche, penetrated into the valley of the Segre. After the death of Dagobert in April, Dugommier, a competent general and a member of the Convention, succeeded to the command. He was well supported by Perignon and Augereau, and wisely counseled by the Representative Debrel. With forty thousand men in May, he recaptured the line of Tech, and drove the enemy across the Pass of Perthes and entered Catalona, where he was confronted by the great Spanish lines at the Pass of Banyuls, which covered Figueras. The French army was destitute and the capture of Figueras was imperative. Orders for the attack were given for November 18. Dugommier was killed in the action,[140] but Perpignon carried out the plans and Figueras surrendered on November 26.[141] By the beginning of 1795 the fortresses of northern Catalona were in French hands.

Muller, a careful general, commanded the Western Army, which was strengthened by the receipt of recruits in 1794. The army was relatively inactive until mid-summer. On July 28, Carnot, for the Committee of Public Safety, announced to the Representatives that it was time for the army to strike a great blow.[142] "Tell Muller," he wrote, "that the French manner of making war ought to be much less by employing ruses and obstination, than by pouncing on the enemy with intrepidity, bayonet in hand." Carnot's friend, Garrau, Representative with the Western Army, wrote to him on the 29th, announcing important victories.[143] On July 31 the French stormed the Spanish camp of San Martial, captured all the artillery and crossed the Bidassoa. Irun, Figuier and Fontarabie fell with San Martial.[144] The vast valley of Bastan was invaded and occupied. Fuenterrabia and San Sebastien fell in the first week in August.[145]

The Committee of Public Safety sent detailed directions to the Western Army on August 16.[146] Muller was replaced by Moncey in the command. Contributions were to be imposed only upon the wealthy. All public and corporation funds were to be confiscated. "All acquisition of territory to the Republic is rejected," the despatch read, "other than that found within the new limits fixed for defense; but one should not neglect anything in enlightening the neighboring peoples, up to the River Ebre, in order to detach them from Spain and encourage them to independance under the protection of the Republic."

Baudot and Garrau inquired from the Committee on November 11 whether the siege of Pampeluna should be laid at once, or delayed until spring, giving the various pros and cons.[147] If delayed, they said, an invasion of Biscay would be made at once. The Representatives informed the Committee on December 5 that "your desires and your wishes have been fulfilled. . . . The Biscayans have been defeated and routed."[148] The Spanish began to lose heart. Peace negotiations were started but brought no immediate result. The Armies, however, remained inactive in the spring, as peace seemed immanent. Operations recommenced on June 25. On July 6 the French cut the Spanish army in two at Irurzon. By July 13 Moncey had driven the Spanish in rout before him, entered Vittoria, and took Bilboa. Peace ended the campaign on July 22.

There were three republican armies located in the West, to cope with the Vendéans and Chouans—the Armies of (Côtes de) Cherbourg, (Côtes de) Brest, and the West. In 1794 there were 136,000 men in these three armies.[149] The bloody feud went on unabated in fury and ruthlessness, after Savenay.[150] Gradually, a more lenient policy of persuasion was evolved.

The Committee of Public Safety transferred twenty-five hundred cavalry to the Army of the West on February 12, 1794, "to operate with the troops there to the entire destruction of the rebels."[151] Garrau, then Representative to this Army, reported to Carnot on the 16th that the brigands in the Vendée were mistreated in every way, and that "our reverses have been exaggerated and have been repaired immediately."[152] He informed Carnot on March 18 from Nantes that Carnot's measure relative to Cholet had produced a good effect.[153] On April 5 he complained to Carnot of the perpetual conflicts of authority that disturbed the ensemble of operations.[154] The Committee of Public Safety, on April 6, informed Representatives Hentz and Francastel of the criticisms it had received concerning the measures of severity that had been used in the West. The Committee gave no instructions but expressed the hope that the war would soon be over. "See everything for yourselves;" they wrote, "there are generals who do not wish to terminate this war; it is of importance to the Republic that it no longer be a question of this execrable Vendée."[155] Vachot was named to command all the troops operating against the Chouans on May 13.[156]

The Committee of Public Safety issued an important order to the Army of the West on July 2.[157] The twenty-five thousand men ordered transferred from the Army to Chalons-sur-Marne were to be reduced to fifteen thousand. The troops were to be taken out of cantonments and put into camps, held constantly ready for action. The generals were to report daily to the Representatives what they had done to exterminate the brigands. Every day of inactivity was to be considered a crime. Generals were to be held accountable for the indiscipline of the troops, as well as for the acts of inhumanity which would only aggravate the civil war rather than conclude it. Carnot, in the name of the Committee, repeated these admonitions on July 23.[158] No indulgence was to be shown to the brigands, but women, children, and the aged were to be treated less severely. The only objective the Committee had, he said, was "that of finally terminating the horrible war of the Vendée, an object which is being avoided, whether by a loose indulgence, or by executions which, in falling upon the weak, can only revolt justice and humanity." On August 16 a lengthy regulation of affairs in the West was decreed.[159] Dumas was made general-in-chief, and other changes in personnel were made. "The Representatives of the people," the decree read, "shall restore justice and impartiality as the order of the day; respect for local customs, the method of persuasion, and good faith will be exercised. . . . Those who have only been misled, or coerced into rebellion by violence will be pardoned." Similar instructions were sent to the Representatives with the Army of Cherbourg on August 18.[160] In its session of August 16, the Committee of Public Safety, in an order written and signed by Carnot, suspended Vachot, and appointed Hoche to the task of destroying the Chouans, as commander of the Army of Cherbourg.[161] Representative Ingrand wrote to the Committee from Niort on August 16, calling the Vendée a "leper for the Republic which will end by tainting the blood of the body politic."[162]

The more humane policy of the Committee of Public Safety was further revealed in its directions to the Representatives with the Armies of Brest and Cherbourg on October 12, which were written by Carnot, although he was temporarily not a member of the Committee.[163] "Our object ought to be to reconcile all hearts to it [the Republic] and to rally to the Government all those whom error or bad treatment have alienated. . . . The way of persuasion and of enlightenment is everywhere preferable to that of violence. . . . Your prudence, your love for order, and for the internal peace of the Republic are a safe guaranty of the rectitude of the measures that you will take, as well as of the firmness with which you will have them executed."

Carnot, in the name of the Committee, announced the provisional union of the Armies of Brest and Cherbourg, under the command of Hoche, who was heartily in accord with the policy of diplomacy and persuasion, and who was to recommend an amnesty to the rebels in the West.[164] On December 1, nine members of the Convention from the Departments in the West, in a letter to the Committee, accused the Convention of never having understood the war in the Vendée. They repudiated the method of total extermination as the solution of the war, and proclaimed that "the other [way] is to listen to the voice of humanity, to use persuasion rather than arms."[165] The Convention, on the following day, decreed an amnesty to all the Vendéans who would lay down their arms within a month.[166]

Ruelle, Representative to the Army of Brest and Cherbourg, wrote to Carnot on December 8, "This [amnesty] has been acclaimed with a joy and an enthusiasm that would be difficult to describe. Congratulate yourself on having contributed particularly to this act of national generosity. I thought that I detected in our last interview that this was already in your heart, and I swear that it was in mine."[167] He wrote to the Committee of Public Safety from Nantes on December 12, "Your decree of amnesty . . . has been received with transport; the more than eighty thousand persons comprising this city have spontaneously blessed this great act of national generosity."[168] Carnot replied to Ruelle on December 14, for the Committee.[169] "The amnesty accorded by the Convention," he wrote, "excepts none and extends to the leaders of the brigands as well as to all others. We invite you to continue actively the fine work of pacification that you have already started, in combining indulgence with vigor and prudence, and particularly in maintaining among our troops the spirit of morality and of discipline that might have prevented such great misfortunes, had it always been present." Carnot instructed the Representatives on February 7 to entrust the entire disposition of the troops to the general-in-chief of the Army of Brest and Cherbourg.[170]

By the treaty agreed to by Charette and the Vendéans on February 15, 1795, the rebels were to recognize the Republic and lay down their arms. In return, freedom of worship was granted, the royal assignats were redeemed, a local militia of two thousand was authorized, and the Vendéans were to be exempted from all other military service. Of the leaders, only Stofflet held back. The Representatives to the armies in the West reported to the Convention from Nantes on February 27.[171] "The Vendée has returned to the bosom of the Republic," they announced. "Charette and all the chiefs of their armies . . . have just solemnly declared that they will submit to the laws of the Republic. . . . In your name, we have spoken the language of humanity, and we have been listened to. The grand and imposing attitude of the Convention since 9 Thermidor has developed in . . . the Vendéans what the defenders of the *patrie* could not obtain from them by the spilling of blood. These unfortunate regions have need of a new life. We are going to superintend them, reviving agriculture and restoring trade. . . . The return of the Vendée . . . brings with it the return of the Chouans." On April 20 the Breton rebels accepted the conditions of February 15, at La Mabilais. Stofflet finally acquiesced on May 2. That unhappy chapter in the Revolution was nearly closed, and Carnot had had an important part in its satisfactory conclusion.

Both Carnot's rôle, and his methods, have been revealed in the descriptive development of the feats of French arms in 1793, and, particularly in 1794. In his direction of the movements and the personnel of the armies Carnot, in the name of the Committee of Public Safety, usually worked through the Representatives of the People with the armies. The political control of the armies was close throughout the period of the Convention. Not only was the safety of France at stake, but also the destiny of the Republic. A unitary control, political and revolutionary, was imperative. The Army was the instrument of the Convention and its great Committee of Public Safety. The correspondance to and from the Representatives is voluminous and attests the minute supervision given from Paris to the military operations.

Infrequently, Carnot, for the Committee, communicated directly with the generals.[172] In most instances, however, the will of the Committee was made known to the generals through the Representatives. In some despatches it was definitely stated that the plan of operations or other instructions were to be noted by the Representatives and then be transmitted to the generals.[173] Conferences between the Representatives and the generals, which must have been very frequent, were often reported.[174] A few of the Representatives wrote directly and personally to Carnot, in addition to the official despatches that they sent to the Committee. This was particularly true of the able and frank Gillet, and of Carnot's former associates-on-mission, Garrau and Lacombe Saint-Michel.[175] The Representatives were free with their counsel to the Committee of Public Safety on plans for military operations.[176] There is no doubt, however, that the decisions lay with the Committee of Public Safety.[177] Modifications in plans, due to changing circumstances, were not only tolerated but encouraged.[178] The Representatives made provisional appointments, promotions, demotions, and dismissals in the field, but these were subject to the approval of the Committee of Public Safety. Their criticisms of the generals were usually free and candid.[179] The mandate to the Representatives was usually a large one. Saint-Just and Le Bas were sent to the Army of the North on April 29, 1794, "to execute the views of the Committee of Public Safety.[180] Lacombe Saint-Michel was sent to the same army on June 26, 1794 "to follow and to supervise operations."[181] The Committee of Public Safety, of course, made the appointments of command.[182] These were usually exclusive and original with the Committee, but the Representatives sometimes nominated a provisional commander-in-chief.[183]

The promotions made by authority of the Committee were usually in the handwriting of Carnot and were usually signed by him. During his direction of personnel and operations, the majority of the generals who made names for themselves in the Revolution and under Napoleon received ample opportunities to display their talents and advance to preferment.[184] The arrests and dismissals of officers and generals were handled in the same way,[185] as were reinstatements.[186] After 9 Thermidor many of the liberations of arrested officers, high and low, were signed by Carnot alone. In September, 1794, in the reorganized Committee of Public Safety, Charles Cochon was associated with Carnot in the conduct of military affairs. Many of the orders having to do with the army personnel were signed by both of them, and many were signed by Cochon alone. In November and December, 1794 and in January, 1795, Dubois-Crancé alone signed many of the orders having to do with the personnel of the armies. Carnot throughout gave himself to the minutiae of personnel as well as to the matters of large import. Memoranda orders signed by him relating to leaves of absence, to indemnities, to minor promotions, and to prisoners of war are legion.[187] These reveal a sympathetic and humane understanding. Carnot's interest in public education was manifested, even in his preoccupation with military affairs, by the order written by him, requiring the great Lamarck, professor of Zoology, to remain in Paris to continue his work in public instruction.[188]

The work of Carnot and his associates was not unavailing. At the beginning of 1795 a general peace seemed possible. France had certainly filled out to her natural boundaries. The first outburst of propagandist zeal had expired. The urge to expand had not yet been inculcated by Bonaparte. Some of the Allies desired peace. Prussia had definitely withdrawn from the contest on October 16, 1794, in order to pursue her interests in Poland. The shadow of the Armed Neutrality of the North had already fallen across the path of the English sea power. On April 5, 1795, Barthélemy, the French ambassador to Switzerland, and Hardenberg, for Prussia, signed the famous Treaty of Basel, whereby Prussia gave France a free hand on the left bank of the Rhine and France, in return, undertook to respect the line of demarcation which virtually put North Germany under Prussian control. By a secret article Prussia was to be compensated should French territory be extended to the Rhine. On May 16 Holland was glad to accept the hard terms offered to her. By them she became virtually dependent on France and had to bear her share in the war against England. Spain made peace with France on July 22, 1795. France evacuated her conquests in Spain and received in return the Spanish half of San Domingo. By the end of 1795, Saxony, the two Hesses, Naples, Portugal, the Duchy of Parma, and the Pope had all made their peace with the French Republic.

Carnot had had no mean part in this defense of France and of the Revolution. The political path of the Revolution was more tortuous and there the leaders are less easy to follow.

Chapter VII

TERROR AND REACTION

THE NATION, welded into a powerful war machine in 1793 and 1794, successfully defended itself and the Revolution. But the Government, despite the virtual monopoly of power in the Committee of Public Safety, was tormented by factions, even after the Girondin leaders had been executed on October 31, 1793. The two titans of the period, Danton and Robespierre, so temperamentally unlike, could not resolve their differences. Steadily their paths, programs, and followers diverged. With Marat and the Girondins gone they faced each other irreconcilably although the final dissolution of their association was yet months in the future.

The Dantonists had favored purging the Convention of the Girondins in order to insure a strong government. The Robespierrists wanted to set up a Jacobin government and the Girondins had stood in the way. Danton went into temporary retirement on October 12 at Arcis-sur Aube. When he returned to Paris on November 21 a precarious *rapprochement* was effected between him and Robespierre.

It was Danton who put the capstone to the arch of the Great Committee's power through the legislation of December 4, by which all constituted authorities were put under the control of the Committee of Public Safety, local officials were replaced by national agents, local authorities were prohibited from levying taxes, public meetings were prohibited, representatives-on-mission were to correspond regularly with the Committee, no central committee of the sections was to be formed in the Commune, and the sections were to correspond no longer with the Commune but with the Committee of General Security. Thus was the work of establishing the dictatorship of the Committee of Public Safety completed.

Hébert and Chaumette were the powers in the Commune at the

moment who dominated the Hôtel de Ville. Their center was the Cordeliers Club. Hébert's vigorous journal, *Père Duchesne,* wielded a great influence in the sections and had a large circulation elsewhere. Chaumette, as *procureur*, was the official head of the municipal council of Paris. This young man of thirty-one had a mind of "the puritanical type which frequently comes to the front in revolutions."[1] He was sincerely a Republican, devoted to the interests of the people, and with a deep compassion for the poor. He lacked courage, on occasion, to defend his convictions. Hébert, the substitute *procureur*, was also a resolute champion of the poor. Robespierre detested him because he thought him to be an atheist and probably a communist. Among the Hébertists were included Vincent, secretary to Bouchotte, Ronsin, the Prussian Anacharsis Clootz, and the representatives-on-mission, Fouché, Carrier, and André Dumont. This faction had well-defined aims and professed decided views on matters of policy. These revolutionaries favored war to the bitter end, the overthrow of all monarchs, the repression of all suspects, and finally they developed a great suspicion of the Committee of Public Safety because of the policy of leniency towards conspirators supposedly advocated by some of its members. Chaumette proclaimed a Law of the Suspects for Paris that amounted to a declaration of martial law.

The anti-Christian movement of the fall and early winter of 1793 was largely the result of the leadership of Chaumette, Fouché, and André Dumont. They were partly prompted to this by the subversive activities of the juring priests, largely Girondins, and of the non-juring, refractory priests who were mostly Royalists. The Convention attempted to remain indifferent to this movement, although the adoption of the republican calendar on October 5 was an anti-Christian measure. This calendar gave no listing of the religious holidays and it abolished Sundays. The Hébertists, however, had a more complete program in mind. They declared Christianity to be a "moribund superstition." Churches were sacked and the riches were poured into the national treasury. Great numbers of priests felt moved to unfrock themselves. The Commune of Paris issued anti-ecclesiastical decrees. The movement spread beyond the Hébertists and became general.

The Department of Paris and the Commune staged a Festival of Reason at the cathedral of Notre Dame on November 10. After the celebration Chaumette addressed the Convention: "Legislators, fanaticism has given place to reason . . . for the first time . . . the French have celebrated their true religion, that of Liberty, that of Reason." The Goddess of Reason was introduced to the Convention, and the deputies repaired to Notre Dame for a second festival. Other cities followed the lead of Paris. In all these festivals the Supreme Being was carefully mentioned, and Reason was usually given as one of his principal attributes. Rather than being atheistic the general tone was deistic, or pantheistic. Hébert went so far as to make Jesus out to be a brave *sansculotte*.

The deputies and the members of the Committee of Public Safety did not associate themselves officially with this anti-religious movement, for political reasons. Robespierre, alone, strongly opposed the dechristianization campaign in its most sensational manifestations. He did this on both religious and political grounds. He had turned his back on the old religion but his essentially religious temperament was shocked by some of the excesses of the movement. He also had scant respect for the leaders of the movement. The campaign was adding fuel to the enmities of France's external foes, and was antagonizing neutral countries. It would, no doubt, intensify the troubles in the Vendée. Robespierre wanted to reduce these possibilities. As a matter of fact, the monarchs did combine to issue a joint manifesto against atheist republicanism. Robespierre and Danton succeeded in persuading the deputies on November 22 to abolish the unseemly popular anti-religious demonstrations and masquerades in the Convention. Chaumette and the Commune even acceded to Robespierre's request for a moderation of the anti-Christian activities. Finally, he got the Convention to issue a reply to the monarchs on December 5, and to promise the complete freedom of all worship.

Danton and Desmoulins were preparing the ground for a general policy of moderation in early December. They wanted a general relaxation of severity and a "dilution of proletarianism," by which they hoped to secure control of the government, conclude peace with Europe, and set up their own bourgeois kind of Republic. Thuriot, Bourdon (Oise), Philippeaux and other discontented persons in the Convention, some of whom had a none too savoury reputation, gravitated to Danton and Desmoulins. Danton tried to win his way back into influence in the Jacobin Club and on December 3 Robespierre cautiously defended him, at a time when the Jacobins were being purged of suspected members. Desmoulins was in bad odor at the Jacobins because of the reputation of some of his associates.

The Moderates (or Indulgents) now launched their attack upon the government. The new weapon was the *Vieux Cordelier,* edited by Desmoulins, and issued for the first time on December 5, with the purpose of attacking the ultra-revolutionaries, rousing public opinion against them, and championing modifications in the existing régime. The plan was that Camille was to work through his new journal, while Danton was to advocate the new policy in the Convention and in the Jacobins. Desmoulins submitted the proof of the first two numbers of the *Vieux Cordelier* to Robespierre, and he dedicated the first number to Danton and Robespierre. The second number contained a violent attack on Clootz. The paper achieved an immediate success and a large circulation, particularly among those who personally feared a continuation of the régime of severity, including a goodly number of aristocrats, speculators, profiteers, and royalists.

Desmoulins did not submit the copy for the third number of the *Vieux Cordelier* to Robespierre. It appeared on December 15 and contained a vigorous attack on the atrocities of the Hébertists and on the whole revolutionary system, and called upon the Committee of Public Safety to put a stop to the work of the extremists. This aroused the Hébertists and the feud waged between Desmoulins in the *Vieux Cordelier* and Hébert in the *Père Duchesne* became bitter. In the fourth number of the *Vieux Cordelier* on December 20, the young pamphleteer agitated the release of the suspects. Robespierre began to mistrust Camille although he was no more attracted to the policies of the extremists than to those of the indulgents. Billaud-Varenne was already calling for Danton's head, but Robespierre was trying to steer a course between the two factions.

The lines, however, were gradually tightening. Collot d'Herbois censured Philippeaux severely in the Jacobins on January 5, but dealt gently with Desmoulins. Danton was cautious and did not openly defend Philippeaux. The members took no action. Two days later Robespierre called upon the Jacobins to rally to the support of the Committee of Public Safety, and he had an enthusiastic response. At a meeting of the Jacobins on January 8 Robespierre denounced Fabre d'Eglantine, an intimate friend of Danton, whose duplicity and corruption he had just discovered. Fabre was expelled from the Club and Robespierre began definitely to draw away from Danton and Desmoulins. Two days later, Desmoulins, whose obstinacy in the meeting of the 8th had antagonized Robespierre, was excluded from the Jacobins. At the same time the Cordeliers Club was expelling Fabre, Philippeaux, Bourdon (Oise), and Desmoulins. In vain, the Cordeliers tried to compel Desmoulins to change the name of his journal.

Fabre d'Eglantine was arrested on January 12, and Danton's efforts in his behalf in the Convention on the 13th only served to compromise himself. Desmoulins' printer was so frightened by events that he refused to print the pending number of the *Vieux Cordelier*. The ultra-revolutionaries, in the meantime, were working vigorously for the release of their fanatical leaders, Vincent and Ronsin, who had been imprisoned in the Luxembourg by order of the Convention as a result of the efforts of Bourdon (Oise) and his friends. Danton, hoping to capitalize later on the gratitude and possible conversion of some of the extremists, succeeded in getting the Convention on February 2 to order their release.

Robespierre read a report on the situation of the Republic in the Convention on February 5. The report was directed against the policy of moderation and repeated Robespierre's favorite explanation of the ills and dangers of the nation—the machinations of the Coalition. In the course of his speech he turned to the Moderates: "Indulgence for the royalists! cry certain people; mercy for rascals! No! Mercy for the innocent, mercy for the weak, mercy for the unfortunate, mercy for humanity." He concluded by appealing for confidence in the wisdom and patriotism of the Convention and the Committee of Public Safety.

Saint-Just took a similar line in his report of February 26 to the Convention, in which he proposed, and the Convention agreed, to confiscate the property of suspects for the benefit of poor patriots. These enemies of the Republic were to be imprisoned until the peace and then banished for life. The Committee of General Security was authorized to release patriots mistakenly imprisoned, on its own authority. There were 300,000 suspects who would come under the possibilities of this order, and it would take months to investigate them. Saint-Just got another decree through the Convention on March 3 ordering every commune to draw up a list of needy patriots. The beginnings of a "revolution in property,"[2] a "vast expropriation of one class for the profit of another,"[3] is detected in this legislation by one authority, who attributes an advanced social program to Robespierre. In any case this decree was a direct bid to the *sansculottes,* hitherto championed by the Hébertists. It was hoped that thus the Committee of Public Safety would strengthen itself against both factions.

The extremists, meanwhile, took a new tack. They tried to increase their influence at the Jacobins for the purpose of persuading the Club to demand the punishment of the seventy-four deputies who were in prison because they had expressed sympathy for the Girondins. These were being kept from the scaffold through the protection of Robespierre. The effort of the extremists was fruitless. Carrier returned to Paris, and he and Collot d'Herbois in the Cordeliers Club endeavored to bring the two clubs together with the view of directing the government to the Left. The deplorable conditions in Paris gave them some hope for success. Paris was suffering its worst food crisis. Bread did come in in meager quantities; but no meat was to be had. Vegetables, butter, fruit, eggs and fish were almost non-existent. Coal and wood were scarce and their cost was exorbitant. Hébert poured forth stinging denunciations in the *Pére Duchesne* of the merchants for hoarding and profiteering. The liberated Vincent and Ronsin began advocating a popular insurrection against the Convention in order to free it from the Moderates. Rumors of such an insurrection spread in the early part of March. Plans for the insurrection centered in the Cordeliers Club. On February 22 Hébert addressed the members: "Increase the revolutionary army, let it march with the guillotine in front and I'll guarantee abundance."[4] Beginning on March 1 placards in the congested quarters in Paris advised the people to dissolve the Convention and replace it by a dictator who would bring back prosperity. One of the posters called for an end "of all the rascals who govern the Republic; they are all conspirators and merchants of Paris."[5] The soldiers became unruly and threatened to free the prisons of patriots, and destroy those whom they thought to be counter-revolutionaries, and whom they accused the Convention of protecting.

Vincent denounced a new conspiracy of the Indulgents on March 4. Hébert now came out flatly for an insurrection. The Cordeliers followed this lead, and issued a call for an uprising. But only Marat of the forty-eight sections responded favorably. Paris refused to be stirred and maintained an unprecedented calm. The members of the Cordeliers Club sought the support of the Commune at the Hôtel de Ville on March 15, but Pache, the mayor, had foresightedly absented himself, and the delegation was received without warmth. General Hanriot, commander of the Parisian Guard, had already declined their advances. Chaumette urged the leaders to move cautiously.

The Committee of Public Safety decided on prompt action in the face of these subversive activities of the extremists, even though Robespierre and Couthon were ill, and Billaud-Varenne, Prieur (Marne), and Saint-André were absent on mission. Barère reported to the Convention on the foreign conspiracies on March 6, and made it a point to criticize both the extremists and the moderates. Decrees to investigate the Cordeliers and to arrest conspirators were adopted. That evening Collot d'Herbois attempted to explain to the Jacobins that the Cordeliers had been misled by intriguers. The Jacobins visited the Cordeliers on the following evening and the Cordeliers tried to explain away the plot, although Vincent did his best to prevent the Cordeliers from capitulating too easily to the Jacobins.

Robespierre, Billaud-Varenne, and Couthon were in attendance when the Committee of Public Safety met on March 12. On the following day Saint-Just presented the report of the Committee on the factions to the Convention. He used the favorite theme of Robespierre, namely, that the threatened conspiracy could be traced directly to the Coalition, which, by some miraculous means, was maintaining two seemingly opposing factions in France, but which, in reality, were concerting their plans against the Republic. The Convention immediately named certain large categories of persons as traitors. Ronsin, Vincent, Hébert, Momoro, Mazuel and a few other leaders were arrested at once. Carrier was left unmolested because of his intimacy with Collot d'Herbois. Clootz and some other foreigners were arrested in order to lend color to the fiction of the foreign connections of the conspiracy. Twenty persons in all were arrested. Their trial began on the first of March. One of the accused was acquitted and the others were condemned. These were executed on March 24, as accomplices of Pitt and Coburg. The aristocrats and royalists were publicly joyful at the event, for they seemed to sense that the Revolution was turning from the *sansculottes* and in their direction. Congratulations poured into the Committee of Public Safety and into the Convention, for their prompt action against the plot of the Hébertists. The Committee was not at all pleased by the fact that the Indulgents were exultant over the destruction of the extremist leaders. The Committee set about reasserting its revolutionary leadership.

Robespierre and Saint-Just had been careful to assess responsibility and guilt equally on both factions. The Committee now let it be known that it would complete its case against the moderates. On March 17 the two revolutionary Committees ordered the arrest of Chaumette,[6] although he had had nothing to do with the insurrection projected by the Hébertists. Couthon and Lindet were present at the session, but did not sign the order. On the same day Saint-Just informed the Convention of the arrest of Herault-Séchelles and of his friend, Simond. The order for the arrest had actually been given on the 15th, on the grounds that an *émigré* had been found secreted in Herault's apartment. Seven members, including Carnot, had signed the order.[7] Prieur (Côte d'Or) and Lindet were present but did not sign. On the following day the Convention decreed that the two Committees investigate the conduct of the Paris authorities.[8] The unsavory East India Company scandal, involving Chabot's group, to which Fabre d'Eglantine belonged, was being officially aired at the time. Billaud-Varenne and Collot d'Herbois in the Great Committee, and Vadier, Amar, and Vouland in the lesser Committee, kept demanding Danton's head. They gradually wore Robespierre's resistance down. Mutual friends brought the two great figures together in the hope of a reconciliation but the meeting only aggravated their differences. "They represented," writes Professor Kerr, "two different worlds; Robespierre stood for the Puritan sansculotte Republic and the strict enforcement of his conception of justice, while Danton, loose and easy-going towards offenses even against himself, stood for the lax bourgeois Republic which triumphed in Thermidor."[9]

Danton had urged a purging of the "sham patriots in red caps" in the Committee of Public Safety as early as the 26th of February. His stirring speeches on March 3 and 4 in the Convention had thrown their old-time spell over the deputies, and they accorded him their enthusiastic acclaim. They expressed some warmth to him as late as March 19. The next day the Moderates returned to their attack on the government. They did this by concentrating on the agents of the Minister of War. Bouchotte had long been the most consistent object of their criticism. Couthon defended the government while Robespierre contented himself with certain veiled insinuations. He carried his alarms, however, into the Jacobin Club. The election of Tallien as president of the Convention on March 21, and Legendre as president of the Jacobins, strengthened the Moderates.

The Great Committee, in the meantime, had prompted the Convention to dissolve the revolutionary army in Paris, and it appointed Robespierre's partisans, Fleuriot and Payan, to the places of Pache and Chaumette at the Hôtel de Ville. General Hanriot, of the Parisian Guard, was also devoted to Robespierre. Collot d'Herbois and Billaud-Varenne had now completely won Robespierre over. It is not probable that he believed Danton to be a conspirator, but he believed him to be a dangerous man and he certainly was a vigorous critic of the government. Robespierre also knew that if the present government were overthrown Danton would head its successor.

Despite their decisive cooperation in some of the most acute crises of the Revolution, Robespierre was now to abandon Danton to the natural revolutionary fate. By doing so his own head inevitably became the price of Danton's head.

The two revolutionary Committees were busy during the week of March 23-30 preparing for the destruction of this last faction. It was decided to include Desmoulins with Danton, Philippeaux, and Westermann, and associate them all with the notorious Chabot group in order to implicate them the better in the so-called conspiracy sponsored by the Coalition. Saint-Just and Robespierre prepared the report of accusation which was read to a full session of the two Committees on the evening of March 30.[10] There is some evidence that Carnot at first stood with Robert Lindet in opposing the arrest of Danton.[11] Carnot's son says that, while Carnot had no "sympathy for Danton, a man violent and theatrical, and particularly none for his entourage,"[12] he protested the accusation in words which the son quotes from notes kept by his father. "You accuse Danton of treason and you have no proof against him. . . . Let us not start bloody quarrels among the men who have worked together to establish the Republic. . . . Reflect well, that a head such as that of Danton will carry along many others. . . . If you trace the road to the scaffold for the Republic of the people, we all shall pass in succession on the same route."[13] Carnot signed the order finally, his son says, because he "remained faithful to his doctrine of solidarity in the united government."[14] Carnot had remained consistently outside of, and opposed to, the factions, for which he had a deep aversion. Aulard says that Carnot's colleagues evidently agreed with him, "that it was necessary at all costs, even by a crime, to preserve the governmental unity, and by this, the unity of national defense."[15] Carnot's signature was third in order of the eighteen given. Robert Lindet refused to sign, crying, "I am here to supply the citizens, not to kill patriots."[16] Rhul also declined to sign because of his friendship for Danton. The arrests were to be made at once. The order for this was signed by all but Lindet and Rhul, with Robespierre signing last. Rhul risked his life in warning

Danton but the latter quietly, even somewhat apathetically, permitted himself to be arrested. Desmoulins, Philippeaux, and Delacroix (d'Eure-et-Loire) were also arrested that night, and all were incarcerated in the Luxembourg.

Paris was all agog at these sensational arrests. Danton, one of the great heroes of the Revolution, had been considered impregnable against the threats of suspicion and the nemesis of the guillotine. The Convention assembled at eleven the next day, with Tallien presiding. Legendre courageously undertook to defend his friend, Danton, but just when he was proposing that Danton be permitted to appear at the bar of the Convention to speak in his own defense, Robespierre entered. As he spoke he won back the deputies who had been wavering under the persuasiveness of Legendre. Even the shadow of the Danton of old before the Convention might have turned the tide. Saint-Just then presented the twenty-eight page statement of accusation, "Report on the conspiracy plotted to secure a change of dynasty," in which he said, "The Revolution resides in the people, and not in the reputation of certain individuals. . . . Your Committees have charged me to ask justice from you on men who for a long time have been betraying the popular cause." The Convention subserviently confirmed the arrests. The trial commenced on April 2 in the Revolutionary Tribunal. Fifteen men stood trial, there being the usual number of foreigners to lend plausibility to the charge of the alien connections of the conspiracy. Danton spoke powerfully in his own defense on the third of April, but to no avail. The trial was a mere formality, a matter of simple question and answer, with no witnesses, and virtually without documentary evidence. Condemnation came speedily and on March 5 the executioner Sanson led the victims to the guillotine while David nonchalantly sketched them from the terrace of an adjacent cafe. The shaggy head of the mighty Danton was the last to fall into the basket, just as the compassionate curtain of darkness fell.

The Convention in the days to follow gave a stunned submission to the Committee of Public Safety. The provinces—probably poorly informed of all that had happened and ignorant of what it meant—sent in their loyal approbation. Robespierre was now supreme. He dominated the Jacobins and the Revolutionary Tribunal, but his predominance was less marked in the two Committees. In the Convention the Plain seemed to be increasingly friendly to his leadership. No leader was left to dispute the power of the Committee of Public Safety or to criticize its government. The bourgeoisie, however, was ceasing to lick its wounds, and was stirring itself to devise means whereby it could achieve a political control commensurate with its undoubted economic power in the nation.

The insatiable Government continued to warn against the counter-revolutionaries. The Terror obsession seemed to have some of the leaders in its grip. Collot d'Herbois harangued against the enemies of the Republic in the Jacobin Club on April 10, and Saint-Just read a report in the Convention on the 15th against the foreigners. The resultant decree provided that all prisoners accused of conspiracy throughout the country should be transferred to Paris for trial before the Revolutionary Tribunal. This decree practically did away with the provincial guillotines, although a few did continue their bloody work.

The Convention took a decisive step on April 1 in consolidating the Revolution and completing the centralization of power and control in the Government, by unanimously decreeing the abolition of the six ministries and of the provisional Executive Council. It was Carnot who presented the report in the Convention that resulted in this decree that broke so completely with the past. This was a task congenial to Carnot. In the report that he made to the Convention on January 29, 1793, for the Commission to the Pyrenees he had advocated the abolition of the provisional Executive Council and the centralization of control.[17] Since that time the powers of the ministries and of the Council had declined steadily before the growing power of the Convention and its two great Committees. The natural conflicts between these governmental organs were a decided hindrance to efficient government. The ministries were a hold-over from the old régime and represented the principle of the division of power,[18] that was incompatible with the exigencies of the moment with their need for strongly centralized government. By the decree the six suppressed ministries were to be replaced by twelve commissions which were to be appointed by the Committee of Public Safety.

These included civil administration, police and courts of justice, education, agriculture and the arts, commerce and provisions, public works, public relief, transport, finance, army and navy, munitions and foreign affairs. Details of administration, only, were confided to these new commissions. April 20 was the date for the extinction of the ministries and the Council.

Carnot built up a strong case for this action.[19] He said that the ministries were an institution created by the kings for the hereditary government, for the maintenance of the three orders, and for the preservation of distinctions and prejudices, and that therefore they were "incompatible with the republican régime." He questioned the capacity of the old hierarchy to develop a new order built upon reason and the consent of the people.

"It is only by binding, closer and closer, the 'fasces' of the republic," he said, "by a nervous organization and by indissoluble bonds that the unity of the state can be guaranteed and that it can be protected from becoming the prey of external enemies. Isolation, deprivation of all aid, civil wars, and enslavement are the prompt and inevitable consequence of the failure of harmony and of united action. . . .

"The people establishes a governmental system as a convenience to itself; this is to remedy, as much as is possible, the inconvenience of not being able to deliberate in general assembly. The government is, then, properly speaking, but the council of the people, the custodian of its revenues, the sentinel charged to protect it from the dangers that beset it.

"It is by the disregard of these elemental and eternal truths that all the thrones and all the tyrannies of the world have been established. In the beginning no people wanted to give itself a master. Power, however, has everywhere passed from the hands of the people and the sovereignty has passed from its legitimate possessor to an agent. . . .

"It is necessary to protect the people against its assassins. The means to secure this end are, first, the choice of proper men to compose the government, then their rotation and their responsibility, and the subdivision of executive functions in so far as is possible without destroying the unity and rapidity of action."

Carnot spoke of the Committee of Public Safety as a "direct

emanation, an integral and responsible part" of the Convention, to which should be delegated "all those tasks of a secondary importance that cannot be discussed in the general assembly." He described the organization of the Committee of Public Safety and stated its delegation of powers to the new commissions. He went on to show the responsibility of the legislators to the people and in doing so he painted a glowing picture of popular sovereignty. He developed, in detail, the membership and functions of the twelve commissions. He announced that this revolutionary system would prevail until a "solid peace" made it possible to reduce gradually the methods that crime, the factions and the late convulsions of the aristocracy had forced upon the Convention. This, then, was the decree that consummated the centralization of absolute power in the hands of the Committee of Public Safety.[20]

The Government proceeded to restrain the new popular clubs, and now that active opposition was destroyed or greatly reduced, it warned the Jacobins to tread lightly in their criticisms. The economic policy was lightened and liberalized but the policy of regulation was continued. The maximum was variously enforced, according to the interest and effectiveness of the local authorities and popular societies.

Robespierre, with the Hébertists and the Dantonists finally out of the way, set himself to realize the politico-religious system which he had in mind. The religious policy of the Committee of Public Safety had been to oppose the violent destruction of Catholicism and to try to maintain the freedom of cults.[21] Robespierre now wanted a distinctive religion for the nation. He needed a central moral force of some kind for his ideal of the state with its reign of justice and virtue, and this unifying force must be found in religion. On May 7 he was ready to read his report on the new religion in the Convention. In it he attacked the atheists but he avoided discussing the existence of God on philosophical or scientific grounds. His position was utterly utilitarian. The new religion was to have but two positive beliefs, one in the Supreme Being, and the other in the immortality of the soul.

In his pragmatic report, Robespierre said: "There is no question here of judging any particular philosophical opinion. . . . In the eyes of the legislator anything which is of use to the world and good in its effects is the truth. The idea of the Supreme Being and the immortality of the soul is a continual recall to justice; it is therefore social and republican. . . . The motives of duty and the bases of morality are necessarily linked with the idea of a Supreme Being, and to banish him is to demoralize the people." After attacking the priests, he continued, "the real priest of the Supreme Being is nature; his worship, virtue; his ceremonies, the joy of a great people assembled under his eyes to draw tighter the sweet bonds of universal fraternity and to present to him the homage of sensitive and pure hearts."

This peroration drew extended applause from the Convention, among whose members a general deistic sentiment prevailed favorable to the new cult. Robespierre then read his proposed decree. The French people were to recognize the existence of the Supreme Being and the immortality of the soul, and the worthy worship of the Supreme Being was recognized as the practice of the duties of man. The complete liberty of all religions was reaffirmed. There would be no priesthood in the new cult. Thirty-six annual festivals were to be celebrated on the *décadis*, at which the magistrates of the nation were to "inculcate patriotic and republican virtues in the minds of the regenerated people." Suitable hymns and civic chants were to be composed for the new cult. June 8 was to be an inaugural fête to the new deity, to be staged under the direction of the painter, David.[22] The Convention ordered that the inscription "Temple of Reason," wherever it appeared was to be replaced by "To the Supreme Being," or "The French People recognize the Supreme Being and the Immortality of the Soul."

Carnot was president of the Convention on May 16, when the Jacobins presented their address congratulating the Convention on this decree. "Replying coldly," writes Professor Aulard, "[Carnot] spoke more as a disciple of Diderot than as an admirer of the Savoyard Vicar, appeared to confound God with nature, and by the shades of his language, showed as well as he could without risking his head, that he did not adhere to the new cult."[23] Carnot said, in part, "Justice, humanity, love of country, consolation for the one who suffers, hope of a better future . . . all these things together make the Supreme Being; he is the unification of all thoughts which are the happiness of man, of all sentiments which spread flowers in the way of life.

"To deny the Supreme Being is to deny the existence of Nature; for the laws of Nature are supreme wisdom itself. What is the Supreme Being, if it is not the great final truth which contains all truth, the eternal order of nature, immutable justice, the sublime virtue which includes all the virtues, the love which embraces all pure affections. . . . To invoke the Supreme Being is to call on the spectacle of nature."[24]

Carnot had expressed similar feelings on May 12, when he had replied, as president, to the deputation from Geneva, honoring Rousseau.[25] This was likewise true in his response to the fraternal society that presented itself on May 19 to adhere to the cult of the Supreme Being.[26] In this address he implied that some such belief was of real social value for the masses: "The vows which have come to the Convention from many sources since it solemnly proclaimed this principle, prove that such a belief is a necessity of man and that without it a great void would exist in his heart. The Supreme Being is the compass which ought to guide man's desires, and immortality is the harbour toward which his hopes ought to be directed. The Convention notes with satisfaction that public opinion, already established on this point, grows with each specific adherence. It rejoices particularly at those that are made as a result of enlightenment and meditation."

The enlightened, scientifically-minded, practical but compassionate and poetical Carnot quite apparently had his tongue in his cheek so far as this new cult is concerned. At a later date Carnot's son summarized the religious beliefs of his father: "Without seeking a metaphysical explanation of God, Carnot accepted the idea of a Supreme Wisdom, working together with love for the conservation of the world. He did not question that man was the master of his own destiny, and because of that belief, he disdained all speculation which did not lead directly to the improvement of the individual or to the progress of the social order: his philosophy took a very practical direction."[27]

The Fête of the Supreme Being transpired, as planned, on June 8. Robespierre, as president of the Convention, mounted an outdoor tribune in the Tuileries and delivered "an ecstatic Rousseauist harangue,"[28] after which he led the great procession to the Champs de Mars where he climbed an artificial mountain to the chanting of a hymn specially composed for the occasion by André Chénier. Robespierre was blissfully happy.

The "Incorruptible" now turned from this harmless diversion to the completion of the structure of the Terror. Since prisoners accused of conspiracy in the provinces were now sent up to Paris for trial, the Revolutionary Tribunal was overburdened with work. To meet this problem and to satisfy his own obsession concerning the enemies of the State, Robespierre got through his decree of 22 Prairial (June 10), in the face of some opposition. By this decree all forms of evidence were permissible, and when there was material evidence, witnesses were dispensed with. Public defenders were no longer to be provided. The right to denounce conspirators was accorded to all citizens, and that of delivering persons to the Revolutionary Tribunal was extended to the two Committees, to the public prosecutor, to the representatives on mission, and to the Convention. Only one punishment, that of death, was to be meted out. The Revolutionary Tribunal was divided into four sections, each with its complement of president, judge and jurors, sitting simultaneously and steadily delivering judgments. "Justice" was to be done wholesale. On June 11 Bourdon (Oise), in desperation, secured approval of a decree providing that the Convention alone had the inalienable right to issue an order of accusation against one of its own members, but Robespierre got this action reversed in favor of an earlier provision permitting the Committees of Public Safety and of General Security to call any and all persons before the Revolutionary Tribunal.

At the time that the internal crisis was developing to its climax, Carnot made an important and sensible pronouncement on foreign policy in the name of the Committee of Public Safety, on July 16, after the capture of Dinant, Ypres, and Charleroi.[29] "The majority of people," he said, "whom it would be necessary to unite to France in order to advance to the Rhine are not yet ready for our revolution. The factions, therefore, which are forming in the interior of these regions would join with our enemies beyond to render us the victims of our own success. . . .

"It appears to be much more wise to restrain our projects of expansion to that which is entirely necessary to bring the maximum of security to our country, to break the coalition against us, to assure our commerce, and to reduce our enemies to impotence."

Meanwhile, resistance developed rapidly against Robespierre in the Convention. The leaders included such men as Tallien, Barras, Legendre, Cambon, Dubois-Crancé, Merlin de Thionville, Siéyès, and Fouché. Some of these men, of course, feared for their lives.

From the time of the execution of Danton the number of executions had mounted daily in Paris.[30] After 22 Prairial (June 10) the Terror became a veritable massacre. From April 5 to June 10, 723 persons had been sentenced to death by the Revolutionary Tribunal, while there were 288 cases of acquittal or "no case." From June 10 to July 28 (10 Thermidor), a period of six weeks, 1376 unfortunates were condemned and executed in Paris. On June 11 there were 7321 persons confined in Paris prisons. Up to the spring of 1794 the majority of the executions under the Terror had been in the provinces, particularly in those where the opposition to the Revolution was the most intense, or where the pressure on the frontiers was greatest.[31] It was only in June and July, 1794, that the majority of the executions took place in Paris, and fifty-seven per cent of all the victims in Paris were condemned in these two months. In the Terror as a whole, roughly seventy per cent of the victims belonged to the lower classes, and thirty per cent to the upper classes. But in Paris in these two months fifty-seven per cent of the victims belonged to the upper classes, and only forty-three to the lower classes. In this period the trials were, even more than ever, a travesty on justice. The prisons were purged of suspects, many of whom had been in prison for a considerable period. Few new arrests were made. On July 5, Saint-Just alone signed an order of the Committee of Public Safety, ordering 157 persons to be sent to the Revolutionary Tribunal to be judged with the "least delay possible."[32]

The public was satiated after the execution of Danton, and

popular revulsion to the guillotine developed. In June and July it was necessary to move the guillotine two or three times because of popular feeling. Fear was everywhere. The Convention was nearly deserted. When Prieur was elected to the Presidency, there were 117 members in attendance. The deputies sought obscurity and hiding. The arrest of Catherine Théot, "Mother of God," a religious maniac patronized by Robespierre, on June 15 constituted a rebuff to him, and held him up to ridicule. In the Committee of Public Safety, Collot d'Herbois and Billaud-Varenne stood opposed to Robespierre in this affair. After considerable difficulty, Robespierre succeeded in getting the proceedings against Théot quashed. Hurt to the quick, Robespierre absented himself from the Convention and the Committee of Public Safety, and only frequented the Jacobin Club. He attended his own bureau to June 30, and after that he attended but one meeting of the Committee of Public Safety before July 18.

There was "open war"[33] in the Committee of Public Safety after the middle of June. Serious differences had developed between Carnot and Saint-Just, and Robespierre supported Saint-Just, thus alienating Carnot,[34] although a contemporary annalist comments that Carnot was odious to Robespierre because he feared the power that Carnot exercised over the army.[35] Friction had developed between Carnot and Saint-Just over military matters. Saint-Just was a very energetic representative on mission to the armies. Carnot was inclined to be jealous, and he preferred to work alone. In April Saint-Just had protested against the arrest of a contractor of gunpowder whom Carnot had had incarcerated in the Luxembourg. More serious difficulties between the two developed in June.

Hamel believes that the dissensions between Carnot and Robespierre dated from their differences of opinion in the case of Lazare Hoche in April.[36] It was Carnot who had discovered the genius of the young soldier, and he considered "the General as his protégé."[37]

As early as December 10, 1793 Hoche recognized Carnot's trust in him, even after the set-back at Kaiserslautern.[38] Politically, Hoche seems to have been enamoured of Robespierre. In the winter there was jealously and a lack of cooperation between

Pichegru and Hoche.[39] There is some evidence that Saint-Just and Bouchotte preferred the docile Pichegru to the masterful, successful Hoche.[40] In the early spring Hoche, as Commander-in-chief of the Army of the Rhine, declined to execute orders of Carnot having to do with the offensive against Treves. Hoche was thereupon deprived of his command of the Army of the Rhine and on March 10 he was ordered to the army of Italy at Toulon to take command of the expedition to Oneglia. The suspicions of the Committee of Public Safety followed him there and on March 20 it ordered the Representatives to arrest Hoche and sent him to Paris under guard. The order was signed by Carnot and Collot d'Herbois.[41] On the same day the Committee wrote to the Representatives at Toulon, "We have the proof that General Hoche is a traitor. We are replacing him." This despatch was signed by Collot d'Herbois, Robespierre, Carnot, Billaud-Varenne, and Barère.[42] Robespierre, jeune, wrote to his brother Maximilien from Nice on April 5, "Hoche is arrested and is on his way to Paris."[43] In the same letter he praised Bonaparte as a patriot.

The Committee of Public Safety ordered Hoche to be put in the Prison des Carmes, on April 11, to be held until further order.[44] Hamel makes Carnot responsible for the arrest of Hoche and states that Robespierre alone opposed his imprisonment.[45] Carnot makes the exactly opposite case in a subsequent polemical defense of himself.[46] In any case, the order of April 11 was signed by Collot d'Herbois, Saint-Just, C.-A. Prieur, Billaud-Varenne and Barère. Carnot was present at the session of the Committee but did not sign. After 9 Thermidor, on August 4, Hoche was freed and the seals on his papers were lifted.[47] Carnot signed this order with six others. On the 8th Carnot wrote and signed, alone, an order keeping Hoche in Paris for instructions.[48] Carnot wrote and signed an order on August 16, suspending Vachot, and appointing Hoche to command the expedition against the Chouans.[49] On the 21st the Committee appointed Hoche to the command of the Army of Cherbourg, succeeding Vialle.[50] He was made Commander-in-chief of the provisionally-united armies of Brest and Cherbourg on the tenth of November.[51] Carnot, for the Committee, wrote to Bollet, representative with these two armies, on

January 18, 1795, "The correspondence of General Hoche . . . reveals a man, active and enlightened, who desires, as we do, the end of this deplorable war."[52] It is apparent that Hoche had completely rehabilitated himself with Carnot.

The differences between Carnot and Saint-Just came to a climax in June over orders having to do with the siege of Charleroi. Saint-Just had two important missions to the Army of the North after the execution of Danton. On April 29 he and Le Bas were sent to this army to "execute the views of the Committee of Public Safety."[53] Saint-Just began making suggestions on strategy, which Carnot "rejected tactfully."[54] Considerable liberty, however, was left to the Representatives. Carnot sent instructions to the two representatives on May 2,[55] "We present another idea, which you can make use of if it seems suitable to you; we ask you only to consider it carefully." On the following day, Saint-Just, in the name of the two representatives, wrote to the Committee from Réunion-sur-Oise,[56] "Hasten to send us a plan of operations from Cambrai to Beaumont. . . . Reply at once; do not lose an hour. We are trying to reestablish order." Carnot acknowledged this on May 4, in his own handwriting.[57] "We invite you to secure the most exact information on this subject [of the faithlessness and incompetency of officers and officials], and replace them as promptly as possible by worthy men who have your confidence. . . . You ask of us a plan of operations; up until now these have not been wanting. . . . Detailed operations cannot be directed from here, because they depend on the daily movements of the enemy, which one cannot anticipate. The general plan is as follows. . . . What is now necessary is to reestablish order in the army, to prevent the passage of the Sambre from Beaumont to Landrecies, to press the enemy on his left flank in order to prevent him from taking the Capelle hill and thus cut your communications with Avesnes. . . . Cover Cambrai, press the enemy if it is possible as you propose, to the gates of Valenciennes, and march on Bavay."

Shortly thereafter Saint-Just returned to Paris. On June 1 he attended his first meeting of the Committee after his return. At that session he wrote and signed an order,[58] naming General Dejardin to the command of the right of the Army of the North and of the Army of the Ardennes, under Pichegru, and ordering General Charbonié to come to Paris in order to receive a command. On June 5 the Committee of Public Safety ordered the arrest of General of Division Delmas of the Army of the Rhine.[59] Carnot wrote and signed an order on July 2, releasing Delmas from arrest,[60] and on the following day, Carnot ordered him to the Army of the North as General of Division.[61] Choudieu, representative with the Army of the North, wrote to Carnot on June 3 from Lille,[62] "The letter from the Council of Landrecies reminds me of a matter on which it is necessary that the Committee advise me. Saint-Just and Le Bas arrested the magistrates of Menin and of Courtrai by the following order: 'The magistrates of Landrecies having been assassinated, the magistrates of the conquered territory are to be arrested as a reprisal.' It appears that this fact is not true, since the above-mentioned magistrates are in Paris." Carnot replied in a few days that the detained magistrates were to be released.[63]

Saint-Just was sent back to the armies on June 6, by the Committee of Public Safety, to range the frontiers of the North and East, from the sea to the Rhine, in order to "superintend the armies and see to the execution of the decrees of the Convention and the orders of the Committee of Public Safety."[64] Carnot wrote and signed this order. Decisive engagements were being prepared for. Carnot had urged Jourdan, commanding the combined Armies of the Moselle and the Ardennes, on May 27, to take Dinant and Charleroi.[65] Saint-Just arrived at the siege camp before Charleroi on June 12. Jourdan suffered a reversal on the 16th. Carnot, on June 18, after the capture of Ypres, without consulting Saint-Just, ordered the Army of the North to demand reinforcements of 15,000 infantry, and 1,500 cavalry from the Army of the Moselle. The order was not carried out. Saint-Just wrote to the Committee of Public Safety on June 23, "After Charleroi we shall fall upon Namur and Mons."[66] On June 25 Charleroi was taken, and on the following day the important battle of Fleurus was won. Then Pichegru wrote to Jourdan asking for the reinforcements ordered by Carnot, and sending him Carnot's despatch. Jourdan, supported by the representative Gillet, declared that he needed these troops. Gillet protested to the Committee in letters on July 2 and 3, and also addressed himself personally to Saint-Just, asking him to have the order revoked. Saint-Just had returned to Paris in the night of June 28-29, just after Fleurus. The order was revoked in the Committee, but only after violent explanations and recriminations. Saint-Just referred to the order as inept,[67] and said that had it been carried out the battle of Fleurus would have been lost. It was in these sessions that Saint-Just accused Carnot of liaisons with the aristocrats and threatened to have him guillotined. Carnot evidently defied Saint-Just and accused him and his friends by crying, "You are ridiculous dictators."[68] At another time, in the presence of Levasseur (de la Sarthe), Carnot said to Robespierre, "You commit only arbitrary acts in your office of general police. You are a dictator."[69] The representative Richard wrote from Antwerp on August 5, to the Committee, "Saint-Just made the greatest efforts to prevent the execution of the plan adopted by the Committee of Public Safety, which produced such victories for the Republic. I had many lively scenes with him on this subject."[70]

The animosities between Saint-Just and Carnot must have developed rapidly. But tempers were short and nerves taut in those days. Carnot evidently appreciated the invaluable services of Saint-Just as a representative with the armies, particularly in inflaming the troops, reestablishing morale and order, and in purging the armies and the local administrations of unfaithful and corrupt officers and officials. These services, however, had to remain limited because of Saint-Just's ignorance of engineering, tactics, and strategy. Saint-Just was sensitive to the fact that he was not kept completely informed in late June, and this omission grew in his mind to have a "sinister significance,"[71] for which he held Carnot responsible in his speech on the ninth of Thermidor.

After the important victory of Fleurus on June 26 there was less justification than ever for the continuation of the Terror. Fouché and his associates began spreading the rumour that the Great Committee was drawing up extensive lists of proscription containing many Montagnards. Couthon discounted this in the Jacobin Club on June 14, saying that only four or six traitors, whom he did not name, needed to be punished. This merely aggravated the fear among the Montagnards. Fouché and his friends now began to concentrate on Robespierre as the person to hold responsible for the Parisian Terror and for the threatened accusations. The members of the Committee of Public Safety were in a dilemma. They were sure that Robespierre was determined to sacrifice them, if need be, and they knew that if the Montagnards overthrew Robespierre that would be but a prelude to the overthrow of the whole Committee, and a reorganization of the Government.

Fouché made friends with Vadier and Amar in the lesser Committee. Saint-Just began talking of the necessity of establishing a dictatorship. On June 24 Carnot foresightedly despatched a large part of the Parisian artillery to the front. These artillery men were friendly to the *sansculottes*. Couthon hotly denounced this action in the Jacobin Club. That same day the Jacobins denounced Robespierre's enemies in the Convention. On June 29 there was a violent disagreement in the two Committees. Barère reports that the majority of the members besought Robespierre and Saint-Just to have the Law of Prairial repealed. These two remained adamant and threatened to appeal to popular opinion against the new combination. The attacks on Robespierre doubled in the Convention. On July 1 Robespierre defended the continued use of reprisals and executions in the Jacobin Club. By now almost the entire Committee of General Security opposed Robespierre, as did several members of the greater Committee. Robespierre withdrew almost entirely from active participation in the Government. Although he attended meetings of the Committee of Public Safety, he refused to give his signature. He signed only five decrees from July 3 to July 27, and these were unimportant. There is some evidence in these days that he was willing to tolerate some let-up in the work of the Terror.

Fouché and his crowd began tentative negotiations with the Right. The Jacobins, his friends in the Commune, and Hanriot, all urged Robespierre to put down his enemies by force, but he declined. A feeble attempt at reconciliation in the two Committees on July 23 was fruitless. Some of the members now feared a dictatorship by Robespierre. On the 24th Robespierre again complained of the conspiracy, in the Jacobin Club. The Club addressed the Convention in such vague and general terms on the next day as only to intensify the general alarm.

Robespierre addressed the Convention on July 26 (8 Thermidor). Excepting for the financiers, Ramel and Mallarmé, he accused no individuals, but he left everyone uncomfortable. He concentrated his spleen on the proconsul conspirators. He handled his colleagues on the Committee of Public Safety lightly, but he did attack the management of the war (Carnot) and the direction of the finances (Cambon). This was the first time a member of the Committee had reproached his associates publicly. Despite differences in the Committee before this there had been a careful preservation of apparent harmony, and the principle of united responsibility had determined all public utterances of the Committee. The address, in general, was vague and not specific, and it was extremely weak. Robespierre finally proposed his remedy: "Punish the traitors, renew the officials of the Committee of General Security, purify that Committee itself and subordinate it to the Committee of Public Safety; purify even that Committee, constitute the unity of the government under the National Convention and crush all factions."[72] That was all .When the opposition got the floor, Billaud-Varenne asked to have the speech referred to the Committees, saying, "I had rather my dead body should serve as a footstool to an ambitious man than by my silence to authorize his misdeeds!" This constituted a challenge from the highest quarters in the Government. Robespierre was asked to name the conspirators but "he evaded once more, made a general statement and lost the day."[73]

Affairs moved rapidly and inexorably to their climax in the next few hours. Robespierre went off to orate for two hours in the Jacobin Club, where his confreres listened to him, with enthusiasm and fidelity. Billaud-Varenne and Collot d'Herbois attended the session for the first time in months but were denied a hearing. They were finally driven from the hall. Robespierre's friends urged him to have the members of the two Committees arrested, but he refused. Saint-Just stayed on at the Committee of Public Safety, drafting a speech, while the other members seemed to be too paralyzed to do anything. When Collot d'Herbois came in from the Jacobin Club he accused Saint-Just of being engaged in writing an accusation against his associates on the Committee. Saint-Just finally admitted as much and "turning upon Carnot with calm arrogance," he added, "'You are not forgotten either, and you will find that I have treated you in masterly fashion.'"[74] Meanwhile the conspirators were working furiously elsewhere, and finally won over the Right. Then they secured the support of the Mountain, and they knew they could count on the president, Collot d'Herbois, and on Tallien.

The Convention met at ten o'clock on nine Thermidor (July 27). Robespierre was there in the clothes he had worn at the fête of the Supreme Being. Saint-Just had promised to submit his speech to the Committee of Public Safety before delivering it to the Convention, but he went directly to the hall. He did not get far into his speech. One reads in it, however, a passage criticizing the war management, with Carnot, no doubt, particularly in mind. "I find it very deplorable . . . that the liberty of moving the troops is concentrated in very few hands and in impenetrable secrecy, to the extent that all the armies might be transferred, with only a few persons informed of it."[75]

The opposition refused to let Saint-Just go on with his speech. Tallien interrupted him first, and then the ultra-bloodthirsty Billaud-Varenne got the floor to denounce Robespierre as a moderate. Robespierre demanded the right to be heard but was hooted down. Tallien's motion to arrest Robespierre's followers was adopted. Barère mounted the tribune and temporized until the disorder became too great in the hall. Finally, Louchet, an obscure Montagnard from Aveyron and an extreme terrorist, was recognized, and moved the arrest of Robespierre. Augustin Robespierre asked to be included with his brother, and the decree including both was passed. Le Bas also offered himself for arrest, and he, Couthon, and Saint-Just were ordered arrested. Hanriot had been suspended earlier in the day as commander of the Paris guard.

Payan and Fleuriot feverishly organized the Commune against the Convention, and Hanriot spent the day inflaming the masses, until he was finally put under arrest. Fleuriot signed a decree outlawing fourteen deputies, including Collot d'Herbois, Freron,

Tallien, Carnot, and Fouché. Robespierre broke his detention at the Mairie and went to the Hôtel de Ville, but took no action against the Convention. Hanriot was released at eight-thirty but remained inactive. The Jacobins stood shoulder to shoulder with the Commune. The Convention, in night session and in the face of these alarming developments, declared Robespierre and his associates *hors la loi*. Barras was empowered to lead the armed forces against the insurrection. Carnot had already signed an order that day that the young patriots in the camp at Sablons were to come, armed, to the Convention.[76]

Now that he was outlawed Robespierre consented to lead the insurrection, but it was too late. By one-thirty in the morning Barras had enough troops to face the mob and to enter the Hôtel de Ville where he surprised and arrested Robespierre, his associates, and about forty members of the Commune. The outlaws were taken to the Tuileries into a room adjoining the Convention hall. They needed only to be identified to be condemned. At four o'clock in the afternoon on Ten Thermidor (July 28) the condemned leaders and their friends in the Commune were driven to the guillotine. There were twenty-one of them, for Le Bas had shot himself at the Hôtel de Ville. The last head to fall was that of Robespierre. Now he would know whether his own soul was immortal or not. Men would never be able to forget him.

The Committee of Public Safety at once informed the Representatives of the Armies of the North, and the Sambre-et-Meuse of what had happened.[77] Carnot sent a similar despatch to the Representatives with the Army of the Western Pyrenees at the same time, in which he spoke of the "intrigue of the treasonable Robespierre brothers," and concluded, "These rascals are no more."[78] On August 13 Carnot sent an illuminating despatch to the Representatives with the Army of Italy: "We do not doubt that the new conspiracy, which has just been destroyed, spread one of its most dangerous branches in those places [Italy] where the Robespierres exercised such a perfidious and active influence. The project that the younger Robespierre came to persuade us to . . . through the tyranny of his brother, to invade Piedmont and thus abandon our natural frontiers and give up Corsica. . . . This project, I declare, seems to us to be the fruit of the intrigue of these conspirators. . . . What astonishes us, dear colleagues, is to see that this system of Robespierre found some favor among you."[79]

Three groups had combined to overthrow Robespierre. There were the anti-Robespierrists of the Committees, such as Collot d'Herbois and Billaud-Varenne, who opposed him as a person, but who were, many of them, extreme terrorists. Then there were the anti-Robespierrist Montagnards, the so-called Thermidorians, many of whom were former friends of Danton. These wanted to seize power in the Government. Finally, there were the Moderates of the Plain, men who had hitherto been passive.

Reorganization was started immediately after Nine Thermidor. The Commune of Paris was abolished on that very day, and the National Guard was reformed. On July 29 it was decided that one-fourth of the Committee of Public Safety should retire each month, and that no retiring member could be re-elected until a month had elapsed. Two days later the Committee was reconstituted. The six new members were Eschassériaux, Thuriot, Tallien, Laloy, Bréard, and Treilhard. Four of these were Thermidorians. Barère, Lindet, Prieur (Côte-d'Or), Carnot, Billaud-Varenne, and Collot d'Herbois completed the twelve on the Committee. Their policy was to modify and to moderate, but not to stop the Terror, to pursue the war, and to maintain the Revolutionary Government, with a purged Jacobin Club and a reformed Revolutionary Tribunal. On August 1 Legendre proposed the reopening of the Jacobin Club, which he had himself locked up on the night of 9-10 Thermidor. Carnot opposed the reopening, but the motion was adopted.

Fouquier-Tinville was impeached on August 1, and the Law of 22 Prairial was repealed. Decrees of August 12 and 28 curtailed the powers of the representatives on mission. On August 23 the whole system of government was reorganized. The twenty-one committees in the Convention were replaced by sixteen, and the executive power hitherto monopolized by the two Committees was widely distributed among them. The Committee of Public Safety was particularly restricted to the direction of war and foreign affairs. The 132 prisoners from Nantes turned over to the Paris Tribunal by the blood-thirsty Carrier in January were acquitted on September 14, and the Nantes Tribunal was impeached. This alarmed Billaud-Varenne and his associates and they fulminated in the Jacobin Club. On November 12, the Club was closed. Carrier was put on trial and on December 16 was sentenced to death.

On October 6 Prieur (de la Marne), Guyton- Morveau, and Richard had been elected to succeed Carnot, Lindet, and Prieur (Côte-d'Or) on the Committee of Public Safety. Carnot and Robert Lindet, however, continued their activities with the personnel, movements, and provisioning of the Armies. Carnot returned to the Committee on November 5, along with Cambacérès and Pelet (de la Lozière) succeeding Laloy, Eschassériaux, and Treilhard. Carnot left the Committee finally on March 5, 1795, along with Cambacérès and Pelet, succeeded by Reubell, Siéyès, and Laporte.

Gradually, three groups began to take form in the Convention after Nine Thermidor. One group was made up of independents, comprising certain Thermidorians and Jacobins, members of the old Mountain, who represented extreme republicanism and inclined to the Left, but a Left freed of Billaud-Varenne and Collot d'Herbois. Merlin (Douai), Barras, Cambacérès, and Siéyès were in this faction. The second group included the Thermidorians proper, the ones who had taken the lead in the recent violent measures against the Robespierrists. They inclined more and more to the Right. Tallien and Fréron were influential in this group. The third faction was made up of the old Center and Right, and its members favored the restoration of the Monarchy and the Constitution of 1791. The seventy-three deputies who had been imprisoned in the previous year for protesting against the expulsion of the Girondins on June 2 were released on December 9, and were welcomed back into the Convention. This increased the number of moderates.

Persistent efforts were made to impeach the Terrorists on the two Great Committees as they were constituted before Nine Thermidor. As early as August 29 Lecointre, a very excitable Thermidorian, had proposed this step, but at that time the Convention would have nothing to do with the accusation. Lecointre spoke again on October 7, and this time he included Carnot in his vigorous attack.[80] On December 24 the two Committees reported that there were grounds for investigating the suspicions against Billaud-Varenne, Barère, Collot d'Herbois, and Vadier. A commission of twenty-one was appointed. Its report was not ready until March 2, when it recommended that these four revolutionaries be arrested.[81] The arrest was voted.

In the debate in the Convention on the guilt of these four men, the other former members of the two Great Committees were gradually involved. It was on March 22, 1795 that Carnot first asked to be heard in defense of his accused colleagues.[82] Their defense, of course, was also his own defense. The central question was the one of responsibility for the political decrees, arrests and acts of the Committee of Public Safety. Carnot had signed most of the orders and decrees of the Committee. He had attended most of its meetings. The question by 1795 was whether he was to be held equally accountable with Robespierre, Saint Just, Barère and others for what appeared to the Moderates of 1794 to be the excesses and abuses of the Terror. Carnot, as his own advocate and fighting for his life, denied his responsibility. He made out a case that has been generally accepted by posterity.[83]

Carnot's principal statement was given on March 23, after the unfriendly Larivière had proposed that Carnot be heard at length.[84] After announcing that he wanted to stand with his accused associates and share their fate, Carnot plunged into the heart of his long address.[85]

"For a long time I personally attacked Robespierre and Saint-Just in the meetings of the Committee of Public Safety. . . .

"I have served the democracy as best I could. I am passionately devoted to the popular cause; but wherever my duties called me, I maintained the dignity and character with which I was endowed. . . .

"I was not in Paris the 2nd and 3rd of September, nor on the 31st of May. I remained isolated. I never missed an occasion to pronounce against the factions, against every sort of tyranny, against the permanence of power. . . .

"Malevolence tries in vain to cite any signatures given by me for acts that are found to be reprehensible. It is necessary to explain, once and for all, to the National Convention, what the signatures of the former members of the Committee of Public Safety really were.

"The signatures given by the members of the former Committee of Public Safety (I speak of the signatures 'en second') were a formality prescribed by law, but absolutely insignificant for him who was bound to fulfill it; on his part it was neither an express adherence, nor even a granted acquiescence of confidence. . . . Precisely they were only and had never been more than simple *vues,* an operation, purely mechanical, which proves nothing, which attests nothing, excepting that the reporter, that is to say, the first signer of the Minute, was acquitted of the prescribed formality of submitting the document in question to the examination of the Committee.

"I am asked why one signed papers without knowing them. I reply—by absolute necessity, by the physical impossibility of doing otherwise. The press of business was too great for deliberation in the Committee; we were forced to distribute the work. . . ."

Carnot proceeded to elaborate some of his political philosophy. He questioned the right of the Convention to judge the accused for opinions which they had expressed in the Convention. To do so, he said, was an attack upon public liberty. The freedom of opinion on the part of a representative of the people must be guarded sacredly. He concluded his speech, "The crime of tyranny was expiated the Tenth Thermidor; whoever loves the *patrie* will no longer hunt for further guilty persons, and will not jeopardize the Republic under the pretext of avenging it. I conclude that the Convention should decree that there are no grounds for the accusation against the prisoners." The Convention ordered this speech printed and distributed. Three days later Carnot spoke again quite briefly. "In order to prove to you," he said, "the manner of giving signatures in the Committee of Public Safety, I will say that I signed their [his own secretaries'] arrest without knowing it. It was impossible to sign otherwise than through confidence, because it was necessary to give five- to six-hundred signatures each day."

At the session of the Convention on May 28, Gamon, after declaring that "the presence of assassins of the *patrie* in the bosom of the Convention dishonored the national representation," proposed a Commission of nine to report on all the deputies "denounced and accused of complicity with the late tyrants."[86] Henri Larivière then proceeded to make a violent attack on Carnot, although he admitted the specialties in the Committee of Public Safety, and put Carnot in that one of the three groups that included Prieur (Côte-d'Or) and Robert Lindet. He stated that he did not want the head of Carnot but he wanted him expelled from the Convention.[87] "How could you be so indifferent," he said, "or so imbecile as not to open your eyes to the projects of the cannibals with whom you associated daily? Not to prevent crime, is to commit it." Carnot replied, "I was confined constantly to the task for which I was responsible; I worked sixteen hours a day, and I had no ear for anything but what happened in my offices. . . . As for the signatures, I gave them as of confidence, and that is still done today; it was impossible to examine the papers that were presented to me to sign."[88]

After Carnot had finished Gouly moved the arrest of Robert Lindet, Voulland, Jean-Bon Saint-André, Jagot, Elie Lacoste, Lavicomterie, David, Carnot, Prieur (Côte-d'Or), Barbau-Dubarran, and Bernard (de Saintes), all former members of the two Revolutionary Committees.[89] The Convention proceeded to vote on these names separately. Carnot spoke again, briefly, just before his name came up for vote.[90] Arrest had been voted for all those who had preceded him. When the vote was called on Carnot, an anonymous voice cried out, "Carnot organized the victory," and the Convention, shamed by the cry, refused to press the matter to a vote.

Carnot had been committed to the policy of the Terror. He believed in a strongly centralized government for the crisis, and he was responsible for the defense of France, both within and on the frontiers of the Nation. He saw the need for absolute control at home. He opposed tyranny but he favored the virtual dictatorship of the Committee of Public Safety. He claimed only to be a specialist. He said that he had only formally signed the various general decrees of the Committee.[91] Some authorities have agreed that there were specialties in the Committee and that on functional matters signatures were given by the members not particularly concerned, by confidence. These authorities have contended, however, that general policies were decided in the full sessions of the members, and that, therefore, the Committee as a whole was responsible.[92] Sorel has written of Carnot in this regard, "He confined himself to his rôle, achieving a sort of stoicism of state and imposed upon himself as a duty, . . . this capitulation of his humanity; letting the Terrorists guillotine so long as they let him defend France."[93] Some of Carnot's contemporaries separated him from Robespierre, Couthon and Saint-Just, but yet held him fully accountable for conscious knowledge of what he signed in the Committee.[94] Others acquitted him of all responsibility and praised him for his courage in offering to share and suffer the responsibility with the accused.[95]

Naturally, Carnot could not have lived in France in 1793 and 1794, much less have been a member of the Revolution's dictatorial Government, without being aware of the conscious policy of the Terror, which the Committee of Public Safety was pursuing. Solidarity within the nation, the consolidation of the Revolution, and the defense of the country were survival necessities in the period of the Convention. The policy of the Terror and the guillotine as an instrument were designed to serve these vital ends of the nation. The Terror did work.[96] Carnot recognized its necessity and its validity fully as well as any. Charged with the defense of France and needing a nation united in itself, a veritable "nation in arms," and believing as thoroughly as he did in a strong central government for the emergency, Carnot was probably as committed as any other to the use of the ruthless means of the Terror. He recognized that the crisis of war, to be met successfully, called for national solidarity, even at the expense of the usual constitutional guarantees of safety, freedom, opinion, and liberty.

Carnot's great responsibility lay in his having once and for all, at some time, given his consent to the policy of the Terror. He was sincere and honest in that consent. Having once approved a general policy it seems too severe to hold him responsible for the manifold individual injuries and tragedies wreaked through the means of decrees, arrests and executions. These abuses were bound to appear. Carnot had the mammoth task of reorganizing the existing armies, of organizing the *levée en masse,* of controlling and directing the personnel and the campaigns of the fourteen armies, and of repelling strong invading foes, with a rough but patriotic republican national army. He signed a multitude of decrees and orders to the armies and to the representatives with the armies, for which he assumed personal responsibility. He devoted himself conscientiously to the minutest details of his office. He had little time left for the careful perusal of the individual decrees and orders which needed the signatures of the members of the Committee. He did sign most of these. It may be near the truth to say that the members of the Committee of Public Safety are to be held jointly responsible for general policies, and personally responsible for those individual and specific acts with which each was specially charged. It should be added that once Carnot felt that the Terror had served its purpose he opposed its continued use. This was certainly true after the execution of Danton, if not before.

Gradually but unmistakably, during the winter of 1794-5, the pendulum was swinging back in a conservative direction. The Moderates were assuming control more and more. The *maximum* was repealed on December 23. The sale of the property of relatives of *émigrés* was discontinued on December 21, and on the 29th the sequestrated property of German, English and Spanish subjects was restored. In January the Moderates got Boissy-d'Anglas onto the Committee of Public Safety. On January 12 the priests and nobles condemned to deportation were released. Peace was made with Tuscany on the ninth of February. By the Law of 3 Nivôse (February 21) freedom of worship was conceded. On March 8 the surviving Girondin deputies were restored to their seats. Sixteen returned to the Convention.

In these months the country had gone from bad to worse. Professor Madelin vividly describes France in that winter, "France lay sick: the fever of 1789, the superhuman effort of 1792, the blood-letting of 1793 and 1794, the never-ceasing starvation of all those years, had brought on a kind of anaemia complicated by neurasthenia."[97] Prices in Paris were frightful and bread was scarce. A cart load of wood cost 500 livres, a pound of brown sugar forty-one, a bushel of flour 225, and one had to pay 1248 livres for a leg of mutton. The price of bread rose to forty-five livres a pound. In January a gold louis brought 130 livres in *assignats.* In March it brought 227 livres.

The Jacobins were greatly alarmed at conditions and at the developments in the Convention. They began clamoring for the Constitution of 1793, but the Moderates replied that they wanted a new constitution. The Jacobins brought matters to a head on April 1 when a mob of angry citizens broke into the Convention and cried out for "bread and the Constitution of 1793." They kept up their shouting for four hours until the National Guard dispersed them. The Convention immediately voted the deportation of Billaud and his associates, and a long list of others. It ordered the arrest of sixteen Jacobins who had been ringleaders in this latest insurrection. Pichegru, who happened to be in Paris, was given troops and told to restore order. The National Guard was revamped into a bourgeois body. On April 3 the Committee of Public Safety was increased to sixteen members. The departmental authorities were restored. On April 15 it was proposed to restore property confiscated from victims of the Terror, to their surviving relatives. Action on this was delayed to the third of May. Trade in gold and silver was freed from restrictions on April 25. This premature action, however, only further depreciated the *assignats.*

The Convention appointed a Constitutional Committee on March 21. Cambacérès, reporting for the Committee on April 18, proposed that an entirely new constitution be drafted. The Convention accepted the recommendation and named a new committee of eleven. This committee contained only one extreme Republican, and at least three members favorable to the monarchy.

The White Terror broke out sporadically all over the South. On May 20 a popular uprising occurred in Paris, stimulated by both the Royalists and the Jacobins in the Convention. The Committee of Public Safety and the bourgeois National Guard finally succeeded in dispersing the mob, but the disorders continued in the city. The Committee called in troops, from the outside, and by May 3 General Menou commanded 20,000 men. The mob had withdrawn in the meantime to the faubourg Saint-Antoine where it was forced to surrender to this overwhelming number of soldiers. Sixty-two Montagnards were arrested for complicity in this insurrection, and six of these were condemned to death. In every direction the last vestiges of the Terror were extirpated. The Revolutionary Tribunal was abolished. Churches were restored to their cults on the condition that the priests declare their obedience to the laws. A permanent guard of troops was assigned to protect the Convention. On June 10 the Dauphin died after suffering unspeakable deprivations.

Boissy-d'Anglas presented plans for a new constitution on June 23, and these were adopted. Universal suffrage was to be abolished, and residence and tax-paying qualifications were established for the franchise. The Legislative Corps was to be composed of two councils, the Five-Hundred, and the Elders.[98] The members of the larger body were to be elected by the primary assemblies for three year terms with one-third retiring every year. The minimum age limit was thirty. The 250 members of the Council of Elders were to be elected from and by the entire Legislative Corps, for a similar term and with the same system of retirement. The Elders must be at least forty years of age. The Five-Hundred alone could initiate legislation and the Elders could veto any measure for one year. There was to be an executive Directory of five members, selected by the Council of Elders from a list of fifty presented by the Council of Five-Hundred. The Directors were not to sit in the Legislative Corps, nor were they to control the finances. In practice they assumed the direction of the Ministries, but this was not stated in the Constitution. One director was to retire annually by lot. The Directors could not dissolve the Legislative Corps and call for new elections, nor could the Legislative Corps hold the Directors responsible. A Declaration of the Rights of Man was included in the Constitution. Clubs were expressly prohibited by the Constitution.

Carnot evidently did not like this Constitution. His son is our principal authority for this and he evidently wrote down what his father told him long after the event when the facts had amply proven the father to be right.[99] The Constitution was debated in the Convention from July 1 to August 17, but Carnot did not figure in this discussion. It is reported that Carnot thought that the great separation of powers would result in deadlock in the processes of government. His filial biographer says that Carnot preferred a single legislative body, frequently renewed. There would be another elected assembly, composed of the élite men of science and experience.[100] This would be a more permanent body and would interpret and maintain the law. A censorial magistrature would also be established to hold the officers of the state to account. Carnot, his son reports, also criticized the executive Directory. His son quotes him as saying, "Your executive will discuss as a legislature, with the result that the destinies of the State will depend on the humors of five persons and the more these humors are in disagreement, the more the State will suffer fluctuations."

On August 18 it was decreed that two-thirds of the members of the Convention were to pass into the new Legislative Corps. This was prompted by the Republicans, by the Thermidorians, and by all the regicides, 300 of whom remained, who wanted to protect themselves against the Royalist movement. Many of these "republicans in possession," such as Tallien (and his glamorous mistress Cabarrus), Barras, Merlin, and Barère had enriched themselves and had a material stake to preserve. More than that, however, they needed power in order to save their necks. It was decreed on August 22 that the primary assemblies were to nominate this two-thirds. Carnot voted for these two measures, on the grounds that the membership, so guarded, would prevent the reopening of all of the questions of the Revolution. He feared the capture of seats by the counter-revolutionaries. He explained his votes in these words, "What is most important is that the traditions not be interrupted. . . . We cannot, without danger, confide the task of sustaining the Republic to a majority which is a stranger to its foundation."

The Constitution was submitted hurriedly to the primary assemblies and approved by 914,000 out of 958,000 votes. The unpopular "decrees of the two-thirds," however, were accepted by 167,000 out of 263,000 voting on them. There is evidence of considerable fraud and doctoring of the vote. In any case the number of abstentions was enormous. The Convention proclaimed the Constitution on September 23 and fixed October 2 for the nomination of the Electoral Colleges, October 12 for the election of deputies, and November 6 for the initial meeting of the Legislative Corps.

The Paris sections were particularly angered by the "two-thirds" and other decrees, and revolted on October 4. The Convention appointed Barras and forty others to preserve order. The Convention raised 1500 "patriots" and had 4000 regulars available. Barras got hold of some artillery, and with the help of Bonaparte, put down the insurrection. The victorious Convention avoided the system of reprisals. Bonaparte was named commander-in-chief of the Army of the Interior.

The Convention dissolved itself on October 26 and on the following day those Conventionals who had been elected to the Legislative Corps assembled. On October 30 the candidates for the Directory were listed, and on November 4 the new government was completed.

Carnot was elected to the Council of Elders in fourteen departments. The notification of his election by the electoral college of la Sarthe reached him first. Characteristically, he accepted that mandate. He had had no connections there. This choice demonstrated his conviction that a legislator should not be considered a representative of a locality, but of France the Nation. He did not know that he was to be one of the Directors, on the refusal of Siéyès to accept his election.

Chapter VIII

THE BOURGEOIS REPUBLIC

THE DEMOCRATIC republic came to an end on October 26 when the Convention laid down its functions. The bourgeois republic, established upon a property qualification for the suffrage, began the next day with the organization of the two Councils comprising the Legislative Corps.

The nomination and election of the executive Directory occupied the Councils on October 30 and 31. The Five-Hundred presented a slate of fifty to the Council of Elders. Five of these were strong characters and the rest were purposely insignificant figures. The Elders elected Larevellière[1] (216 votes), Reubell (176 votes), Siéyès (156 votes), Letourneur (189 votes), and Barras (129 votes). The enigmatical and oracular Siéyès characteristically declined the election. The other four Directors asked Carnot to become Minister of War, thinking thereby to dispose of him safely.[2] Carnot declined, probably because he doubted the intentions of his political enemies, Barras and Reubell.[3] Finally, he permitted his name to be considered for the Directory, and it was included on the list of nine sent by the Five-Hundred[4] to the Elders.[5] The Elders elected him on November 3 with 117 votes out of the 213 voting.[6] The newly-elected "Third" considered Carnot "a zealot who had cooled down." He was installed in office on the following day.

All five of the Directors were regicides. The former Vicomte Paul de Barras was tall, handsome, and elegant. He was wildly extravagant and lived luxuriously; was cruel, base, and shameless; was a sensualist and a refined debauchée, with a succession of mistresses whom he palmed off on others when he was satiated with them. He had no political principles; had a lust for wealth, and retired with a considerable fortune. Reubell was an Alsatian *avocat* and was the least repentant of the Jacobins. He ever favored violent measures. He had sat in the Constituent

Assembly and in the Convention. In the latter he had been a member of the Committee of War. He was decidedly unfriendly to Carnot. He favored a despotism similar to that exercised by the Committee of Public Safety and he supported the policy of conquest in order to achieve the "natural frontiers" of France. He had a strong, masterful will and really dominated Barras and Larevellière. In the Directory he was constantly surrounded by army contractors and speculators, and he retired with a considerable fortune.

Larevellière, an *avocat* by profession, had also sat in the Constituent Assembly and in the Convention. He was an old Girondin. He was physically ill-favored for he was hump-backed, had a head too large for his body, and spindly legs. He had an irrepressible hatred of priests although he had really a religious mind, and was absorbed in his dream of founding a natural religion. He was a Theophilanthropist. He was an upright man, and seemingly was very vain. He favored the policy of conquests as a means of emancipating peoples. Letourneur was an engineering officer who had graduated from the School of Engineering at Mézières shortly after Carnot. He had been a member of the Committee of War in the Convention. He was an honest man of mediocre ability, and simply followed Carnot in the Directory. Carnot[7] favored an early and definitive peace, opposed propaganda and annexation, was "disposed to be contented with Belgium and Luxembourg,"[8] favored a policy of moderation internally, and believed that there should be concord and agreement between the will of the majority in the Councils and the will of the Directory. The "three matadors of the Directory,"[9] Reubell, Barras, and Carnot were immediately and constantly in conflict. The first two, with Larevellière, constituted the majority.

The Directory was installed in the Palace of the Luxembourg on November 2, the day before Carnot's election. The palace was in a lamentable condition, just having been vacated by the agency of weights and measures, and by the Commission of Public Instruction. The Directors had to borrow a table from the *concierge* in order to conduct business. Shortly, however, they had surrounded themselves with princely furnishings in the apartments they occupied. With a great deal of pride and vanity they wore the official costume designed by the painter, David, and they instituted a pomp and a ceremonial for the performance of their various duties. A guard of 120 cavalry and 120 infantry was under their orders. Each director received about $25,000 a year.

In the distribution of labor in the Directory, Carnot was given the direction of war. Larevellière had public instruction, national fêtes, and manufactures. Reubell was assigned justice, finance, and foreign affairs. Barras had the police, and Letourneur the marine. Each of the Directors was also responsible for one-fifth of France, and Carnot was assigned the departments in the North, with which he was well acquainted. The Directory was represented by commissaires in all departmental, municipal, and judicial units throughout France. These officers attended all sessions of the local bodies. The appointment of these agents was a considerable task for there were nearly a thousand cantons in France.

The Directors immediately appointed the original six ministers. These were quite subordinate to the Directory and were actually only heads of departments. They never met together, and they were not responsible in any way to the Legislative Corps. Merlin (Douai), as Minister of Justice, was the only one with any real authority. When he was shifted to the newly-established Ministry of Police, he was succeeded by Genissieu, a vigorous Jacobin, who held the post until the time of the Babeuf plot, when Cochon, a friend of Carnot, became Minister of Justice. Bénézech was Minister of the Interior, Delacroix of foreign affairs, Admiral Truguet, of the navy, and Faipoult of finance. Aubert-Dubayet was named Minister of War. He had fought with La Fayette in America, had been a member of the Legislative Assembly, and had been active in the defense of Mayence and in the Vendéan civil war. He had had a period in prison as a suspect, and was released after 9 Thermidor. He was named commander-in-chief of the army of Cherbourg on February 4, 1795. He was replaced as minister by Petiet, a member of the Elders, on February 8, 1796, when he was named ambassador to Constantinople. Aubert-Dubayet was a handsome man, who knew it, and who liked the ladies.

Trouvé, a light-weight youngster, was the first secretary-general of the Directory. This was an important position since the incumbent edited the *procès-verbaux* of its sessions, countersigned the expedition of all its acts, and directed its bureaux. Carnot soon proposed Lagarde, an *avocat* of Douai and a friend of Merlin, for the position. He was appointed and served faithfully and discreetly throughout the period of the Directory. Many secret deliberations were held by the Directory without Lagarde being present. Under Lagarde's direction the Directory organized six distinct bureaux. Two others were added later, one for military topography directed by General Clarke, under the supervision of Carnot, and the diplomatic bureau directed by Bonnier and supervised by Reubell. Each of the Directors had personal secretaries. Barras had seven, Carnot nine, and Reubell had four.

In military affairs, Carnot demonstrated his usual acumen and his passion for details. He continued to write many of the military despatches, which bore the signatures of two members besides himself. He remained experimental, and in 1795 Clarke, Hoche, and he ascended in a balloon in the presence of the entire Directory.[10] His hands were not as free as they had been in the Committee of Public Safety, and the generals pursued a more independent line of action. There was a close connection between military operations and diplomatic objectives and negotiations. This was partly because of the centralization of both in the Directory, and partly because of the fact that the military operations were serving a large political purpose. Instructions to Bonaparte were inextricably military, political and diplomatic. In the autumn of 1795 Pichegru commanded the army of the Rhine et Moselle, Jourdan the Sambre et Meuse, Moreau the army of the North, Schérer that of Italy and Hoche the army of the West. Bonaparte had command of the army of the Interior.

French society was demoralized and broken-spirited, corrupt, enervated, profligate, pleasure-mad, and suffering during the Directory. Every extreme flourished. There was pathetic and squalid poverty, there was lavish extravagance and luxury, there was shameless vice, open corruption, and widespread profiteering. Morals were depraved and the family was shattered. Everything seemed to contribute to the degradation of the national character.[11] The "rotten bellies"—the profiteers, exploiters, and politicans, and the "empty bellies"—the starving masses, stood in sharp contrast and in sullen opposition to each other.

"Pleasure is the order of the day," wrote Charles de Constant. There was a mad rush for pleasure and all Paris was bent on amusement. Bagatelle, Tivoli, Frascati, the Elysée-Bourbon, and the village of Chantilly were all centers of fashion and gayety. There were circuses and games everywhere. The numerous theatres were crowded. Gambling was universal and the play was high. There were three hundred public dance halls. Dancing became a mania, and crowds even danced in the streets. There was a great amount of rich and heavy eating, and the famous *restaurateurs* appeared to cater to the epicures and the gourmands.

Captivating "ladies of easy virtue" had their great public moment. "It was 'Therezia I,' 'Her Most Serene Highness,' who really held the sceptre."[12] Barras installed her in the Luxembourg to reign, as she was about to divorce Tallien. From that lofty place "her soft eyes held government, society, and populace in captivity."[13] She did the honors at the Luxembourg, for Barras was the only Director who received company on a large scale. That company was very mixed—a huge demi-monde. Only Madame Barras was not there. Contractors and speculators were much in evidence. Speculation was so much in the air that all the ladies trafficked in sugar, coffee, land and assignats. Therezia set the fashions, too. These changed with bewildering speed. Dresses were very *décolleté*. It was the period of the women "sans-chemises." "The reign of the sans-culottes," writes Madelin, "had been followed by the reign of the sans-chemises," and that is an apt characterization of the altered society and its mood.

Divorces were numerous. The decree of September 20, 1792, establishing divorce, had been liberalized considerably on May 17, 1794. Fifteen months after the passing of the first decree, 5994 divorces had been granted. During the Directory this figure steadily mounted. The foundlings in Paris became a serious problem. Despite the dissolution of the family, pompous Festivals of Marriage, and of Filial Piety were held. There developed a widespread irreverence for the dead—a strange perversion, indeed, among the French.

The Directory inherited bad finances, and it never solved the problem of finance.[14] When the Directors took office twenty-four gold francs (louis d'or) brought 2500 francs in assignats. Four days later the gold louis brought 3400. The depreciation of the assignats was steady.[15] Twenty-four livres in specie bought 238 livres in assignats in April, 1795, 808 in July, 1205 in October, 3575 in December, and 7200 in the following March. Those who suffered most from this inflation were first the poor, the weak, the aged—the wards of the state, then those with fixed incomes, investors, *rentiers,* functionaries, officers, and the soldiers. There was much industrial unrest and there were many strikes, until the Directory reverted to the severe legislation of the monarchy to deal with them.

On November 8, 1795, a sort of budget was presented, amounting to 3000 millions of expenses in paper money. There was to be a further forced loan of 600 millions, one-half of which was to be payable in grain. Actual expenses were listed at 618,512,624 livres, and receipts at 561,820,176 livres (specie money). The next year's budget amounted to 1000 million livres (specie value) of which 550 million livres was for war. The wealthy classes prevented the Directory from regulating the finances for they profited from the fluctuations and manipulations of the currency. The Directory came more and more to depend on the contributions levied by the victorious armies and conquest thus became the principal resource of the nation. "It was necessary that victory pay."[16] This policy increased the hatred of France outside and prolonged the war. The Directory had joined its financial policy with its general politics.

Truly, France was in an unhealthy state in 1795 and the Directory only aggravated her disorders.

In the first months of the Directory Babeuf symbolized the effort to bring the Revolution back to a popular base, with some commitment to a program of social reform. The movement led by him climaxed its activities in the winter and early spring of 1796. Babeuf's communism had developed gradually over the years, but even as a youth he had dreamed of the socialization of property. He owed a great deal to Morelly's *Code de la Nature* (1775). After Thermidor he began publishing his popular *Tribun du peuple*. In the period of the Directory the "ardent Democrat"[17] began agitating the downfall of the Government and the restoration of the Constitution of 1793.

The Panthéon Club[18] assembled on November 16, 1795 for the first time. This Club was the product of a coalition of the Terrorists and the adherents of Babeuf. There is evidence that the Club was suggested by the Directory.[19] It included many of the amnestied Montagnards, who wanted their revenge on those who had imprisoned them. Carnot had tried to place some of these in government service, but they had refused. Many of the members of the Club, particularly those around Amar, were social radicals. Babeuf, evidently, did not meet with either the Panthéon Club or with the older Amar group. The Club gradually went over to the Left, opposed to the Directory. The friendly journal *Amis des Lois* led an active and systematic campaign against the financial policy of the Directory. Babeuf's own *Tribun du peuple* was very widely read. Its subscription list included many of the wealthy. These followed Babeuf not because of his communism, but in spite of it.[20]

In the early spring of 1796, the Directory became greatly alarmed at this latest popular movement. It ordered the Panthéon Club closed on February 27, and on the next day Bonaparte, as commander-in-chief of the army of the Interior, promptly executed the order. The decree included the other clubs of the day. Partly as a reward for his services on this occasion, Bonaparte was shortly thereafter named commander of the Army of Italy. After this closure of the Panthéon Club the *Journal des Hommes libres* became friendly to Babeuf. Carnot was particularly active in opposing the movement led by Babeuf.[21] This was due, primarily, no doubt, to his consistent dread of factions,[22] and his dislike of extremists. He felt that it was high time for stability and order to prevail in France. The papers friendly to Babeuf constantly levelled their invectives at Carnot.[23] Larevellière and Letourneur were also strong in their opposition to Babeuf and his followers, and Larevellière wanted to go further and include a much larger number of those to be run down and prosecuted.

Babeuf felt that time pressed if he wanted to accomplish anything, and so on March 30 he organized the *Comité insurrecteur.* The members were Buonarrati, who was more communistic than Babeuf, Antonelle, Debon, Dorthé, Félix le Pelletier, and Sylvain Maréchal, "obscure men, . . . men of the pen, more than of action." The sympathizers of the new conspiracy included former Robespierrists, such as Bouchotte. "The Tribune" and his followers launched a vigorous popular campaign that utilized placards and popular songs among its techniques. The purpose of the plot was less a communistic one than a last desperate effort of the Terrorists to seize power.[24] They spread far and wide their theoretical program which started out:

"Nature has given each man an equal right to the enjoyment of all property. Inequality is the cause of all the evils of society. The conservation of equality is the purpose of association because it is only by equality that organized men can be happy. . . . Nature imposes on everyone the obligation to work. . . . No one can, short of a crime, appropriate exclusively the possession of the soil or of industry. The rich who will not renounce their superfluity to the poor are the enemies of the people. Those who have repudiated the Constitution of 1793 are guilty of popular *lèse-majesté.*"

The Directory appointed Cochon, a friend of Carnot, as Minister of Justice on April 3, succeeding Genisseau, who was considered to be too friendly to the Jacobins. On the 14th the Directory issued a proclamation, drafted by Larevellière, to the inhabitants of Paris denouncing the "anarchists." The Legislative Corps passed a special Law of Public Safety on April 16, giving the Directory the power to put down subversive activities. The newly-organized Legion of Police, friendly to the conspirators, was ordered to join the armies on April 23. They preferred to stay in Paris and, on the instigation of the Babeuvists, they mutinied. Carnot took energetic measures and on May 2 the Directory ordered that the Legion be disarmed and dissolved. Brune executed these orders.

The conspirators now began to mature their plans more rapidly. Grisel, a captain of infantry, and a spy, who had gained the confidence of Darthé, on May 4 revealed their plans to Carnot, president of the Directory. Grisel was granted 10,000 livres in assignats in a secret deliberation of the Directory on May 6, for confidential expenses. A few days later he was granted a sum of 50,000 livres. Carnot Feulins, who was attached to the Ministry of Police at the time, aided in the repressive measures now laid down. It was arranged to arrest the conspirators on May 7 in the home of Drouet, but they had left a few minutes before the police arrived. But on May 10 the leaders of the "Egaux," Babeuf, Buonarrati, and Pillé, were arrested, followed shortly by others. The documentary evidence of the plot was confiscated. In all, 245 orders of arrest were issued. Carnot's name was signed to all of them.[25] In the provinces the repression was severe.

The arrested conspirators languished in prison for months. Friends of Babeuf made an attempt on the camp of Grenelle in the night of September 9-10, in order to raise an insurrection against the Government. A false alarm that they were moving on the Palace of Luxembourg prompted Carnot and Letourneur to arm themselves and prepare to direct the defending forces.[26] Thirty-two arrests were made. These persons were condemned to death by a military commission, contrary to the laws, The Court of Cassation later, on April 10-11, 1797, nullified these judgments, but the men had long since been executed. It was not until a year after their arrest, on May 26, 1797, that Babeuf and Darthé were condemned to death. They were executed on the following day. Seven others were deported, and the rest were acquitted.

The Directory oriented itself more and more to the Right after the arrest of Babeuf and his followers.[27] Carnot seemed to have something to do with this.[28] The Directory became more friendly to the "new-third," whose members it had hitherto shunned because of their suspected royalism. The administration was cleared of Jacobins, who were replaced by former Girondins and royalists.

While these disturbing and recurrent events had been transpiring affairs had gone on regularly in the war office. On April 12, 1796, the Directory authorized the publication of a special journal for the armies, called *Journal des defenseurs de la Patrie.*[29] Its first number appeared five days later. Instead of the old representatives-on-mission, the Directory maintained important commissioners with the armies, such as Joubert with the Army of Sambre-et-Meuse, and Saliceti with the Army of Italy. On March 30, 1796 is was necessary to reduce and regulate the manufactury of arms and supplies at Paris, because of oversupply. Personnel was also to be reduced.[30] In the same session the Minister of War was urged to discover and prosecute the wasters of the public monies, and the public thieves.[31]

Conflict in the West remained acute in the the early months of the Directory. Charette and Stofflet were still active in leading the rebels. Hoche commanded the republican army of the West.[32] Hoche was told to give the command provisionally to General Willot on December 3, so that he could be given an important mission. The Directory had in mind the command of the army of Italy for him. Hoche came to Paris on December 18, for a few days, but he refused the command.[33] When Hoche returned to the West, the Directory instructed him to exercise a "just severity which will secure respect for the government, and display humanity which will win hearts and bring them into the Republic."[34] In March the Directory discussed with him the advisability of taking the islands of Jersey and Guernsey from England.[35] On April 4 they acknowledged the receipt of the news of the capture of Charette.[36] On April 18 the Directory communicated to Hoche an idea for sending a thousand to fifteen hundred men to England to retaliate with instigating a *Chouannerie* there.[37] On receipt of Hoche's agreement, he was given authority to direct this expedition.[38] On the previous day the rebel Scépeaux and his followers had submitted. Hoche was instructed to pacify the inhabitants "more by persuasion than by force and to employ every means that his wisdom and his knowledge suggested to him."[39] Dumas, the Commissioner of the Directory in certain departments of the West, was instructed in similar fashion,[40] concluding: "Make the republican government cherished; let justice, good faith, and honesty be the guides of all the magistrates and public servants, so that calm and confidence will be restored, and superstition will struggle in vain to overthrow the constitution, whose purpose ought to be to assure the happiness of all Frenchmen." On July 30 the Directory completely lifted the state of siege in the West in those departments that had submitted to the Republic.[41]

With the West finally pacified, and Hoche available for other projects, the Directory turned seriously to the plan for an expedition to Ireland, "ripe for insurrection against England." The Directory wrote to Hoche to this effect in June.[42] A secret agent had already been sent to Ireland to lay the foundations. The Directory stated that if Ireland were detached from England, the latter would be no more than a second-rate power. Two expeditions were to sail from France and land in the province of Connaught. A third expedition was to sail from Holland. Hoche was to supervise the execution of the enterprise. Carnot wrote a personal letter to Hoche on June 22:[43] ". . . . As for myself in particular, I see in the success of this operation the downfall of the most irreconcilable and the most dangerous of our enemies. In it I see the security of France for centuries and, between us, General, I am pleased to see in it another object that touches we deeply, namely the new career of glory that is opened up for you." After calling attention to the wholesome dread and respect that the English have for Hoche, he concluded, "This task is worthy of you. I have resolved to propose to the Directory that you be put in actual command of the expedition. . . . If this project is agreeable to you, let me know, and from that moment plan the means of execution. . . . In the meantime, secrecy."

Théobald Wolfe Tone, an Irishman, offered his services for this expedition, and on July 12 he and Hoche had decisive interviews with the Directors in the Palace of Luxembourg. One of these was with Carnot, in whose apartment "they dined with the brother of the Director, the Minister of Marine Truguet, General Clark, General Lacuée, the Secretary-General Lagarde, ect."[44] On the 16th Wolfe Tone was made a *chef de brigade*. Important instructions were sent to Hoche on July 19, decided upon in a secret deliberation.[45] A republican government was to be established in Ireland as the best guarantee of a firm alliance between Ireland and France. The reins of government in Ireland were to be in the hands of the French until general peace was secured. Hoche was to lead the Irish insurrectionists, who would rise in great numbers. He was to organize at once a simple and effective financial system in Ireland and raise an Irish fleet. When Ireland was in a proper state of revolution, Hoche was to descend upon England, if his troops and the reinforcements from the new Irish government should give the promise of success. Hoche was formally made commander of the expedition on July 20, and was ordered to choose 15,000 men for the enterprise.[46] On September 16, it was ordered that these 15,000 were to be debarked in Ireland as soon as possible, and 5,000 men under General Quentin were to be landed on the east coast of England.[47] Things were hanging fire when Hoche wrote to the Directory on December 8, urging that the expedition be given up because of the delay in the fleet and in the transports. The Directory, reluctant to give up this project, replied that it was sending the Minister of Marine, to see if the obstacles could be overcome.[48] Finally, on December 17, the Directory abandoned the expedition in a despatch to Hoche, praising him for his zeal, and asking him to come to Paris for a new command.[49] The Directory announced the same news to the Minister of Marine, saying that undue publicity, and the bad faith of some had compelled the abandonment of the expedition.[50] Hoche had actually sailed in December, but had gotten separated from his fleet during a violent storm. He was tossed to the Island of Ré and finally debarking at La Rochelle, he journeyed up to Paris for his new assignment.

The outstanding successes of French arms during the time that Carnot was a member of the Directory were achieved by the Army of Italy under the command of Bonaparte. The armies in the East were unable to fulfill the plans of the Directory, and their concerted efforts with the Army of Italy came at a later time. The command was frequently changed in these armies and the fatal jealousies that had long retarded action in the East continued.

Moreau was transferred from the Army of the North to command the Army of the Rhine et Moselle on March 25, 1796.[51] Jourdan continued in command of the Army of the Sambre et Meuse. Moreau was instructed to take the offensive as soon as possible and to force a passage of the Rhine at either Huningue or at Brisach. On April 10 the Directory sent an important despatch to Moreau, written by Carnot.[52] The two armies in the

East were to collaborate and the two were to concert their actions with those of the Army of Italy. Jourdan's army, debouching on Dusseldorf, was to seek by an audacious march on the right bank of the Rhine, to attract to it the main forces of the enemy, so that the Army of the Rhine et Moselle could seize this moment to cross the Rhine and enter the Brisgau and the Souabe. The enemy before abandoning the Palatinate would try to force a battle with the Rhine et Moselle, but the Directory forbade any general engagement. At this point the Directory lay down some general principles, in accord with those championed by Carnot in the campaigns in 1794 and 1795:

The Directory injects a fundamental reflection to which it invites your attention. This is that attacks directed against the entire line of an army usually produce little effect and sacrifice a great number of men as a pure loss. . . . It is important, therefore, to avoid them with care, as well as those attacks that have as their unique object the center of the enemy and which almost always are disadvantageous to the armies undertaking them. But attacks made with force against a wing of the enemy, which it is often possible to turn, make it possible to dislodge the adversary from his positions and give the aggressor the means to constrain all of the enemy's movements and compel him to take positions that expose him to a complete route. . . .

You will occupy a new country whose resources, wisely husbanded, can provide for most of the needs of the army.

A passage of the Rhine near Strasbourg will assure us of the possession of the fort of Kehl and from there Strasbourg can become the center of your supplies and furnish you incalculable resources.

The Directory used various means to stimulate the armies in the East. On April 12 a newspaper, *Journal des défenseurs de la Patrie* was established particularly for the troops.[53] The victories of the Army of Italy were used to inspire the other armies.[54] On May 25 the Directory sent to Joubert, its able commissioner with the Sambre et Meuse, leaflets to be distributed widely among the enemy troops in order to incite them against the prince and to expose to them the perils of breaking the armistice that the Allies had asked for.[55] In June Joubert was instructed to encourage the timid Jourdan, who was disheartened because of the retreat of the left wing of his army.[56] The Directory's acknowledgment to Jourdan on June 28 of the passage of the Rhine near Strasbourg and the capture of the fort of Kehl by Moreau's army was largely devoted to encouragement and flattery.[57] Carnot added a personal postscript to this message. "The despatch of Moreau has just arrived. Forward, brave Jourdan; it is your turn! You see that your movements have not been useless. The moment is decisive. Seize it, and move like lightning, and strike like a thunder-bolt." Jourdan, however, was unable to execute the plans sent to him and the Directory had to remind him on July 6 that his task was to take a position parallel to the course of the Acher River and then to penetrate beyond the Rhine as far as possible, moving rapidly towards Franconia.[58]

The Directory acknowledged Moreau's successes at Gmund, Aalen, and Heydenheim, on August 12, and revealed to him its great conception for concerted action on the Danube.[59]

"The moment has come to unite the three armies of the Sambre et Meuse, the Rhine et Moselle, and of Italy, and direct them in a manner to conquer an honorable and permanent peace. . . . First, you are to defeat completely the army of Archduke Charles, pursue him energetically, cross the Danube and the Lech, take possession of the great road that goes from Innsbruck to Ratisbon and that passes by Munich and Neustadt, and support your Left on the Danube at Ingolstadt, . . . in order to cut off the retreat of Wurmser in the Tyrol." The Directory instructed Jourdan on the same day that he was to move on Ratisbon with the greatest celerity.[60]

Joubert was instructed on August 20 to circulate proclamations among the Bohemians and Hungarians in the Austrian Empire, taking advantage of their discontent against the oppressive régime of the House of Hapsburg to promise republican aid to their insurrection.[61]

Beurnonville was appointed to succeed Jourdan in the Sambre et Meuse in September. In addition to his own incompetency, Jourdan had been troubled by the jealousies of Pichegru who had been attached to the Sambre et Meuse after he had resigned as commander-in-chief of the Rhine et Moselle.[62] The Directory sent Beurnonville detailed instructions on October 1, concluding:

"It is not necessary to remind you that it is in moving against the flanks and the rear of the enemy that we can hope for success. The constant practice of this by General Bonaparte has given him the means of annihilating two Austrian armies in a single campaign in Italy."[63]

The matter of an effective command in the armies of the East long baffled the Directory. On October 12 Kléber was named to succeed Beurnonville in the Sambre et Meuse.[64] On the day before Christmas the two armies were united under the single command of Moreau.[65] On Christmas Day the Directory ordered Moreau to send 30,000 infantry and 1500 cavalry to Bonaparte, and justified this with the remark that "The conquest of Italy is so precious and offers such powerful means of delivering even more terrible blows to the Emperor. . . . Our position on the Rhine, nevertheless, remains important. The enemy will be forced to withdraw a great number of troops from there, to check the progress of Bonaparte."[66] On February 1, 1797, the two armies were again separated and Hoche was sent to command the Sambre et Meuse.[67] During this period Willot commanded the troops located in the Midi whence he sent long reports to the Directory of the political agitation in the departments of the Midi, with particular reference to the anarchists.[68] Willot was full of ideas for the solution of these local problems.

The military program of the Directory that was moving steadily in the direction of French imperialism achieved its greatest success in Italy, where the amazing victories of the young Bonaparte were confounding the enemy and astonishing the world. This young, undersized Corsican of the lesser nobility, who spoke French badly, had served a competent apprenticeship in the fighting of the Revolution. As a captain of artillery he had contributed materially to the recapture of Toulon from the English. Later, as commander of the artillery in the Army of Italy, he had shared in drafting the memorable plan of Colmar on May 21, 1794, for uniting the Armies of the Alps and of Italy, and abandoning the defense for a vigorous offense. He took a prominent part in the campaign that gradually edged the Austro-Sardinian forces from the Col di Tendi and the coast, back to Savona. Later he was instrumental in driving the Allies from the pass of Savona and from their position at Dega.

At the time of Thermidor Bonaparte was imprisoned because of suspicions arising from his friendliness with the younger Robespierre. In March, 1795 he was ordered to take an infantry command in the Vendée. Bonaparte delayed taking this post, and then pled ill health. In July, 1795 he drew up two important *mémoires* for the Committee of Public Safety. In the first he urged that the army of Italy receive strong reinforcements from the army of the Pyrenees; that Loano and Vado be recaptured; that Lombardy be overrun and its fertile territory exploited; that Mantua be blockaded; and that the Army penetrate the Tyrol, join hands with the Army of the Rhine, and compel the Emperor to accept terms from the Republic. The second *Mémoire* was more detailed. Bonaparte demonstrated that the way in which the French troops were then distributed in a semi-circle in a barren and mountainous country, made defense far more costly than a vigorous offense would be. The Allies, he said, must be separated by driving a wedge between the Austrian and Sardinian forces. He proceeded to fill in the details for the general plans suggested in the first *Mémoire*.

Within a month, on August 19, Bonaparte was called to Paris as assistant in the Topographic Bureau of the Committee of Public Safety, in close association with Carnot and Clarke. Schérer succeeded Kellermann as commander-in-chief of the Army of Italy, and with 16,000 troops from the Army of the Pyrenees, won the striking victory of Loano. He failed, however, to follow up the victory. Bonaparte was of material assistance to Barras on 13 Vendémiaire in protecting the Convention and in putting down the Paris insurrection. He continued to advise on the Italian campaign, and his counsel was incorporated in the instructions sent to Italy. Schérer, however, declined to follow the plans from Paris.[69] It was finally decided to supplant him with Bonaparte, himself. It seems that Carnot, as early as 1794, had seen the need for plans comparable to those proposed by Bonaparte, but had not been able to find the man to execute them.[70] Carnot was probably most responsible for the appointment of Bonaparte.[71] The decision of the Directory to appoint Bonaparte was ratified on March 2. In January he had become engaged to Joséphine de Beauharnais, a young widow of Creole extraction, and a habituée of the salon of Madame Tallien. Bonaparte was madly in love with Joséphine, and on March 9 they were married. After a brief honeymoon of two days, Bonaparte set out for Italy. He was twenty-seven years of age. He arrived in Nice on the 27th, and took command of the army. Officers whom he inherited in Italy included Augereau, Masséna, Sérurier, La Harpe, and Cervoni. Bonaparte took with him Berthier, Murat, Marmont, Junot, and Duroc. Bonaparte faced the Austrian and Sardinian armies in Italy. The former comprised 32,000 men, and the latter 20,000, and both had a considerable number of reserves, Beaulieu, a septuagenarian Belgian subject of the Emperor, commanded the Austrian forces.

Bonaparte wrote immediately, on March 28, to Carnot, to announce his cordial welcome by the army, and to suggest that Schérer, "a man, pure and enlightened, but tired out by the war which has affected his health," be given an appointment somewhere as an ambassador.[72] He assured Carnot that, in conformity with his wishes he had sent a company of light artillery to Nice.

Within a fortnight of his assumption of the command, Bonaparte won his first victory over the Austrians in the pass that separates the Alps from the Appennines, and on April 23 the Directory wrote to congratulate him on the victory of Montenotte.[73] Two days later the Directory sent him an important despatch touching upon the authority of the Directory, and outlining its general plans.[74] "A republican government," wrote the Directors, "knows how to acclaim those who render essential services to the *patrie*. . . . One more effort, Citizen General, and nothing can stop the triumphant advance of the army you command. . . . A great career opens up before you. . . .

"The instructions which the Directory gave to you when it appointed you commander-in-chief . . . have already established the bases of action. It outlines today, rapidly, the conduct that you should follow in the various circumstances that it is natural to suppose military events may put you. . . .

"The Directory reserves exclusively the power given it by the Constitution to negotiate peace; but it believes it is useful to inform you, Citizen General, of some of the principles on which it relies to establish it. An offensive and defensive alliance with the King of Sardinia would, no doubt, be of the greatest advantage to the Court of Turin. . . ." In another despatch to Bonaparte on the same day, the Directory requested exact and full reports of battles, topography, and movements of the troops for the purpose of writing the history of the triumphs of the Republic.[75] It concluded: "No rest until our enemies are completely dispersed."

Bonaparte had already written to Carnot on April 20 to announce the suspension of arms between the King of Sardinia and the French and to ask for his orders for the army, saying that his own proposal would be "to contact the Austrians, and give battle before your reply."[76] On May 1 the Directory sent Bonaparte a long despatch filled with instructions and observations.[77] Before this, on April 28, Bonaparte had forced the Piedmontese to sign the Armistice of Cherasco which detached the Court of Turin from the Coalition. Bonaparte did this on his own responsibility, without the participation of Saliceti, and in disobedience to the orders of the Directory, which reserved such matters to itself or to its Commissioners. Bonaparte again exceeded his authority on May 9 when he granted an armistice to the Duke of Parma in return for a heavy ransom. The Directory became alarmed at Bonaparte's assumption of authority and began trying to restrain him. This alarm prompted the Directory to propose the division of command in Italy.

In a long despatch to Bonaparte on May 7,[78] the Directory commented on the Armistice of Cherasco, giving its approval and remarking that it was advantageous from every point of view. It stated that it was pleased that Saliceti had been consulted before the conclusion of the armistice. "Such transactions," read the despatch, "in cases of urgency where the Directory itself cannot be consulted are particularly the prerogative of the Commissioner of the Government with the armies. The French generals, however, ought to be the only direct agents with whom the enemy generals should communicate. . . . The plan of campaign that you outlined in your letter of the 9th is worthy of the French and of the army which you command and lead to victory; but it presents major obstacles and insurmountable difficulties. . . . It is necessary to confine them to a circle less extensive than the one your propose. . . ." The Directory then proceeded to give both military and diplomatic instructions. A shorter despatch on the same day requested Bonaparte to send monuments of art to Paris.

Bonaparte wrote to Carnot on May 9 from Plaisance.[79] After giving a full report on recent military events, he remarked: "I owe you particular thanks for your courtesies to my wife; I commend her to you; she is a sincere patriot, and I love her madly. I hope, if all goes well, to send ten millions to Paris; that will do you no harm for the use of the army of the Rhine. Send me 4,000 unmounted cavalry. . . ."

The Directory arranged a public audience on May 9 to receive the captured Piedmontese and Austrian flags brought to Paris by Bonaparte's aides, Junot and Murat, and decreed a fête of Reconnaissance and Victory for May 29.[80] In the ceremony on the 9th the Minister of War eulogized the intrepid "young warrior who leads the French from victory to victory, and who combines the impetuosity of youth and the talent and the sang-froid of experience." After Junot had spoken, Carnot, as President, charged the two young officers to "rejoin your brothers in arms; crown your glory by the wisdom of your conduct, imitate the young and valiant general whom the Minister of War has just eulogized so justifiably. . . ." The two aides-de-camp were promoted by the Directory on the following day.[81]

The victory of Lodi on May 11 and the entrance into Milan followed in short order. Bonaparte announced to the Directory from Lodi on May 14 that he would next execute its orders for the movement on Leghorn and on Rome.[82] He then came to grips with the proposal to divide the army and establish two commands.[83] The plan was to bring all of the active part of the Army of the Alps down into the plains, amalgamate the two armies, and then divide them between Bonaparte and the venerable Kellermann, the victor of Valmy and now the commander-in-chief of the Army of the Alps. Kellermann would operate in the North and push on into the Tyrol, while Bonaparte would subjugate the South Italian states.

Bonaparte vigorously opposed this plan in his despatch and expressed his willingness to leave Italy. "I owe to the Republic," he wrote, "the sacrifice of all of my own ideas. If I have been put in bad odor in your opinion, my answer is in my heart and in my conscience. . . . I can only be useful if I am invested with the same esteem that you had for me in Paris. Whether I fight here or elsewhere is indifferent to me: to serve the *patrie*, to merit from posterity a page of our history, to give to the Government the proofs of my attachment and of my devotion, constitutes all of my ambition. I have begun with some glory, and I only desire to continue to be worthy of you. . . ."

In a letter from Carnot to Bonaparte on the following day, the Director said, "Let Italy see only Republicans in her conquerors, friends of order, full of admiration for all peoples."[84] The Directory strengthened itself in Italy on May 16, by announcing to Saliceti that Carnot's old friend, Garrau, would join him.[85] The Directory also congratulated Bonaparte on his recent victories,[86] and spurred him on to destroy completely the Austrian army. With Beaulieu crushed, "the House of Austria will think finally of peace, which hitherto the perfidious counsels of England have prevented. . . . Venice, as you have suggested to the Directory, ought to be treated as a neutral power, not as a friendly power."

The Directory waxed eloquent in a despatch to Bonaparte on May 18, acknowledging the victory of Lodi.[87] Instructions then followed for the entire route of Beaulieu and the conquest of Milan. The Directory also wrote of the actions to be concerted by the armies of the Alps and of Italy. The Directory had not yet abandoned its plan for a division in the command. It announced to Bonaparte that the armistice still operated on the Eastern front but that it would be broken as soon as the enemy began to divert troops to the Italian front. It was probably Carnot who prompted the question in the despatch: "Eh! What are your young engineering officers doing?"

Popular enthusiasm in Paris and in France for Bonaparte and the army of Italy was too great for the fearful Directory to insist upon its plan for a division in command. In its despatch to Bonaparte on May 21 acknowledging the taking of Cremona and all of Lombardy the Directory accepted Bonaparte's case against the dual command and continued the single command under him.[88] In concluding this despatch the Directory expressed magnanimously its confidence in Bonaparte by delegating considerable latitude to him, probably as a belated and grudging acknowledgement of the independence of his conduct in military operations and in diplomacy. "The rest of the military operations" the despatch reads, "towards Germany and in Mantua depend absolutely on your success against Beaulieu. The Directory recognizes how difficult it is to direct these operations from Paris and it leaves to you the widest possible latitude, while recommending the most extreme prudence. Its intention, nevertheless, is that the Army shall not penetrate the Tyrol until after the expedition into Southern Italy."

Carnot wrote to Bonaparte on the same day:[89] "The Directory, my dear General, to which I communicated your letter, has decided that it is suitable for you alone to continue to command the entire army of Italy." Carnot proceeded to discuss a more personal matter: "It is with great regret that we accede to the wish of citizeness Bonaparte who is going to join you. We feared that your solicitude for her might distract you from the tasks to which glory and the safety of the *patrie* call you, and for a long time we resisted her desire. . . ." He concluded on a practical, paternal note for the army: "Strive to rest the army in regions that are healthy and fresh; take care that they do not eat much acid fruit because this can bring on very dangerous disorders."

Meanwhile, Bonaparte had granted an armistice on his own responsibility to the Duke of Modena on the condition of a payment of 750,000 francs, the surrender of valuable stores, and a gift of valuable paintings. He then violated the neutrality of Venice and on May 27 he made a secret treaty with that state whereby the French were permitted to pursue the Austrians through Venetian territory and to besiege them in Venetian fortresses. Bonaparte laid siege to Mantua, while Vienna replaced Beaulieu by Wurmser, another old man, and detached 25,000 troops from the Rhine for massing in the Tyrol.

The tremendous contributions levied by Bonaparte against the states in Italy were an almost miraculous boon to the Directory with its fatal financial policy. These unexpected additions to the national treasury helped to reconcile the Directory to Bonaparte's independence, and to his usurpation of authority. On June 11 the Directory informed him that it could profitably dispose of the six millions that he had announced that he was sending to Paris.[90] In its letter of June 22 to Bonaparte, the Directory opined that he had probably already concluded an armistice with the Pope.[91] The armistice was actually signed on the following day.

Carnot wrote a friendly letter to Bonaparte on June 22, in which he re-stated a conviction to which he consistently held.[92] "I have received, worthy General, your letter of June 10. . . . Nothing is more in conformity with my wishes than to see the principles of democracy, which are the foundation of our government, propagate themselves among us; but it is necessary for us to guard against compromising our own liberty by attempting to establish that of others. The Directory believes that so long as our army remains in Italy it is essential to consider that country as a conquered territory. . . . We desire peace and we want it this year; do nothing that will postpone it. . . .

"The political horizon is clearing up materially at Paris and I take great satisfaction, my dear and worthy General, in assuring you that your triumphs have been more responsible for this than everything else. . . .

"Your dear wife, not yet fully recovered, will join you soon; she carries with her the particular regrets of my family; I beg of you to so assure her when you see her, as she will equally give to you the assurance of my inviolable attachment to everyone who belongs to you."

Two days later passports were issued by the Directory to Joséphine, to four persons attached to her service, and to certain others, including Junot, aide-de-camp, Joseph Bonaparte, and to Nicolas Clary, brother-in-law of Bonaparte.[93] Bonaparte concluded a letter to Carnot from Bologna on July 2 on an intimate note: "I am told that Madame Carnot is in confinement; if this be true, I beg of you to accept my congratulations."[94]

The Directory acknowledged the news of the occupation of Leghorn on July 11.[95] Shortly thereafter, the Directory severely reminded Bonaparte of its orders that regular and exact reports on the military situation and historical bulletins were to be furnished to it.[96] The Directory saw "with regret that, since the beginning of the campaign, it had received nothing of the nature required. It is important hereafter that this task be scrupulously followed and executed in conformity with the model submitted. . . ." In its session of July 31 the Directory took cognizance of the evil rumors prevalent suspecting the motives and the conduct of Bonaparte, insinuating particularly that he was working only for himself and that he was not accounting accurately for the contributions levied in Italy.[97] The Directory decided to write to Bonaparte to "deny these perfidious insinuations and to assure him that it maintained the confidence and admiration that his loyalty and rare military talents inspired in all true republicans." In its letter to Bonaparte the Directory stated that it was well acquainted with Bonaparte's principles and with his "inviolable attachment to the Republic."[98]

Before replying formally to this assurance of the Directory's faith in him, Bonaparte wrote more intimately, though no doubt equivocally, to Carnot on August 9, from Verona:[99] ". . . The heat is excessive here, and my health is somewhat impaired. If there is a single honest man of good faith in France who suspects my political intentions and doubts my conduct, I shall renounce instantly the happiness of serving my country. Three or four months of obscurity will subdue envy, will restore my health, and will prepare me all the more advantageously to fulfill whatever tasks the Government will confide to me. . . . In entering into public life I adopted this principle: Everything for the *patrie*.

"I beg of you to believe the sentiments of esteem and of friendship that I have professed for you."

In acknowledging the victory of Castiglione, on August 12, the Directory outlined its further military plans to Bonaparte. The young conqueror was to push his conquests to Innsbruck, shattering Wurmser's army in the process, thus leaving nothing but Austria for the enemy troops to fall back upon. In order to assist this drive, Moreau, who had pushed Prince Charles back upon Donauworth, would have his right occupy the line from Innsbruck to Ingolstadt. This would cut the communication between the imperial armies of Italy and Germany and would facilitate the French advance to the Inn. Meanwhile, General Kléber, who was temporarily commanding the Sambre et Meuse during the illness of its commander-in-chief, would march on Ratisbon, after having dispersed the army corps of General Wartensleben. In conclusion, the Directory urged Bonaparte to increase the contributions and to send to Paris the amount beyond that necessary to support the army [100]

Carnot bared his feelings in a letter on September 19 to Bonaparte, prompted by the latter's victory of Bassano: [101] "Although accustomed to the most extraordinary achievements on your part, our hopes have been surpassed by the victory of Bassano. What glory for you, immortal Bonaparte! What a terrible blow to haughty Austria! She would not be able to rise again if all our armies had had the same success as that of Italy; but the miserable retreat of Jourdan disconcerts all of our plans. . . . However, Beurnonville, who replaces Jourdan, comes with considerable reinforcements. . . .

"It is in your own energies that we find fresh means. Advance to Trieste if your left is protected and if your rear is safeguarded. . . ."

In its despatch to Bonaparte on September 29 the Directory commented on the Pope's refusal to accept the conditions of peace, and stated that it would not modify them.[102] It repeated that it wanted to terminate the campaign by the capture of the besieged Mantua, which would help in the dictation of terms to central Italy. On October 12 the Directory replied[103] to a letter from Bonaparte on October 3, in which he had accused Willot of being a royalist.[104] The Directory stated that Willot's distinguished services in helping pacify the Vendée had destroyed all suspicions of his loyalty to the Republic.

By now Alvintzy had succeeded Wurmser as commander-in-chief of the Austrian forces in Italy. The Archduke Charles had severely defeated the French in Germany and was able to send reinforcements into the Tyrol. The Directory informed Bonaparte on October 12 that indiscipline and the desire to pillage had been the principal causes for the retreat of the Republican armies in Germany and that he should be on his guard against the same evils in Italy.[105]

Bonaparte took time to refer to family concerns in a letter to

Carnot on October 25 from Verona:[106] "I have received, my dear Director, your letter of October 8. You have seen, from the letter of my brother [Lucien] what a swelled head he has. . . . I ask your pardon for troubling you with these petty domestic annoyances. . . . I beg you to present my respects to your family."

The Directory took the important step in a secret session on November 15 of appointing General Clarke, director of the historical and topographical cabinet, as envoy extraordinary to Vienna for the purpose of proposing a general armistice between the two powers.[107] At the same time, the Directory sent a despatch to the Emperor proposing such an armistice.[108] On the next day, the Directory gave instructions to Clarke.[109] He was to go to Vienna by way of Italy so that he could consult with Bonaparte. He was not only to arrange an armistice but he was also to propose to the Emperor a congress of ministers plenipotentiary to conclude a general peace. The armistice was to be made for as long a period as possible, but at least to May 20, 1797. It should guarantee the status quo of the moment.

Bonaparte gave proof of his solicitude for the bereaved relatives of his men in a letter of November 19 to Carnot:[110] "You will find enclosed, my dear Director, two letters which I beg you to read and transmit to their addresses. That to the widow of Muiron [announcing the death of her husband at Arcole] ought to be delivered to her by a relative who could prepare her for this bad news." The other letter was to General Clarke announcing the death of his nephew, Elliott, at Arcole. In a letter to Carnot from Milan on December 28, Bonaparte again referred to the widow Muiron:[111] "I recommend to you, Citizen Director, the widow of Citizen Muiron, whom this brave young man left, in confinement, in order to rush to the defense of the *patrie*. I have made a request to the Directory in her behalf that I beg of you to consider seriously."

Carnot wrote to Bonaparte on December 29 in great concern lest Bonaparte conclude that he was an "enemy to his glory" because of certain "absurd" and "impudent" stories that certain "perverse writers" were circulating.[112] "It will suffice, I believe," wrote Carnot, "to assure you that all this is but an affair of intrigue and cabal, and that you, Bonaparte, your wife, and all that belong to you, have no friends more warm, more sincere, more absorbed in your personal affairs than I and mine. Your interests have become those of the Republic, your glory that of the entire nation. . . . Adieu, my dear General, count on me as I count on you, along with all wise men who love the Republic for her own sake and not for theirs.

"A thousand remembrances from my family to your dear helpmate."

Bonaparte was reminded by the Directory in a despatch of December 30 that the new campaign should be opened, if the Court of Vienna was not going to welcome the propositions Clarke was authorized to make.[113] "You know our desire for peace;" wrote the Directors, "it is live and constant; . . . our moderation, however, must not decline to weakness." The despatch went on to reveal that General Clarke had reported on the state of mind and loyalty of Bonaparte's general officers. "These indicate certain necessary reforms," the despatch stated, "but you should be the one to name the persons who ought to be included in these changes, whether their services have become useless to the Republic, or whether they have become more dangerous than useful. The strength of an army derives principally from its moral organization and from the choice of its leaders."

Early in the new year, the Directory gave its approval to certain important political arrangements largely consummated by Bonaparte.[114] "The peace with Naples was in part the result of one of your despatches," wrote the Directors, "in which you developed all the advantages of its conclusion. . . . Your opinion on Rome seems to us to be right. . . . The arrangement proposed for the evacuation of Leghorn merits equally our approbation." Another despatch from the Directory on the same day approved Bonaparte's recommendations for promotions.[115]

The Directory informed Bonaparte on January 19, 1797, that General Clarke was to collaborate with him in all diplomatic activities so that there would be no contradictions between these and the military operations.[116] In the following days the general instructions of Clarke for negotiations with the Emperor were modified and enlarged,[117] and he was told to decide on no proposition without the advice and consent of Bonaparte.[118] It is apparent that the proposed preliminary articles of peace were drafted by Bonaparte, in concert with Clarke, and approved by Barras.[119]

Bonaparte replied to Carnot's letter warning him of the malicious gossip that sought to alienate them, on January 28 from Verona:[120] "I received your letter, my dear Director, on the field of battle of Rivoli. I have read with pity in the papers all that one debits to my account. . . . I believe that you know me too well to imagine that I can be influenced by all of this. I have always been satisfied with the marks of friendship that you have given to me and to mine, and I shall always preserve a deep appreciation of them. . . . The esteem of a small number of persons like you, that of my colleagues and of the soldiers, sometimes also the opinion of posterity, and above all the promptings of my own conscience and the welfare of my country, alone interest me."

In the face of the general misgivings concerning the disinterestedness of Bonaparte, Carnot wrote to him on the very same day that Bonaparte had defended the purity of his feelings and motives in his letter to Carnot.[121] "Return and enjoy the benediction of the entire French people" wrote Carnot, "who call you its benefactor; return and astonish the Parisians by your moderation and your philosophy. A thousand projects—each more absurd than the other—are attributed to you; no one believes that a man who has done such great things can come down to live as a simple citizen. As for me, I believe that it is only Bonaparte become simple citizen who can reveal the general Bonaparte in all his grandeur.

"Believe me to be the surest and the most inviolable of your friends."

There was little correspondence between Carnot and Bonaparte between this time and Carnot's exile after 18 Fructidor. Bonaparte wrote Carnot a short letter from Goritz on March 22, in which he concluded, "My respects to your family."[122] His next letter to Carnot was on 17 Fructidor (September 3) and contained only military news. Carnot instructed Clarke on May 5,[123] and Moreau on June 13,[124] to try to obtain the release of La Fayette, Bureaux-Pusy,[125] and La Tour-Maubourg from the prison of Olmutz. On August 1 Carnot wrote to Bonaparte for the same purpose.[126]

The fortunes of war continued in favor of the French in Italy. When Mantua fell on February 2 after a siege of seven months the conquest of Italy was virtually complete. Archduke Charles succeeded Alvintzy in command of the Austrians. Bonaparte was reinforced by troops from the Army of the Rhine under Bernadotte, and he now had more than 70,000 men in Italy. On February 19 the Pope sued for peace. On April 18 Bonaparte compelled the Austrians to sign preliminaries of peace at Leoben, within eighty miles of Vienna. Clarke was in Italy at the time, and Bonaparte took this important step on his own authority.[127] Carnot and Letourneur alone in the Directory completely approved the preliminaries of Leoben.[128] The Emperor gave up all claims to his Belgian Provinces and "recognized the limits of France as decreed by the laws of the French Republic." For his losses in the North, he was to receive an "equitable indemnity" on the signing of a definitive treaty. The French were to restore other Hapsburg lands and were to retire to Italy. Peace was to be made definitely in a general Congress. In the middle of May, Venice, after a campaign of pressure, treachery, and intrigue, fell to the French and became virtually a French dependency. In June Genoa was transformed into a republican state under French control. It was subsequently named the Ligurian Republic. In the previous October the Cispadine Republic had been established to embrace Modena, Bologna, and Ferrara. In December Bonaparte had set up the Lombard Republic. This became the Cisalpine Republic on July 9, 1797, and on July 15 the Cispadine and Cisalpine Republics were united.

After 18 Fructidor, Bonaparte dictated the Peace of Campo Formio on October 17. Austria got Venice and the whole of Venetia as far as the lines of the Adige and the lower Po, together with Dalmatia and Venetian Istria. France got the Ionian Isles. The Emperor renounced all claims to the Netherland Provinces. He recognized the Cisalpine Republic, and promised to call a Congress at Rastadt for the settlement of German affairs. The secret articles stipulated that the Emperor would use his influence at the Congress to procure the extension of the eastern boundary of France to the Rhine, while the French Government was to help him acquire the archbishopric of Salzburg and a frontier strip of Bavaria.

This treaty was signed by Bonaparte alone for France. Clarke had been recalled in disgrace after 18 Fructidor because of his connections with Carnot. France was now on the high road to imperialism and Carnot's consistent championship of a policy of no foreign conquests beyond the natural frontiers or what was necessary for the safety of France was relegated to the historical discard. Bonaparte left Italy in the middle of November for Paris where greater imperial plans were to germinate.

Chapter IX

18 FRUCTIDOR

AMIDST THE frivolity and luxury of the period of the Directory the Carnots lived simply in the Luxembourg. Madame Carnot's two sisters and their families lived with them in their Directorial apartment. Carnot's wife was in poor health during much of the period. The three sisters became pregnant at about the same time. The Director's first child, Nicolas Léonard-Sadi, was born on June 1, 1796.[1] Carnot humored the religious beliefs of his family and let his children be baptised quietly. Those who gathered habitually in the Carnot salon were scientists, artists, and writers: Bougainville, Berthollet, Prony, Costaz, Charles Bossut, Fourcroy, Valmont de Bomare, Lemercier, Lebrun, and Beffroy de Reigny (Cousin Jacques). Two long-time friends and benefactors also frequented the Carnot home. These were M. de Longpré, his old professor of mathematics, and the dame Delorme, who as the head of the d'Aumont household had befriended Carnot when he first came to Paris as a student.

The political atmosphere of the Carnot home was one of toleration. Beffroy de Reigny, who wrote as Cousin Jacques, was an old friend of Carnot, having met him first in 1786 in Arras. He was the medium for many of Carnot's anonymous benevolences. Beffroy de Reigny was no friend of the Revolution and this was well known. Carnot's friendship for Beffroy de Reigny was used against him at the time of 18 Fructidor. In the suppressed third volume of his *Dictionnaire néologique,* Cousin Jacques has left an intimate picture of Carnot.[2]

He, a very pronounced patriot, and I, a well-known aristocrat, maintained an acquaintanceship so little suspect that one could not say that any partisanship . . . entered into it whatsoever. . . . I had the permission of bringing on Mondays one or two friends of my own choice to dine with the Carnots. I did not abuse the privilege, but from time to time I profited by it to bring persons, particularly of talent, who wanted to know him. I took d'Alayric, la Houssaie, Valmont de Bomare, and even merchants, respectable by their habits and their probity. Everyone was received there with frankness and simplicity. An officer, arriving from his department, imagined that the pomp of the Director Carnot would equal that of the kings. He was singularly astonished at the simplicity, the frugality, the patriarchal good will that prevailed there, and he was still speaking of it two years later. . . .

Portalis and Tronson-Duçoudry,[3] who came to see me often, drove in a carriage with me and my family to dine at the Luxembourg. Our guests were received without ceremony, without fawning, without affectation, but with that decency and that patriarchal simplicity of which Carnot was never able to rid himself completely, even when he wished to appear very serious. . . .

His great delight was to relieve the unfortunate anonymously; I do not know how many persons of all parties I have helped for him, and always with the express command of absolute silence. . . .

One saw in his home Royalists, Jacobins, Moderates; everyone enjoyed himself, because no one was permitted to express extreme opinions, and because tolerance was the spirit of the place.

On certain fixed days he received the most distinguished savants, particularly the mathematicians, from seven to ten in the evening. . . .

One knows his songs, his couplets, his fugitive poems; I put twenty-one of his songs to music. . . . One recognizes in the literary productions of Carnot a style, flowing and pure, and a spirit, delicate and cultivated. . . .

As for the morality of Carnot, it suffices for me to say that I have never seen in my whole life a son more respectful, a father more tender, a husband more obliging, a friend more frank, and a man more decent; never was a word spoken in his home that could shock modesty, and one was not even permitted those pleasantries with a double meaning, that usage often seems to tolerate in society that poses as respectable.

Joséphine Bonaparte had been an occasional visitor to the Carnot home and Carnot had taken a sincere interest in her welfare. Her last letter to Carnot was dated 18 Fructidor, and was intended to introduce Serbelloni to Carnot.[4] Joséphine wrote that she wanted to send some statuettes and vases of alabaster and marble that she had picked up in Florence and Leghorn to

Carnot and to his sisters, but that it was impossible to send them. She concluded: "Adieu, amiable citizen, count on my real and sincere devotion." As a postscript, she added: "Remember me, I beg of you, to your brothers, and I embrace your charming children. Be good enough . . . to accept a case of Turin *liqueur,* which M. Serbelloni is commissioned to give to you for me."

Carnot, unlike so many others during the Convention and the Directory, did not materially aggrandize his fortune. He had listed his possessions on September 29, 1795 in conformity with the law of September 26.[5] These possessions consisted of a vineyard property in the village of Bouzeron, near Chagny, Saône-et-Loire, a heritage from his mother, which before the Revolution brought in from five- to six-hundred livres a year; the "dot" of Sophie Dupont, fixed by the contract at 30,000 livres, carrying interest at 1500 livres; furniture, effects, and silver valued at 4000 livres. In 1795, he said, this was all that he had left, excepting that, because of his absence and neglect, he had lost totally the income from his mother's inheritance, and the interest on his wife's "dot" was but 1500 livres in assignats. While he was in the Directory he invested in a farm near Montdidier, but this was sequestrated on 18 Fructidor.[6]

Carnot maintained his deep interest in science during the Directory. The Directors attended the first public session of the National Institute on April 4, 1796, which was held in the Salle des Antiques and lasted for four hours. Vandermonde, one of the members, died shortly thereafter, and Carnot was elected to fill his place. In May the Directory had ordered 1500 copies of Bossut's *Differential and Integral Calculus* printed by the Government and three hundred copies sent to the engineering officers.[7] Bossut was a friend of Carnot, a member of the National Institute, and examiner of the military corps of engineers. At the time of his own election to the Institute in August, Carnot published his lucid *Reflexions sur la metaphysique du calcul infinitesimal,* which he had written some years before.[8] Carnot displayed a great interest in the new *École Polytechnique,* as well as in the National Institute. He was constantly in the company of the leading scientists of the time.

In his periodic presidency of the Directory Carnot was occasionally called upon to speak formally for the Government. At the celebration of the Fête of the Victories on May 29, 1796, at the Champ de Mars, Carnot gave the principal address.[9] This, of course, was a further revelation of his thought. "We exist only as a result of a long train of blessings," he said, "and our life is nothing but a continual exchange of services. . . . He who is a good son and a good father is also a good citizen: he loves his *patrie* and joyfully renders it the tribute of his services; he rejoices in affording his brothers the protection he has received." After praising the "courageous philosophers who prepared the Revolution by their writings, breaking the chains of slavery and expelling the furies of fanaticism," Carnot eulogized the armies: "A young republic arms its children to protect its independence; nothing can withstand their impetuosity. . . . After a host of victories, they push back our boundaries to the limits set by nature . . . and make of an oppressed enemy nation a free and allied people. . . . The ardor of the soldier is seconded by the genius and the audacity of their leaders."

Carnot was President on the occason of the first annual celebration of 9 Thermidor (July 27, 1796) when the celebrations of July 14, and August 10, were combined with this commemoration of 9 Thermidor. The entire day was given over to the fête. The Directory led the procession to the *École Militaire* where a heavy rain halted proceedings for half an hour. The sun then came out and the weather was glorious. On an outdoor tribune in front of the *École Militaire,* in a "profound silence," Carnot delivered a fervid republican speech, in the florid style of the Revolution, while it was still in full tide:[10] "The excess of oppression brought its own end . . . . The liberty which receives our homage merits the fidelity of all friends of humanity. She is a child of Nature, gentle as she is, mother of tender affections as well as of sublime virtues; her cult is as pure as it is simple, her salutary maxims are lodged in our hearts, where they are ineffacable. . . . Frenchmen, worthily conserve this gift of heaven, this liberty that our constitution assures us, that guarantees for us the innumerable triumphs of our arms and that has determined forever the great epochs which we celebrate today. . . ."

The report of the affair concludes that "this discourse was acclaimed by the cries of *Vive la Republique*, a thousand times repeated. Then the President of the Directory lighted on the altar of the Republic a flame representing the sacred fire of Liberty, while the Conservatory of Music chanted the Hymn of Liberty."

In the early period of the Directory there were two parties among the Directors. Carnot and Letourneur wanted an early and definitive peace, while the other three wanted a continuance of the war, partly because they felt that their power needed war and expansion, and partly because of their fear of the generals, if released from military activities. There was considerable enmity between these two groups.[11] The latter group, with the majority in the Five-Hundred, wanted to go on being revolutionary, even at the expense of alienating public opinion, while Carnot and Letourneur were sympathetic to the policy of moderation and justice championed by the majority in the Council of Elders. There was uncertainty among the public as to the factions in the Directory and this increased the general anxiety.[12] In one café in the early winter of 1795 the patrons dubbed all of the Directors but Carnot as royalists in disguise.[13] In the early spring of 1797 there seemed to be an accord between the Jacobin journals and Barras, between the royalist journals and Reubell, and between the moderate papers and Carnot.[14] In May, 1797, Carnot was praised in certain quarters as the author of the victorious military plans and also because he was inaccessible to advances, and was incorruptible even vis-a-vis his own family.[15] Partisan lines were steadily tightening. Pichegru had been given a leave on February 6, and he had been in Paris since the end of March, where he was the object of advances and solicitations from various parties, particularly those hostile to the Republic. The Directory, on April 3, appointed him ambassador to Sweden.[16] Pichegru made no acknowledgment to this appointment for two weeks. He then accepted it in principle but asked for some months of rest. He never assumed the post. In a secret session on April 22 the Directory ordered the arrest and exile of Madame de Staël, reported on the verge of reentering France to foment new troubles.[17] She was sympathetic with such Moderates as Lanjuinais, Daunou, Cabanis, Boissy-d'Anglas, Dupont de Nemours, and Lacretelle jeune.

In 1796 there were two well-defined royalist groups. One of these supported the claims of the Pretender, the Comte de Provence, who was in direct line after the dealth of the Dauphin. The Pretender's cause was being subsidized by the English, through Wickham, their minister in Switzerland. The future Louis XVIII issued a proclamation promising the restoration of absolutism in France. In the fall his agents in Paris began plotting a military overthrow of the Directory.[18] The Pretender's conduct was most inept at the time. The plotters approached Hoche in October, but he declined their advances, and informed the Directory of what had happened. The plot failed, but the Council of War gave fourteen acquittals and light sentences to the others implicated.

The constitutional royalists, on the other hand, feared the Pretender because of his promise to restore absolutism. These royalists wanted a return to the Constitution of 1791. They could not unite on a candidate. One faction was for Orléans, the "Austrian" faction favored the marriage of Louis XVI's daughter, Mme. Royale, to the youngest Austrian archduke, the famous Archduke Charles, while a third group favored the Spanish Bourbon family.[19] The Constitutional Royalists included such figures as General Dumas, Portalis, Troncon-Duçoudry in one group, and Le Mérer, Durand de Maillane, Henri-Larivière, and Thibaudeau in another. This latter group met regularly in the rue Clichy. Negotiations between these Royalists and the Pretender were futile.

General Dumas often dined with the Carnots. He and Carnot agreed on the necessity of a definitive peace. Dumas met weekly with a dozen of the best men among the Constitutional Royalists. These wanted Delacroix replaced as Minister of Foreign Affairs, and Dumas was named to persuade Carnot to present their suggestions. Carnot agreed, and suggested Barthélemy to the Directory, but the Triumvirate decided to keep Delacroix. This rebuff was the first case of disagreement between the Directory and the Constitutional Royalists. When the Directory proposed laws for the censorship of the press on October 30, 1796, these Royalists strongly opposed them, believing that the Directory wanted to control opinion in its favor. The legislation was not passed. Carnot was consistently opposed to the censorship of the press during the Directory.[20] After the defeat of the press laws the Constitutional Royalists urged the Directory to permit free elections in the impending elections.

During the period of rapprochement with the Right, the Directory had given up its anti-clericalism. Carnot was eager for the religious pacification of France and wanted peace with Rome so that the Pope might help bring the Catholics into the Republic.[21] That the Pope was amenable was indicated by his letter *Pastoralis Sollicitudo* of July 4, 1796. This letter called for cooperation with the civil government. When negotiations broke down between Rome and France the letter remained unfulfilled. Both the constitutional bishops and the submissive refractory clergy seemed to be in accord with the letter. But the royalist, unsubmissive refractory priests were stupefied and enraged at the papal letter. After the downfall of Babeuf, the Directory had sponsored liberal and tolerant legislation in favor of the clergy. Only on the eve of the elections did they discover that this legislation had but contributed to the development of Royalism. This prompted the Directory to begin again to oppose the clerical peril.

The elections of 1797 were the first "electoral consultation" since the establishment of the Directory. The complicated system of elections began on March 31. The issue of the elections was the character of the majority in the two Councils. The present majority came from the two-thirds of the Conventionals and one-half of these were now retiring. After the elections one Director would retire by lot, and would be replaced by the Councils.

The Directory labored under no illusions and turned to every expedient it could think of to guarantee its majority and reduce the number of royalist deputies. It tried to restrict the franchise even further than it was. A proposal was made to have the new Director chosen before the elections. When nothing came of this Reubell proposed an immediate secret lot in the Directory and the resignation of the member so designated by chance. This would force an election in the current Councils. The Directors, however, would not agree to this. The sessions of the Directory in this period were stormy and the journal *Gardien de la Constitution*, reporting the heated session held during the night of April 4-5, spoke particularly of the "courage of Carnot," in defending the "Constitution which he swore to defend against all attacks no matter from what quarter they came."[22] On that occasion Letourneur stood with him, and they won over another to constitute a majority. On May 14 the Clichyens got a law passed obliging the Directors to conduct the lot publicly. Larevellière and Reubell protested this and tried to obstruct its promulgation, but Carnot and Barras combined to compel their consent. The expedients of the Directory availed little. The pure Royalists and the constitutional Royalists concluded an electoral alliance. Even Louis XVIII, the Pretender, issued a conciliatory manifesto. The clergy, particularly the returned *émigrés,* were active, supported by English money. Pichegru, who was in indirect contact with Wickham, was an important figure in the elections.

The newly-elected Third was unfavorable to the majority in the Directory. Of the 216 Conventionals who retired only eleven were reelected and two of these were members of the Clichy group (Clichyens). Very few republicans were elected. Even in Paris those elected favored a modified monarchy. The new Legislative Corps was largely made up of men who had had political and administrative positions under the Constitutional Monarchy before August 10. The Bouches-du-Rhône elected General Willot, who had openly protected the royalists and *émigrés.*[23] He was to be a very determined royalist in the Legislative Corps. When he knew how the elections had gone, Reubell wanted to invalidate them and hold new ones in which the returned *émigrés* would be disfranchised. Discussions in the Directory became violent.

Mathiez says that Carnot became surrounded by Royalists, more or less disguised, such as Dumas, Lacuée, and Beffroy de Reigny.[24] He and they agreed on the necessity of peace. Carnot also believed it was possible to work with the new majority in the Legislative Corps and to make the necessary concessions. He did not have the repulsion against the priests that Larevellière and Reubell had, and he found it difficult to fear the priests. He was ready to make peace with Austria and England, and to restore French conquests.[25]

The new Third took its place on May 20. The Council of Five-Hundred elected Pichegru president, and the Council of Elders elected Barbé-Marbois. The majority of the members did not want to overturn the Government, at least not at once. They preferred to temporize for a time. A minority, however, whom Thibaudeau called the "White Jacobins" wanted immediate action. Dumas and his friends restrained the impatience of these Clichyens:[26] Jourdan des Bouches-du-Rhône, Camille Jordan, Boissy-d'Anglas, Merson, Pastoret, Imbert-Colomès, Willot, Le Mérer, and Quatrienière. The Directory was supported by the army, the purchasers of national property, and the army contractors. The Legislative Corps had the whip hand through the control of funds.

The Clichyens, believing that Carnot had prevented the coup of Reubell and Barras against them, tried to win Carnot over. They wanted a majority in the Directory. They were favorable to Letourneur, but the lot fell to him. Carnot favored the election of Cochon or of Bénézech to the Directory.[27] Dumas and his friends, and the Clichyens supported the candidacy of Barthélemy, the minister to Switzerland who had negotiated the Treaty of Basle.[28] There is evidence that Barthélemy was a convinced Royalist.[29] The Five-Hundred put Barthélemy at the head of their list with 309 votes out of 458 voting. On May 26 the Elders elected him with 138 votes out of 218 voting. Barthélemy hastened from Switzerland to his new post, and the Royalists fêted him along the route. Barthélemy did not warm up to the Directors, not even to Carnot.[30] In his *Mémoires* he wrote: "The idea of seating myself alongside the great rascals who occupied the Luxembourg revolted my soul."[31] He remained aloof and isolated and only infrequently participated in the deliberations. Instead of being a help to Carnot, he was a "dead weight." Carnot, as President of the Directory, had welcomed Barthélemy on June 6:[32] ". . . Your wide acquaintanceships and the spirit of toleration that characterizes you, are a sure guarantee of the success with which you will work in concert with us. . . . Having been far from the theatre of the factions that have so long afflicted our country, you can judge with impartiality, and the efforts that you join to ours to suppress them will impart to them a character infinitely favorable to their destruction."

That Carnot pursued an independent line, and was sensitive to the crisis in the government is attested by the letter he wrote on July 2 to his friend, the Constitutional Royalist Mathieu Dumas: [33] "I have never departed from this principle, that a constitutional government can only be founded upon confidence. . . . I cannot adequately express to you my concern: everything presents to me the vision of dissolution; anarchy and royalism dispute which will bathe in the blood of republicans; everywhere these [republicans] suffer the blows of fanaticism, of the *émigrés*, of Babeuvism."

The Directory and the Legislative Corps clashed in July over the question of the personnel of the ministers. Although the Ministers were appointed by and responsible to the Directory, the Legislative Corps believed that the Ministers should be persons in accord with the will of the majority in the two Councils. Carnot agreed with this contention for the purpose of securing effective government. It seems that Dumas, Portalis, and Siméon finally waited upon Barras to gain his consent to certain changes in the ministries, and that Barras, whose "principal objection was his inveterate hatred" for Carnot, at last gave his consent, only to break his word later.[34]

On July 17 Carnot moved to dismiss the ministers of foreign affairs, justice, marine, and finance and replace them by men acceptable to the majority in the Legislative Corps.[35] In replying to Reubell's objections, Carnot stated that while the Legislative Corps had no constitutional right to share in the appointment of the ministers "without harmony between the Directory and the majority in the Legislative Corps, the Constitution could not function."[36] Carnot and Barthélemy were outvoted on this issue and from that moment the schism in the Directory was irremediable.[37] These two did not believe in either the royalist or the clerical peril, and Carnot wanted only to oppose the factions with the laws. The other three believed in the peril and saw no other means to adjure it than by a *coup d'état*."[38]

Talleyrand-Périgord received a letter from the Directory on July 18, asking him to succeed Charles Delacroix as Minister of Foreign Affairs, and on the following day he assumed office. Carnot alone had opposed this appointment in strong terms: "Let no one mention him! He betrayed his Order, his King, his God! This Catiline of a priest will sell out the Directory completely."[39] But in Talleyrand "Reubell admired a diplomat, Larevellière chose a convert, Barras sought an accomplice,"[40] and the deed was done. Ironically, as President of the Directory Carnot had to sign the appointment.[41] A week later Schérer was named Minister of War.

Bonaparte interjected himself threateningly into the political crisis in a letter from Milan on July 18, in which he proclaimed the devotion of the soldiers to the Constitution of 1795, and their alarm over the trend of events as they discovered them in letters from home.[42] "I believe that the peace and tranquillity in the armies depends upon the Council of Five-Hundred," he wrote. "If this leading body of the Republic continues to lend a willing ear to the Clichyens, it will lead as directly to the disorganization of the Government; we will have no more peace, and this army will be almost unanimously motivated by the desire to march to the aid of liberty and the Constitution of 1795." In a letter on July 27 Bonaparte announced that he was permitting Augereau to go to Paris on personal affairs, but that he would carry with him petitions to the Directory from the soldiers, in which they revealed their "absolute devotion to the Constitution of 1795 and to the Directory."[43]

Before this, on July 11, Bonaparte had sent his aide-de-camp Lavallette to Paris to observe affairs, remain aloof, and report back to him. Lavallette reported a conversation which he had with Carnot:[44] "It is impossible," Carnot said, "to go on any longer on the revolutionary road. If a lasting system of moderation is not adopted, all is lost. . . . The faction against which I am struggling does not blush to charge me with being a royalist; and nevertheless, no one is more convinced than I am of Pichegru's treason, and the necessity of punishing him; but they want to govern France as they would a club. . . . My situation is painful; for I am forced to move with a party in which, exclusive of Pichegru, there are men to whom I am obnoxious, who perhaps conspire with him, and who will ruin the Republic without obtaining the secret aim of their endeavours."

Lavallette urged Bonaparte to remain neutral in the violence planned against the Councils. Bonaparte finally decided to do nothing, except to permit Augereau to go to Paris. He ceased corresponding with the Directory, and he held back the transmission of money. The Triumvirate in the Directory turned to Hoche who responded favorably to their advances.[45] On July 16 he was nominated Minister of War, and on the 18th he reached Paris. Troops were concentrating around Paris, and when Carnot inquired severely of Hoche what they were doing there, the latter withdrew in confusion.[46] After personal interviews with Carnot, Larevellière, and Barras, Hoche left Paris in utter disgust. The opposition then discovered that he was not yet thirty and so was ineligible for a ministerial post.

Barras turned to Bonaparte for a general to assist in the intended coup. It was then that Bonaparte let Augereau, whom he did not quite trust, go to Paris. In the meantime, the Directory had made Schérer Minister of War. Augereau arrived in Paris on August 5, and three days later was appointed to command the Military Division of Paris. Augereau made no secret of the fact that he had come to Paris to kill the Royalists, and that he wanted five or six heads.[47] His fellow conspirators were alarmed at his enthusiasm and tried to restrain his impetuosity. Bernadotte suddenly appeared from Italy with colors captured at Rivoli. The Directory received him on August 27. Bernadotte and Augereau did not get on well together. Kléber, a consistent republican, was also in Paris at the time.

Carnot, as President of the Directory, made an important speech in the Directorial palace on August 10, commemorating the great August 10, 1792.[48] His words are particularly illuminating in the face of the royalist sympathies and connections of which he was accused, and for which he was to be proscribed and exiled within a month.

". . . . In these short years, what memorable events follow one upon the other! What triumphs! What tragic scenes! What a combination of sublimity and feebleness! What prejudices destroyed! What a harvest of talent! What united efforts to try to crush the new-born liberty! What cowardly attempts to destroy the Republic! What vipers smothered in the arms of the giant! . . .

"Misfortune on those," he continued, "who conceive the plan to restore the throne!" He doubted that those who had helped destroy the monarchy and establish the Republic would now aid the "vile instruments of a faction that would destroy liberty," and the imprescriptible rights of the people.

"No, Frenchmen! You will not forget" he said, "what it cost you to become free; you would not hazard the same catastrophies, or even greater, to again become slaves." He warned against those who argued that it was easy to substitute a hereditary for a Constitutional Government, but who neglected to speak of the deadly opposition the desperate republicans would put up, or of the difficulty of reestablishing the inequalities and the feudal institutions that are the foundation of monarchies, or of the effort to snatch away the national property from those who had acquired it under the guarantee of the laws, or of the sanguinary struggle that would ensue between the pretenders to the throne. He elaborated many other essential readjustments, punishments, and banishments that would result if the Kings were restored. He swore that the Government, despite differences of opinion on other matters, would stand united in preventing any movement to overturn the Republic. He concluded by declaring that "peace would be achieved when the enemies of the Republic discover that they have no support among us, and when all of us are convinced that the happiness of the people is in the extinction of all parties, that the people wants tranquillity, that it is tired of being the plaything of the passions and the vain promises of the factious."

The public was materially comforted by this address and by the peace concluded with Portugal at the same time.[49] "The speech of Carnot was to the taste of everyone," read the official report, "excepting the determined royalists who were tempted to believe themselves reconciled with the Triumvirate. . . ."[50]

The differences, however, between the majority in the Directory and the majority in the Legislative Corps were fundamental and profound. The conflict was social as much as political and governmental, for the material advantages and possessions gained by the revolutionary bourgeoisie were at stake.[51] The Royalists wanted a positive financial program, with a reduction of expenses and an end to profiteering. They wanted also to veto the legislation against the priests and *émigrés,* permit them all to return to France and either restore to them their confiscated property or reimburse them for it. They also wanted peace at once.[52] This program alarmed the "interests"—all the interests produced by the Revolution and now grouped around the Government.

The Legislative Corps immediately laid down its challenge to the Directory. The financial policy of the Directory was attacked. This alienated the creditors of the state. A law was passed to limit the financial responsibility of the Directory, but the Directors still had their source of supply in the generals.

The Council of Five-Hundred voted a new bill of amnesty, but the Council of Elders, by a vote of 112 to 90 rejected it on August 29. The two Councils voted to abrogate all discriminations remaining against the relatives of *émigrés* and against the former Terrorists who had been amnestied. The revolutionary legislation against the refractory clergy had already become a dead letter in three-fourths of the departments. The tribunals favored the priests and the Directorial Commissaires and gendarmes were apathetic. The legal assimilation of the refractory and juring priests was voted by the Legislative Corps. A simple submission to the laws sufficed for this reintegration into the State. This act was adopted in the Five-Hundred by a margin of only six votes, and was confirmed in the Council of Elders on August 24.

Acts of sabotage were frequent against the possessors of national property. Assassinations were numerous and a White Terror spread rapidly. Republicans who had acquired national property were everywhere in danger. To those who had a material stake in the preservation of the revolutionary arrangements it began to look as if a counter-revolution was under way. In their own defense they began organizing clubs, called "Constitutional Circles," in which activity they were encouraged by the majority in the Directory. The Jacobin experience of many of the members stood them in good stead. The first club to be organized was made up of members of the former Club de Noailles in which Siéyès had been an important figure. These "Montmerenciens" numbered three-hundred in the beginning, and included Republicans of all shades. Clubs were soon established all over France, and were particularly strong in the Midi. The Legislative Corps pretended to see great danger to the social order, and a return to terrorism in these clubs, and therefore voted the temporary closure of all political organizations, including the Club de Clichy with the rest.

In these critical days it is apparent that Barras was negotiating with the Pretender and with the English, and had an ear open to the Clichyens.[53] Finally he had repudiated his promise to Dumas and his friends to vote with Carnot to replace the ministers by those agreeable to the majority in the two Councils. He had received documents from Bonaparte proving Pichegru's treason and he returned to republicanism. Barras revealed these papers to Reubell and Larevellière but he kept Carnot and Barthélemy in ignorance of them. Barras then heard of the relations between the Clichy group and the Pretender. When the changes were actually made in the ministries, Carnot's friends Bénézech, Cochon, and Petiet, were replaced by persons agreeable to the Triumvirate. It was at this time that Barras, anticipating trouble from the two Councils, enlisted the support of Hoche, and got troops as near Paris as Reims. This naturally alarmed the Councils, but Carnot and Barthélemy reassured them and they discontinued their own plans for defense. Pichegru proposed a plan to expose Hoche and the Triumvirate, absolving Carnot, on the grounds that Hoche's troops had penetrated within the twelve league zone prohibited by the Constitution. Carnot, as President of the Directory, in reply to an inquiry from the Council of Five-Hundred for an explanation, signed a message stating that this unconstitutional approach of the troops was due to the error of the Commissioner of War in overlooking the constitutional law, and to his ignorance of geography. Barras had finally informed Carnot of Pichegru's treason, and Carnot felt that he could not blame the Triumvirate and seem to stand with Pichegru.

As a price for his support in this instance Carnot got Barras to promise to give up his idea of a *coup d'état*, and when Hoche presented himself on the next day to the Directory, Carnot immediately lectured him severely. Pichegru may have gotten wind of the evidence the Directory had on him, for he immediately moderated his conduct. This alarmed the English who were subsidizing him. Dumas was pursuing a moderate line at the time, and was in correspondence with Moreau, commander-in-chief of the Rhine et Moselle. Moreau had discovered papers incriminating Pichegru but he said nothing to the Government of these until after 19 Fructidor. He had informed Dumas of them, however, through General Desaix, who was friendly to the Clichyens. Bonaparte had become angry at the Clichyens because their journals had criticized Joséphine and had exposed her collusion with the army contractors and provisioners. One journal had even accused Bonaparte of being a thief. Bonaparte used these attacks as the excuse for the leave he asked for on June 30. The Directory insisted that he disregard these attacks and continue in command. These events prompted Bonaparte to issue a political proclamation to his troops on July 14: "Mountains separate us from France; you will leap them with the speed of the eagle, if it is necessary in order to defend the Constitution, defend liberty, and protect the Government and the Republicans."[54] The armies of Bonaparte and Hoche sent addresses to Paris, fulminating against the Clichyens. Moreau's troops abstained. For a time Bonaparte continued to send money to Paris, and the troops of Hoche, destined for Ireland, still hovered around Paris.

The preponderance of evidence concerning Carnot, himself, is that he had not gone over to the Royalists and their plans for a restoration of the monarchy, but that he remained a republican at heart. The Triumvirate, of course, called Carnot a Royalist, and Larevellière recorded this conviction in his *Mémoires*.[55] These three men had good reason for clouding their antagonism towards Carnot. Cambacérès gave as his opinion: "From certain facts that came to my knowledge, I was warranted in concluding that the three Directors, who constituted the majority, were less averse to the royalists than to Carnot, whose inflexible integrity cut them off from all hope. His lofty disinterestedness was a severe censure on their corrupt proceedings."[56] Many of those who denied the allegations against Carnot were of the royalist or moderate groups and were therefore in a position to know whether Carnot was one of them, or not.[57]

Carnot concluded his Presidency on August 23. It was the turn of Barthélemy, but the Triumvirate demanded a formal vote, and Larevellière was chosen. The Royalists knew that trouble was brewing but the Clichyens were in disagreement, and the majority in the Councils were opposed to the resort to force.

Some of the partisans of direct action in the Legislative Corps wanted to wait for the reorganization of the national guard which had not yet begun. These temporizers did not want to alienate Carnot and so counselled their more impatient colleagues to abide by legal means. But while the Clichyens debated among themselves the Triumvirs acted with resolution. Barras had Fouché organize a secret police for him, and the Triumvirs collected arms, and gathered around them officers in Paris on leave.

Events moved rapidly. On September 1, Raffet, royalist commander of the section of la Butte des Moulins, proposed to Dumas the capture of Barras and Reubell that night, and if they resisted, kill them. The Triumvirs were immediately informed of this and they had Raffet arrested and imprisoned at once. This opened the eyes of the temporizers among the Royalists and in the night of 16-17 Fructidor (September 2-3) their leaders agreed upon a plan of action with the Inspectors of the two Councils. Vaublanc was to accuse the Triumvirs in the Five-Hundred on 19 Fructidor. The Five-Hundred would declare the country in danger, assemble the Parisian National Guard and other troops under the command of Pichegru and Willot,[58] and march on the Luxembourg.

Two hours after this plan was concluded, the Triumvirs decided to meet on the evening of 17 Fructidor in the home of Reubell, with Augereau and all of the ministers present. They assembled as scheduled, without having informed Carnot and Barthélemy, and declared themselves in "permanent session." They immediately ordered all services, such as the posts, discontinued, called for troops from the Sambre et Meuse, and since Moreau was suspect, they called him to Paris, and gave his command to Hoche. These proclamations were placarded throughout Paris during the night, along with certain compromising documents. Augereau closed the barriers and at three in the morning of 18 Fructidor his troops surrounded the Tuileries and imprisoned the Inspectors of the Councils. The Guard of the Legislative Corps offered no resistance and helped arrest the deputies, who were sent to the Temple. The operations went off quietly, without any firing, and by seven o'clock it was all over. Barthélemy had been arrested, but Carnot was warned at the last moment and fled in the night. Besides these two Directors, forty members of the Council of Five-Hundred, and thirteen of the Council of Elders, and certain others, to a total of sixty-five, were condemned to deportation to Cayenne. Eighteen only were actually deported.

On 19 Fructidor the deputies friendly to the Directory were convened and were informed of the most serious documents revealing the Royalist plot. After a pretence of deliberation, the Councils voted a lengthy act prepared by Merlin de Douai, which invalidated the elections of all kinds in fifty-three departments and restored the law of 3 Brumaire against the relatives of *émigrés*. The Councils also approved the wholesale deportations, and passed severe laws against the priests. The publishers and printers of thirty-two journals were arrested and the Legislative Corps assumed the control of the press. François de Neufchateau, a protégé of Reubell, and Merlin de Douai, were chosen to replace Carnot and Barthélemy in the Directory. Augereau was named to command the united armies of the Sambre et Meuse, and the Rhine et Moselle, after the death of Hoche on September 19. Paris had remained quiet and indifferent to these illegalities. This was the first great change in the Revolution in which the people had no significant rôle. Brumaire was to be another.

With a Legislative Corps purged of fully two-hundred of its members, the Directory was now supreme. In the name of defending the Constitution of 1795, the Triumvirate had resorted to force, had abandoned the Constitution, and established a dictatorship. It was now plainly the representative of that part of the bourgeoisie that had profited from the Revolution for its own enrichment.[59] The generals were filling the coffers of the State. They had saved the Government by their direct intervention in politics. For the moment, the generals neutralized each other, and the Directory was safe. As Phipps so aptly puts it: "With the army master of the situation, and the purged Directory and Councils ready to carry out its will, we are getting very near Brumaire."[60]

Carnot escaped from Paris and fled to Geneva.[61] Thence he went on to Coppet, and was at Nyon when Bonaparte went through on his way from Milan to the Congress of Rastadt.[62] Carnot evidently lighted his windows as a part of the illumination in honor of the young conqueror, but he made no effort to meet with Bonaparte, because of the embarrassment it might cause the latter.[63] The exile then continued on to South Germany with a passport carrying the name Pasquier. He stopped in a village near Augsburg. He was kept in view there by the diplomatic agents of the Directory.[64] It was in this village that Carnot secured a copy of the *Report of Bailleul* on the 18 Fructidor. Carnot wrote his *Réponse*[65] to that Report and the local bookseller had the important reply printed.[66] The Directory tried to suppress it in France. The original was widely translated, including one by William Walton, an American, under the title, *The Justification of Carnot, or the republican system displayed*, and dedicated to President Jefferson.

The reply of Carnot was, naturally, a political document. It is important as the statement of Carnot's defense against the accusations of the Directorial majority in 1797. In general, the argument is consistent with the previous pronouncements of Carnot. He branded the Report of the Commission as a "tissue of abominable impostures,"[67] and claimed that it was totally unsupported by documentary evidence of which there was an abundance to call upon. Carnot went so far as to say that the documents which Bailleul claimed to have seen and read did not even exist. Carnot disposed of Bailleul's statements and accusations, one by one.[68] He explained his relations with Willot and Pichegru, and he spoke of the Triumvirs as follows: "Republican directors; I knew none among the Triumvris; I knew only assassins of the Republic and of the Constitution."[69] His repeated criticisms of the Triumvirs were severe and detailed.

Carnot gave some attention to the anti-Catholic program of the Triumvirs, with particular reference to the religious policy of Larevellière. In doing so he revealed his own position on religion. He wrote:

"I had the misfortune not to admire the dogmas of the new sect [Theophilanthropy], but I did not ridicule them, either. Universal tolerance is the only dogma that I profess. I believe that there is just about a balance between the good a sincere religion does and the harm which the abuses of a religion effect.

I abhor fanaticism, and I believe that the fanaticism of religion . . . is the worst of all.

"I believe, in a word, that you must not kill men in order to force them to believe; nor kill them to prevent them from believing; but that it is necessary to tolerate the frailties of others, because each of us has his own; let prejudices disappear with time, if they cannot be cured by reason."[70]

In his defense of the freedom of the press, on which he had insisted in the Directory, he wrote: "I find that the abuse of this liberty is a great wrong, but that it is a much greater wrong to limit it. I believe that the freedom of the press finds in itself, in the long run, the remedies for the evils which it produces; that there is no civil liberty, no political liberty, where there is not the liberty of the press."[71] He concluded his passages on religion and the press, by saying: "Our republican directors wanted France to be a country with a political inquisition, to be a vast tomb of living beings similar to the prisons of Genoa, over the doors of which was written, in derision, the word 'Libertas.'"[72]

Carnot aptly summarized the foreign policy of the Triumvirate:

"The system of the Directory is not equivocal for whoever has observed its development with some attention. It is to establish the national power less upon the real grandeur of the Republic, than upon the weakening and the destruction of its neighbors; to let them fight each other, and to treat them as friends so long as the Republic has need of paralyzing them, or has need of their help; and, when the time has come, destroy them."[73]

He explained his opposition to the plan of forcing the French Constitution or death upon the Swiss who preferred their own constitution under which they had lived for three hundred years and had found it to be more democratic than that of the French.[74] In mentioning the peace with Austria, Carnot replied to Bailleul: "I observed to Revellière that I could only remind him of what Bonaparte had written many times: that a peace could not be enduring so long as the clauses were not at least tolerable for the vanquished party; otherwise a germ of irritation would be left which would, sooner or later, produce a fatal explosion."[75]

Carnot declared that the Directory had followed the same policy internally that it had externally, that of inflaming, dividing, and destroying, rather than of pacifying and uniting. He called particular attention to the needless conflict between the Directory and the Legislative Corps. He pointed out the ineffective financial policy of the Directory. Carnot said, "I know of no social pact strong enough to withstand cannon shots; no constitution strong enough to survive, when those who are made its guardians, are so sacrilegious as to want to destroy it themselves."[76] Further along, he added: "When a constitution is good the very means of saving it are found, in it, itself."[77] This was entirely possible in 1797, he said, because the majority in the Legislative Corps wanted to proceed in the spirit of the Constitution. It was the Directory that wanted to repudiate it and establish its own dictatorship. He proceeded to demonstrate how an insurrection, even, could be reconciled with the Constitution, if such a means was necessary to save the Constitution. But he declared that the coup of 18 Fructidor was unnecessary and unconstitutional, and that the proscription was completely unconstitutional. He called the law of 19 Fructidor an "unjustified outlawry" against a part of the national representation and some of the leading magistrates.[78] He made the Triumvirs guilty of high treason.

Carnot accused Barras of being a member of a faction which he detested. This faction, he said, wanted to put the Duke of Orleans on the throne. He proceeded to state his own longstanding aversion to factions and concluded: "I have been successively exposed to all the factions, because I have never failed to oppose them all. I have been attacked by the publicists of all the parties."[79]

Carnot went on to say that the restoration of the finances and the stability of the laws ought to command the attention of the legislators. He then made one of his rare statements concerning property and property rights: "It is time that the right of property cease to be uncertain. The guarantee of possessions can alone make agriculture flourish, and bind the citizens, through peaceful enjoyment, to the *patrie* that protects them; finally resulting in making the love of country the sovereign passion of their hearts."[80]

In his reply Carnot repeated an idea which he had presented

in his Declaration of Rights: "It is when the obligations of the citizens are reduced to a small number of simple and immutable duties that each one can know them and can conform to them with pleasure, train one's children in the fulfillment of these same practices, and there develops a public morality which identifies itself with the very existence of the nation, gives it its true character, and perpetuates its duration. That is why all great legislators have seen less inconvenience in an imperfect but immutable code, than in better laws that are constantly changing. The best government is the one where everything is done by habit, by education, and not by following variable precepts."[81]

Carnot summarized what happened on 18 Fructidor in terms of political philosophy:

"Before Fructidor, agitation was pushed to the excess, because there was a schism between the two principal constituted authorities. Those are storms that one must expect in a democracy. There were two ways to calm the agitation: one was to use the voice of conciliation, to bring the authorities together through love of country and the sentiment of the common danger; this way would preserve the powers intact, would be in accord with the republican system, and would establish confidence in the social pact. The second was that one of the authorities destroy the other; it is this that the executive Directory took for its own profit. . . . What resulted? A monarchy in five persons."[82]

After developing the analogy between the dictatorial Directory after Fructidor and the monarchical system, Carnot revealed his own purposes as a republican legislator and magistrate:

"My object was to propagate the love of the republic by giving to it a real liberty for its foundation. . . . I wanted to guarantee for the national representation of the people the supreme place which the nature of things ordains and that the Constitution designs for it. I desired that the citizens be directed in their conduct by institutions converted into habits, more than restrained by the menaces of the law; finally, I thought that it was better to let prejudices gradually disappear by the light of reason, than to destroy them by violence."[83]

Carnot concluded by speaking in modest terms of himself and of his public career. "I have surely made many mistakes," he wrote, "in a career for which I was not at all destined; but I have never departed from the principles which have served me as a guide in all the torments of the Revolution. . . . I have never used the long exercise of power . . . to amass riches, to elevate my relatives to lucrative employments; my hands are clean and my heart is pure. . . . My only crime, I repeat . . . is to have tried to protect the French people from having tyrants."[84]

Carnot waxed patriotically prayerful in his conclusion to this polemical writing:

"O France! My Fatherland! O great people, truly great people! It is on your soil that I had the happiness to be born; I cannot cease to belong to Thee excepting by ceasing to exist. You embrace all the objects of my affection, the work that my hands have contributed to establish. . . . Receive this vow to serve Thy immortal glory, and Thy constant prosperity, which I renew each day [and] which I address at this moment to all that Thou containest of virtuous and honest souls, to all those who preserve within themselves the sacred spark of liberty."[85]

Considering the provocation under which Carnot wrote, this polemical document is remarkably free of rancour and bitterness. He did castigate severely his opponents but in general his writing was dignified and breathed a philosophical spirit. The ideas which he developed agreed with those which he had enunciated and followed earlier in the Revolution. His single-minded devotion to the Republic and his unbounded love and patriotism for France stand out transparently.

The *coup d'état* of Bonaparte and the subsequent law of 3 Nivôse an VIII (December 24, 1799) were finally to bring the homesick exile back to his beloved France.

Chapter X

FROM EXILE TO EXILE

THE MONTHS in France were crowded during the more than two years Carnot was in exile in Bavaria. The dictatorial Directory did very little to meet the internal problems that remained upon the agenda of urgent public business. Carnot was finally to return to France after another *coup d'état* in which a virtual military dictatorship was to supersede the thoroughly discredited Directorical one.

After getting the Treaty of Campo Formio under way, Bonaparte left Rastadt for Paris on December 1, 1797. The conqueror was enthusiastically received by the Directory and the people. He was elected to life membership in the National Institute in place of the proscribed Carnot. On December 10 he delivered the Treaty of Campo Formio, ratified by the Emperor, to the Directory. Then, in order "to keep his glory warm," as he put it, and because the time was not yet ripe for his capture of power, Bonaparte proposed the Egyptian adventure, having concluded that the preferred descent upon England was impossible. With considerable relief, the Directory sent Bonaparte his commission as general-in-chief of the Army of the Orient on April 12, 1798. Bonaparte sailed shortly with 40,000 troops, and 120 mechanics, scholars, and engineers, including Monge and Berthollet.

In its attempt to brook no opposition the Directory excluded fifty Radical deputies on May 11, 1798. On March 12, 1799, the Directory formally renewed the war on Austria, and the Congress of Rastadt came to an end. In the same spring, the elections brought Siéyès into the Directory. A serious struggle developed between the Directory and the Legislative Corps, and Treilhard, Larevellière, and Merlin (de Douai) were forced out of the Directory, and two pronounced Radicals, Gohier and Moulins, and Roger-Ducos, a partisan of Siéyès, were elected in their places. This overturn in the Government was due to a coalition between the two principal parties in the Five-Hundred, the Radicals (lumped together as Jacobins), and the Moderate Republicans under the leadership of Boulay de la Meurthe, and to which Bonaparte's brothers Lucien and Joseph belonged. Siéyès, Ducos and Barras were classed as Moderates.

The French suffered a series of reverses in Italy, and the Cisalpine Republic was dissolved. The Archduke Charles led his troops to victory on the Rhine, and the Russian allies of the Emperor contributed to the victories against the French. Bonaparte's grandiose plans had gone awry in the East, but France was ignorant of these disasters. Bonaparte decided that the moment was ripe for his reappearance in France and he "escaped" from Egypt on August 21, 1799, landing in Corsica early in October. On October 9 he debarked in France and began his triumphal journey to Paris.

Siéyès had been reviving his Constitutional suggestions of 1795. The executive power would be vested in three consuls, elected for ten years, and there would be a Senate with life members, and a Chamber of Deputies elected by universal male suffrage. To achieve this new constitution the Council of Elders was to move that the Legislative Corps assemble outside of Paris and there adopt the new constitution, which would then be submitted to a plebiscite. But would the Five Hundred consent?

Lucien informed the newly-arrived Bonaparte of the contemplated reforms, for which Bonaparte immediately expressed his sympathy. "He himself stood in need of a new Constitution in order to come into power, and Siéyès was in want of a general esteemed by the army to establish his Constitution."[1] Talleyrand brought the two men together secretly on November 1 in the home of Lucien Bonaparte. They met together again on November 6 to perfect their plans.

On 18 Brumaire (November 9) the Council of Elders decreed the transferal of the Legislative Corps to Saint Cloud on the following day, with the provision that no deliberations be held elsewhere. Bonaparte was appointed to execute the decree, with troops assigned to him for the purpose. He was to appear before the deputies to take the required oath. When the Five-Hundred, under the presidency of Lucien Bonaparte, was informed of this decree it immediately adjourned. Siéyès and Ducos resigned from the Directory. Bonaparte sent Talleyrand and Bruix to the detested Barras to demand his resignation, which was acceded to. Moulins and Gohier were now rendered powerless and Moreau was told to detain them in the Luxembourg.

The two Councils assembled in Saint Cloud at noon on 19 Brumaire (November 10). The Radicals in the Five-Hundred protested the unlawful acts of 18 Brumaire. Bonaparte, in alarm, rushed in and addressed the Elders in a strangely incoherent and very inconclusive speech. In the meantime the Five-Hundred had received the resignation of Barras, and the members had renewed their oath to the Constitution. Suddenly Bonaparte stalked in unannounced and accompanied by four grenadiers. The uproar against him overwhelmed him. He momentarily lost consciousness and was carried out into the open followed by cries of *"Hors de la loi."*

Lucien Bonaparte, besieged by motions against his brother, resigned his chair to the vice president, so that he could speak from the tribune, but he could not be heard in the din. He sent word to Bonaparte that he had been compelled to relinquish his seat and needed military protection. Bonaparte sent soldiers in to "rescue" him and bring him outside where Bonaparte waited with his officers, at the head of a battalion of the Guard of the Legislative Corps. Siéyès, Ducos, and Talleyrand were already seated in a carriage by the gate, ready for flight. Lucien saw that the fate of the *coup* depended upon the reluctant troops. He addressed them extravagantly and called upon them to defend the majority of the deputies against the "terrorizing" minority. Bonaparte almost ruined the effect by a grandiose pronouncement, but Lucien's vow to be the first to strike down Bonaparte if he should ever violate the liberties of the French, finally won over the grenadiers, and the day was won. For a second time in little more than two years Paris was indifferent. Generally, France approved the *coup-d'état.*

The reorganization of the Government moved rapidly. Siéyès, Bonaparte, and Ducos were the three consuls. The Five-Hundred, after excluding sixty-two members, elected a commission of twenty-five, to meet with a like number from the Elders, and with the three Consuls, for the purpose of taking care of urgent business, formulating a new constitution, and drafting a new civil code. The Legislative Corps then adjourned until February 20, 1800. Ducos soon became inactive, and Siéyès contented himself with his usual pastime of elaborating a constitution. Bonaparte chose his own ministers. He appointed Gaudin, minister of finance, Talleyrand, minister of foreign affairs, Laplace, the mathematician, minister of the interior,but soon replaced him by Lucien Bonaparte, Berthier, minister of war, Fouché, minister of police, Cambacérès, minister of justice, and Forfait, minister of the navy. Bonaparte provisionally reformed the finances. The vicious compulsory loans were abolished and the capitalists became more easy in their minds.

Siéyès' proposed constitution was based on the principle that the different branches of the government should counterbalance one another. The people were declared sovereign and universal suffrage was guaranteed. The election of representatives was to be indirect. The 5,000,000 adult voters were to choose one-tenth of their number as notables of the Communes, eligible for communal offices. These were to elect one-tenth of themselves as notables of the Department, eligible for departmental offices. These were to elect one-tenth of their number as notables of France, candidates for the legislative body, and for central administrative offices up to that of minister. All lists were to be valid for ten years. There were to be two legislative bodies, one of which would discuss but not vote on bills originating in their own body or presented by the Government, while the other would vote but not discuss such bills. At the head of the state there would be a Grand Elector and two Consuls chosen by him. Each of these would appoint his own subordinates. A constitutional jury of eighty members, appointed for life and self-perpetuating would serve as guardian of the Constitution, would annul unconstitutional laws, would appoint the Grand Elector, and would elect the members of the two legislative bodies.

Bonaparte made some significant changes in this proposed constitution. The Grand Elector was replaced by a First Consul as head of the Government and responsible for the execution of the laws. This magistrate was to be elected by the Senate for a ten year term. The First Consul would appoint and dismiss ministers, ambassadors, councillors of state, administrative officers for all of France, and all judges excepting for the Court of Cassation, the highest court of appeals. The will of the First Consul would be law when promulgated in the form of a decree. He would direct diplomacy and would be the commander-in-chief of all military forces. He would sign treaties and laws on their adoption by the legislative body. He was to appoint a Council of State as a part of the executive agency. Two Consuls would be associated with him.[2] Siéyès' Constitutional Jury was transformed into a Senate with eighty life members chosen from the Notables of France. From these same Notables the Senate would choose the three hundred members of the Legislative Corps, and the one hundred members of the Tribunate. Neither of these bodies could initiate legislative measures. The Senate was to elect, also, the Court of Cassation, and the Court of the Exchequer.

The fifty members of the Commission assented to this Constitution as modified by Bonaparte. The Commission then chose Bonaparte as First Consul, and Cambacérès and Lebrun as his associates, Siéyès refusing to be a candidate. The latter was made president of the Senate and Ducos was made a senator. The Commission finished its tasks on December 12. Siéyès, Ducos, Cambacérès, and Lebrun chose thirty-one Senators, and these elected others up to a total of sixty, which remained the number for a time. This Senate then elected the members of the Tribunate and the Legislative Corps. Bonaparte appointed his Council of State, which met for the first time on December 25. A Manifesto of December 15 presented the consular constitution to the people of France for their ratification. The law of 3 Nivôse an VIII (December 24) permitted most of the exiles to return to France.

Bonaparte addressed letters to the King of England and to the Emperor on December 25, in which he expressed his desire for peace, but without making any definite propositions. The revolt in the Vendée still burned. The Austrians were victorious in Italy, but Masséna inflicted a defeat on the Russians at Zurich, and the campaign in Holland was successful, releasing that army of 30,000 for other fields. By February, 1800, through threat and conciliation, the Vendée was quieted, and the Army of the West was ready for transfer. The British had the French blockaded in Egypt and Malta. Early in 1800 Bonaparte laid down his masterly plans for the ensuing campaign. Bonaparte, himself, was to cross the Swiss Alps with the reserve army, penetrate into Lombardy and there cut off communications between Vienna and the Austrian army. After a decisive blow the Austrian army would be forced to capitulate. These plans were under way in February and March.

Carnot was one of those permitted to return to France by the law of 3 Nivôse an VIII (December 24, 1799). His joy in being again in France was unbounded. He wrote to his brother in Dijon, on January 20, 1800: "I hasten, my very dear friend, to announce my arrival in Paris. My wife arrived a quarter of an hour after me. You can easily imagine our joy. . . ."[3] He was still expressing his happiness to members of his family in March.[4] Bonaparte restored Carnot to military service on February 7, 1800, with the functions of inspector general of reviews and with the rank of general of division. The Consuls offered him the position of first inspector of the military administration, but Carnot declined. A few months later Bonaparte offered him the ministry of war, then held by Berthier. Carnot demurred, saying that he would want more liberty of action than Bonaparte would be willing to give. On the latter's word to give him complete control, Carnot accepted. He was Minister of War during the second Italian campaign, from April 2 to October 8.

The story is told that, for a mission to Moreau, commanding the Army of the Rhine, on May 5, the Consuls gave Carnot 24,000 francs for expenses. Carnot, on his return to Paris, turned back 12,200 francs unspent. His son remarks that this was embarrassing for there was no place to enter such an unprecedented proceeding in the books and a new chapter had to be opened for it.[5] Bonaparte had sent Carnot on a delicate mission to Moreau to get his consent to sending 30,000 troops to the Army of Italy.[6] "Bonaparte hoped to profit by the mutual esteem that united Moreau and Carnot; he determined to send to him this able minister, this excellent conciliator."[7] Carnot arrived just after Moreau's success at Stockach, and he was present at the victory of Biberach. Carnot won Moreau's reluctant consent to send the troops away, but had greater difficulties in convincing the other generals. "All the generals had a high regard for Moreau, and they loved Carnot, and when they saw the accord that reigned between these two illustrious chiefs, they consented with a true zeal."[8] The timid General Moncey was chosen to command the reinforcements. Moreau and Carnot spent two days in going over their instructions to him. Bonaparte, whom Carnot met at Lausanne, was highly pleased at the outcome of this mission.[9] Murat requested Carnot to escort his wife back to Paris, a task which Carnot fulfilled with "a gayety, a delicacy and even with a kind of gallantry that contrasted with the profound reflections that the contemporary situation in France inspired in him."[10]

On June 16 Carnot wrote to Bonaparte that on the previous day he had given an audience to Fulton, the inventor, who had displayed a model of a submarine which he proposed as a means of attacking the English navy and merchant marine.[11] Carnot reported that the experiments promised success and that he saw nothing any more contrary to the rights of men in attacking a fleet under water than in attacking a fortress by mines. General Lomet reports that on his return from Italy, Bonaparte gave scant attention to Fulton, who took his invention and his genius to the United States.[12] Later, when he presented his plan for steam vessels to Bonaparte, the latter rejected it, in exasperation.[13]

Bonaparte's letters to Carnot during these months when Carnot was minister of war were terse, explicit orders to send troops, to outfit the soldiers, to appoint generals and officers named by Bonaparte, and like commissions, making of Carnot but a bureaucratic agent of his own will. These impersonal letters do give evidence, however, of the confidence Bonaparte had in Carnot. Carnot's own official correspondence during this period was voluminous.[14] This covered not only business conducted with the armies and the army services, but also a great deal with the other ministers. Much of this was with the Ministers of Police, of the Interior, and of Foreign Affairs, with particular reference to the governance of occupied territories, with treaties, and the subsistence of the troops, particularly in the Helvetic and Batavian Republics. The connections between the ministries were many and intricate, and Carnot regulated his relations with his colleagues with circumspection and with a fine regard for these associates. His correspondence with them was courteous, precise, friendly, and efficient. His letters to the generals in the field were written on the same high level.

There was a great deal of discussion in Paris among the politicians while Bonaparte was in Italy and before the Battle of Marengo on June 14 as to who his successor would be in case he should be killed. In the circles where this was the most considered, Carnot emerged as the candidate the most likely to command the confidence of the people and best direct the government. In a discussion at Talleyrand's, with Siéyès present, Carnot and Lafayette were put forth as possibilities.[15] Miot de Melito left Paris on May 19 to spend several days with Joseph Bonaparte at Morfontaine, where they talked of the implications of the possible death of Bonaparte. Miot reports an interesting conversation on May 31 that included Girardin, a member of the Tribunate, at which Joseph Bonaparte reported a meeting of partisans of Siéyès where "Finally, Carnot was proposed and it seems that everyone was already so well disposed in his favor that the proposition was not so much debated as supported by every argument that the meeting could adduce in his favor. . . . So much reciprocal suitability [to the regicides, Moderates, Army, Jacobins], so many pledges given to all parties, placed Carnot in a unique position. His elevation to power would be a security for all, without being alarming to any. . . . Finally the opinions of all . . . were brought into unanimity."[16] The group in Joseph Bonaparte's home did not agree with this conclusion. "Objections [to Carnot] were indeed plentiful; but while making them, we knew not whom to propose."[17] Roederer reports that he and Bonaparte were discussing this matter after Marengo, and Bonaparte said: "Whom to name? If I had been killed at Marengo, it is said the Senate would have named Carnot. *Eh bien!* Carnot, perhaps, would do better than any other."[18] Fouché, on the other hand, reports that these rumors angered and prejudiced Bonaparte. "I affirmed that the conduct of Carnot had been unimpeachable; and I remarked that it would be very hard to render him responsible for the extravagant projects engendered by sickly brains, and of which Carnot had not the least idea. He was silent; but the impression had sunk deep. He did not forgive Carnot, who some time after, found himself under the necessity of resigning the portfolio of war."[19]

Carnot was evidently ignorant of the fact that he had been discussed as a possible successor to Bonaparte. His duties had become intolerable to him. He had had to oppose the policies of the First Consul on occasion,[20] and he had not had the independence of action that he thought he had been promised. After the decisive victories in Italy he felt himself more useless than ever. The great victory of Marengo on June 14 climaxed the French successes. An armistice was signed in Italy on June 15, and the Cisalpine and Ligurian Republics were reestablished. Bonaparte was back in Paris early in July. Carnot offered his resignation on August 29, but was persuaded to remain. Bonaparte wrote him on September 1: "The Consuls desire . . . that you continue the functions that you have exercised for six months with as much zeal as usefulness for the *patrie*. You have improved the administration of the war office, but there are greater improvements to be accomplished."[21] But on October 8 Carnot was permitted to resign. He wrote to his brother in Nolay on October 30 that he had "left a difficult post where he could no longer do any good."[22] Bonaparte at a later time commented on Carnot as Minister of War: "He showed few talents and had many quarrels with the Minister of Finance and the director of the Treasury, Dufresne, in which he was usually wrong. . . ."[23] Bourrienne remarked at the time that Carnot was "no favorite of Bonaparte, on account of his decided republican principles."[24] Lacuée served as *interim* Minister until Berthier could resume the post. It was suggested that Carnot's rank be regularized as general of division and chief of engineers as a recognition of his services. Berthier agreed and prepared the papers, but Bonaparte vetoed the plan.[25]

The Treaty of San Ildefonso had been signed with Spain on October 1. The Battle of Hohenlinden was won on December 3, and the road to Vienna was open. Moreau signed an armistice on December 25. On February 9, 1801, the definitive peace of Luneville imposed more severe terms on Austria than had that of Campo Formio. Bonaparte could now turn to the domestic affairs of France.

Following his resignation, Carnot retired to Saint-Omer where he took up again his scientific studies, and corresponded with Charles Bossut concerning some new ideas in trigonometry he was working out. Carnot had been re-elected to the National Institute on his return from exile, and he now had time to renew relations with his scientific colleagues. In 1801 he published his *De la Corrélation des figures de géométrie*, that was soon translated into German and published at Dresden.

The Carnots lived quietly in Saint-Omer. Their second son was born on April 6, 1801,[26] and was named Hippolyte.[27] Carnot wrote to Bonaparte on May 27 that "although returned to private life, by taste as well as by need, I am far from being indifferent to public affairs and to the success of the Government."[28] His tenure of private life was to be short-lived.

The Department of Pas-de-Calais presented Carnot's name to the Senate and in March, 1802, that body elected him to the Tribunate as one of the twenty annual replacements. Carnot was reluctant to leave his private affairs,[29] but his sense of duty was too great to be disregarded. Carnot joined the small group of members in the Tribunate opposed to the growing autocracy of Bonaparte.[30] He opposed the establishment of the Legion of Honor with thirty-eight others. He cast the only vote in the Tribunate in 1802 against the Consulate for life. When he advanced to vote the members crowded round, but he wrote: "Were I to sign my proscription by it, nothing could force me to disguise my sentiments. No."[31] *Puis il sortit.* Lucien Bonaparte destroyed the register and another vote had to be taken.

Carnot continued his scientific studies while fulfilling his duties as a tribune. In 1803 he published his important *Géométrie de Position*,[32] and his *Principes fondamentaux de l'équilibre et du mouvement*.[33]

Bonaparte proposed the transformation of the Consulate for life into the hereditary monarchy in the spring of 1804. This man who had risen as a result of the Revolution's principle of "careers open to talent," wanted to found a dynasty. The republican Carnot now had his greatest opportunity to register his opposition to the monarchical principle and to summarize his own political faith. Before casting the sole vote against the hereditary monarchy,[34] Carnot supported his vote in a lengthy speech.[35]

Carnot praised Bonaparte for his services to the nation, saying that had he done nothing but establish the civil code, his name would be honored by posterity. "If," he said, "this citizen has restored public liberty . . . is it a proper recompense to offer him the sacrifice of this very liberty? Would it not destroy his own work to transform the nation into his personal patrimony?"[36]

Carnot proceeded:

"I voted against the consulate for life; I shall vote the same against the establishment of the monarchy, as I believe my position of tribune compels me to do; but this will always be with the precautions necessary to prevent the awakening of the partisan spirit; it will be without personalities; without any passion other than for the public good, always remaining true to myself in the defense of the popular cause.

"I have always professed to submit to the existing laws, even when they displease me the most; more than once I have been the victim of my devotion, and I shall not now follow another practice. I declare at once that, in opposing the proposal, from the moment a new order of things is established and shall have received the consent of the majority of the citizens, I shall be the first to conform all my actions to it, and give to the supreme authority every mark of deference that the constitutional hierarchy demands."[37]

Carnot declined to discuss the merits of the different kinds of governments, remarking that volumes had been written on this subject. He then summarized the arguments for the restoration of the monarchy, as outlined by its proponents; it would guarantee stability of government, assure public tranquillity, put down civil strife, and repel the external enemy, achievements that the republican system had failed in after a very thorough trial. Carnot proceeded to attack these arguments. "I shall first observe," he said, "that the government of one man is nothing more than a gauge of stability and tranquillity."[38] He described the transition of Rome from Republic to Imperial Monarchy: "Republican pride, heroism, and sturdy virtues were replaced by the most ridiculous conceit, the vilest adulation, the most shocking cupidity, and the most absolute indifference to the national prosperity."[39] He turned to France under the Bourbons: "Whenever an entire nation espouses the particular interests of a family it is obliged to intervene in a multitude of events which, without this relationship, would be of the utmost indifference to it."[40] He attributed the weaknesses of the Republican systems before 18 Brumaire to the fact that they were born in the midst of factions and in extraordinary times.

After 18 Brumaire, he said, the time was ripe to "establish liberty on solid bases proven by experience and reason. . . ."[41] "After the Peace of Amiens Bonaparte could have chosen between the republican and the monarchical systems; he could have done anything that he wished; he would have met only the slightest opposition. The shrine of liberty was confided to him, and he had sworn to defend it; in fulfilling his promise he would have had the loyalty of the nation, which had judged him alone capable of solving the problem of public liberty. He would have been covered with incomparable glory. Instead of that what is it that is proposed today? It is proposed to make of the nation a property absolute and hereditary. . . . Is this the interest of the First Consul himself? I think not."[42]

Carnot admitted that the state was falling into dissolution before 18 Brumaire and he commented "that political bodies are subject to diseases which can only be cured by violent remedies; that a temporary dictatorship is sometimes necessary to save liberty."[43] He went on to say that it was not because of their nature that the great republics lacked stability, but because they were improvised in times of crisis, and exaltation presided too exclusively at their establishment. He made one exception: "One only was the work of philosophy, and was organized in tranquillity; this one has persisted full of wisdom and vigor—the United States."[44] "It is less difficult," he said, "to form a republic without anarchy than a monarchy without despotism. How can any limitation that is not illusory be put upon a government in which the head has all the executive power in his hands, and all the positions to fill."[45]

Carnot admitted that the majority of the French would vote for the monarchy but he denied that this would be a free vote and he questioned the validity of a public opinion manufactured by the propaganda of state functionaries. He went on to call attention to the fact that the new order, instead of ushering in the epoch of general peace, would aggravate the international tension because the other great Powers would not tolerate the new *régime*. "Would not," he said, prophetically, "the Emperor of the French soon want to be emperor of other Powers?"[46]

He enquired whether liberty was a fruit always to be snatched away from man, or not. He replied: "No, I cannot consent to regard this good, so universally superior to all others and without which the others are nothing, as nothing but an illusion. My heart tells me that liberty is possible, that a free *régime* is easy to maintain, and more stable, than any arbitrary government, than any oligarchy."[47] He concluded his speech with the assurance: "However, I repeat, I am always ready to sacrifice my dearest affections to the interests of the *patrie*, and I am contented to have spoken again with the voice of a free spirit. . . . I vote against the proposition."[48]

The courageous words and the acute observations of this inveterate republican commanded universal respect.[49] Their austere, lofty and disinterested tone struck a sobering note against the times ahead. Napoleon remarked later that Carnot had "spoken and voted against the Empire, but his ever upright conduct gave no offense to the Government."[50]

In June, 1804 the members of the Tribunate were included *en bloc* in the new nominations for the Legion of Honor, and Carnot without any expression of gratitude[51] took the required oath, which read; "I swear on my honor to devote myself to the Empire, to the conservation of its territories in their integrity, to the defense of the Emperor, of the laws of the Republic and the property that they uphold, to combat with all the means that justice, reason, and the laws authorize, all efforts tending to reestablish the feudal *régime*, or to restore the titles and the privileges associated with it; and finally to collaborate with all my power to the maintenance of liberty and equality."[52]

Carnot continued to sit in the Tribunate until it was suppressed in 1807. He then retired to private life without civil or military pension. The Carnots left Paris for an estate "Presles," that Carnot had bought near la Ferté-Alais and Étampes, and close by the estate of his friend, General Canclaux. "Presles" had been stripped, and then abandoned by speculators, so that a complete restoration was necessary. Carnot wintered in Paris and journeyed there frequently for his work at the National Institute and at the Council of the Polytechnic School. At "Presles" he devoted himself to science, history, and agriculture. He also assumed the exclusive instruction of his two sons. In these years he translated Horace and read Plutarch, Marcus Aurelius, Mably, Hume, Harrington, Pope's *Essay on Man*, and Lloyd's *Memoirs*. In 1810 the electoral college of the Côte-d'Or presented his name for the Senate but Napoleon did not approve the recommendation.

The modest circumstances of Carnot were brought to the attention of Napoleon and on June 17, 1809, the latter wrote from Schönbrun to the Duke de Feltre, suggesting a pension of ten thousand francs for Carnot, and this was arranged. Napoleon then suggested that Carnot write a treatise on the fortification of places for the military school of Metz. Carnot accepted and four months later had the work ready. Napoleon received the study in an ungracious manner and not a single copy was sent to the school at Metz. The demand for the book at home and abroad, however, called forth second and third editions in short order, and it was translated for the use of almost every army in Europe.

In this *De la Défense des Places Fortes*[53] Carnot, in a technical sense took Montalembert as his ground work, but without the latter's antipathy for the bastioned trace, and his partiality for high masonry *caponiers*. Carnot followed out the principle of retarding the development of the attack, and provided for the most active defense. To facilitate sorties in great force he abandoned the counterscarp wall, and provided instead a long gentle slope from the bottom of the ditch to the crest of the *glacis*. Carnot believed that this would compel the assailant to maintain large forces in the advanced trenches, which he proposed to attack by vertical fire from mortars. Along the front of his fortress he would build a heavy detached wall, loop-holed for fire, sufficiently high to be a most formidable obstacle. This came to be called "Carnot's wall." This, and Carnot's principle of active defense, played a great rôle in the rise of modern fortifications.

Carnot quoted liberally from Vauban,[54] the Duke d'Alba, d'Arçon, Maigret, de Cormontaingne, and a great deal from Caesar's *Commentaries.* He went back into antiquity to cite the defensive strength of Troy, Nineveh, Babylon, and Sardis, and he gave a detailed analysis of famous sieges and defenses in history, beginning with the siege of Syracuse by the Athenians in 413 B. C., and including ten in ancient times, and thirty-seven in modern times. He revealed a fine comprehension of the art of siege throughout history.

The treatise is largely technical, quite dry and unimaginative excepting for the professional. Carnot did, however, propound some general maxims, and he devoted a chapter to the psychology and the morale of the troops. His most repeated text is on the duty "to defend to the last extremity the post confided to you," and the epigraph of his work is: "In the defense of fortresses valor and industry, separately, suffice for naught, but together they accomplish all. Valor! Industry! all the defense of fortresses is in these two words."[55]

"With the French," Carnot wrote, "obedience is not blind, and yet none are more heroic."[56] Intelligent obedience, based on confidence in leadership, accounts for the success of French arms. Fortresses are the most important of all military posts, for they are the watch towers (or, fortified sentinels) distributed on the frontiers. "War," Carnot continued, "is a violent condition that brings extraordinary measures and a multitude of inevitable misfortunes in its train, that are tolerated only to avoid others much greater."[57]

Fortresses are not placed by chance on a frontier, but they constitute a unified ensemble, all of whose parts are related, and connected organically with the general system of the war. Carnot classified the various kinds of fortresses, designed for different purposes. "He who has an effective cordon of fortresses," he wrote, "is always master of accepting or refusing battle. . . . Fortresses dispense with the necessity of having the total active army in readiness, for in taking the first assault of the enemy they afford time for the forces to be assembled."[58] Further along, Carnot wrote: "With us . . . by the system of fortresses the ensemble is saved by the momentary sacrifice of a single point; while in the rest of the Empire the citizens live in the most profound security."[59] But with an undefended people a single battle can decide the fate of an empire.

Carnot described the kind of officer who inspires trust and devotion, and he remarked that "it is necessary to have enthusiasm, and a great passion ought to be the spirit of a great ensemble. . . . All famous actions have been due to some kind of exaltation. In antiquity, when an entire people defended its capital, this exaltation was imperative necessity, the first of all laws. With the Greeks and Romans, this was the love of country; at the time of the Crusades and of chivalry, this was a sentiment composed of piety, honor, and gallantry; with the Swiss and Dutch Republics, it was the hatred of tyranny; . . . finally, the sieges of Calais, Orleans . . . proved that the fidelity to a Prince could also become a great and generous passion. Do not hope to obtain effects without a cause, a heroic devotion without a source that lifts man powerfully above himself. How wrong are those who seek to confine this energy, to argue when it is time to act, to weaken the impulsion of a sentiment that is indefinable, but which is the unique principle of all that is good and great in the world."[60]

In the years 1807-1814, the Carnots maintained a simple *ménage* at "Presles." Carnot's brothers often came to visit him for they were warmly devoted to each other.[61] Carnot's best friends at the time were Prieur (Côte-d'Or), a Republican, and Louis de Lespinasse, a Royalist. All three had a common passion for music. Many others frequented the Carnot home during this period, including the Comte de Serrent, M. de Sermaise, M. de Bellonet, Admiral Bougainville, Dupont de Nemours, Gail, Gengembre, Girard, the engineer, Adet, the chemist, Lacroix, the mathematician, Palissot de Beauvois, the botanist, Bouffleurs, and Humboldt, the famous scientist. In 1812, Sadi, who was a very precocious and a very lovable boy, was admitted to the *École poly-*

technique at the age of sixteen, while the eleven year old Hippolyte was placed in the *Institution polytechnique* of M. Lemoine d'Essoies.

In February, 1813, Carnot's wife died in Paris after a long illness. Carnot communicated the sad news to his brother, the mayor of Nolay, on February 7: "I have just lost the most virtuous of wives and my children the most tender of mothers. The companion of my happiness and of my troubles for twenty-one years has succumbed after a long and painful illness. I am twelve years older than she, and she should have closed my eyes, and yet I have had to close hers. She retained consciousness and her loving heart to the very last . . . as she tenderly held my hand. . . . Announce this sad news to our relatives. I embrace you with all my heart."[62] Carnot announced the news to the Empress Joséphine, for his wife had cherished in her memory the kindnesses of Joséphine years before.[63]

At the beginning of 1814, when Napoleon had his back to the wall, Carnot came forward to offer his services to help stem the invading tide, in a characteristic letter on January 24:

"Sire, so long as success crowned your enterprises, I abstained from offering services to Your Majesty, which I did not think would be agreeable to you. Today, Sire, that bad fortune puts your constancy to the proof, I no longer hesitate to offer the feeble means that are still mine. The effort of a sexagenarian arm is a small thing, no doubt; but I thought that the example of a soldier whose patriotic sentiments are known, might rally to your eagles many persons uncertain as to the part they should take and who might be persuaded thus to serve their country rather than to abandon it. There is still time for you, Sire, to achieve a glorious peace, and to secure the love of a great people."[64]

Napoleon gladly accepted the offer, and assigned Carnot to the important command at Antwerp. Carnot left Paris on January 30 for his new post. He had but the rank of chief of battalion in engineering. His *entourage* was very simple, and consisted of his aide-de-camp Joseph Ransonnet, a secretary, and a domestic, the faithful Joséphine Briois, who had raised his children. "The simplicity of this equipage, which responded to the customs of the country, helped win all hearts."[65]

Antwerp was being besieged by the Prussians under Bulow and by the English under Graham, and the Swedes, under Bernadotte, were approaching. On February 3-5, the city was bombarded and on the 6th the siege became a blockade. Bulow wrote Carnot on the 11th that the Empire was over and that he might now desert it. Carnot received this communication on the 18th and refused to follow its suggestions. On March 16, General Maison, in the name of Napoleon, wrote Carnot that he should evacuate Antwerp, leaving only 3,000 marines in the city. Napoleon needed the other troops elsewhere. Carnot protested and asked for permission to retain 15,000. This was granted and only the imperial guard was removed. Bernadotte wrote to Carnot on April 8, signing himself, "Your affectionate," and urging Carnot to join forces with the Allies in the march on Paris, where, he said, the abdication of Napoleon had taken place, followed by the restoration of the Bourbons.

Carnot refused all these overtures and awaited definite confirmation of the rumors of abdication, and orders from whatever constituted authorities existed in Paris. On April 7 the provisional government appointed General Dupont as Minister of War and he requested the garrison at Antwerp to adhere to the new order. Napoleon's formal abdication was dated the 11th. On April 12 Carnot received Dupont's message. He replied that at first the Council had voted to submit to the new order but on second vote had decided to send a delegation to Paris to determine whether the action had been free and abdication formal, with a quorum of the Senate and Legislative Corps present. If not, and civil war impended, it would be a calamity to leave Antwerp. Maison wrote Carnot again on April 16, but Carnot continued to suspend judgment until official word arrived from Paris. When this came his order of the day called for obedience to the new *régime*:

"The army does not deliberate, it obeys, and is sees that the laws are executed.... The moment approaches, no doubt, when we must take a new oath to him whom the general consent of the nation will name King; but we must prevent all disorder, avoid all agitation, and obey unanimously. The precise moment will be fixed; it will be consecrated by a fitting ceremony. Until then we can enjoy no change. . . . We will remain strong at our post; we will religiously guard the sacred shrine that has been entrusted to us, and we will await, as faithful and incorruptible soldiers, the hour when we can transfer our trust to the legitimate sovereign."[66]

The English General Graham wrote to him to congratulate him on the wisdom of this decree.[67] On April 18 another decree arrived from Paris announcing the restoration of the Bourbons. Because of the division among the troops Carnot had to move tactfully, but he finally brought the soldiers around to the acceptance of the new order. Carnot's administration of the city as its governor in these critical days had been decidedly successful and popular.[68]

Carnot left Antwerp on May 3, 1814 for Paris. He was reconciled to the Restoration. He pinned his Cross of Saint Louis back again upon his uniform and presented himself at a solemn audience in the Tuileries. The King received him coldly. Carnot passed before him and left without saying a word. Carnot retired from public life and again became one of the most active members of the Institute. He prepared a new edition of his *Géométrie de position.*

As a protest against the threatened abuses of the restored Bourbons, Carnot prepared a frank appeal to Louis XVIII for liberalism in government, and for the union of all parties, which he evidently intended only for the attention of the King. The document was released, however, due, evidently, to the hostility of the courtiers to Carnot. It was soon published without the consent of Carnot, under the title *Mémoire au Roi.*[69] This widely-read pamphlet called forth many replies, including an attack on it by Chateaubriand, to which Carnot replied. His first reply appeared in *le Censeur Européen,* and his second remained unpublished. Carnot also sent to *le Censeur Européen* an article entitled "Considerations on the means of giving birth to the national spirit of France." He contributed, in this period, some satirical dialogues to a small sheet, *le Veredique.*

Carnot's opening words were striking: "The social state as

we see it is nothing but a continual struggle between the urge to dominate and the desire to escape domination."[70] In a later passage he put this idea in another way: "This history [of man] is nothing but the monotonous picture of the eternal abuse of power; the people only figure as the instruments and the victims of the ambitions of their rulers."[71] Carnot wrote of the disorders that naturally follow from the conflict between the partisans of undefined liberty to whom all restraint is illegitimate, and the partisans of absolute power, to whom all liberty is an abuse. He commented on the disillusionments of the Revolution which had resulted from the failure of the hopes engendered by "a multitude of purely philosophical writings."[72]

Carnot condemned the royalists for having deserted Louis XVI. He said that they should have remained in France to help stop the torrent, and they have no right to blame others for not having stopped it. Carnot called these aristocratic *émigrés* the real regicides for they had taken arms against their very "mother-country."[73] He held this class responsible for the abuses of the Revolution. Carnot admitted the general enthusiasm in France for the return of the Bourbons after the Napoleonic oppression, but he called attention to the fact that the returning *émigrés* expected to find the France of 1789. They had not expected to find a new generation nurtured in other principles, but for twenty years this process has been going on. Those now in control have reversed the rôles. The twenty-five million Frenchmen who stayed at home and protected the *patrie* are now called traitors and the *émigrés* are honored as patriots.

Carnot reminded Louis XVIII that one can be King either by the consent of the people or by the grace of God. The sanction for the latter is really the sanction of force, with its resultant adulation. He called attention to the fact that the parties, at first willing to forget their old quarrels, were reviving. He bewailed the fact that the King, forgetting his promises, was banishing the liberals. While Carnot made a plea for the dissolution of the parties he indicated that the King was behaving in a way to aggravate their revival. Carnot revealed what the Revolution meant to those who had remained in France and had participated in it:

"The French Revolution was a composite of heroism, of cruelties, of sublime traits and of monstrous disorders. All families that remained in France were compelled to take a part, more or less active, in this revolution; each of these made sacrifices more or less significant; each of these furnished children for the defense of the *patrie;* and this defense has been glorious. All were, consequently, interested that success crown the enterprise."[74]

Carnot made himself the champion of the longings and desires of these loyal Frenchmen who had won such a stake in the Revolution and its aftermath. He indicated that there were adequate guarantees in the Constitutional Charter for all that these patriots wanted. The provisions for representation in the document should be thoroughly adhered to. Carnot affirmed that "the majority, by its instinct, judged that that person had the right to rule who governed well, and that he lost that right when he governed badly; that he who made the people happy was the legitimate ruler."[75]

"In the state of nature," Carnot wrote, "man is cruel only through necessity; in the state of society, he is cruel by caprice in order to satisfy his fantasies, and the passions that result from his contacts with his fellows."[76] While he demurred from preferring the state of nature, he pointed out that the social state is susceptible to an infinitude of gradations, of which one extreme is that of total isolation, and the other that of absolute despotism. The real problem is to find the proper place between these two vicious extremes, where can be found a just liberty and a legitimate power. Liberty properly restrained he called social liberty, and power properly tempered he called legitimate power. Carnot remarked that only on experience could man establish solid principles, and that the science of government perfects itself unconsciously by experience and by reflection. Carnot insisted that national prosperity was the great and unique object of the social state. This could be realized in a monarchy satisfactorily limited, as well as in a republic satisfactorily balanced. The actual way in which it was done would depend somewhat on the nature of the government of each country.

Carnot inquired what motive could possibly be strong enough to unite individual, selfish efforts toward a common good. This, he said, would call for a noble and strong passion. It could be nothing else than a profound love for the *patrie*. A national spirit, so rooted, was lacking in the France of the times, and it was imperative to develop such a spirit. A nation to be great must have a great passion dominating it. This had been proved historically. In one case it had been the passion of liberty, in another that of conquest, in yet another, that of religious fanaticism, but, he concluded, "with us it must be the love of the very soil that gave us birth."[77] This he found easy for the predominately peasant population of France, for whom it was entirely natural to love and worship the very soil of the *patrie*.

This *Mémoire* is objective and restrained. It is virtually free of personalities. It is philosophical in temper and the political principles of Carnot are repeated in general form. It revealed a profound understanding of what had actually happened in France during the Revolution. This candid *Mémoire* is a protest against the arbitrary abuse of the Constitutional Charter, against the irresponsibility of the ministers, and against their efforts to divide the country by arousing the factions. To a large extent, it is a plea for a common, united patriotism. Carnot stood forth in this *Mémoire* as an unqualified and uncompromising republican.[78]

Napoleon left Elba on February 26, 1815, and landed on French soil on March 1. While he was marching on Paris, Carnot went to see Prince Cambacérès, and the two discussed the turn in events. "General," said Cambacérès, "what do you mean to do?" "I shall serve Bonaparte [replied Carnot]. Between me and the Bourbons an implacable war must henceforth exist. . . . However, Bonaparte must be held in check. He must not be allowed to recommence the system of the Empire."[79] Napoleon was at Fontainebleau on March 18, and on the 20th he entered the Tuileries in Paris. Napoleon issued promises of substantial reform and expressed his willingness to become a well-limited constitutional ruler.[80] On the very day of his arrival Napoleon called Carnot in for an interview. On returning home Carnot was immediately recalled and offered the portfolio of minister of the interior. Carnot accepted. He had high hopes for the honesty of Napoleon's change of mind. Shortly thereafter the ministers presented a joint *Mémoire* to Napoleon for which Carnot drafted the rough minute: "Your Majesty has traced the route that we should follow: no external war, excepting to repel an invasion; no reaction internally, no arbitrary acts, the serious but not meticulous responsibility of the custodians of power, the security of persons and property, the abolition of censorship: these are the principles that your proclamations have consecrated."[81]

Napoleon offered Carnot the title of count on March 22 through his chancellor, Cambacérès. Carnot made no reply to this and the patent remained uncalled for in the archives.[82] Carnot was, however, sometimes called Count during the Hundred Days and although he did not use the title, at least one of the official documents during his ministry used the title *Comte* over his signature.[83] Carnot had a deep-seated aversion to titles of nobility and confided to private notes that "hereditary nobility is a principle of hatred and of jealousy between citizens. . . . Those who accept noble distinctions thereby reveal their own inferiority."[84] When Carnot received his patent as Peer of France on the day of the Battle of Waterloo, he accepted it as a matter of duty so that he might serve the nation in the Chamber of Peers.[85]

Napoleon deputized Benjamin Constant to prepare the modification of the Constitution necessary to fulfill his promises of reform. On April 22 this "additional Act to the Constitution of the Empire" was ready, and on June 1 its acceptance by popular vote was celebrated in appropriate ceremonies. When Carnot discovered that the additional Act was not coming up to what he had been led to expect from Napoleon he protested vigorously against it, telling Napoleon that it "would do his cause more harm that the loss of a battle, and that those who signed it would compromise, with him, some of their popularity."[86] When Napoleon asked him, then, whether he would sign it, Carnot replied: "I shall sign it because the interest of France dominates every other consideration with me."[87] This signature was the pretext for his proscription by Louis XVIII.[88]

Carnot, in response to Napoleon's request, hastily set down certain suggestions of constitutional changes.[89] The major principles were: the French nation is sovereign and independent; the people give themselves a political constitution in order to assure the national prosperity and the happiness of each; the constitutional charter should be accepted by the majority of the citizens; the government is monarchial under the name "French Empire;" the monarch is chosen by the people and he takes the title "Emperor of the French;" the monarchy is hereditary in the male line; no other title or dignity is hereditary in France. Carnot provided for a senate and a chamber of deputies. The former would be composed of members over forty years of age, with life terms. The members of the latter were to be at least twenty-five, and were to be elected for five years. The president of the senate would stand next to the Emperor in importance. The executive power would be vested in the Emperor and the Ministry, and the Ministers would be responsible. The laws would be initiated by a Council of Legislation composed of five commissioners from each of the Chambers, five from the judiciary, and five councillors of state. This Council would be presided over by the Emperor. The Chamber of Deputies could discuss and vote, but not amend proposals. When passed by the Chamber, proposals immediately became law. The Senate would have the duty of maintaining the Constitution, and it would exercise a censorial power over all authorities. The judiciary would be independent and would be named by the Emperor for life. Nothing came of these proposals.

Carnot wrote to Napoleon on May 4 to warn him of the general discontent and of the civil revolt that threatened.[90] He proposed that Napoleon proclaim two decrees which Carnot outlined. These announced that Napoleon would permit the Chamber of Representatives to amend the Additional Act and submit the modified constitution to the people for ratification. Napoleon declined this counsel.

Carnot, as minister of the interior, interested himself in popular education, a matter always close to his heart. In February and March, before the final advent of Napoleon, the Society for Elementary Instruction had been formed in Paris. Lasteyrie, de Laborde, and Gérando had been the pioneers in these months in introducing the methods of Bell and Lancaster into France. Carnot embraced these new ideas, and three days after his installation in office he communicated with Gérando. The latter had been urging the Society for the Encouragement of National

Industry to support a society devoted to the promotion of elementary education. The Society agreed on condition that the approval and patronage of the minister of the interior was secured. Carnot was enthusiastic and immediately established a scholarly Council of Benevolence and Welfare for these general purposes. Its first session was held on April 13 and the initial discussion was almost exclusively devoted to education.

Carnot prepared two decress on education in April. The first one, of indeterminate date, was the most important. The second was a mutilated copy of the first. It is dated April 27 and appeared in the *Moniteur* of that date.[91] Something had evidently intervened to alter Carnot's original proposal. It may have been the reactionary Additional Act that accounted for the changes in these decrees. Carnot prefaced the first proposal by a report to Napoleon, in which he said: "This discovery [to give the greatest degree of simplicity, rapidity, and economy to primary education] is of great importance for the interests of civilization, for worthy customs and public order, for liberty, and finally, for the interests of agriculture and manufacturing."[92] The result of this program of popular primary education, he said, would be to inculate the sentiments of duty, of justice, of honor, and respect for the established order in the hearts of the children. He told Napoleon that this establishment of primary education would complete the system of liberal institutions which "Your Majesty prepares for Your Empire. This will give the first and the surest guarantee for the future."[93] He suggested that the decree start out: "Napoleon . . . considering that: (1) Education is the principle of all order and of all enduring happiness, and that the enlightenment that assures the liberty and the dignity of man cannot be too widely diffused; (2) there exist methods of primary instruction so perfected that they can easily embrace all classes of society. . . ."[94]

The decree proposed went on to set up specifically the new system of primary education, that was to be supported, initially, by the state, under the supervision of the minister of the interior. Ultimately the localities would assume the entire support of these institutions. Government inspectors would insure centralized control and uniform standards. The decree that Napoleon did finally issue on April 27 established an experimental primary school in Paris. This was to serve as a model and was intended to become a normal school for primary training.[95]

Carnot busied himself with a wide variety of duties during his ministry.[96] He gave himself to such problems as roads, public works, the National Guard, exports, a new system of weights and measures, public education, professional schools, scientific institutes and museums, libraries, public health, and cults. He submitted frequent reports to Napoleon, and he worked out a careful budget, arranged in twelve chapters.[97] He conducted a wide official correspondence with administrative officers throughout France, and with the bishops of the Church. He gave public audience to all kinds of petitions at stated times, and was always accessible. He performed his duties with his characteristic thoroughness, and devotion to details.

Carnot was presiding over the Commission of Instruction at the Ministry when the news of Waterloo came to him.[98] On June 21, after his return to Paris after the defeat of Waterloo, Napoleon tried to persuade the Assemblies to consent to a Commission composed of Caulaincourt, Carnot, and Fouché, to open negotiations with the enemy and conclude the war. The Chamber of Representatives, however, refused to deal with Napoleon because the Powers had outlawed him. It insisted that only the Legislative Corps could negotiate, and that Napoleon must either abdicate or be deposed. Napoleon abdicated on June 22 in favor of his son, but the Assemblies disregarded this reservation. Napoleon deputized Fouché to read his abdication to the Chamber of Representatives, and Carnot to the Chamber of Peers. Carnot related to his son the scene in the garden of the Elysée when he reported back to the Emperor: "Sire, I said with emotion, I have just performed the dolorous mission that Your Majesty charged me with. Napoleon looked at me for some time and then said in an affectionate tone: 'M. Carnot, I have discovered you too late'."[99]

After the abdication the two Chambers elected a provisional Commission of Government, composed of five members. The Chamber of Representatives elected Carnot, Fouché, and Grenier, with Carnot at the head of the list with 324 votes. The Chamber of Peers elected Caulaincourt and Quinette. This Commission finally decided to yield to force.[100] Fouché, on his own responsibility, announced to Louis XVIII that the provisional Government would dissolve as its only duty, and this appeared in the *Moniteur* on July 8.

Louis XVIII dissolved the two Chambers on July 8. On July 24 the King ordered fifty-seven persons to leave Paris and to be kept under police surveillance.[101] The cases of these persons were to be disposed of finally by the Chambers when they convened on September 25. Carnot was on the King's list, and he was the only one of Napoleon's recent ministers to appear on it. Carnot retired to Cerny and it was there that he issued on September 12 his *Exposé* of his political conduct since the First of July, 1814.[102]

Carnot denied that his purpose in this work was to plead his case beforehand with the members of the Chamber. He wrote: "I want to preserve the esteem that the public has for me in spite of the many persecutions to which I have been subject; I comfort my own heart in proving to the people that I do not merit losing its confidence, that I have not ceased to consecrate all my thoughts and all my wishes to the happiness of my country."[103] Carnot claimed that Louis XVIII had picked him out from among Napoleon's ministers because of the publication of his *Mémoire au Roi* in the previous year. He denied all connection with its publication and said that, as minister of the interior, he had discouraged its further distribution. He reviewed the entire history of the appearance of the pamphlet. Carnot then denied that he had anything whatsoever to do with the return of Napoleon from Elba.

Carnot replied to the natural question as to why he had accepted a portfolio under Napoleon: "I will say frankly that I accepted without regret the place offered me by the Emperor because I had the hope of doing some good in it. I believed, and I still believe, that the Emperor had returned with the sincere desire to preserve the peace and to govern paternally."[104] In a subsequent passage he wrote: "I flattered myself to see our disasters ended; to see the resources of the state directed to the progress of industry, to the relief of the indigent, to the perfecting of public instruction. I rejoiced in the thought that as minister of the interior, I could become one of the principal agents of these happy changes."[105] He commented that it was the policy and the activity of the allies that forced Napoleon to deviate from the line of moderation that he had marked out to follow. Carnot went into a thorough explanation of the conduct of the Provisional Commission of Government after Napoleon's abdication.[106] The Commission honestly tried, he said, to save Paris and France from their enemies until some regularly constituted government could assume control. This was imperative, he claimed, and it was only patriotic devotion that motivated the members.

Carnot was only repeating an old conviction when he wrote: "It is the duty of a good citizen to abide by the established government. In the crises of state, there can be moments of uncertainty as to which side to take; one can hesitate or choose between opinions, without being guilty of a crime, but when the majority has once decided, the minority is only a faction if it persists in its opposition. It is this principle of eternal justice that constitutes the essence of every political society; without it there would be nothing but anarchy and civil war in the entire world."[107]

Carnot concluded his brief and dignified *Exposé* by recapitulating the salient facts in his political career, with the recurrent accusations or punishments that had repeatedly denied the quality and the motive of his acts. He finished by prophesying for himself a final denial of justice: "I have idolized my country, and soon, perhaps, I shall be forced to solicit the generosity of foreign princes for an asylum in their states."[108]

The event came about as Carnot had predicted. He anticipated the final verdict and fled the country in October. He took his fourteen year old son, Hippolyte, with him. Sadi, the older, was a captain in the engineering corps. Alexander of Russia had offered him an asylum and Russian passports were issued to him. He arrived in Brussels on October 20, and left Belgium on November 4 for Munich and Vienna, arriving in the latter city on December 19. Thence he traversed Moravia to Cracow. The travelers left there on December 31 and arrived in Warsaw on January 6, where they abandoned their incognito. It was in Warsaw that Carnot learned that the Chamber of Deputies had violated the charter by condemning the Conventionals to perpetual exile.

Carnot's reception in Poland had been most cordial.[109] He spent over six months in Warsaw, and then journeyed to Silesia, on a safe conduct from the King of Prussia. Traveling via Berlin and Frankfort-on-the-Oder, he finally arrived at Magdebourg, the place nearest to his beloved France in which he was permitted to reside.[110] Attempts in France to permit the proscribed to return to their *patrie* were decisively defeated on May 17, 1819. Carnot's brothers had been active in the effort to have this question reopened in France.

Carnot led a simple life at Magdebourg. His financial resources were very limited. Besides his son, the household included the faithful *domestique*, Joséphine, who followed these two in exile. Carnot followed affairs in France with intense interest, and he corresponded regularly with his brothers. Carnot visited among new friends, both in the French colony made up of descendants of Huguenot *émigrés*, and among the Germans, of whose society he remarked: "In Germany one does not know how to give his talent in conversation; society counts for little."[111] He was particularly happy in those homes where there was music. Carnot took up versification again and in 1820 friends of his published a first edition of his collected poems in Paris,[112] and in the following year his heroic-comic poem *Don Quichotte* was published in Paris and Leipzig.[113]

Carnot devoted himself to flowers, and he and his son took long walks into the country. It was during this period that he met Dr. Wilhelm Körte of Halberstadt, with whom his relations became very cordial.[114] Dr. Körte requested the privilege of writing Carnot's biography. This was granted and the work was completed in October, 1819, and was published in Leipzig in 1820.

Carnot jotted down his reflections under the heading, "Solitary Promenades."[115] "Morality consists in the recognition and the accomplishment of our duties. . . . The word 'duty' seems to be opposed to that of 'pleasure,' and the latter is always the principal object of our wishes. One is tempted to believe at first that morality is nothing but a long sermon, a continual exhortation to repress our desires, to resist nature, to impose on ourselves every form of privation. . . . But the true morality does not have this austerity of principles; it is, on the contrary, founded upon the personal interest, and the end that it serves is to reconcile this personal interest with the general interest, to identify them, to make all the individual inclinations and passions contribute to the happiness of society in general, without depriving anyone of his rightful pleasures.

"Society ought to be like a beehive, where each bee, in obeying its own instinct works for the good of all the bees. The workers deal justly with the loafers, those who do not have the instinct to work, by killing them. Reason, which is superior to instinct, ought to suggest to men other means whereby they can harmonize the interest of the individual with that of society. . . . Follow the dictates of your conscience. Love your neighbor as yourself. . . . Do nothing to others that you would not want done to you. . . . It is assuredly the most sublime of all arts, and the most difficult, perhaps, to do for others through reason, what the bees and the ants do through instinct. . . ."

Carnot includes in these notes his reflections on the writings of Rousseau and Mme de Staël. His son kept notes on the thoughts of his father under the title, "Meditations of a Solitary Walker."[116] "It is necessary to be useful to society. Therein is all the law, and all the prophets. This morality is that of all civilized peoples, no matter in what clime, or of what religion. He who is useless is shamed by others; he is a parasite who encumbers the earth with his uselessness. . . . Tolerance is a sacred duty. All cults are good and all, at bottom, teach the same morality. . . . Impartiality is the basis of all government. . . . True individual interests are also those of society. . . . Institutions unite the power of example to that of habit, to form a second nature. . . . Time changes, destroys, and renews everything. . . . Morality is designed for the happiness of man. . . . The device of man is hope. The art of making men happy it that of having them ever hope. Happiness is a perspective, and hope puts us in the proper place to enjoy it. . . . The germ of benevolence put in us by nature is the principle of all morality. . . . Politics consists in the recognition of the true interests of the social order. . . . The morality of savages is a state of war, where each seeks his own advantage at the expense of others. The morality of social man on the contrary is a doctrine that unites men through a reciprocity of services. . . . Right is the advantage accorded by the law; duty is the obligation imposed by the law. Duty is the condition of right. . . . The nobility is a paper money that is valuable to those who have it, and that the others depreciate as much as they can. The nobility is in the world what the 'zero' is in arithmetic, it is nothing in itself. . . . We are all made of the same dough. . . . Each of us has the right to believe himself important. The difficulty is to persuade others to think the same. . . . I have lived in a century of enlightenment; I have seen the dawn of human reason break through, and eternal truth triumph over ancient prejudices. I have discovered that beneficence is the most perfect of the virtues . . . and that morality is nothing but the art of reconciling the personal interest with the general interest."

Carnot, as a person, is not easy to know. It is his character, however, that gave whatever unique tone and quality there is to his ideas as these became translated into the public life of a great citizen.[117] There is general agreement on certain characteristics of bearing and character. He was tall, with a certain dignity and nobility of bearing and presence. His forehead was high; his eyes were blue and full of sagacity; his nose was slightly aquiline; his lips were serene; his face was mobile in expression; often it would light up with a sudden movement of vivacity, but the calm of his eyes was constant; his diction was precise and clear; he spoke rapidly and with feeling.[118]

There is evidence that Carnot was temperate, modest, just, virtuous, austere, and of simple tastes.[119] In his home life he was patient and indulgent, but towards himself he was severe. He made his conscience the supreme guide of his life. He was an indefatigable worker with a tremendous capacity for work and he had a veritable passion for details. As a politician Carnot was usually direct in his dealings and had little gift for intrigue.[120] He has been called an engineer in politics as in war,[121] and more a mathematician than a politician.[122] His style in writing was lucid, forceful, and pointed. Some of his war proclamations anticipated those of Napoleon for pungency and force.[123] His speeches were usually forceful and simple, although oftentimes they were replete with classical allusions. On infrequent occasion he became quite declamatory and demagogical in his utterances. In his mathematical and philosophical thought Carnot analyzed with clearness, surety of judgment, and with fineness of perception.[124] He was meditative and studious by nature. Carnot was oftentimes inflexible and stubborn, and sometimes intractable. His amiability was not constant, for he was harsh, even irascible and difficult, on occasion.[125] He worked alone better than with others, and he was not always approachable.[126]

Sorel calls Carnot the most resolute and incorruptible of the republicans.[127] Madelin speaks of him as the "solid Burgundian," the savant type of officer, very capable, fearless before the enemy, a methodical and perspicacious calculator, not easily susceptible to discouragement, even less to fatigue, calm to the point of being glacial.[128] He concluded by calling him a "veritable man of destiny for France." Thibaudeau called him aptly a "caractère antique,"[129] and Lamartine's characterization coincided with this: "Carnot, républican des temps antiques."[130] Napoleon described Carnot as a sincere worker in all that he did, and as a man without intrigue and easy to mislead; that he was useful in directing the operations of war in the Committee of Public Safety, but that he did not merit all the praise that men had given him; that, as minister of war, he had displayed few talents; that in the Tribunate he spoke and voted against the Empire, but his conduct was always correct and gave no concern to the government; and that he conducted himself well at Antwerp.[131]

Carnot was not a political figure of the first rank. He never attached himself positively and definitely to a party and he was not magnetic enough in personality nor was his political program unique enough for a party to form around him. This lack of the partisan spirit in him, his general inability to plan and work with others, his spirit of moderation, and his temperamental reticence combined to make his political position seem quite equivocal on certain critical occasions in the Revolution. This was particularly true in the months before and after 9 Thermidor, in the period before 18 Fructidor, and in the Hundred Days, times when his behavior aroused suspicions as to his motives and ambitions. His uncertainties in crises, however, came from an honest attempt on his part to find what was actually the best and most patriotic way to serve the *patrie* without compromising too much, and preserve all that was then possible of the achievements of the Revolution. The ultimate decisions of Carnot verify the conviction that his political conduct was thoroughly consistent with the central principles of his political faith.[132] No matter how one evaluates his other services, Carnot did "organize" effectively the victory in the decisive years of 1793 and 1794.

Carnot might, with the moral authority that he wielded, have been the "man of the hour" at certain times in the Revolution. He would, however, have had to call upon talents and traits that he quite evidently lacked. His immediate and his final significance in and for the Revolution might have been less vital and less enduring had be become the leader and the storm center of a particular period of the Revolution. By pursuing the path which his character, more or less unwittingly, compelled him to follow, he became a living symbol of the purest republican principles and virtues. Part of this, no doubt, was legend, even in his own day. Later it was magnified out of proportion. As real and legendary figure and symbol, however, he has wielded a significant power over the minds and imaginations of men. The particular consummation of character, ideas, and conduct in this man may well make him, from one point of view, the "French citizen par excellence."[133] Niebuhr said of this man: "Carnot is, on some scores, the greatest man of this century; his virtue is of an exquisite quality. My political ideas differ from his and my love for him seems to be an anomaly; but this love does exist. If but a crust of bread were left to me, I would be proud to share it with Carnot."[134]

At the very center of Carnot's political, moral, spiritual, and philosophical convictions was love of country.[135] This was the real dynamic of his emotional life as well. This profound affection amounted almost to idolatry and was the absorbing passion of his life. Carnot almost personalized the very soil of France into a living, organic being that merited all the virtuous service and worship that the child of the nation could give it.[136] This worship of country was the only real cult that Carnot adhered to.[137] It must be remembered that Carnot was physically and spiritually born of a sturdy, independent bourgeois stock that was rooted deep in the soil of France.[138] From such loins as his have sprung a race of narrow yet devoted Republican patriots.

It was this single-minded devotion to the *patrie* that made Carnot insist upon the autonomy of states. He lacked the evangelistic fervor of many of the Revolutionaries, who wanted to transform the institutions of other states on the French Revolutionary model. This was a subtle form of imperialism that Carnot feared. His passion for humanity at large and his belief in the rights of self-determination compelled him to take issue with it. He was fearful lest the very ideas of the Revolution be defeated in the means taken to spread them. More than that, no doubt, his emotional feeling for France compelled him to protect and preserve her, inviolate and sacred. This was not a narrow nationalism for Carnot believed that the mission of the Revolution to other peoples would be accomplished best by the means of demonstration in France.

This religion of the *patrie* called for civic righteousness of a very high order. On this Carnot constantly insisted. No other leading republican in the Revolution so thoroughly and so consistently combined the principles and practices of the cult of the state as did Carnot in his own character and conduct. He was always a Republican but the nation was not always republican. No matter, for the *patrie* was always there and it was always the same. Carnot, therefore, was the profoundest kind of patriotism incarnate. His being was identified with the living being that France was to him. He made himself one with France. This identification of the virtues and the essence of a country and of a citizen, as that citizen defined them, is, no doubt, Carnot's greatest contribution to the Revolution and to France.

Carnot died at Magdebourg on August 2, 1823, at three score years and ten. On June 10, 1889, in the Presidency of his grandson, Sadi, the ashes of the "impenitent republican" and "organizer of victory" were brought home to the *patrie*, to rest in the Pantheon in Paris.

NOTES

CHAPTER I.

THE FASHIONING

[1] Rene Girard—"Carnot et l'Education Populaire Pendant le Cent Jours," *La Révolution Française,* LII, (1907), p. 430.

[2] Jules Toutain—*La Gaule Antique vue dans Alesia,* (Le Charité-sur-Loire, 1932), p. 130.

[3] *Travels through France and Italy,* (London, 1907), p. 72.

[4] *op. cit.,* p. 71.

[5] *Ibid.,* p. 72.

[6] Tyson and Guppy, ed.—*The French Journals of Mrs. Thrale and Doctor Johnson.* (Manchester, 1932), p. 209.

[7] *Travels in France* (New York, 1915), p, 183.

[8] *Ibid.,* pp. 183-184.

[9] *Ibid.,* p. 184.

[10] W. E. Mead—*The Grand Tour in the Eighteenth Century.* (Boston, 1914), p. 44.

[11] Donald Greer—*The Incidence of the Terror during the French Revolution* (Cambridge, 1935), p. 68.

[12] M. Roustan—*The Pioneers of the French Revolution* (London, 1926), Preface.

[13] *Ibid.,* p. 16.

[14] P. F. Willert, in "Philosophy and the Revolution," *Cambridge Modern History,* Vol. VIII (1904), p. 10.

[15] M. Arago, *Biographie de Lazare-Nicolas-Marguerite Carnot* (Paris, 1850), pp. 3-4.

[16] L'Abbe Augustin Sicard, *Les Études Classiques avant la Révolution* (Paris, 1887), p. 417.

[17] *Ibid.,* appendix, pp. 559-561: Plan d'Études de l'Oratoire. D'Apres le *Ratio Studiorum,* dressé par le P. Morin, en 1745.

[18] H. T. Parker, *The Cult of Antiquity and the French Revolutionaries.* (Chicago, 1937).

[19] M. Carnot. *Mémoire adressé au Roi en Juillet 1814,* pp. 16, 17, 20, 34; Carnot, Lazare—"Discours prononcé par le citoyen Carnot, séance extraordinaire du 11 floréal an 12," *Tribunat,* 1804 (Pamphlet); *Réponse de L. N. M. Carnot . . . au Rapport Fait sur la Conjuration du 18 fructidor an 5 . . . par J. Ch. Bailleul . . .* Londres, 1799, pp. 33, 38, 49, 64, 89, 118, 156, 203, 207, 212.

[20] Sadi Carnot, ed.—*Centenaire de Lazare Carnot, 1753-1823,* Notes et Documents Inédits (Paris, 1923), pp. 11-13.

[21] *Ibid.,* p. 17.

[22] Hippolyte Carnot, *Mémoires sur Carnot* par son Fils, 2 Vols. (Paris, 1861-1863), I, p. 5.

[23] Moniteur (réimpression) XX, p. 456; *Ibid.,* p. 518; F.-A. Aulard,—*Histoire Politique de la Révolution Française* 1789-1804, Paris, 1901, p. 492.

[24] Archives de la famille Carnot.

CHAPTER II.

APPRENTICESHIP

[1] Arago, *op. cit.,* p. 10.

[2] *Correspondance de Napoléon ler* (Paris, 1858-1870), XXIX, p. 59.

[3] *Mémoires sur Carnot, op. cit.,* I, pp. 96-99.

[4] Ernest Hamel—*Histoire de Robespierre,* 3 Vols. (Paris, 1865-1867), I, pp. 25-30. Hamel writes of this society that it "had the glory of counting in its membership two of the most indefatigable pioneers of the new social order," Carnot and Robespierre. *Ibid.,* I, p. 27.

[5] *Ibid.,* p. 30:

"Amis, de ce discours usé
Concluons qu'il faut boire;
Avec le bon ami Ruzé
Qui, n'aimerait a boire?
A l'ami Carnot,
A l'aimable Cot
A l'instant je veux boire;
A vous, cher Fosseux,
Au groupe joyeux
Je veux encore boire."

[6] *Ibid.,* p. 62.

[7] A. Cornereau,—*Deux Lauréats de l'Académie de Dijon* (Dijon, 1903), p. 14.

[8] Ferdinand Dreyfus, *Vauban Économiste* (Paris, 1892), pp. 25-26.

[9] *Mémoires de Saint-Simon* (1899), XIV, p. 324.

[10] Jacques Roujon, *Louvois et son Maitre* (Paris, 1934), p. 150.

[11] C.-A. Sainte-Beuve, *Causeries de Lundi* (Troisième Éd.) (Paris, 1885), XIV, p. 14; XV, p. 247.

[12] M. Carnot, capitaine au Corps—Royal du Génie.—*Éloge de M. le Maréchal de Vauban,* etc. (Dijon, 1784), p. 2. There are forty-five pages of text and fourteen of notes. On the last page one finds these words: "Approbation. Cortot, censeur royal . . . je n'y ai rien trouvé qui en doive en empecher l'impression."

[13] *Ibid.,* p. 10.

[14] *Ibid.,* p. 44.

[15] *Ibid.,* p. 6.

[16] *Ibid.,* p. 16.

[17] *Ibid.,* pp. 24-25.

[18] *Ibid.,* p. 25.

[19] *Ibid.,* p. 9.

[20] *Ibid.*

[21] *Ibid.,* pp. 27-28.

[22] *Ibid.,* p. 29.

[23] *Ibid.,* p. 30.

[24] *Ibid.,* p. 31.

[25] *Ibid.,* p. 32.

[26] *Ibid.,* p. 37.

[27] *Ibid.,* p. 43.

[28] *Ibid.,* p. 34.

[29] Chapter V is largely devoted to a discussion of the military forces and policies in France on the eve of the Revolution.

[30] Cornereau, *op. cit.,* pp. 20-21.

[31] Quoted at length in *Mémoires sur Carnot, op. cit.,* I, pp. 130-140.

[32] *Mémoires sur Carnot, op. cit.,* I. pp. 146-148.

[33] Early in the Revolution, Montalembert emigrated for a time. After his return and during the Convention Carnot often called him into consultation on military affairs. He was promoted general of division. The following item is significant: Le comité de salut public arrête que Montalembert, ancien officier général, demeurant à Paris, rue de la Roquette, faubourg Antoine, section Popincourt, est invité à continuer ses travaux relatifs à l'artillerie et aux fortifications, et que les gardes qui lui ont été donnés

seront tenus de se retirer sur-le-champ. Thuriot, Carnot (main de Thuriot) F.-A. Aulard,—*Recueil des Actes du Comité de Salut Public*, etc., (Paris, 1889), XV, p. 785, *séance* of August 9, 1794.

[34] Quoted in *Mémoires sur Carnot, op. cit.*, I, pp. 155-156.

[35] *Ibid.*, p. 156.

[36] Étienne Charavay,—*Correspondance Générale de Carnot* (Paris, 1892), I, p. xv; *Mémoires sur Carnot, op. cit.*, I, pp. 157-160.

[37] Léon Hennet,—*État Militaire de France pour l'Année 1793* (Paris, 1903), pp. 310-313.

[38] Claude-Marie Carnot, born January 15, 1755; aspirant in the engineering corps January 1, 1771; second lieutenant in the engineering school at Mézières on January 1, 1774; first lieutenant, January 1, 1776; Captain, May 25, 1788; administrator of the Pas-de-Calais in 1790; deputy of this department to the Legislative Assembly on August 27, 1791; member of the military committee attached to the depot of fortifications on September 1, 1792; commissioner of the executive council to the Armies of the Moselle and of the Rhine from October to December, 1792; named lieutenant-colonel and director of the depot of fortifications on December 20, 1792; commissioner of the executive council for the purpose of inspecting fortifications in the Nord and in the Pas-de-Calais, from May to July, 1793; named chief of brigade on August 31, 1795; general of brigade on June 4, 1796; retirement on September 22, 1797; returned to active service on February 22, 1800; second in command of the engineering corps in the Army of Reserve on March 10, 1800; inspector of fortifications, from April 23, 1800 to September 7, 1801; resigned on March 28, 1802; retired on October 24, 1810; named inspector general of the engineering corps on April 23, 1814; deputy of Châlon-sur-Saone on May 12, 1815; provisional Minister of the Interior on June 23, 1815; retired on September 9, 1815; named honorary lieutenant-general on December 24, 1817; died at Autun on July 17, 1836.

CHAPTER III.
CARNOT—LEGISLATOR AND ON MISSION

[1] *Mémoires sur Carnot, op. cit.*, I, p. 198.

[2] F. A.-Aulard in his *La Société des Jacobins,* (Paris, 1889-97), 6 vols., only mentions Carnot once as a member, III, p. 161, reporting the *séance* of Monday, October 3, 1791, under the presidency of Brissot, in which one of the secretaries read a list of ninety-five deputies who had just been received into the Paris society, which included the names of the Carnot brothers.

[3] Claude-Antoine Prieur du Vernons was born at Auxonne on December 22, 1763; became an under-lieutenant of engineering at the school at Mézières on January 1, 1782; deputy to the Legislative Assembly and to the Convention from the Côte-d'Or; named member of the Committee of Public Safety on August 14, 1793; was one of the founders of the Polytechnical School, and contributed to the establishment of the decimal system and to the standardization of weights and measures; deputy to the Council of Five Hundred; retired on April 25, 1811; died at Dijon on August 11, 1832.

[4] Paul Arbelet,—"La Jeunesse de Prieur de la Côte d'Or," *Revue du Dix-Huitième Siècle,* 1918, pp. 99-100: ". . . Prieur de la Côte d'Or, qui plus tard composait la musique des élégies ou des Chansonnettes dont Lazare Carnot faisait les vers. . . ."

[5] *Moniteur* (Réimpression), X, p. 327.

[6] *Ibid.*, XI, p. 35.

[7] *Mémoires sur Carnot, op. cit.*, I, p. 197.

[8] *Moniteur* (Réimpression), XII, pp. 171-172. Subsequent references to the *Moniteur* are to this edition, unless otherwise noted.

[9] *Correspondance Générale, op. cit.*, I, p. xvi.

[10] J.-C. Colfavru; "Opinion de Robespierre sur la necessité et la nature de la Discipline militaire," *La Révolution Française*, VII, 1885, p. 268.

[11] *Moniteur* (Réimpression), XII, pp. 401-402.

[12] *Moniteur* (Réimpression), XII, pp. 620-621.

[13] *Moniteur* (Réimpression), XIII, p. 241.

[14] *Moniteur* (Réimpression), XIII, p. 301.

[15] *Correspondance Générale, op. cit.*, I, pp. 4-23.

[16] *Ibid.*, pp. 5-6.

[17] *Ibid.*, p. 8.

[18] *Ibid.*

[19] *Ibid.*, pp. 10-23.

[20] *Moniteur* (Réimpression), XIII, p. 383.

[21] Armand-Louis de Gontaut, duc de Biron, executed in Paris on December 31, 1793.

[22] *Correspondance Générale, op. cit.*, I, pp. 28-148.

[23] *Ibid.*, footnote, p. 28; *Mémoires sur Carnot, op. cit.*, I, pp. 266-267, quoting Prieur, who said to Hippolyte Carnot: "Toutes ces lettres sont de votre père, quoiqu'elles portent nos signatures collectives."

[24] *Correspondance Générale, op. cit.*, I. p. 96.

[25] *Ibid.*, p. 100.

[26] *Ibid.*, p. 112.

[27] *Ibid.*, pp. 148-157 (with appendices, to p. 173).

[28] *Ibid.*, pp. 156-157.

[29] Among the other nine were Duquesnoy (the only other, with Carnot, who had sat in the Legislative Assembly), and Thomas Paine. Robespierre also headed the list elected from Paris and he chose to accept the election from the capital.

[30] cf. Albert Mathiez—*Girondins et Montagnards.* (Paris, 1930), pp. 6-19; Crane Brinton—*A Decade of Revolution, 1789-1799* (New York, 1934), pp. 109-112.

[31] For an illuminating treatment see Crane Brinton—*The Jacobins* (New York, 1930).

[32] *Ibid.*, p. 183.

[33] *Correspondance Générale, op. cit.*, I, p. 179.

[34] Lamarque had been born in the Dordogne in 1753. He was a deputy to the Legislative Assembly, to the Convention and to the Council of Five Hundred from the Dordogne. He was exiled in 1816 as a regicide, but returned to France in 1819, and died at 86, in 1839, in the place of his birth.

Garrau had been born in the Gironde in 1762. He was deputy suppléant to the Legislative Assembly, and deputy to the Convention and to the Council of Five Hundred. He was inspector of reviews in 1806, was proscribed in 1816, returned to France in 1819, dying in that year in the Gironde.

[35] *Correspondance Générale, op. cit.*, I, pp. 181-322.

[36] F.-A. Aulard—*La Révolution Française, op. cit.*, p. 641; P.-F. Tissot—*Mémoires Historiques et Militaires sur Carnot* (Paris, 1824), p. 206; F.-A. Aulard—A Review of M. Bonnal's *Carnot D'Après Les Archives Nationales, Le Depot de la Guerre et Les Séances de la Convention* (Paris, 1888), in *La Révolution Française*, XV, 1888, pp. 567-571.

[37] *Ibid.*, p. 568.

[38] *Correspondance Générale, op. cit.*, I, p. 265.

[39] *Ibid.*, p. 347.

[40] *Ibid.*, pp. 207-214.

[41] *Archives Nationales* AF III 133, signed by Garrau and Carnot.

[42] *Correspondance Générale, op. cit.*, I. p. 203, signed by Carnot and F. Lamarque.

[43] *Ibid.*, pp. 281-282, and in the final report, *Ibid.*, p. 331.
[44] *Ibid.*, pp. 289-306.
[45] *Ibid.*, p. 306, footnote.
[46] *Ibid.*, pp. 354-362; 382-386.
[47] *Ibid.*, pp. 323-348; Bibl. Nat. Le. 39/400; *Moniteur*, XV, 308; F.-A. Aulard,—"Les Idées Politiques de Carnot," *La Révolution Française*, XIV, 1888, pp. 640-656.
[48] Tissot, *op. cit.*, p. 48: "Le rapport . . . parut un modéle de clarté et de precision: il était rempli des meilleures vues d'administration, contenait en raccourci la statisque de cette vaste contrée et indiquait tous les moyens d'amélioration dont elle pouvait être susceptible."
[49] Aulard, *La Révolution Francaise, op. cit.*, p. 641.
[50] *Correspondance Générale, op. cit.*, I, p. 323.
[51] *Ibid.*, p. 332.
[52] *Ibid.*, p. 334.
[53] *Ibid.*, p. 335.
[54] *Ibid.*, p. 337.
[55] *Ibid.*, p. 338.
[56] *Ibid.*, p. 339.
[57] *Ibid.*
[58] *Ibid.*, p. 341.
[59] *Ibid.*
[60] *Ibid.*, p. 342.
[61] J. B. Bury—*The Idea of Progress* (London, 1920), for the history of this theory and the significance of the Eighteenth Century for its development; Carl L. Becker—*The Heavenly City of the Eighteenth Century Philosophers* (New Haven, 1932).
[62] *Correspondance Générale, op. cit.*, pp. 345-346.
[63] *Ibid.*, p. 348.

CHAPTER IV.
THE REVOLUTION TIGHTENS

[1] *Archives Parlémentaires de 1787 à 1860* (Première série), LVII, p. 63.
[2] *Ibid.*, p. 366.
[3] *Ibid.*, p. 462.
[4] Archives de la famille Carnot, quoted in *Centenaire de Lazare Carnot, op. cit.*, pp. 46-47.
[5] *Correspondance Générale, op. cit.*, I, p. 360.
[6] *Ibid.*, pp. 363-380; Arch. Nat. F7 4402; Impr. Bibl. Nat. Le. *38* 2414.
[7] C. J. H. Hayes,—*Essays on Nationalism* (New York, 1926), p. 44.
[8] Albert Sorel,—*L'Europe et la Révolution Française* (Paris, 1891), III, p. 311.
[9] *Correspondance Générale, op, cit.*, pp. 386-389; Copie, Arch. des affairs étrangèrs, Pays-Bas, CLXXXI, p. 147; Moniteur, XV, p. 590; *Journal des Debats*, No. 164, p. 5. The reunion was ordered on the same day, the decree being signed by Carnot (Minute aut. Arch. Nat. F 7 4402; orig. aut. Arch. Nat. C. 248).
[10] *Correspondance Générale, op. cit.*, pp. 390-397; 401; 408-409.
[11] *Ibid.*, pp. 398-400; orig. aut., Arch. Nat., C. 248.
[12] *Correspondance Générale, op. cit.*, pp. 397-398; *Journal des Debats*. Supplément au No. 172, p. 1; *Moniteur*, XV, p. 663.
[13] *Correspondance Générale, op. cit.*, pp. 401-407; Impr., Bibl. Nat., Le38 2552.
[14] *Mémoires sur Carnot, op. cit.*, II, p. 619. In his thinking in this matter Carnot found himself to be in accord with D'Alembert. Cf. Jules Barni—*Histoire des Idées Morales et Politiques en France au Dix-Huitième Siècle* (Paris, 1865), p. 429.

[15] Eleven of the thirteen colonies adopted constitutions between 1776 and 1789. The first one to set forth a declaration or bill of rights properly so called was Virginia, and its declaration was one of the most influential. As early as 1778 a French translation of these Colonial constitutions, dedicated to Franklin, appeared in Switzerland. Another translation was published in 1783 at Franklin's own instigation.

[16] Aulard, *op. cit.*, pp. 21-23; Georg Jellinek,—*The Declaration of Rights of Man and of Citizens.* (New York, 1901).

[17] Lazare Carnot, "Discours prononcé par le citoyen Carnot, séance extraordinaire du 11 Floréal an 12," *Tribunat,* 1804, p. 6.

[18] These comparisons are derived from the following sources: Aulard, *op. cit.*, pp. 19-23; 283-308; Jellinek, *op. cit.*, A. C. O'Connor et M. F. Arago. —*Oeuvres de Condorcet;* H. M. Conaway—*The First French Republic* (Columbia University Dissertations, v. 39); *Constitutions de France* (1791-1830), (Paris, 1830); F. A. Aulard et M. B. Mirkine-Guetzevitch,—*Les Déclarations des Droits de l'homme, Textes constitutionnels concernant les droits de l'homme et les garanties des libertés individuelles dans tous les pays,* (Paris, 1929); A. Mathiez,—*op. cit.*, pp. 82-108.

[19] For a competent summary of Rousseau's political ideas see F. W. Coker,—*Readings in Political Philosophy,* (New York, 1914), pp. 478-479; also, G. H. Sabine,—*A History of Political Theory* (New York, 1937), ch. XXVIII.

[20] C. E. Vaughan, ed.,—*The Political Writings of J. J. Rousseau,* (Cambridge, 1915), I, Introduction, p. 4.

[21] *Ibid.*, II, p. 437.

[22] Leon Say,—*Turgot,* p. 95; Charles Henry,—*Correspondance Inédite de Condorcet et de Turgot,* 1770-1779, p. xviii.

[23] *Barni, op. cit.*, p. 429.

[24] *Ibid.*, p. 445.

[25] The entire second volume (474 pages) of the *Correspondance Générale de Carnot,* is devoted to this mission of Carnot in the Departments of the North and the Pas-de-Calais, from March 12 to August 6, 1793.

[26] *Correspondance Générale, op. cit.*, II, p. 40; Arch. Nat., C. 359, No. 1906.

[27] *Correspondance Générale, op. cit.*, II, pp. 43-44; Procès-verbal, p. 356.

[28] *Correspondance Générale, op. cit.*, II, pp. 55-56.

[29] *Ibid.*, p. 57.

[30] *Ibid.*, footnote, p. 61, quoting the journal, *Le Républicain,* for April 6, 1793 (No. 156, p. 676), to indicate the help which they gave to General Duval and to the civil authorities in Lille and Valenciennes: "Carnot, le digne Carnot, and Lesage-Senault, commissaires de la Convention dans ses contrées, les ont secondés par des measures vigoureuses que dans des circonstances aussi critiques exigeaient."

[31] The Procès-verbal of April 18 mentioned this recommendation. The Committee of Public Safety ordered a fixed limitation on the number of women allowed in the train of the army. (Aulard, *Recueil,* III, p. 309). On the 30th legislation was passed permitting only laundresses, vendors of foodstuffs and wines to be attached to the armies. *Correspondance Générale, op. cit.*, II, footnote, p. 117; pp. 135-136; *Moniteur,* XVI, p. 270.

[32] *Correspondance Générale, op. cit.*, II, pp. 182-185.

[33] *Ibid.*, pp. 245-247.

[34] *Ibid.*, pp. 280-282; Arch. Nat. AF II 238, No. 163.

[35] *Correspondance Générale, op. cit.*, II, p. 287.

[36] *Ibid.*, pp. 294-295; elaborated upon by Carnot on June 1 to the Committee of Public Safety, *Ibid.*, pp. 299-303; reported on by Carnot-Feulins to Bouchotte on June 1, *Ibid.*, pp. 305-306. For an interesting contemporary

account of this engagement, written by an inhabitant of Furnes, see *Ibid.*, pp. 457-474.

[37] *Ibid.*, pp. 297-298.

[38] *Ibid.*, p. 375.

[39] *Ibid.*, pp. 400-402.

[40] *Ibid.*, p. 451; Arch. Nat., reg. du Comité de salut public séance du 11 Aout 1793.

[41] *Correspondance Générale, op. cit.*, II, pp. 452-453, taken from Paul Foucart,—*La Défense Nationale dans le Nord* (Lille, 1893), II, p. 7.

[42] Crane Brinton,—*A Decade of Revolution, 1789-1799* (New York, 1934), p. 116.

[43] *Moniteur* (Réimpression), XVI, pp. 522-554.

[44] *Mémoires sur Carnot, op. cit.*, I, p. 328. Unfortunately the letter which the son says Carnot sent to the Convention does not appear in the edited Correspondence of Carnot and the writer has been unable to find any reference to this episode other than in the Memoirs by the son.

CHAPTER V.
THE DICTATORSHIP IN COMMISSION

[1] Louis R. Gottschalk,—*The Era of the French Revolution* (Cambridge, 1929), p. 243.

[2] Leo Gershoy,—*The French Revolution and Napoleon* (New York, 1933), p. 273.

[3] Aulard, *op. cit.*, p. 341.

[4] F.-A.Aulard,—*Recueil des Actes du Comité de Salut Public avec la correspondance officielle des Représentants en Mission et le registre du conseil exécutif provisoire.* (Paris, 1889), I, xv. These indispensable volumes will hereinafter be referred to as *Recueil,* with the proper volume.

[5] *Moniteur,* No. 190, p. 773.

[6] *Ibid.*, No. 253, p. 1021.

[7] Aulard, *op. cit.*, p. 339; Brinton, *op. cit.*, p. 121; *Recueil,* I, xv.

[8] Geoffrey Bruun,—*Saint-Just—Apostle of the Terror* (Cambridge, 1932), p. 60.

[9] Brinton, *op. cit.*, p. 122.

[10] *Cambridge Modern History,* VIII, pp. 344-5.

[11] *Ibid.*

[12] Bruun, *op. cit.*,

[13] *Girondins et Montagnards* (Paris, 1930), p. 51.

[14] *Ibid.*, p. 32.

[15] *The French Revolution* (New York, 1928), p. 349.

[16] *The Fall of Robespierre* (New York, 1927), pp. ix-x.

[17] *The French Revolution*, p. 349.

[18] *The Revolutionaries* (London, 1930), p. 209.

[19] *Ibid.*, pp. 196-227.

[20] *Mémoires sur Carnot,* I, pp. 347-348; Lacretelle, jeune,—*Présis Historique de la Révolution Française. Convention Nationale* (Paris, 1803), pp. 141-2; Taine,—*Les Origines de la France Contemporaine—La Révolution* (Paris, 1885), III, pp. 234-244.

[21] Aulard, *op. cit.*, p. 341; Madelin, *La Révolution* (Paris, 1912), p. 316; Hamel, *op. cit.*, III, p. 170; Arne Ording,—*Le Bureau de police du Comité de Salut public, Étude sur La Terreur* (Oslo, 1930), reviewed by P. Caron, *La Révolution Française,* LXXXIV, 1931, pp. 84-86, a letter of Col. Sadi Carnot on the same (pp. 177-179), replied to by Ording (pp. 352-354).

[22] For Carnot's absorption in his military labors see: Aulard, *op. cit.*, p. 338; *Correspondance Générale, op. cit.*, I, pp.x-xi; *Ibid.*, III, p. ii; Sorel, *op. cit.*, III, pp. 513-515; Pierre de la Gorce,—*Histoire Religieuse de la Ré-*

volution Française (Paris, 1921), IV, p. 90; Bruun, *op. cit.*, p. 60; Wilhelm Körte,—*Das Leben L. N. M. Carnots* (Leipzig, 1820), p. 44; p. 60; A. H. Jomini,—*Histoire Critique et militaire des Guerres de la Révolution* (1820), V, p. 24.

[23] *The Revolutionaries*, p. 247.

[24] *Ibid.*, p. 248.

[25] Mathiez, *The French Revolution* p. 373.

[26] Because of his close supervision of all of the armies he has been called "a permanent representative on mission to the armies," Henri Wallon,—*Les Représentants du Peuple en Mission et La Justice Révolutionnaire* (Paris, 1890), IV, p. 135.

[27] L. N. M. Carnot,—*Campagne des Français depuis le 8 Septembre 1793* (Paris, An III), pp. 6-7.

[28] Particularly important for the military thought and practice of the eighteenth century in France are the following: André Dussauge,—*Le Ministère de Belle-Isle, Etudes sur la guerre de Sept Ans* (1914); Liddell Hart,—*The Ghost of Napoleon* (1934); Spenser Wilkinson,—*The French Army before Napoleon* (1915), although Wilkinson only treats of the physical organization of the army after the Revolution is once under way, disregarding the achievements of the armies in 1793 and 1794, and the vigorous and successful apprenticeship served by the new officers, many of whom Napoleon used later. Wilkinson does say, however (p. 20): 'When Bonaparte, in 1796, took over the command of the army of Italy, the generals, officers and men of that army had been trained during four arduous years of mountain warfare. He made no changes, and none were needed, in its methods of fighting, in the formal tactics of any of the three arms, or in the methods of movement and supply."

Walter Dorn,—*Competition for Empire*, 1740-1763 (New York, 1940), Ch. III, an admirable chapter on "Eighteen Century Militarism."

[29] Dorn, *op. cit.*, p. 83; "Everywhere, therefore, soldiers represented the dregs of society. . . . It will explain the savage discipline and inhuman punishments characteristic of all armies of the old regime."

[30] Professor Dorn has an illuminating passage on the social structure of the armies of the eighteenth century: "An explanation [for military strategy and tactics] must be sought rather in the social composition and military structure of the armies themselves, in the narrowly political purpose of warfare and in the social and economic milieu in which wars were fought . . . . So long as legally unequal social classes were superimposed one upon another it was utterly impracticable to exact the obligation of military service from all citizens alike. . . . [mercantilist] statesmen, therefore, had to make the effort to recruit their armies as far as possible from among those elements which stood outside the productive organization of society, to take their officers from the nobility who stood above it and their soldiers from the unemployed, vagabonds and beggars who stood below it." *op. cit.*, p. 80.

[31] *Cambridge Modern History*, VIII, pp. 401-402.

[32] Belle-Isle, who was named Minister of War in the critical year, 1758, at seventy-four years of age, and at the end of a distinguished military career, made some important reforms. *cf.* Dussauge, *op. cit.*

[33] *Ibid.*, p. 264, "En realité le Gouvernement royal, inconsciement, a fait de la hiérarchie militaire une transposition de l'ordre social."

[34] Wilkinson, *op. cit.*, p. 93.

[35] Dorn, *op. cit.*, p. 88.

[36] Wilkinson, *op. cit.*, p. 103, "Of 285 members elected to the Chamber of Nobles—[in 1789] 154 were officers. Of these one-third were in sympathy with the popular ideas." The lesser provincial nobles in the army, holding

the inferior officerships, were generally friendly to the Revolution, and to equalization of officerships in the army.

[37] Liddell Hart, *op. cit.*, p. 16. The writer's treatment of the pre-Revolutionary French army owes a great deal to this lucid essay.

[38] *Ibid.*, p. 164.

[39] Dorn, *op. cit.*, p. 91: "The inadequacy of his means did not permit him to revolutionize the tactics and strategy of his century. But he applied his resources with rare intelligence and exceptional finesse. In spite of his mastery of the military literature and science of his day and his accurate study of the strategy of the ancients, his art was above all personal and spontaneous."

[40] Hart, *op. cit.*, p. 20.

[41] In the very heat of the war, on July 11, 1794, the members of the Committee of Public Safety charged with the conduct of military affairs ordered forty copies of the five volumes of the *Lettres et Mémoires* of Marshal Saxe, for the use of the Committee. *Recueil,* XIV, 258-9, signed by Carnot, C.-A. Prieur, Robert Lindet.

[42] Wilkinson, *op. cit.*, p. 33.

[43] *Ibid.*, p. 54, "[This work] at once attracted universal attention and holds a place in the history of the French army like that occupied in the history of French social and political thought by the writings of Jean-Jacques Rousseau, which it resembles in the stimulating power of its ideas. It appeals with almost as much effect to the soldier today as it did to the officers of the ancien régime."

[44] Quoted in Wilkinson, *op. cit.*, p. 79.

[45] *Ibid.*, p. 120.

[46] *Cambridge Modern History,* VIII, p. 407.

[47] *Moniteur,* XVII, 412; Aulard—*Recueil,* VI, pp. 3-4.

[48] *Moniteur,* XVII, 474-478.

[49] *Procés-verbal,* XIX, 191.

[50] The Committee of Public Safety authorized the preparation of an observation balloon for the Army of the North on October 25, 1793 (*Recueil,* VIII, 3), and on November 24, it authorized further experimentation with balloons at Meudon (*Ibid.*, 672-4). On April 2, 1794, after a successful demonstration at Meudon, a Company of balloonists was decreed (*Ibid.*, XII, 349-350), signed by Carnot and C.-A. Prieur.

[51] For the important private manufactury of arms at Moulins, see *Correspondance Générale, op. cit.*, III, pp. 103-104 for instructions on September 8, to Representative-on-Mission Legendre (de la Nievre) signed by Carnot; *Ibid.*, pp. 218-220.

[52] *Ibid.*, pp. 453-561.

[53] *Moniteur,* XVIII, 331.

[54] *Correspondance Générale,* III, p. 461-485.

[55] Étienne Charavay,—"Lazare Carnot, D'Après Sa Correspondance," *La Révolution Française,* XIX, 1890, p. 495.

[56] Ramsay W. Phipps,—*The Armies of the First French Republic and the Rise of the Marshals of Napoleon* I (London, 1926-1935), II, pp. 121-122.

[57] Particularly the following cartons: AFII 203; AFII 204; AFII 66.

[58] *The Revolutionaries,* p. 247.

[59] W. B. Kerr,—*The Reign of Terror* (Toronto, 1927), p. 190.

[60] *Op. cit.*, II, p. 112.

[61] *Ibid.*, p. 54.

[62] Archives Historiques du Ministère de la Guerre, B^{1}322; B^{1}323.

[63] Archives Nationales, AFII^{204}.

[64] *Ibid.*, AFII^{203} and AFII^{204}.

[65] Phipps, *op. cit.*, I, p. 62.

[66] "Ce plan conçu surs de bons principes et attribué à Carnot, etendit sa reputation," A. H. Jomini,—*Histoire critique et militaire des Guerres de la Révolution,* IV, p. 52.

[67] Phipps, *op. cit.,* I, p. 246.

[68] *Ibid.,* p. 247.

[69] *Op. cit.,* p. 379.

[70] *Op. cit.,* II, p. 140.

[71] Phipps gives the numbers as 26,000 and 37,000, respectively; *op. cit.,* I, p. 251.

[72] This mission is fully documented in *Correspondance Générale, op. cit.,* III, pp. 261-342.

[73] *Ibid.,* p. 261.

[74] *Ibid.,* p. 271.

[75] *Ibid.,* p. 283.

[76] Wilfred B. Kerr,—*The Reign of Terror, 1793-4,* p. 216.

[77] *Ibid.,* pp. 216-218 for a good report of this engagement.

[78] Phipps, *op. cit.,* I, p. 252.

[79] *Ibid.,* p. 253, probably derived from Jourdan's own description of the battle, see *Correspondance Générale, op. cit.,* III, pp. 312-318, Archives de la guerre, mémoires autographes et inédits de Jourdan. Jourdan did note that "dans d'autre circonstances Carnot et son frère donnerent au général en chef des conseils utiles."

[80] *Correspondance Générale, op. cit.,* III, p. 316.

[81] *Op. cit.,* p. 218.

[82] *Op. cit.,* pp. 258-261; cf. Soult, *Mémoires,* I, p. 55.

[83] *Correspondance Générale, op. cit.,* III, pp. 332-3.

[84] *Ibid.,* p. 314.

[85] *Ibid.,* p. 323.

[86] *Ibid.,* p. 326.

[87] *Moniteur,* XVIII, p. 166.

[88] *Correspondance Générale, op. cit.,* III, pp. 328-330.

[89] *Ibid.,* pp. 336-7.

[90] *Ibid.,* p. 347.

[91] *Ibid.,* pp. 373-4.

[92] *Ibid.,* pp. 374-5.

[93] *Ibid.,* pp. 383-4.

[94] *Ibid.,* p. 397.

[95] *Ibid.,* pp. 407-408.

[96] *Ibid.,* pp. 430-433.

[97] *Ibid.,* pp. 433-435.

[98] *Ibid.,* p. 444.

[99] Aulard, *Recueil,* VIII, p. 126.

[100] *Correspondance Générale,* III, pp. 442-443.

[101] Aulard, *Recueil,* VIII, p. 199.

[102] *Ibid.,* p. 202.

[103] Quoted in Phipps, *op. cit.,* I, p. 269.

[104] Aulard, *Recueil,* VIII, p. 440.

[105] Laurent, Representative-on-Mission in the Army of the North, wrote to the Committee on November 12, to inquire why General Jourdan was in Paris, Aulard, *Recueil,* VIII, p. 363.

[106] *Ibid.,* p. 485.

[107] Kerr, *op. cit.,* p. 220.

[108] *Recueil,* VIII, p. 60.

[109] *Ibid.,* p. 123.

[110] *Ibid.,* pp. 179-180 (November 2); pp. 416-7 (November 14).

[111] *Recueil,* VII, 565, appointment of Hoche written by Carnot and signed

by Carnot, Collot d'Herbois, C.-A. Prieur, and Robespierre; *Ibid.*, VIII, pp. 261-2.

112 *Correspondance Générale,* III, p. 111, despatch of the Representatives-on-Mission to the Committee of Public Safety on September 9.

113 *Recueil,* VII, p. 564; Phipps, *op. cit.*, II, p. 88, "Carnot considered the General (Hoche) as his protege."

114 Madelin, *op. cit.*, p. 251.

115 *Recueil,* IX, pp. 19-20; 35; 54-5; 89-91; 116-117.

116 *Ibid.*, VIII, pp. 610-614.

117 *Ibid.*, IX, p. 204.

118 *Ibid.*, IX, pp. 559-560.

119 Announced by them in a despatch from Sultz to the Committee of Public Safety on December 25. *Recueil,* IX, pp. 662-664.

120 *Ibid.*, pp. 698-9.

121 *Ibid.*, p. 699.

122 *Ibid.*, X, 56-7.

123 *Recueil,* X, 239-241, in Carnot's hand, and signed by four members of the Committee, and empowering the Representatives to execute the dispositions of the decree "severely."

124 Phipps, *op. cit.*, II, p. 118.

125 *Ibid.*, p. 117.

126 Madelin, *op. cit.*, p. 251.

127 *Recueil,* VIII, pp. 222-224.

128 *Ibid.*, IX, pp. 505-7; 537; 556-7; 617-619; for reports of the siege and capture.

129 *Cambridge Modern History,* VIII, p. 434.

CHAPTER VI.
LA PATRIE IS DEFENDED

1 *Moniteur,* XIX, pp. 169; 171-2; *Recueil,* X, pp. 120-1; 157-164; *Procès verbal,* XXIX, pp. 138-159.

2 *Recueil,* XIII, 103, Pomme, to a member of the committee of Public Safety, from Carentin, on April 27, 1794.

3 Phipps, *op. cit.*, I, p. 2.

4 *Ibid.*, pp. 4-5.

5 Madelin, *op. cit.*, p. 255, quoting from Erckmann-Chatrian's *Madame Thérèse;* cf. Gustave Le Bon,—*The Psychology of Revolution*, p. 227, "To realize the causes of the success of the revolutionary armies we must remember the prodigious enthusiasm, endurance, and abnegation of these ragged and often barefoot troops. Thoroughly steeped in revolutionary principles, they felt that they were the apostles of a new religion, which was destined to regenerate the world." Lyford Edwards.—*The Natural History of Revolution*, p. 162, "The fusion of national patriotism with the social myth is the most important spiritual cause of the success of the military campaign under the radical government."

6 *Considérations sur les Principaux Evénéments de la Révolution Française, ouvrage posthume de Madame de Baronne de Staël* (1818), II, p. 12.

7 *Recueil,* XII, 634.

8 Arch. Nat., AFII66. This order was written by Couthon and signed, in addition, by Barère, Saint-Just, Collot-d'Herbois, and Carnot.

9 Léonard Gallois—*Histoire des Journaux de la Révolution Française, 1789-1796* (Paris, 1845-1846), II, p. 489. The paper was started in November, 1789. Deschiens mentions 1980 numbers, and termination on May 19, 1795, but Gallois saw only 1735 numbers. The Bibliothèque Nationale has a partial reimpression of Volumes II, and VI-XXXIII; Lc²295.

10 Carnot cuts no figure in its pages.

[11] *Recueil,* XIII, 570-571.

[12] Monseignat du Cluzel,—*Un Chapitre de la Révolution Française, ou histoire des Journaux en France de 1789 à 1799,* p. 225.

[13] Bibl. Nat'le., Lc2733.

[14] *Recueil,* XIV, 774-5. Barère, C.-A. Prieur, and Collot-d'Herbois signed the order.

[15] *Recueil,* XV, p. 8, signed by Carnot alone, but initialled also, evidently by Barère; *Ibid.,* p. 166, for a further order, signed only by Carnot, on July 14.

[16] *Arch. Nat.,* AFII66, pièce 66. This is one of the most important memoranda of the Committee of Public Safety not published by Aulard.

[17] *Ibid.,* pièces 70, 73, 74.

[18] Deschiens,—*Collection de Materiaux pour l'Histoire de la Révolution de France, etc., Bibliographie des Journaux* (Paris, 1829); Gallois, *op. cit.,* p. 177. *Recueil,* XVI, 506, Séance of September 4, 1794, authorizing payment of 5373 livres to the printer of the journal, signed by seven members, including Carnot.

[19] Arch. Nat., AdxxA549, No. VIII, of July 27, 1794, No. XII, of July 31, 1794, and No. XXIV, of August 25, 1794.

[20] *Op. cit.,* p. 361.

[21] *Recueil,* XVI, 185.

[22] The most of these orders are found in Arch. Nat., AFII66; some are found in *Recueil,* XII, 143; 215; XIII, 46; 587; 715; XIV, 19; 26; 259; 376; XV, 582; XVI, 24-25; 230.

[23] *Recueil,* VIII, 432-3; IX, 720; X, 414. These particular orders were signed by Carnot among others.

[24] *Recueil,* 25-6, signed by Barère, Carnot, C.-A. Prieur, Collot-d'Herbois, Billaud-Varenne, Saint-Just, and written by Barère.

[25] Jomini, *op. cit.,* IV, footnote, p. 14; Phipps, *op. cit.,* I, p. 213.

[26] Kerr, *op. cit.,* p. 174.

[27] Archives Historiques du Ministère de la Guerre, B[13]22.

[28] *Recueil,* XI, 603-4.

[29] *Ibid.,* XI, 699-700, The Representatives Richard and Choudieu wrote to Carnot on March 14 that Pichegru "a reçu avec une véritable satisfaction les orders d'attaque qui lui ont été donnés par le Comité et va les exécuter."

[30] *Ibid.,* XIII, 101-2, Guiot to the Committee of Public Safety from Lille, on April 27: "Nos braves soldats marchent au combat en chantant et dansant la Carmagnole."

[31] *Ibid.,* XIII, 134, Choudieu to the Committee from Lille on April 29.

[32] *Ibid.,* XIII, 155-6; 156-8.

[33] *Ibid.,* 130, séance of April 29, decree signed by Billaud-Varenne, Carnot, C.-A. Prieur.

[34] *Ibid.,* 153-4.

[35] Viz., *Ibid.,* 271-3, May 4, 1794.

[36] *Ibid.,* XIII, 678-9. Saint-Just and Le Bas to the Committee of Public Safety on May 22; *Moniteur,* XX, 552, for the *compte rendu* of Jourdan.

[37] *Ibid.,* XIII, 149, séance of April 30, order written by Carnot, and signed by Robespierre, Saint-Just, Collot-d'Herbois, Barére, Lindet.

[38] *Ibid.,* XIII, 660-2.

[39] *Ibid.,* 778-9, May 27, 1794.

[40] *Ibid.,* XIV, 212-213, séance of June 8, 1794.

[41] *Ibid.,* 171, written by Carnot and signed only by him.

[42] *Ibid.,* 277-8, Gillet and Guyton to the Committee of Public Safety. Saint-Just arrived back in Paris on the night on June 28-29.

[43] *Ibid.,* 364; 388, Richard to the Committee, praising the parts Macdonald, Daendels, and particularly Souham, had had in the victory.

[44] *Ibid.*, 385-6, written and signed by Carnot.
[45] *Ibid.*, XIV, 473-5.
[46] *Ibid.*, 525-6, Gillet, Saint-Just and Guyton to the Committee, on June 25.
[47] Colonel Phipps gives the number as 52,000, *op. cit.*, II, p. 155.
[48] *Recueil*, XIV, 563, Guyton to the Committee on June 27. Phipps denies the effectiveness of its use, but remarks that it is the first appearance of a balloon on a battlefield, *op. cit.*, II, p. 170.
[49] *Ibid.*, XIV, 542-3, Guyton, Gillet, Laurent and Saint-Just to the Committee of Public Safety, on June 26.
[50] *Ibid.*, 540. The order was written and signed by Carnot.
[51] *Ibid.*, 629.
[52] *Ibid.*, 641-2; 667-9.
[53] *Ibid.*, 666-7, on July 2; 669-670, in a despatch to Saint-Just, on July 2; 696-7, Gillet and Guyton to the Committee in the same vein.
[54] *Ibid.*, 711-2. In this despatch Carnot advised Lacombe Saint-Michel that the "principles of humanity and of politics of Bergé are very good and I believe that you would do well to listen to his advice, with the wise mistrust that one should always have." Lacombe Saint-Michel referred to Bergé in a letter to Carnot on September 21, 1794: "Cet animal de Bergé m'embarrasse; il coute cher à la nation; je t'ai demandé déjà ce que tu voulais que j'en fisse, et tu ne m'a pas repondu. Il n'est utile qu'a bien boire et bien manger. Adieu, je t'embrasse"; *Ibid.*, XVII, 5-6.
[55] *Ibid.*, XIV, 717-8, Richard to the Committee from Bruges. On July 5 the Committee sent instructions to the Army of the Sambre-et-Meuse. "Never forget in battle to hold a large force in reserve that . . . can protect the retreat, if this is necessary, or can pursue the enemy if the battle is won. The immensity of the forces at your disposal gives you the possibility to fulfill this object." *Ibid.*, 741-3, signed by Carnot, C.-A. Prieur, Couthon, Collot-d'Herbois, Billaud-Varenne, and Barère.
[56] *Ibid.*, XV, 86-89, Gillet to the Committee.
[57] *Ibid.*, XV, 6.
[58] *Ibid.*, 84-5, written and signed by Carnot.
[59] *Ibid.*, 85, written and signed by Carnot.
[60] *Ibid.*, 141-2, written and signed by Carnot. "Send her the superb collection of paintings in which that country abounds. . . . The people alone, who are everywhere the same, everywhere the friends of liberty, should be respected—in their manners, customs, and even in their oddities, the effect of their prejudices and ignorance."
[61] *Ibid.*, XVI, 14.
[62] *Ibid.*, XV, 159, written by Saint-Just, and signed, also, by Billaud-Varenne.
[63] *Ibid.*, 225, Guyton and Laurent to the Committee.
[64] *Ibid.*, 207-9.
[65] *Ibid.*, 224, Gillet to the Committee.
[66] *Ibid.*, 253-4, Hentz and Goujon to the Committee.
[67] *Ibid.*, 268-9, Gillet to the Committee.
[68] *Ibid.*, 269-272; 289-290; 290-1.
[69] *Ibid.*, 382-3, Laombe Saint-Michel to Carnot from Dunkirk on July 23.
[70] *Ibid.*, 294-6.
[71] *Ibid.*, 293-4.
[72] *Ibid.*, 317-8, written and signed by Carnot.
[73] *Ibid.*, 335.
[74] *Ibid.*, 409.
[75] *Ibid.*, 413-4.
[76] *Ibid.*, 502, Gillet to the Committee on July 29.
[77] *Ibid.*, 546.

[78] *Ibid.*, 638-640, signed by five members, including Carnot, This order was followed by detailed instructions on August 13, written and signed by Carnot, in the name of the Committee, *Ibid.*, XVI, 78-79.

[79] *Ibid.*, XV, 665-6, Hentz, Goujon, and Bourbotte from Thionville; *Ibid.*, 773-6, Bourbotte from Trèves on August 8, detailing the victory.

[80] *Ibid.*, XVI, 121-3 to the Committee on August 15.

[81] *Ibid.*, XVI, 174-7, written and signed by Carnot, on August 17.

[82] *Ibid.*, 363-4, to the Committee. On the following day he announced, regretfully, the postponement of the difficult expedition on Walcheren, which would open up the way into Holland. The immediate hazards were too overwhelming. He presented his own suggestions in some detail. *Ibid.*, 372-3, to the Committee; *Ibid.*, 373-5, to Carnot.

[83] *Ibid.*, 370-1, J.-B. Lacoste to the Committee.

[84] *Ibid.*, 461, written and signed by Carnot, non enregistré.

[85] *Ibid.*, 569, written and signed by Carnot. Gillet replied to this on September 13, stating that he was acting vigorously to achieve this end. *Ibid.*, 680-2.

[86] *Ibid.*, XVII, 5-6.

[87] *Ibid.*, 42-44.

[88] *Ibid.*, 30-31, from Hervé.

[89] *Ibid.*, 40-2.

[90] *Ibid.*, 87-88, written and signed by Carnot.

[91] *Ibid.*, 159-160.

[92] *Ibid.*, 160-161.

[93] *Ibid.*, 203-5.

[94] *Ibid.*, 262. In the session of the Committee on the very next day a regulation of affairs in the three armies of the West was signed by Cochon, Richard, and Thuriot, but was written by Carnot, and the restitution of a dismissed officer in the same session was signed by Carnot alone. *Ibid.*, 283-4; 285.

[95] *Ibid.*, 329-330, Carnot, for Committee, sent instructions to Bourbotte for the Army of the Moselle, written and signed by himself, alone; For other instances see among others, *Ibid.*, 385-6; 386-8; 443-4; 563-5.

[96] *Ibid.*, 289-90; 290-292.

[97] *Ibid.*, 345-7. The official announcement to the Committee was made by Bellegarde and Lacombe Saint-Michel, *Ibid.*, 366-8.

[98] *Ibid.*, 513 to the Committee on October 18, from Worms.

[99] *Ibid.*, 563-5, written by Carnot.

[100] *Ibid.*, 657-9, signed by Richard, but written by Carnot.

[101] *Ibid.*, 659-661, written by Carnot.

[102] *Ibid.*, 782-3, written by Carnot. He wrote later to Bourbotte that "nous ne nous dissimulons pas les grandes difficultés de cette expédition." *Ibid.*, XVIII, 24-5, November 8.

[103] *Ibid.*, XVII, 663-4, Lacombe Saint-Michel to the Committee.

[104] *Ibid.*, 794-5, Frécine, Gillet and Bellegarde to the Committee.

[105] *Ibid.*, XVIII, 27-28, Lacombe Saint-Michel and Bellegarde to the Committee.

[106] *Ibid.*, 93-95, written and signed by Carnot.

[107] *Ibid.*, XVIII, 124-5, signed by nine members, including Carnot. Bréard, Carnot and Richard signed a postscript written by Carnot, urging the prompt despatch of Kléber to the Army of the Rhine to aid in the siege of Mayence. Kléber wanted to take Ney with him, *Ibid.*, 309-310, Gillet to the Committee.

[108] *Ibid.*, 307-9.

[109] *Ibid.*, 333-5, signed by Cambacérès, Carnot, Merlin (Douai), and Thuriot. On December 3 Gillet sent a resumé of six months campaigning to

the Committee, *Ibid.*, 494-5.

[110] *Ibid.*, 145, written and signed by Carnot.

[111] *Ibid.*, 811-3, written and signed by Carnot.

[112] *Ibid.*, XIX, 94, Feraud and Merlin (de Thionville) to the Committee.

[113] *Ibid.*, XIX, 600-3, Bellegarde, Gillet, Lacoste, Portiez (de l'Oise), and Joubert to the Committee from Amsterdam.

[114] *Ibid.*, XX, 152-3, written and signed by Carnot.

[115] *Ibid.*, 185, The Representatives, from the Hague.

[116] *Ibid.*, 276-7, to the Committee.

[117] *Ibid.*, 632-8.

[118] *Ibid.*, 465-7, written and signed by Carnot.

[119] *Ibid.*, 627, written and signed by Carnot, non-enregistré. The same was planned for the other frontiers, *Ibid.*, 628.

[120] *Ibid.*, XII, 167.

[121] *Ibid.*, 480-2.

[122] *Ibid.*, 526-8.

[123] *Ibid.*, 676-7.

[124] *Ibid.*, XIII, 43-44.

[125] *Ibid.*, 146-148, Robespierre, jeune, and Ricord to the Committee.

[126] Phipps, *op. cit.*, III, p. 183.

[127] Robespierre jeune had written to his brother, Maximilien, on April 5, 1795 from Nice, referring to Bonaparte as a patriot, and as a man of "transcendant merit." He mentioned the arrest of Hoche in the same letter. *Recueil,* XII, 421.

[128] Carnot wrote to the Representatives on August 13, expressing his alarm at the reduction in the garrison of Toulon to 1600 men. *Recueil,* XVI, 80-81, written and signed by Carnot.

[129] *Ibid.*, XV, 717-720. Albitte and Saliceti announced the arrest of Bonaparte, from Nice on August 12, *Ibid.*, XVI, 65.

[130] *Ibid.*, XVI, 327-8.

[131] *Ibid.*, XVI, 80-81.

[132] *Ibid.*, XVI, 247-8, written and signed by Carnot. Non enregistré.

[133] *Ibid.*, XVII, 507. Carnot was not a member of the Committee at this time. The same message was conveyed to all of the Representatives on October 22. *Ibid.*, 565, written and signed by Carnot.

[134] *Ibid.*, 799.

[135] *Ibid.*, 788-790.

[136] *Ibid.*, 800-801, November 5. This order was written by Carnot, and signed by three members in addition to Carnot.

[137] *Ibid.*, XVIII, 96-97, written and signed by Carnot.

[138] *Ibid.*, XIX, 204-206. Written and signed by Carnot.

[139] *Ibid.*, XX, 254, written and signed by Carnot.

[140] *Recueil,* XVIII, 222-3, Delbrel to the Committee from Agullana.

[141] *Ibid.*, 359-61, Delbrel and Vidal to the Committee.

[142] *Ibid.*, XV, 488-9, written and signed by Carnot.

[143] *Ibid.*, 514-5. The same announcement was made to the Committee by Cavaignac, Garrau and Pinet, ainé, *Ibid.*, 516-521.

[144] *Ibid.*, 613-616, the Representatives (unsigned) to the Committee on August 2; Garrau to Carnot, *Ibid.*, 617-8.

[145] *Ibid.*, 689-692, Garrau, Cavaignac, and Pinet, ainé, to the Committee on August 5.

[146] *Ibid.*, XVI, 147-9, written by Carnot, but not signed, non-enregistré.

[147] *Ibid.*, XVIII, 80-81; Garrau wrote personally to Carnot on this matter, *Ibid.*, 83-84.

[148] *Ibid.*, 540-542, signed by Garrau, Baudot, and Delcher.

[149] Phipps, *op. cit.*, III, p. 4.

[150] *Supra.*

[151] *Recueil,* XI, 83, written by Carnot, and signed, in addition, by three others.

[152] *Ibid.,* 192.

[153] *Ibid.,* XII, 50.

[154] *Ibid.,* 413-5.

[155] *Ibid.,* 427, written by Barère, and signed, in addition, by Carnot, Billaud-Varenne, and Collot-d'Herbois.

[156] *Ibid.,* XIII, 493, written and signed by Carnot.

[157] *Ibid.,* XIV, 656-7, written and signed by Carnot.

[158] *Ibid.,* XV, 379-380, written and signed by Carnot.

[159] *Ibid.,* XVI, 145-7, session of the Committee of Public Safety. Order written and signed by Carnot.

[160] *Ibid.,* 190-2, Session of August 18, order written and signed by Carnot. Non-enregistré.

[161] *Ibid.,* 151. Non-enregistré. Boursault wrote to the Committee on September 28, concerning Moulin, who commanded the Army of Brest, and Hoche. He admitted the patriotism of both but said that Hoche had "greater military talents." *Ibid.,* XVII, 122-7.

[162] *Ibid.,* XVI, 156-163.

[163] *Ibid.,* XVIII, 385-6.

[164] *Ibid.,* XVIII, 64, written and signed by Carnot. Boursault recommended to the Committee on November 26 that native volunteers be organized into counter-Chouan companies, to supplement the decimated troops. *Ibid.,* 352-5. On December 6, Carnot approved of this for the Committee, excepting for the name, which might cause permanent trouble. He called attention to the fact that companies of guides had already been authorized with the same end in mind, and on the same principle. *Ibid.,* 554-5.

[165] *Ibid.,* XVIII, 452-8.

[166] *Ibid.,* 477-8.

[167] *Ibid.,* 592-3.

[168] *Ibid.,* 661-2.

[169] *Ibid.,* 712-3, written and signed by Carnot. On January 12, 1795, the Committee ordered the minimum of military activity in the West so as not to jeopardize the success of the amnesty. *Ibid.,* XIX, 431-2, written and signed by Carnot. Non-enregistré.

[170] *Ibid.,* XX, 130-2. Two orders, one to the Representatives with the army, the other to those in the Sarthe and the Orne. Both were written and signed by Carnot.

[171] *Ibid.,* 516-7.

[172] To Jourdan, general-in-chief of the Army of the Moselle, on May 23, 1794, a long memorandum written and signed only by Carnot, Arch. Nat., AFII203; To Vachot, commanding in the Vendée, on May 28, 1794, written and signed by Carnot, Arch. Nat., AFII203; To Moulin, general-in-chief, Army of the West, June 16, 1794, written and signed by Carnot, Arch. Nat., AFII 203; other examples in *Recueil,* XIII, 160-1; XIX, 555-6.

[173] *Recueil,* XIII, 214-5, Carnot for the Committee, to Saint-Just and Le-Bas, on May 2, 1794, instructions to be considered, and then given to Pichegru; *Ibid.,* 778-9, Carnot, for the Committee, to the Representatives with the Army of the Moselle on May 27, 1794, instructions to be transmitted to Jourdan; *Ibid.,* XIV, 741-3, the Committee to the Representatives with the Army of the Sambre-et-Meuse, instructing them to communicate the contents of the despatch to Pichegru and Jourdan. This was signed by six members, including Carnot.

[174] *Ibid.,* XIV, 159-160, June 5, 1794, between the Representatives to the Armies of the North, Ardennes, and the Moselle, and Jourdan and other

officers; *Ibid.*, 786, July 7, 1794, Lacombe Saint-Michel reporting an interview with Pichegru and Richard.

[175] *Ibid.*, XII, 50, Garrau, from the Army of the West, to Carnot from Nantes, on March 18, 1794; *Ibid.*, XIV, 786, Lacombe Saint-Michel to Carnot from the Army of the North on July 7, 1794; *Ibid.*, XV, 117-8, Lacombe Saint-Michel to Carnot from Dunkirk on July 12, 1794; *Ibid.*, 168-171, Florent Guiot, from the Army of the North to Carnot on July 14, 1794; *Ibid.*, 171-2, Lacombe Saint-Michel to Carnot from Dunkirk, July 14, 1794; *Ibid.*, XVIII, 83-84, Garrau from the Army of the Pyrenées Occidentales to Carnot on November 11, 1794.

[176] Viz., *Ibid.*, XVI, 239-240, Gillet, from the Army of Sambre-et-Meuse to the Committee on August 20, 1794, suggested changes in plans; *Ibid.*, XVIII, 350-1, Carnot, for the Committee to the Representatives with the Army of the West, November 26, 1794: "The new reflections that you present to us . . . are decisive, and we are sending an order to you conforming to your proposition; communicate it to your other colleagues and to Generals Hoche and Canclaux, so that each can conform in what concerns him." Written and signed by Carnot.

[177] Viz., *Ibid.*, XI, 307, Lacoste and Baudot, Army of the Moselle, to the Committee on February 20, 1794, submitting Hoche's plan for an expedition on Trèves. The Army, they said, "only awaits the order of the Committee." This plan was vetoed on February 25, *Ibid.*, 389, signed by three members, including Carnot; *Ibid.*, XIII, 246, Saint-Just and Le Bas from the Army of the North on May 3, 1794, "Hasten to send us a plan of movement from Cambrai to Beaumont. . . . .Reply at once; do not lose an hour." Carnot replied to this on May 4, giving the general plan of operation, *Ibid.*, XIII, 271-3; *Ibid.*, XIV, 786, Lacombe Saint-Michel to Carnot from the Army of the North on July 7, 1794, "Everything is prepared to execute the changes you have thought to be necessary;" *Ibid.*, XVIII, 80-81, Baudot and Garrau from the Army of the Pyrenées-Occidentales on November 11, 1794, inquiring whether the siege of Pampeluna should be laid at once or delayed.

[178] Viz., *Ibid.*, 271-3, Carnot, for the Committee, to Saint-Just and Le Bas, with the Army of the North, on May 4, 1794, "The details cannot be directed from here because they depend on daily movements of the enemy, which no one can foresee;" *Ibid.*, XIV, 656-7, Session of the Committee on July 2, 1794, instructions to the Army of the West, "These orders are subject to the modifications judged necessary by the Representatives of the people with the Army of the West," written and signed by Carnot; *Ibid.*, XVIII, 64-5, Carnot for the Committee to Bollet, with the Army of Cherbourg, on November 10, 1794, giving general directions. "The additional measures, or modifications, we leave to you." Written and signed by Carnot.

[179] Viz., *Ibid.*, XVII, 648-9, Gillet, Army of the Sambre-et-Meuse, to the Committee on October 27, 1794, criticizing Moreau and Michaud and wondering why the Committee left such "imbeciles" there when Hoche was available; *Ibid.*, XIV, J.-B. Lacoste, Armies of the Rhine and Moselle, to the Committee on June 3, 1794,—a long report on the military situation, with a frank estimate of the generals.

[180] *Ibid.*, XIII, 130, signed by Billaud-Varenne, Barère, Carnot, C.-A. Prieur.

[181] *Ibid.*, XIV, 540.

[182] Viz., *Ibid.*, XIV, 58, Session of June 1, 1794, the first attended by Saint-Just after his mission to the Army of the North, ordering Desjardin to command the right of the Army of the North, and the Army of the Ardennes, under Pichegru, and ordering General Charbonié to Paris to receive a command. Written and signed by Saint-Just; *Ibid.*, XIV, 518, Session of June 25, 1794, naming Moreau commander-in-chief of the Army

of the Moselle. Written and signed by Carnot; *Ibid.*, XV, 499, Session of July 29, 1794; 604, August 2; 677, August 4; *Ibid.*, XVI, 145, August 16, various assignments in succession for General Dumas, from the command of the Army of Italy, to the École de Mars, to the Army of the West, and as general of division to the Army of the Sambre-et-Meuse; *Ibid.*, XVI, 252, Session of August 21, 1794, sending Hoche as commander-in-chief of the Army of Cherbourg. Written and signed by Carnot non-enregistré; *Ibid.*, XVII, 199, Session of October 3, 1794, Schérer called from the Sambre-et-Meuse to Paris for a new appointment. Written and signed by Carnot, non enregistré; *Ibid.*, XVIII, 89, Session of November 12, 1794, sending Schérer as commander-in-chief to the Army of Italy. Same session—ordering Moulin to his post as Commander-in-chief of the Army of the Alps. Written and signed by Carnot. Non enregistré.

[183] Viz., *Ibid.*, XIV, 101, Session of June 3, 1794, provisionally confirming the nomination of general of division Du Merbion as general-in-chief of the Army of Italy, by the Representatives with that Army. Written and signed by Carnot.

[184] In addition to those mentioned earlier, see: *Ibid.*, XII, 552, session of April 13, 1794, Moreau promoted from general of brigade to general of division, written and signed by Carnot; *Ibid.*, XVI, 473, Session of September 2, 1794, Saint-Cyr confirmed as general of division in the Army of the Rhine, written and signed by Carnot. Non-enregistré; *Ibid.*, same session, Desaix confirmed in the same rank, written and signed by Carnot. Non-enregistré; *Ibid.*, XVI, 600, Session of September 9, 1794, Captain Ney confirmed as adjutant-general, chief of battalion, promoted on the field by Gillet. Written and signed by Carnot, non-enregistré; *Ibid.*, XVIII, 400, session of November 28, 1794, General of Brigade Macdonald promoted to general of division. Written and signed by Carnot. Non-enregistré. Grouchy was mentioned in an order signed by Carnot in the same session.

[185] Viz., *Ibid.*, XV, 650, session of August 4, 1794, Huché, general of division in the Army of the West, dismissed and ordered to appear before the Committee to give an accounting. Signed by Thuriot, Carnot, Tallien, and written by Carnot. Non-enregistré; *Ibid.*, XIV, session of June 5, 1794. generals of division Delmas and Laubadère of the Army of the Rhine, arrested and ordered before the Committee. Signed by Barère, Saint-Just, Robespierre, Carnot, Billaud-Varenne, Collot-d'Herbois, Couthon, and written by Barère.

[186] Viz., *Ibid.*, XIV, 659, session of July 2, 1794, liberating Delmas. Written and signed by Carnot; *Ibid.*, 694, session of July 3, 1794, sending Delmas to the Army of the North as general of division. Written and signed by Carnot; *Ibid.*, XV, 459, Session of February 22, 1795, reinstatement of general of brigade Clarke. Signed by Carnot. Non-enregistré.

[187] Viz., *Ibid.*, XV, 241-6, session of July 17, 1794, a long, humane regulation governing prisoners of war and deserters from the enemy, written and signed by Carnot; *Ibid.*, XV, 422, session of July 25, 1794, "Le citoyen, Nie, meunier de Nolay (Côte-d'Or) est autorisé à faire venir pres de lui pour la mouture des grains celui de ses quatre fils aux armées qu'il jugera necéssaire." Written and signed by Carnot. Non-enregistré; *Ibid.*, XVIII, 304-5, session of November 23, 1794, authorizing citizen Delaitre, a cotton manufacturer of Étampes, to take six prisoners from the depot there for work in his factory. Written and signed by Carnot. Non-enregistré; *Ibid.*, XVIII, 368, session of November 27, 1794, an indemnity of fifty livres to the invalided Dubois, for the loss of his haversack. Written and signed by Carnot. Non-enregistré.

[188] *Ibid.*, XII, session of April 17, 1794. Signed by Carnot and Barére.

CHAPTER VII.
TERROR AND REACTION

[1] Kerr, *op. cit.*, p. 247.
[2] Albert Mathiez, *The French Revolution, op. cit.*, p. 450.
[3] Mathiez, *Girondins et Montagnards* (Paris, 1930), p. 109.
[4] Kerr, *op. cit.*, p. 343.
[5] *Ibid.*, p. 344.
[6] *Recueil*, XII, 19.
[7] *Ibid.*, XI, 712-3.
[8] *Ibid.*, XII, 41-42.
[9] *op. cit.*, p. 352.
[10] *Recueil*, XII, 283; *Moniteur*, XX, 94 ff., *Procès-Verbal*, XXXIV, 304, 331.
[11] *Mémoires sur Carnot*, I, p. 368; Kerr, *op. cit.*, p. 357.
[12] *Ibid.*, I, p. 368.
[13] *Ibid.*, pp. 368-9.
[14] *Ibid.*, p. 369.
[15] *Histoire Politique de la Révolution Française*, (Paris, 1901), p. 464.
[16] *Ibid.*
[17] *Supra.*
[18] Frédéric Masson, *Le Département des Affairs Étrangères pendant la Révolution, 1787-1804* (Paris, 1877), pp. 307-8.
[19] *Moniteur*, XX, pp. 114-117; *Recueil*, XII, 326-330.
[20] On the day after the adoption of this decree the two committees ordered the arrest of Deforgues, minister of foreign affairs (*Recueil*, XII, 344) and appointed Goujon to handle, provisionally, the affairs hitherto cared for by the ministries of the interior, and of foreign affairs. (*Ibid.*, 349). Carnot signed both decrees.
[21] This is clearly stated in a letter to Lanot and Brival, representatives on mission at Tulle, on December 16, and signed by Billaud-Varenne, Carnot, C.-A. Prieur, and Robert Lindet. *Recueil*, IX, 441.
[22] Carnot signed the decree on May 17, with Robespierre and Billaud-Varenne, ordering the Commission of Public Works to construct a hill for this ceremony. *Recueil*, XIII, 576.
[23] *Op. cit.*, p. 492; Kerr, *op. cit.*, p. 405; cf. Hamel, *op. cit.*, III, p. 520.
[24] Lazare Carnot, "Réponse du Président de la Convention, la séance du 27 floréal, an II," *Convention Nationale* (Pamphlet), pp. 4-5.
[25] *Moniteur*, XX, p. 456.
[26] *Ibid.*, p. 518.
[27] *Mémoires sur Carnot*, II, p. 618.
[28] *Cambridge Modern History*, VIII, p. 365.
[29] *Correspondance Générale*, IV, pp. 496-502; Albert Sorel, "Le Comité de Salut Public et la Question de la Rive Gauche du Rhin en 1795," *Revue Historique*, XVIII, 1882, p. 275.
[30] For an able, statistical treatment of the Terror, see Donald Greer,—*The Incidence of the Terror*, (Cambridge, 1935).
[31] There were 16,594 victims of the Terror in all of France, and of these 2,639, or 16 per cent, were executed in Paris.
[32] *Recueil*, XIV, 141.
[33] Albert Mathiez, *Autour de Robespierre* (Paris, 1925), pp. 154-5: "Des le début de Messidor la guerre ouverte était au comité de Salut public. Billaud, Collot d'Herbois et Carnot avaient pris l'offensive contre Robespierre, soutenu par Couthon et bientôt par Saint-Just." Barère and Lindet tried to reconcile the groups, Mathiez says.
[34] Hamel, *op. cit.*, III, pp. 689-690.
[35] Lacretelle, jeune (Charles-Joseph), *Précis Historique de la Révolution Française, Convention Nationale, op. cit.*, II, p. 297.

[36] *op. cit.*, III, p. 501.
[37] Phipps, *op. cit.*, II, p. 88.
[38] Henri Wallon, *Les Représentants du Peuple en Mission et La Justice Révolutionnaire, op. cit.*, IV, p. 195.
[39] Phipps, *op. cit.*, III, p. 123.
[40] *Ibid.*, pp. 121-2.
[41] *Recueil,* XII, 72. Edmond Bonnal, in a book not carefully documented and very partisan to Carnot, claims that this arrest was inspired by Saint-Just—*Carnot D'Après les Archives Nationales, Le Dépot de la Guerre et les séances de la Convention* (Paris, 1888), p. 191.
[42] *Recueil,* XII, 74.
[43] *Ibid.*, 421.
[44] *Ibid.*, 512.
[45] *op. cit.*, Sorel supports this position, *op. cit.*, III, p. 544.
[46] *Réponse de L. N. M. Carnot . . . a Bailleul* [*after 18 Fructidor*] (1799), pp. 146-150; Bonnal, *op. cit.*, pp. 191-3, supports this position.
[47] *Recueil,* XV, 646.
[48] *Ibid.*, 763. Non-enregistré.
[49] *Ibid.*, XVI, 151, non-enregistré.
[50] *Ibid.*, 251. Written and signed by Carnot, non-enregistré.
[51] *Ibid.*, XVIII, 64, written and signed by Carnot.
[52] *Ibid.*, XIX, 555-6, written and signed by Carnot.
[53] *Ibid.*, XIII, 130, signed by Billaud-Varenne, Barère, Carnot, C.-A. Prieur.
[54] Bruun, *op. cit.*, p. 116.
[55] *Recueil,* XIII, 214-5.
[56] *Ibid.*, 246.
[57] *Ibid.*, 271-3.
[58] *Ibid.*, XIV, 58.
[59] *Ibid.*, 155, written by Barère, and signed by seven members, including Carnot.
[60] *Ibid.*, 659.
[61] *Ibid.*, 694.
[62] *Ibid.*, 113-4.
[63] *Ibid.*, 231, signed by Carnot.
[64] *Ibid.*, 171.
[65] *Ibid.*, XIII, 778-9.
[66] *Ibid.*, XIV, 475.
[67] Albert Mathiez, *The Fall of Robespierre* (New York, 1927), pp. 146-7, and Ch. VIII; Mathiez, *The French Revolution,* pp. 497-8.
[68] Hamel, *op. cit.*, III, p. 599.
[69] *Ibid.*, p. 600. Further, on these antagonisms between Carnot and Robespierre, see Jomini, *op. cit.*, IV, 305; Bonnal, *op. cit.*, pp. 157-158; L. N. M. Carnot, *Exploits des Français, etc.*, (Basle, 1796), pp. 107-8.
[70] *Recueil,* XV, 680.
[71] Bruun, *op. cit.*, p. 118.
[72] Kerr, *op. cit.*, p. 469.
[73] *Ibid.*, p. 471.
[74] Quoted in Bruun, *op. cit.*, p. 131.
[75] Quoted in Mathiez, *Girondins et Montagnards, op. cit.*, p. 162, taken from Vellay, *Oeuvres complètes de Saint-Just,* II, p. 482.
[76] *Recueil,* XV, 462.
[77] *Recueil,* XV, 486-8.
[78] *Ibid.*, 488-9, written and signed by Carnot.
[79] *Ibid.*, XVI, 80-81, written and signed by Carnot.
[80] Laurent Lecointre,—"Les Crimes de Sept Members des anciens Comités

de Salut public et de Surété Générale ou Denonciation Formelle, etc." (Pamphlet), pp. 31-32; 160-161.

[81] *Moniteur,* XXIII, 584; 589-592.

[82] *Ibid.,* XXIV, (No. 186), 47.

[83] Aulard denied its validity, *Études et Leçons sur la Révolution Française* (Paris, 1893), Ch. IX, "Les Responsibilités de Carnot."

[84] *Moniteur,* XXIV (No. 186), 47.

[85] *Ibid.,* 49-53.

[86] *Ibid.,* XXIV, (No. 253), 569.

[87] *Ibid.,* 569-570.

[88] *Ibid.,* 570.

[89] *Ibid.,* 570-1.

[90] *Ibid.,* 574.

[91] Aulard, *Études, op. cit.,* pp. 193-194, opposes Carnot's defense here, as does Mathiez, *After Robespierre,* p. 215.

[92] Arne Ording,—*Le Bureau de police du Comité de Salut public, Étude sur La Terreur,* reviewed by P. Caron, *La Révolution Française,* LXXXIV, 1931, pp. 84-86; pp. 352-354, for a reply by Ording to a letter (pp. 177-179) from Colonel Sadi Carnot, criticizing Ording's thesis on the responsibility of Carnot; Aulard,—*Histoire Politique, op. cit.,* p. 341.

[93] *op. cit.,* p. 514.

[94] *Memoirs of Count Miot de Melito,* pp. 172-3; *Mémoires de Barras,* I, p. 167.

[95] A. C. Thibadeau,—*Mémoires sur La Convention et le Directoire* (Paris, 1824), I, pp. 149-151; *Mémoires de B. Barère* (Paris, 1842-1844), Tome II, Vol. IV, pp. 104; 110; *Correspondance de Napoléon ler, op. cit.,* p. 59; Lavalette, *op. cit.,* p. 260; Le Baron de B ****, *op. cit.,* pp. 45; 72-73; 85; 101; P.-F. Tissot,—*Mémoires Historiques et Militaires sur Carnot* (Paris, 1824), pp. xxi-xxii; 60-63; Editorial *Edinburgh Review,* XXIV, November, 1814, pp. 200-2; *Correspondance Générale de Carnot,* I, pp. x-xi; Körte, *op. cit.,* p. 60.

[96] Aulard, *Études, op. cit.,* p. 189: "Dont [the Terror] l'énergie surhumaine et inhumaine sauva l'independance de la France pendant la periode si critique."

[97] *The French Revolution,* p. 441.

[98] *Anciens,* Council of Elders seems to the author to be a better translation than Council of Ancients, as is usually given.

[99] *Mémoires sur Carnot,* I, pp. 585-588; II, pp. 1-5.

[100] Madelin, op. *cit.,* p. 469. Madelin says, however, that Carnot favored separate chambers. But in Carnot's scheme only one chamber would be legislative.

CHAPTER VIII.
THE BOURGEOIS REPUBLIC

[1] Frequently spelled La Revellière-Lepaux.

[2] A. Debidour,—*Recueil des Actes du Directoire Exécutif,* 4 vols., (Paris, 1910-1917), I, p. 5, footnote; *Mémoires sur Carnot,* II, pp. 9-10; L. N. M. Carnot, *Réponse à Bailleul* (1799), p. 174.

[3] *Mémoires sur Carnot, op. cit., Réponse à Bailleul, op. cit.,* Carnot de Feulins,—*Histoire du Directoire Constitutionnel* (1800), p. 8. They had both voted against him in the Convention when he was accused after 9 Thermidor.

[4] He received 181 votes in the Five-Hundred.

[5] *Mémoires sur Carnot,* II, p. 12, quoting a deputy, Villetarde: "Nous ne pouvons former un gouvernement républican sans lui [Carnot]".

[6] Debidour, *op. cit.,* I, 11-13. Hereinafter the name Debidour will be used

simply, in the references to this important collection, with the proper volume and page.

[7] *Mémoires et Souvenirs du Baron Hyde de Neuville,* 3 vols., (Paris, 1888-1892), I, p. 134, "Carnot, seul, élu sur le refus de Siéyès, representait le talent dans le Directoire."

[8] Albert Sorel,—*Bonaparte et Hoche en 1797* (Paris, 1896), p. 4; 151.

[9] Albert Mathiez,—*Le Directoire,* p. 43. For Carnot's characterization of his colleagues see his *Réponse à Bailleul,* pp. 153-154.

[10] *Centenaire de Carnot,* pp. 48-49, from notes inédites du général Lomet, collection Brouwet. Experiments in aerostatics were regularly engaged in. See Debidour, III, 615.

[11] See Madelin, *op. cit.,* ch. XLIV, "Society under the Directory;" Mathiez, *Le Directoire* (1934), ch. VI, "La Politique et les affaires: La République au Pillage;" E. & J. Goncourt,—*La Société Française pendant le Directoire* (Paris, 1876).

[12] Madelin, *op. cit.,* p. 547.

[13] *Ibid.*

[14] See Mathiez, *Le Directoire,* Ch. V, "La Politique Financière du Directoire."

[15] *Cambridge Modern History,* VIII, p. 709, a table showing the value of the assignats in coin of 100 livres; November, 1789—95; January, 1790—96; January, 1791—91; January, 1792—72; January, 1793—51; January, 1794—40; January, 1795—18.

[16] Mathiez, *Le Directoire,* p. 117.

[17] Inscription on the statue of Babeuf in Dijon.

[18] Its formal name was "Réunion des Amis de la République."

[19] Mathiez,—*Le Directoire,* p. 142.

[20] *Ibid.,* pp. 196-7.

[21] Madelin, *op. cit.,* p. 503.

[22] Mathiez,—*Le Directoire,* p. 215, "[Carnot] était avant tout un homme d'ordre. Il avait pour les babouvistes et pour les clubistes en général le même genre d'aversion qu'il autrefois professé à l'egard des enragés, des hébertistes et des dantonistes. Il détestait les factieux."

[23] Aulard,—*Paris pendant la réaction thermidorienne et sous le Directoire,* 5 vols., (Paris, 1898-1902), IV, 3; 106; 141-4; 161; 165; 172.

[24] Mathiez,—*Le Directoire,* p. 212.

[25] Mathiez,—*Le Directoire,* p. 211.

[26] Debidour, III, 589-590.

[27] Mathiez, *Le Directoire,* p. 213.

[28] *Ibid.,* p. 215.

[29] Debidour, II, 133, signed by Carnot, Larevellière, Reubell.

[30] *Ibid.,* 60.

[31] *Ibid.,* 61-62.

[32] The Directory sent him important instructions on November 18, 1795, and asked for his views. Debidour, I, 85-86. The despatch was written by Carnot, and signed also by Letourneur and Barras.

[33] *Ibid.,* 172-3.

[34] *Ibid.,* 558.

[35] *Ibid.,* 830, March 16, 1796.

[36] *Ibid.,* II, 91-92.

[37] *Ibid.,* II, 176, signed Letourneur, Carnot, Barras.

[38] *Ibid.,* 374, May 13, 1796.

[39] *Ibid.,* 388, signed Carnot, Reubell, Barras.

[40] *Ibid.,* 390-1, signed Carnot, Letourneur, Barras.

[41] *Ibid.,* III, 217.

[42] *Ibid.,* II, 659-662, June 19, 1796, signed Carnot, Reubell, Barras.

[43] *Ibid.*, 688-9.
[44] *Ibid.*, III, 112, footnote.
[45] *Ibid.*, 140-4.
[46] *Ibid.*, 150-1.
[47] *Ibid.*, 629.
[48] *Ibid.*, IV, 448-9, December 12.
[49] *Ibid.*, 477-8.
[50] *Ibid.*, 476-7.
[51] Debidour, II, 25, signed by Letourneur, Carnot, Barras. Beurnonville succeeded Moreau in the command of the Army of the North.
[52] *Ibid.*, 124-128. Signed by Carnot, Letourneur, Barras.
[53] *Ibid.*, 133, signed by Carnot, Larevellière, Reubell. This journal first appeared on April 17.
[54] *Ibid.*, 360-361.
[55] *Ibid.*, 468.
[56] *Ibid.*, 702-703, June 23.
[57] *Ibid.*, 740-1.
[58] *Ibid.*, III, 28-30, signed Letourneur, Carnot, Larevellière.
[59] Ibid., 336-7, signed Carnot, Barras, Reubell.
[60] *Ibid.*, 338-340.
[61] *Ibid.*, 410-411, signed by Carnot, Reubell, Barras.
[62] *Ibid.*, 689-691, September 25.
[63] *Ibid.*, 731-4, signed Letourneur, Carnot, Larevellière.
[64] *Ibid.*, IV, 41, signed Letourneur, Carnot, Larevellière.
[65] *Ibid.*, 517, signed by Carnot, Barras, Larevellière.
[66] *Ibid.*, 524-5, signed Carnot, Reubell, Larevellière.
[67] *Ibid.*, 769, signed Carnot, Barras, Reubell.
[68] *Ibid.*, 41, October 12, 1796, two despatches to Willot. The footnote calls attention to the numerous letters from Willot to the Directory and to Carnot, found in Arch. Nat., AFIII, 407, dossier 2239.
[69] In a letter full of detailed instructions, on January 20, Carnot concluded: "It is not a member of the executive Directory who speaks to the commander-in-chief of the Army of Italy; it is a Republican, jealous of the glory of his fatherland, who expresses himself openly to another Republican." *Mémoires sur Carnot,* II, p. 29.
[70] *Cambridge Modern History,* VIII, p. 563.
[71] Phipps, *op. cit.,* IV, p. 5, stating that Carnot, not Barras, proposed Bonaparte for the Italian command; Madelin, *op. cit.*, p. 508, "It would seem that it was Carnot who proposed the man to his colleagues." Madelin writes further: "Carnot wanted a fiery war-chief; Reubell a bold man of action; Larevellière an enemy of all 'shaveling priests'; Barras, a man of compliant character; and each of them suggested Bonaparte; and each of them, within a year, vowed that he it was who had discovered him;" J. H. Rose, *The Life of Napoleon I* (New York, 1916), I, p. 68.
[72] *Correspondance de Napoléon Ier,* I, pp. 110-111. This citation will be given hereafter as *Corr. Nap.*
[73] Debidour, II, 210-211, signed Letourneur, Carnot, Larevellière. The Directory sent him another despatch on the same day.
[74] *Ibid.*, 227-230, signed Letourneur, Carnot, Reubell.
[75] *Ibid.*, 230-1, signed Letourneur, Carnot, Reubell.
[76] *Corr. Nap.*, I, pp. 207-8.
[77] Debidour, II, 277-9, signed by Letourneur, Carnot, Larevellière, and evidently written by Carnot.
[78] *Ibid.*, 328-333, signed Letourneur, Carnot, Larevellière.
[79] *Corr. Nap.*, I, pp. 251-2.
[80] Debidour, II, 345.

[81] *Ibid.*, 352, written by Carnot, and signed also by Reubell and Larevellière.
[82] *Corr. Nap.*, I, p. 279.
[83] Phipps thinks that it was Carnot's plan to have a divided command. *op. cit.*, IV, p. 41.
[84] *Mémoires sur Carnot,* II, p. 63.
[85] Debidour, II, 389, signed Carnot, Barras, Reubell.
[86] *Ibid.*, 392-5.
[87] Debidour, II, 415-9. "Gloire immortelle aux vainqueurs de Lodi! Honneur au général en chef qui a su préparer l'attaque audacieuse du pont de cette ville. . . . Honneur à l'intrépide Berthier. . . . Honneur aux généraux Masséna, Cervoni, Dallemagne. . . . Gloire à la brave division que commandait le général Augereau et à la brave division que commandait le général Augereau et à son chef! Gloire au commissaire du gouvernement Saliceti."
[88] *Ibid.*, 437-9, signed Letourneur, Carnot, Reubell.
[89] Bibliothèque Municipale de Nantes, Vol. No. 659, pièce 148, in the Collection Labouchère.
[90] Debidour, II, 597.
[91] *Ibid.*, 684, signed by Letourneur, Carnot, Larevellière.
[92] Collection Labouchère, pièce 150.
[93] Debidour, II, 706. *Ibid.*, 707. "Le présent arrêté ne sera pas imprimé." Barras, Carnot, Reubell.
[94] *Corr. Nap.*, I, 451-2. Carnot's first child, Léonard-Sadi, had been born on June 1, 1796.
[95] Debidour, III, 61-62.
[96] *Ibid.*, 187, on July 25, signed by Carnot, Reubell, Barras.
[97] *Ibid.*, 225-6.
[98] *Ibid.*, 232-3. All the Directors signed but Barras. Bonaparte replied on August 14, *Corr. Nap.*, I, 549.
[99] *Corr. Nap.*, I, 532-3.
[100] Debidour, III, 332-4, signed by Carnot, Barras, Reubell.
[101] *Ibid.*, 658 [Correspondance inédite de Napoléon Bonaparte (Panckoucke), II, 55-56].
[102] Debidour, III, 718, signed by Carnot, Larevellière, Reubell.
[103] *Ibid.*, IV, 44-45, signed by Carnot, Reubell, Barras.
[104] *Ibid.*, footnote, 45. (*Corr. Nap.* II, 28-32).
[105] *Ibid.*, 44, signed by Carnot, Letourneur, Larevellière.
[106] *Corr. Nap.* II, 73-74.
[107] Debidour, IV, 281.
[108] *Ibid.*, 281-3.
[109] *Ibid.*, 287-9 signed by all five Directors.
[110] *Corr. Nap.*, II, 119-120.
[111] *Ibid.*, 209.
[112] Collection Labouchère, pièce 151.
[113] Debidour, IV, 559, signed by Carnot, Reubell, Larevellière.
[114] *Ibid.*, 628-9, January 7, 1797, written by Carnot, and signed also by Reubell and Larevellière. This despatch acknowledged the receipt of six despatches from Bonaparte.
[115] *Ibid.*, 627, written by Carnot, and signed also by Reubell and Larevellière.
[116] *Ibid.*, 627, written by Carnot, and signed also by Reubell and Larevellière.
[117] *Ibid.*, 710; 715-716, January 23.
[118] *Ibid.*, 727, January 26.
[119] *Ibid.*, 715, footnote; *Corr. Nap.*, II, 267-9. Clarke's presence in Italy

was not entirely popular with the Army of Italy. Aulard, *Paris pendant le Directoire,* III, 773, Rapport du Bureau Central.

[120] *Corr. Nap.,* II, 282-4.

[121] *Mémoires sur Carnot,* II, pp. 127-128, January 28, 1797.

[122] *Corr. Nap.,* II, pp. 410-11.

[123] *Centenaire de Carnot,* pp. 53-54.

[124] *Ibid.,* pp. 54-55.

[125] Bureaux-Pusy and Carnot had been fellow engineering officers, and the wife of the former was a frequent guest of the Carnots in the Luxembourg.

[126] *Ibid.,* p. 55.

[127] Mathiez, *Le Directoire,* p. 293.

[128] *Ibid.,* p. 294.

CHAPTER IX.
18 FRUCTIDOR

[1] The brilliant mathematician and physicist, author of the famous second law of Thermodynamics, who died prematurely on August 24, 1832.

[2] *Centenaire de Carnot,* pp. 62-69.

[3] These two men did not share Carnot's views at the time. Tronson-Duçoudry came over to them later, but Portalis never did.

[4] *Ibid.,* pp. 72-73.

[5] A Mathiez, "La Fortune de Carnot," *Annales Révolutionnaires,* XI, 1919, pp. 123-124; Arch. Nat., C 353.

[6] Carnot Feulins, *op. cit.,* p. 228.

[7] Debidour, III, 488, May 27, 1796, signed by Carnot, Reubell, Larevellière.

[8] Arago wrote of this work: "Carnot analyse les traits fondamentaux et caracteristique de la methode leibnitzienne avec une clarté, une sureté de jugement et une finesse d'aperçus qu'on chercherait vainement ailleurs, quoique la question ait été l'object des meditations et des recherches des plus grands géomètres de l'Europe." Quoted in *Mémoires sur Carnot,* II, p. 86.

[9] Debidour, II, 495-8.

[10] *Ibid.,* III, 198-202.

[11] Carnot Feulins, *op. cit.,* p. 8.

[12] Aulard, *Paris Pendant le Directoire,* III, p. 483. Report of the Bureau Central, September 23, 1796.

[13] *Ibid.,* II, p. 432.

[14] *Ibid.,* III, p. 735.

[15] *Ibid.,* IV, p. 124. Report of the Bureau Central.

[16] Debidour, II, 81, signed by Larevellière, Reubell, Barras.

[17] *Ibid.,* 200-202, signed by Reubell, Letourneur, Barras, Carnot.

[18] Matheiz, *Le Directoire,* p. 258.

[19] Mathiez, *Le Directoire,* p. 248, says: "Tallien était d'accord avec Barras dans cette intrigue."

[20] *Mémoires sur Carnot,* II, pp. 37-38, for an admirable defense of the freedom of the press.

[21] Mathiez, *Le Directoire,* p. 267.

[22] Aulard, *Paris pendant le Directoire,* IV, pp. 43-44.

[23] Willot evidently owed his military command to Carnot, Mathiez, *Le Directoire,* p. 288. Bonaparte had suggested repeatedly to the Directory that Willot should be relieved.

[24] *Le Directoire,* p. 293.

[25] *Ibid.,* "Il croyait sincèrement que cette paix consoliderait la République et la rendait populaire."

[26] *Souvenirs du Lieutenant Général Comte Mathieu Dumas de 1770 à 1836* (Paris, 1839), III, pp. 83-84.

[27] *Mémoires sur Carnot,* II, p. 102.
[28] Mathiez, *Le Directoire,* p. 295; *Souvenirs . . . de Dumas,* III, p. 82.
[29] Mathiez, p. 295.
[30] Barthélemy only mentions Carnot once in his *Mémoires* and that is when he writes, "Carnot disparu (i. e. on 18 Fructidor)," *Mémoires Historiques et Diplomatiques de Barthélemy* (n. d.), p. 84.
[31] Quoted in Mathiez, p. 296.
[32] *Moniteur,* XXVIII, p. 721.
[33] *Mémoires sur Carnot,* II, p. 123.
[34] *Souvenirs de Dumas,* III, p. 106.
[35] Aulard, *Histoire Politique,* p. 604, Note; Arch, Nat., AFII 8.
[36] Sorel, *Bonaparte et Hoche, en* 1787, p. 152.
[37] Aulard, *Histoire Politique,* p. 658.
[38] *Ibid.*
[39] Masson, *op. cit.,* p. 405.
[40] *Ibid.*
[41] *Ibid.,* p. 406, "Carnot a été obligé d'enregistrer sa defaite."
[42] *Corr. Nap.* III, pp. 188-189.
[43] *Ibid.,* p. 201.
[44] *Mémoirs of Lavallette* (London, 1831), I, pp. 251-252.
[45] Phipps, *op. cit.,* IV, p. 282.
[46] *Ibid.,* p. 283.
[47] *Ibid.,* p. 286.
[48] *Moniteur,* XXVIII, pp. 765-766.
[49] Aulard, *Paris pendant le Directoire,* IV, p. 290, Report of the Bureau Central.
[50] *Ibid.*
[51] Mathiez, *Le Directoire,* p. 302.
[52] Imbert-Colomès,—*Au Conseil des 500, à ses Commettans et au Peuple Français sur la journée du 18 Fructidor* (1797), p. 2, "Le Directoire voulait la guerre, les Conseils reclamait à haute voix la paix. . . . Il se forma deslors dans le Directoire un triumvirat pour travailler à la dissolution du Corps legislatif."
[53] Mathiez, *Le Directoire,* p. 314.
[54] Mathiez, *Le Directoire,* p. 326.
[55] *Mémoires* (1895), I, p. 341.
[56] Baron Longon,—*Evenings with Prince Cambacérès* (1837), I, p. 92.
[57] Hyde de Neuville, *Mémoires et Souvenirs, op. cit.,* pp. 180-182; Lavallette, *op. cit.,* I, pp. 251-252; Lacretelle, *Précis Historique, op. cit.,* II, pp. 34-35; *The Diary and Letters of Gouverneur Morris,* (London, 1889), II, p. 366; Bourrienne, *op. cit.,* I, pp. 87-88, giving Bonaparte's testimony of the innocence of Carnot from the cabals of the period; Henri Lemaire, *De La Révolution du Dix-Huit Fructidor* (Pamphlet an VII), pp. 22-23; Madame de Staël, *op. cit.,* II, p. 182; *Mémoires du Chevalier de La Rue* (ed. of 1885), pp. 34-37, quoted in Aulard, *Histoire Politique,* p. 658; Masson, *op. cit.,* p. 305; Brinton, *op. cit.,* p. 216. "The reactionaries were a miscellaneous lot ranging from Carnot, still at heart a republican, to General Pichegru, who was in the pay of Pitt and the Bourbons."
[58] Aulard, *Histoire Politique,* pp. 658-659.
[59] Mathiez, *Le Directoire,* p. 334.
[60] *op. cit.,* IV, p. 317, the last sentence in the book.
[61] Albert Meynier,—"La Journée du 18 Fructidor an V," *La Révolution Française,* LXXX (1927), p. 32, for a detailed description of Carnot's escape from Paris.
[62] *Centenaire de Carnot,* pp. 73-75.
[63] *Ibid.,* p. 75, note autographe de Carnot, Archives Sadi Carnot.

[64] *Ibid.*, p. 76, quoting "Extrait des Notes Inédites du Général Lomet," Collection Brouwet.

[65] *Réponse de L. N. M. Carnot, Citoyen Français, L'un des fondateurs de la République et Membre Constitutionel du Directoire Exécutif: Au Rapport Fait sur La Conjuration du 18 Fructidor an 5, au Conseil des Cinq-Cents, par J. Ch. Bailleul, au nom d'une commission spéciale.* (Signed at the end by L. N. M. Carnot, 18 Floréal, an 6), Londres, 1799. This copy is identical with one which lists no publisher, no date, no place of publication, and no signature at the end. The writer has a personal copy of this edition, which he has compared with the London edition. References are to the unsigned volume.

[66] *A second Mémoire de Carnot* (Hambourg, 1799), was spurious.

[67] *Réponse à Bailleul,* p. 4.

[68] *Ibid.*, pp. 10-97, and résuméd, pp. 98-104. The *Report of Bailleul* had devoted twelve lines of text, and forty-five lines of notes to Carnot.

[69] *Ibid.*, p. 34.

[70] *Ibid.*, pp. 47-48.

[71] *Ibid.*, pp. 48-49.

[72] *Ibid.*, p. 50.

[73] *Ibid.*, p. 105.

[74] *Ibid.*, pp. 106-108.

[75] *Ibid.*, p. 36.

[76] *Ibid.*, p. 116.

[77] *Ibid.*, p. 131.

[78] *Ibid.*, p. 134.

[79] *Ibid.*, p. 215.

[80] *Ibid.*, p. 196.

[81] *Ibid.*, pp. 196-198.

[82] *Ibid.*, pp. 206-207.

[85] *Ibid.*, pp. 227-228.

[83] *Ibid.*, pp. 224-225.

[84] *Ibid.*, pp. 225-226.

CHAPTER X.
FROM EXILE TO EXILE

[1] August Fournier, *Napoleon the First* (New York, 1903), p. 168.

[2] The First Consul was to receive 500,000 francs annually, his two colleagues, 150,000, Senators, 25,000, Tribunes, 15,000, members of the Legislative Corps, 10,000. The Consuls were to live in the Tuileries.

[3] Archives de la famille Carnot.

[4] *Centenaire de Carnot*, p. 81, letter to his brother at Nolay, March 2, 1800: "Je n'ai pu encore, mon cher ami, t'écrire directement pour te faire part de la joie que j'ai ressentie en rentrant dans le sein de ma famille et te remercier de la part que toi et ta chère femme avez constamment prise à mes malheurs pendant la durée de ma proscription. . . . Je désire infiniment revoir la charmante épouse qui fait ton bonheur et embrasser pour la première fois tes beaux enfants. . . . si vous pouvez vous détacher d'un troisième, envoyez-le-moi, il servira de frère à mon petit Sadi qui est tout seul. . . ."

[5] *Mémoires sur Carnot*, II, p. 212.

[6] *Centenaire de Carnot*, pp. 86-90, notes inédites du Général Lomet, May, 1800 (Collection Brouwet).

[7] *Ibid.*, p. 86.

[8] *Ibid.*, p. 89.

[9] *Ibid.*

[10] *Ibid.*, p. 90, "C'était en effect l'un des hommes les plus aimables, les plus gracieux dans le monde et même dans ce qu'on appelle la haute so-

ciété quand il voulait en prendre la peine; toujours simple, modeste, trop confiant par excès de bonté, il était chéri de ceux qui le connaissent bien et même respecté de ses ennemis. Il a souvent été dupe de grands scélérats, mais il fut toujours calme et juste, et ne fit jamais mal à personne."

[11] *Ibid.*, p. 91.

[12] *Ibid.*, p. 91.

[13] *Ibid.*, p. 92.

[14] See Archives Historiques du Ministère de la Guerre B^{12} 39, and B^{12} 41. In the last one of these the author counted 501 letters registered from the Minister of War from April 15 (twelve days after Carnot took office) to the day he left.

[15] J. H. Clapham, *The Abbe Siéyès* (London, 1912), p. 255.

[16] General Fleishmann, *Mémoirs of Count Miot de Melito* (New York, 1881), p. 171.

[17] *Ibid.*, p. 173.

[18] Maurice Vitrac, *Journal du Comte P. L. Roederer* (Paris, 1909), p. 13.

[19] Joseph Fouché, *Memoirs* (London, 1825), I, p. 159.

[20] *Ibid.*, p. 171.

[21] *Corr. Nap.*, VI, p. 449. General Clarke wrote to Carnot on February 9, 1801, saying that Bonaparte had eulogized his service as Minister, *Centenaire de Carnot*, p. 97.

[22] *Centenaire de Carnot*, p. 95.

[23] *Corr. Nap.*, XXIV, p. 60. Étienne Charavay says that Carnot "apporta dans ses fonctions [as Minister of War] une intégrité rare." *La Grande Encyclopédie*, XIX, p. 478.

[24] *Op. cit.*, I, p. 394.

[25] *Mémoires sur Carnot*, II, p. 229.

[26] Carnot wrote to his brother in Nolay on that day: "J'ai différé à te répondre . . . parceque je m'attendais à chaque instant aux couches de ma femme mais elle s'était trompie dans son calcul et ce n'est que d'aujourd'hui qu'elle a été delivrée heureusement. Elle a mis au monde un garçon fort et bien portant." Archives de la famille Carnot.

[27] Deputy for Paris, 1839-1847; in the Revolution of 1848 he was Minister of Education in the Provisional Government until July 5. Under the Empire he refused to sit in the Legislative Corps until 1864 in order to avoid taking the oath. From 1864 to 1869 he was in the Republican opposition. He was a member of the Constituent Assembly of 1871, and in 1875 he was named senator for life. He was a member of the original board of *La Révolution Française*, and he wrote several works on the history of the Revolution. He died on March 16, 1888, three months after the election of his eldest son, Sadi, to the Presidency of France.

[28] *Centenaire de Carnot*, p. 101.

[29] Étienne Charavay, "Autographes et Documents Révolutionnaires," *La Révolution Française*, VI (1884), including an autograph letter from Carnot to Poultier on March 16, 1802; *Centenaire de Carnot*, pp. 101-102, letter to his brother in Nolay on March 23, . . . "Cette nomination contrarie le plan de retraite que je m'étais formé; mais dans les circonstances actuelles je ne puis refuser le poste honorable auquel je suis appelé par le Sénat. Je désire de tout mon coeur y être utile."

[30] Aulard, *Histoire Politique*, op. cit., p. 761.

[31] *Mémoires sur Carnot*, II, p. 236.

[32] Published in a German translation in Mannheim in 1804.

[33] Published in a German translation in Leipzig in 1805.

[34] *Archives Parlémentaires, de 1800 à 1860*. Deuxième Série, VIII, p. 337, "Le Président [Fabre] annonce [in the Tribunate on May 5] que cet extrait est signé par tous les membres présents a l'exception de celui (Carnot)

qui a manifesté son opposition à la tribune."

[35] *Arch. Parl.,* VIII, pp. 288-290; *Mémoires sur Carnot,* II, pp. 240-248; reproduced in *La Révolution Française,* LXXI (1918), pp. 266-271; *Discours Prononcé par le citoyen Carnot, sur la motion relative au Gouvernement heréditaire.* Séance extraordinaire du 11 Floréal an 12. (Pamphlet published by the Government). Hereinafter referred to as *Tribunat.*

[36] *Tribunat,* p. 2.

[37] *Ibid.,* p. 3.

[38] *Ibid.,* p. 4.

[39] *Ibid.*

[40] *Ibid.,* p. 5.

[41] *Ibid.*

[42] *Ibid.,* pp. 5-6.

[43] *Ibid.,* p. 6.

[44] *Ibid.*

[45] *Ibid.,* p. 7.

[46] *Ibid.,* p. 8.

[47] *Ibid.,* p. 9.

[48] *Ibid.,* pp. 9-10.

[49] *Centenaire de Carnot,* pp. 102-103, a letter from Carnot to his brother in Nolay, "Je suis étonné moi-même du succès prodigieux qu'à obtenu ce discours, dans une ville comme celle-çi, depuis longtemps accoutumée à plier sans resistance à toutes les volontés du maître."

[50] *Cor. Nap.,* XXIX, p. 60.

[51] *Centenaire de Carnot,* pp. 139-141.

[52] *Ibid.,* p. 140.

[53] Paris. 1810, 527 pages.

[54] Of whom he wrote, "Marshal Vauban, perhaps the most philanthropic man of his century," *Défense des Places,* p. 28.

[55] *Défense des Places,* p. 502.

[66] *Ibid.,* p. 12.

[57] *Ibid.,* pp. 15-16.

[58] *Ibid.,* pp. 45-46.

[59] *Ibid.,* p. 97.

[60] *Ibid.,* pp. 94-95.

[61] *Mémoires sur Carnot,* II, p. 275, "Il était touchant de voir ces trois fréres, tendrement unis, souriant aux reminiscenses de leur jeunesse. . . ."

[62] Archives de la famille Carnot.

[63] *Centenaire de Carnot,* p. 107, February 6, 1813.

[64] *Mémoires sur Carnot,* II, p. 288; General Clarke, Minister of War, told Carnot the next day that only he could have written such a letter with impunity, *Ibid.;* Carnot et David, *Mémoires de B. Barère* (1842-1844) IV, pp. 111-112.

[65] General Wauvermans, *Napoléon et Carnot* (Bruxelles, 1888), p. 199.

[66] *Mémoires sur Carnot,* II, p. 339.

[67] *Ibid.,* p. 340, "Il est tellement sage et juste dans ses principes, qu'il vous assure l'approbation des soldats de tous les pays."

[68] The city of Antwerp in 1814 voted to name a street for him and erect a statue to commemorate "the wisdom and benevolence with which [he] exercised the military government in grave and difficult circumstances, solemn and rare tribute to a man called to exercise a dictatorship in time of siege," Wauvermans, *op. cit.,* p. 5. Through the vicissitudes of politics these marks of recognition disappeared, but in 1834 they were restored and the new statue was inscribed: "Au Général Carnot, La ville d'Anvers Reconnaissante."

[69] *Mémoire adressé au Roi en Juillet 1814 par M. Carnot, Lieutenant-*

Général, Chevalier de l'ordre royal et militaire de S. Louis, membre de la Légion d'Honneur, de l'Institut de France, etc., Paris, Plancher, 1814. Also published in 1888 in Paris, under the title *La Fusion des Partis, mémoire adressé au Roi en Juillet, 1814,* par Carnot, Isidor Liseux, ed. In his introduction, the publisher of the 1814 edition called the Mémoire "a pendant to the Social Contract of Rousseau."

[70] *Mémoire au Roi,* p. 9.

[71] *Ibid.*, p. 35.

[72] *Ibid.*, p. 10.

[73] *Ibid.*, p. 12.

[74] *Ibid.*, p. 28.

[75] *Ibid.*, p. 34.

[76] *Ibid.*, p. 37.

[77] *Ibid.*, p. 43.

[78] *The Edinburgh Review,* XXIV, November, 1814, reviewed this *Mémoire* (pp. 182-207), p. 186: "It is singular to find an equal unanimity in extolling his [Carnot's] integrity as a public man. . . . His honesty and consistency are denied by no one. . . . In a word, M. Carnot is, and always has been, a sincere republican. . . . It is undeniable, that he has shown himself the most inflexible friend of liberty whom France has produced."

[79] Baron Longon, *op. cit.,* p. 324.

[80] Baron Longon, *op. cit.,* II, p. 234; Bourrienne, *op. cit.,* III pp. 424-425; *Mémoires, Correspondance et Manuscrits du général Lafayette* (Paris, 1838), V, p. 462; Réné Girard, "Carnot et l'Education populaire Pendant le cent Jours," *La Révolution Française,* LII (1907), pp. 424-425.

[81] *Mémoires sur Carnot,* II, p. 424.

[82] *Ibid.*, pp. 427-429.

[83] Arch. Nat., AFIV 1935, a report to the Emperor on April 29, 1815.

[84] *Centenaire de Carnot,* p. 144.

[85] *Ibid.*, p. 145.

[86] *Mémoires sur Carnot,* II, p. 430.

[87] *Ibid.*

[88] *Ibid.*, P. Mantouchil, "Carnot et L'Union Sacrée en 1815," *La Révolution Française,* LXVIII (1915), pp. 444-445.

[89] *Mémoires sur Carnot,* II, pp. 433-435. Carnot's reputation for courage in facing the Emperor is shown by a letter which was written to him on March 29, 1815, by Captain (of frigate) Baudin (afterward Admiral), and quoted in *Ibid.*, p. 413: "Général, de tous les hommes célèbres qui ont traversé la Révolution française, seul vous avez conservé dans tous les temps et sous tous les gouvernements, la noblesse et la fermeté de votre caractère. C'est aussi de vous seul que la France attend aujourd'hui son salut et l'Europe sa tranquillité, parce que seul vous oserez dire la verité à l'Empereur".

[90] *Mémoires sur Carnot,* II, p. 439.

[91] J. B. Duvergier, ed., *Collection Complète des Lois, Décrets, Ordonnances, Réglemens* (Paris, 1834-1837), XIX, p. 415.

[92] Réné Girard, *La Révolution Française, op. cit.,* p. 433.

[93] *Ibid.*, pp. 433-434.

[94] *Ibid.*, p. 434.

[95] *Mémoires sur Carnot,* II, p. 472.

[96] Arch. Nat. AFIV1934, containing the transactions of this ministry during the Hundred Days; *Mémoires sur Carnot,* II, p. 479, quoting M. Grille, chief of the division of the beaux-arts under Carnot; Arago, *op. cit.,* p. 149; Notes de Lecture, "Une lettre de Carnot en 1815," *"La Révolution Française,* LXVI (1914), pp. 160-161.

[97] The total amount provided for was 90,000,000 francs, which included

2,955,000 for public education, 12,000,000 for the cults, 34,000,000 for roads and bridges, 5,250,000 for public works in Paris, 1,200,000 for public health and welfare, 1,535,000 for science and beaux-arts, 460,000 for the National Institute, and 305,000 for four libraries in Paris.

[98] *Mémoires sur Carnot,* II, p. 505; Girard, *La Révolution Française, op. cit.,* p. 442.

[99] *Mémoires sur Carnot,* II, pp. 510-511.

[100] The Prefect of the Deux-Sèvres wrote to Carnot from Niort on July 3: "Napoleon Bonaparte est entré à Niort dans la nuit du ler au 2me de ce mois le rendant à Rochefort. . . . Dans une circonstance pour moi aussi inattendue, j'ai fait, Monseigneur, ce que devait m'inspirer le respect du au malheur et à l'homme qui pendant si longtems a reglé les destinées de la France," Arch. Nat. AFIV1935.

[101] Duvergier, *op. cit.,* pp. 14-15.

[102] L. N. M. Carnot, *Exposé de La Conduite Politique de M. Le Lieutenant-Général Carnot, Depuis le 1er Juillet 1814.*

[103] *Exposé,* p. 6.

[104] *Ibid.,* p. 24.

[105] *Ibid.,* p. 25.

[106] *Ibid.,* pp. 30-47.

[107] *Ibid.,* p. 28.

[108] *Ibid.,* p. 48.

[109] Marcel Handelman, "L'opinion de Lazare Carnot sur le Cent-Jours," *La Révolution Française,* LXXVI (1925), pp. 140-151, quoting a letter from Leon Dembowski, a Polish youth of twenty, who frequented salons where Carnot appeared, to Joseph Dembowski, on January 13, 1816 (Mss. de la bibliothèque Krasinski à Varsovie, t. 4837).

[110] *Centenaire de Carnot,* pp. 130-131, a letter from Carnot to the Marshal Grouchy in New York, from Magdebourg, November 11, 1816: ". . . J'ai fini par me fixer en Prusse pour me rapprocher un peu de notre patrie." (Collection Brouwet).

[111] Archives de la famille Carnot.

[112] *Recueil de poésies diverses, opuscules Poétiques.* These poems represent a wide range of subject matter. Many of them reveal a deep love of nature. Only a few have a political theme. Some of them verify his appreciation of classical antiquity.

[113] *Don Quichotte,* poëme heroi-comique (176 pages). Lazare Carnot, *Poésies* (Paris, 1894) includes both his poems and his *Don Quichotte,* with a preface by J. de Riols: "Et ce n'est pas sans une agréable surpris qu'on lit ces poésies gaies, fines, vives, mordantes, spirituelles, d'un style alerte, semblante écrites d'hier, et sorties de ce cerveau que l'on se figure avoir toujours été occupé aux plus ardus problemes de la stratégie ou du gouvernement d'une grande nation."

[114] Collection A. Bixio, Autog. II C. Fr. nouv. acq. 22735 (Bibliothèque Nationale, Salle des Manuscrits). Letter from Carnot to Dr. Körte, November 29, 1819, exchanging literary notes, and with this postscript: "Les tendres soins que Madame Körte donne à sa chere petite Marie, m'ont fait venir l'idée de lui envoyer une romance que je fit il y a quelques années sur un sujet analogue; et qui fut mise en musique à Paris, ou cette petite pièce eut beaucoup de vogue. . . ." This letter is a fine example of the beautiful, exact script of Carnot.

[115] Archives de la famille Carnot.

[116] Archives de la famille Carnot. Summarized also in *Mémoires sur Carnot,* II, pp. 619 ff.

[117] *Mémoires sur Carnot,* I, p. 8, for an attractive picture of Carnot by his son; cf. Sorel, *op. cit.,* V, pp. 8-9; Körte, *op. cit.,* pp. 350-352, for a full de-

scription.

[118] *Ibid.*, Eduard Chapuisat, "Carnot à Genève," *La Révolution Française,* LIV (1908), p. 337; Larevellière-Lepaux, *Mémoires, op. cit.*, pp. 341-342, for a word picture by a political opponent: "Il est très irascible et vindicatif; cependant il s'echappe rarement; il sait dissimuler. Il est plutôt taquin et opinâtre que ferme et resolu. . . . Il est actif et laborieux au délà de toute expression. Il a une grande intelligence et beaucoup d'aptitude pour l'administration dans toutes ses partis. Il a le coup d'oeil prompt et conçoit bien un plan de campagne. . . . Il est tout à fait homme d'esprit."

[119] *Mémoires sur Carnot,* I, pp. 8-9; p. 51.

[120] Barère, *op. cit.*, IV, p. 104; Tissot, *op. cit.*, p. v; p. ix.

[121] Sorel, *op. cit.*, V, pp. 8-9.

[122] Louis Madelin, *La France du Directoire* (Paris, 1922), p. 39.

[123] Étienne Charavay, *La Révolution Française, op. cit.*, XIX, p. 496; Foucart et Finot, *La Défense Nationale Dans le Nord, de 1792 à 1802* (Lille, 1893), II, pp. 702-704.

[124] Arago, *op. cit.*, p. 66.

[125] Barère, *op. cit.*, IV, p. 105; Longon, *op. cit.*, I, p. 92; Aulard, *Études, op. cit.*, pp. 207-208.

[126] Pierre de la Gorce, *Histoire Religieuse de la Révolution Française,* IV, p. 90.

[127] *op. cit.*, V, p. 9.

[128] *La Révolution,* p. 321.

[129] *Mémoires sur La Convention et le Directoire* (1824), II, p. 9, and I, pp. 52-53 for a glowing picture of Carnot. cf. Tissot, *op. cit.*, p. xv.

[130] *Histoire de la Restauration,* II, pp. 323.

[131] *Corr. Nap.*, XXIX, pp. 59-60; Lavallette, *Memoirs,* II, p. 192. ". . . inflexibility of conscience and the wonderful disinterestedness that have made him hitherto inaccessible both to the seduction and to the threats and severity of power. . . . This austere republican was . . . a good and amiable man; in the bosom of his family he was indulgent to weakness and error;" M. F. Barrière, *Mémoires du général Dumouriez* (Paris, 1848), XII, pp. 81-82, concluding: "Carnot sera regardé de la posterité comme un philosophe austère, un parfait citoyen, bon epoux, et un grand homme."

[132] Editorial, *The Edinburgh Review,* XXIV, November, 1814, p. 186.

[133] J. C. Colfavru, "La Statue de Carnot à Nolay," *La Révolution Française,* (1881), I, p. 81.

[134] *Mémoires sur Carnot,* I, p. 52.

[135] Körte, *op. cit.*, p. 30: Er hatte nur das Vaterland in Auge."

[136] *Mémoires sur Carnot,* I, p. 27, "La vie politique de Carnot se manifeste, en effect, à qui veut bien l'étudier, par un caractère essentielle; c'est le patriotisme qui en fait l'unité. L'indépendance nationale est sa préoccupation incessante."

[137] C. J. H. Hayes, *Essays on Nationalism op. cit.*, p. 102: "For nationalism truly became a religion with the French Revolutionaries."

[138] Lieut-Col. Sadi Carnot, great-grandson of Lazare Carnot, in a letter to the writer, on December 5, 1936: "Mais il [family tree] vous donnera la note de milieu dont est sorti L. Carnot. Ces 18 familles appartiennent toutes à la bourgeoisie rurale de sa province, et même de son canton ou des environs immédiats. C'est une classe qui a été peu étudiée, bien qu'elle forme une base solide de notre nation, par la fermeté de ses traditions." cf. Colfavru, *La Révolution Française,* op. cit., I, p. 86: "Admirable famille de serviteurs de la democratie qui se transmet de génération en génération, comme le seul titre de noblesse, digne de son ambition, le culte de la patrie, le dévouement à la République, et la glorification par les oeuvres de notre immortelle révolution."

BIBLIOGRAPHY[1]

[1] This Bibliography makes no pretense of being exhaustive for the French Revolution and the Napoleonic Era. It comprises the sources, other than the archival material used, and the literature found to be most useful to the writer in the preparation of this biography. Excellent bibliographical essays are to be found in Crane Brinton,—*A Decade of Revolution, 1789-1799* (New York, 1934), and Geoffrey Bruun,—*Europe and the French Imperium, 1799-1814* (New York, 1938).

I. BIBLIOGRAPHICAL.

Caron, Pierre,—*Bibliographie des Travaux Publiés de 1866 à 1897—Sur L'Histoire de la France depuis 1789.*
Paris, Edouard Cornely et Cie., 1912.
Manuel Pratique pour l'étude de la Révolution Française.
Paris, Librairie Alphonse Picard et Fils, 1912.

Deschiens, Francois-Joseph,—*Collection de Matériaux pour l'Histoire de la Révolution de France depuis 1787 jusqu'au ce jour. Bibliographie des Journaux.*
Paris, Barrois L'Ainé, Libraire, 1829.

Gallois, Léonard,—*Histoire des Journaux et Des Journalistes de la Révolution Française, 1789-1796.* 2 vols.
Paris, au Bureau de la Société de l'Industrie Fraternelle, 1845-1846.

Kircheisen, F. M.—*Bibliographie Napoléonienne.*
Paris, H. Chapelot, 1902.
La bibliographie du temps de Napoléon, Comprenant l'histoire des États-Unis.
Paris, Champion, 1908.

Tourneux, Maurice,—*Bibliographie de l'Histoire de Paris pendant la Révolution française.*
Paris, Imprimerie nouvelle, 1890-1906.
Les Sources bibliographiques de l'histoire de la Révolution française.
Paris, Alph. Picard, 1898.

Tuetey, Alexandre,—*Repertoire général des sources manuscrites de l'histoire de Paris pendant la Révolution francaise.* 11 vols.
Paris, Imprimerie nouvelle, 1890-1914.

II. DOCUMENTS.

1. *Archives Parlementaires de 1787 à 1860.*
Première série (1787 à 1799), Paris, Paul Dupont, 1867.
2. *Archives Parlementaires de 1800 à 1860.*
Deuxième série, Paris, Paul Dupont, 1862.
3. Aulard, F. A.—*Paris Pendant la Réaction Thermidorienne et sous le Directoire.* 5 vols.

Paris, Librairie Leopold Cerf, 1898-1902.
4. Aulard, F. A., ed.—*Recueil des Actes du Comité de Salut Public.* 25 vols.
Paris, Imprimerie Nationale, 1889-1918.
5. Charavay, Étienne,—*Correspondance Générale de Carnot.* Paris, Imprimerie Nationale, Vol. I, 1892; vol. II, 1894; vol. III, 1897; vol. IV (ed. Paul Mautouchet), 1907.
6. *Constitutions de France, 1791-1830.*
Paris, Amable Costes, Libraire, 1830.
7. Debidour, A., ed.—*Recueil des Actes du Directoire Exécutif.* 4 vols.
Paris, Imprimerie Nationale, 1910-1917.
8. Duvergier, J. B., ed.—*Collection Complète des Lois, Décrets, Ordonnances, Reglemens, etc., (De 1788 à 1830).* 20 vols.
Deuxième ed., Paris, A. Guyet et Scribe, 1834-1837.
9. *Le Moniteur Universel.*
Original Edition, Reprint Edition of 1796, and Réimpression Edition of 1840.
10. Napoléon Ier, *Correspondance de,* 32 vols.
Paris, Henri Plon, 1858-1870.

III. SOURCES.

1. *Anti-Jacobin Review and Magazine, The*—Vol. I (July to December, 1798), London, 1799.
2. Aulard, F. A.—*La Société des Jacobins.* 6 vols. Paris, Jouaust, puis Cerf, Noblet, Quantin, 1889-1897.
3. Le Baron de B*** (Charles Doris),—*Vie Priveé, Politique et Morale de Lazare-Nicolas-Marguerite Carnot.*
Paris, Imprimerie de Mme. Ve. Perronneau, 1816.
4. Barriere, M. F.—*Mémoires du général Dumouriez.*
Paris, Librairie de Firmin Didot Frères, 1848.
5. Barthélemy, *Mémoires Historiques et Diplomatiques.* n. d.
6. Bourrienne, Louis A. F. de—*Mémoires de M. de Bourrienne, etc.* 10 vols.
Paris, Ladvocat, 1829. Éd. nouvelle, Paris, Garnier frères, 1899.
7. Bourrienne, M. de—*The Life of Napoleon Bonaparte.* 3 vols. London, Henry Colburn and Richard Bently, 1830.
8. de Broglie, le Duc et le Baron de Staël,—*Considérations sur les Principaux Evénéments de La Révolution Française, ouvrage posthume de Madame le Baronne de Staël.* Tomes I and II.
Paris, Delaunay, Libraire, 1818.
9. Carnot, Hippolyte,—*Mémoires sur Carnot, par son Fils.* 2 vols.

Paris, Paguerre, Libraire-Éditeur, 1861-1863.
10. Carnot, Hippolyte et David,—*Mémoires de B. Barère.* 4 vols. Paris, Jules Labitte, Libraire-Éditeur, 1842-1844. London, H. S. Nichols (transl. De V. Payen-Payne), 1896.
11. Carnot, L. N. M.—*Campagne des Français, depuis le 8 September*, 1793, etc. Paris, L'Imprimerie de la République, Messidor, an III (1795).
12. Carnot, L. N. M.—*Don Quichotte.* Paris, F. A. Brockhaus, 1821.
13. Carnot, L. N. M.—*Exploits des Français,* etc. Bâle, J. Decker, 1796.
14. Carnot, L. N. M.—*Exposé de La Conduite Politique de M. Le Lieutenant-Général Carnot, Depuis le I er Juillet 1814.* Paris, Mme Ve. Courcier, 1815.
15. Carnot, L. N. M.—*Mémoire adressé au Roi en Juillet 1814.* Paris, Plancher, 1814, in "Pièces Diverses," vol. 23. Also *La Fusion des Partis,* etc., Paris, Isidore Liseux, Editeur, 1888.
16. Carnot, L. N. M.—*Recueil de Poésies Diverses, Opuscules Poétiques.* Paris, Baudouin Frères, 1820.
17. Carnot, L. N. M.—*Réponse de L. N. M. Carnot, Citoyen Français . . . au Rapport Fait sur La Conjuration du 18 fructidor, an 5 . . . par J. Ch. Bailleul.* Londres, 1799.
18. Carnot, M.—*De la Défense des Places Fortes.* Paris, Chez Courcier, 1810.
19. Carnot, M.—*Éloge de M. le Maréchal de Vauban.* Dijon, Imprimerie de J. B. Capel, 1784.
20. Carnot, Sadi, ed.—*Centenaire de Lazare Carnot, 1753-1823,* Notes et Documents Inédits. Paris, La Sabretache, 1923.
21. Carnot de Feulins—*Histoire du Directoire Constitutionnel.* Paris, an 8 (1800).
22. Chateaubriand, François Auguste Réné,—*Mémoires D'Outre Tombe,* Tome III (Nouvelle edition par Edmond Biré). Paris, Garnier Frères, 1910.
23. Dumas—*Souvenirs du Lieutenant Général Comte Mathieu Dumas, de 1770 à 1836.* (Publiés par son Fils.) 3 vols. Paris, Librairie de Charles Gasselin, 1839.
24. Duruy, George,—*Mémoires de Barras.* 4 vols. Paris, Librairie Hachette et Cie., 1895-1896. New York, Harper and Brothers, 1895-1896. English edition in four volumes, translated by C. E. Roche.
25. Fleishman, General,—*Memoirs of Count Miot de Melito.*

New York, Charles Scribner's Sons, 1881.

26. Foucart, Paul et Finot, Jules,—*La Défense Nationale Dans le Nord de 1792 à 1802.* 2 vols.
Lille, Imprimerie Fefebre-Ducrocq, 1893.
27. Fouché, Joseph,—*Memoirs.* 2 vols.
London, Charles Knight, 1825.
28. Henry, Charles,—*Correspondance inédite de Condorcet et de Turgot, 1770-1779.*
Paris, Charavay Frères, 1883.
29. Hyde de Neuville, Baron,—*Mémoires et Souvenirs.* 3 vols.
Paris, Librairie Plon, 1888-1892.
30. Jomini, A. H.—*Histoire critique et militaire des Guerres de la Révolution.* 6 vols.
Paris, Chez Anselm et Pochard, 1820.
31. Körte, Wilhelm,—*Das Leben L. N. M. Carnots.*
Leipzig, F. U. Brockhaus, 1820.
32. Lacretelle, jeune (Charles-Joseph),—*Précis Historique de la Révolution Française, Convention Nationale.* 2 vols.
Paris, De l'Imprimerie de Didot Jeune, 1803; *Directoire Exécutif,* 2 vols., 1806.
33. Lafayette,—*Mémoires, Correspondance et Manuscrits Du Général Lafayette.* Tomes Quatrième et Cinquième.
Paris, H. Fournier Ainé, Editeur, 1838.
34. Larevellière-Lepaux,—*Mémoires.* (Publié par son Fils) 3 vols.
Paris, Librairie Plon, 1895.
35. Lavallette, Count,—*Memoirs.* 2 vols.
London, Henry Colburn and Richard Bently, 1831.
36. Longon, Baron,—*Evenings with Prince Cambaceres.* 2 vols.
London, Henry Colburn, 1837.
37. Masson, Frédéric, ed.—*Aventures de Guerre, 1792-1809.*
Paris, Boussod, Valadon et Cie., 1894.
38. Michel, Andre,—*Correspondance Inédite de Mallet du Pan.* Tome II.
Paris, Librairie Plon, 1884.
39. Morris—*The Diary and Letters of Gouverneur Morris,* (ed. Anne C. Morris).
London, Kegan Paul, Trench and Co., 1889.
40. Napoléon,—*Correspondance de Napoléon Premier.* Tome Vingt-Neuvième.
Paris, Henri Plon, J. Dumaine, 1870.
41. O'Connor, A. C. and Arago, M. F.—*Oeuvres de Condorcet.*
Paris, Didot Frères, 1847-1849.
42. Rioust, M. N.—*Carnot.*
Gand, G. De Busscher et Fils, 1817.

43. Saint-Beuve, C.-A.—*Causeries du Lundi* (Troisième Édition) XIV et XV.
Paris, Garnier Frères, 1885.
44. Saint-Simon,—*Mémoires.* (Éd. A. De Boislisle), XIV.
Paris, Librairie Hachette et Cie., 1899.
45. Thibaudeau, A. C.—*Mémoires sur La Convention et Le Directoire.* 2 vols.
Paris, Baudouin Frères, 1824.
46. Tissot, P. F.—*Mémoires Historiques et Militaires sur Carnot.*
Paris, Baudouin Frères, 1824.
47. Vitrac, Maurice,—*Journal du Comte P. L. Roederer.*
Paris, H. Daragon, Editeur, 1909.

IV. PAMPHLETS.
1. Anonymous—"De la Tyrannie de Carnot."
Paris, à l'Imprimerie de l'Ami des Lois, an 6.
2. Carnot, "Discours prononcé par le Citoyen Carnot, séance extraordinaire du 11 Floréal an 12." *Tribunat,* 1804.
3. Carnot, "Réponse du President de la Convention, la séance du 27 Floréal, an II," *Convention Nationale,* an II.
4. Chaumontguitry, Guy,—"Essai sur les Causes qui, depuis le 18 fructidor, etc.," *Thermidor,* an VII.
5. Convention Nationale, "Rapport et Projet et Décret, etc., le 9 Juin, 1782," *Recueil des Pièces des l'Assemblé Nationale,* 1792.
6. Faure, P. J. D. C.—"Sur le proces des quatre deputés, etc.," *Convention Nationale,* l'an III.
7. Florville, des Basses-Alpes,—"Vie Politique D'un membre du Directoire ou Les Sécrets Revélés." n. d. (1799).
8. Imbert-Colomes—"Au Conseil des 500, à ses Commettans et au Peuple Français sur la journée du 18 Fructidor," Francfort, 1797.
9. Jordan, Camille,—"A Ses Commettans sur la Révolution du 18 Fructidor," Hambourg, 1798.
10. Lecointre, Laurent,—"Les Crimes de Sept Membres des anciens Comités de Salut Public, etc.," *20 Brumaire,* an 3.
11. Lemaire, Henri,—"De la Révolution du Dix-Huit Fructidor an Cinquième," an VII.

V. SECONDARY WORKS.
1. Arago, M.—*Biographie de Lazare-Nicholas-Marguerite Carnot.*
Paris, Typographie de Firmin Didot Frères, Imprimeurs de l'Institut, 1850.
2. Aulard, F. A. et Mirkine-Guetzevich, M. B.—*Les Déclara-*

tions des Droits de l'homme, Textes constitutionnels concernant les droits de l'homme et les garanties des libertés individuelles dans tous les pays.
Paris, Payot, 1929.

3. Aulard, F. A.—*Études et Leçons sur la Révolution Française.*
(Ch. IX, "Les Responsabilités de Carnot.")
Paris, Felix Alcan, Editeur, 1893.
4. Aulard, F. A.—*Histoire Politique de la Révolution Française* (1789-1804).
Paris, Librairie Armand Colin, 1901.
5. Becker, Carl L.—*The Heavenly City of the Eighteenth-Century Philosophers.*
New Haven, Yale University Press, 1932.
6. Biré, Edmond,—*Legendes Révolutionnaires.*
Paris, Honoré Champion, Libraire, 1893.
7. Bonnal, Edmond,—*Carnot D'Après Les Archives Nationales, Le Depot de La Guerre et Les Séances de La Convention.*
Paris, E. Dentu, 1888.
8. Bonneville de Marsongy, Louis,—*Autour de la Révolution.*
Paris, Librairie Plon, 1895.
9. Borni, Jules,—*Histoire des Idées Morales et Politique en France au Dix-Huitième Siècle.*
Paris, C. Baillière, 1865-1873.
10. Brinton, Crane,—*A Decade of Revolution, 1789-1799.*
New York, Harper & Brothers, 1934.
11. Brinton, Crane,—*The Jacobins.*
New York, The Macmillan Co., 1930.
12. Bruun, Geoffrey,—*Saint-Just, Apostle of the Terror.*
Cambridge, Houghton Mifflin Co., 1932.
13. Bruun, Geoffrey,—*Europe and the French Imperium, 1799-1814.*
New York, Harper & Brothers, 1938.
14. Burdeau, Auguste,—*Les Carnot, Une Famille Républicain,* 1753-1887, Paris, Librairie S. Pitrat, 1888.
15. Bury, J. B.—*The Idea of Progress.*
London, Macmillan & Co., Ltd., 1920.
16. *Cambridge Modern History,* vols. VIII and IX.
Cambridge, University Press. 1904, 1906.
17. Clapham, J. H.—*The Abbe Sieyes.*
London, P. S. King & Son, 1912.
18. Coker, F. W.—*Readings in Political Philosophy.*
New York, The Macmillan Co., 1926.
19. Conaway, Horace Mann,—*The First French Republic,* etc., Columbia University Dissertations, Vol. 39.

New York, Columbia University, 1902.

20. Cornereau, A.—*Deux Lauréats de l'Académie de Dijon.* J. J. Rousseau, 9 Juillet 1750, Lazare Carnot, 2 Août 1784. Dijon, Imprimerie Darantiere, 1903.
21. Dorn, Walter L.,—*Competition for Empire,* 1740-1763. New York, Harper and Brothers, 1940.
22. Dreyfus, Ferdinand,—*Vauban Économiste.* Paris, Librairies-Imprimeries Réunies, 1892.
23. Duruy, Albert,—*L'Instruction Publique et la Révolution.* Paris, Librairie Hachette et Cie., 1881.
24. Dussauge, André,—*Le Ministère de Belle-Isle,* Études sur la guerre de Sept ans. Paris, L. Fournier, 1914.
25. Fournier, August,—*Napoleon the First.* New York, Henry Holt & Co., 1903.
26. Gershoy, Leo,—*The French Revolution and Napoleon.* New York, F. S. Crofts & Co., 1933.
27. Goncourt, Edmond et Jules de,—*Histoirè de la Société Française pendant la Révolution.* (Quatrième ed.) Paris, Didier et Cie., 1875.
28. Gorce, Pierre de la,—*Histoire Religieuse de la Révolution Française,* IV. Paris, Plon-Nourrit et Cie., 1921.
29. Gottschalk, Louis R.,—*The Era of the French Revolution.* Cambridge, Houghton, Mifflin Co., 1929.
30. Greer, Donald,—*The Incidence of the Terror during the French Revolution.* Cambridge, Harvard University Press, 1935.
31. Hamel, Ernest,—*Histoire de Robespierre.* Tome I, Paris, Librairie Internationale, 1865. Tome, III, Paris, Chez l'Auteur, 1867.
32. Hart, Liddell,—*The Ghost of Napoleon.* New Haven, Yale University Press, 1934.
33. Hayes, C. J. H.—*Essays on Nationalism.* New York, The Macmillan Co., 1926.
34. Hennet, Léon,—*État Militaire de France pour l'Anneé 1793.* Paris, la Société de l'Histoire de la Révolution française, 1903.
35. Jellinek, Georg,—*The Declaration of the Rights of Man and the Citizen.* New York, Henry Holt & Co., 1901.
36. Kerr, Wilfred B.—*The Reign of Terror.* Toronto, University of Toronto Press, 1927.
37. M. de Lauwereyns de Roosendaele—*Les Carnots et Saint-Omer.*

Saint-Omer, 1889.
38. Lefebvre, A.—*Les Thermidoriens.*
Paris, Armand Colin, 1937.
39. Mac-Auliffe, Léon,—*La Personalité et L'Herédité.*
Paris, Librairie Scientifique Amédée Le Grand, (1932).
40. Madelin, Louis,—*La France du Directoire.*
Paris, Librairie Plon, 1922.
41. Madelin, Louis,—*The French Revolution.*
New York, G. P. Putnam's Sons, 1926.
42. Madelin, Louis,—*La Révolution.*
Paris, Librairie Hachette et Cie., 1912.
43. Madelin, Louis,—*The Revolutionnaries.*
(Translated by R. J. S. Curtis)
London, Arrowsmith, 1930.
44. Masson, Frederic,—*Le Département des Affairs Étrangères pendant La Révolution, 1787-1804.*
Paris, E. Plon et Cie., 1877.
45. Mathiez, Albert,—*After Robespierre,* The Thermidorian Reaction.
Translated by Catherine Alison Phillips.
New York, Alfred A. Knopf, 1931.
46. Mathiez, Albert,—*Autour de Robespierre.*
Paris, Payot, 1925.
47. Mathiez, Albert,—*Le Directoire.*
Paris, Librairie Armand Colin, 1934.
48. Mathiez, Albert,—*The Fall of Robespierre.*
New York, Alfred A. Knopf, 1927.
49. Mathiez, Albert,—*The French Revolution.*
New York, Alfred A. Knopf, 1928.
50. Mathiez, Albert,—*Girondins et Montagnards.*
Paris, Firmin-Didot et Cie., 1930.
51. Mathiez, Albert,—*La Victoire en L'An II.*
Paris, Librairie Felix Alcan, 1916.
52. Mead, W. E.,—*The Grand Tour in the Eighteenth Century.*
Boston, Houghton Mifflin Co., 1914.
53. Meynier, Albert,—*Les Coups d'État du Directoire.* 3 vols.
Paris, Les Presses Universitaires, 1928.
54. Mortimer-Ternaux—*Histoire de la Terreur, 1792-1794.* 8 vols.
Paris, Michel Levy Frères (and Calmann Levy for final volumes), 1868-1881.
55. Nauroy, Charles,—*Révolutionnaires.*
Paris, Albert Savine, ed., 1891.
56. Ording, Arne,—*Le Bureau de police du Comité de salut public. Étude sur la Terreur.*

Oslo, Jacob Dybwad, 1930.
57. Parker, H. T.—*The Cult of Antiquity and the French Revolutionaries.*
Chicago, University of Chicago Press, 1937.
58. Phipps, R. W.—*The Armies of the First French Republic.* 4 vols.
London, Oxford University Press, 1926-1935.
59. Ritchie, D. G.—*Natural Rights.*
London, Swan Sonnenschein & Co., 1895.
60. Rose, J. H.—*The Life of Napoleon I.*
New York, The Macmillan Co., 1916.
61. Roujon, Jacques,—*Louvois et son Maitre.*
Paris, Grosset, 1934.
62. Roustan, M.—*The Pioneers of the French Revolution.*
London, Ernest Benn, Ltd., 1926.
63. Sabine, G. H.—*A History of Political Theory.*
New York, Henry Holt and Co., 1937.
64. Sagnac, Philippe et Robiquet, Jean,—*La Révolution de 1789.* 2 vols.
Paris, Les Editions Nationales, 1934.
65. Sicard, L'Abbé Augustin,—*Les Études Classiques avant La Révolution.*
Paris, Perrin et Cie., 1887.
66. Smollett, Tobias,—*Travels through France and Italy.*
London, Oxford University Press, 1907.
67. Sorel, Albert,—*Bonaparte et Hoche en 1797.*
Paris, Librairie Plon, 1896.
68. Sorel, Albert,—*L'Europe et La Révolution Française.* 5 vols.
Paris, Librairie Plon, 1885-1903.
69. Taine, H.—*Les Origines de la France Contemporaine—La Révolution,* III.
Paris, Hachette et Cie., 1885.
70. Toutain, Jules,—*La Gaule Antique vue dans Alesia.*
La Charité-sur-Loire, A. Delayance, 1932.
70. Tyson and Guppy, ed.,—*The French Journals of Mrs. Thrale and Doctor Johnson.*
Manchester, Manchester University Press, 1932.
72. Vaughan, C. E.—*The Political Writings of Jean Jacques Rosseau.* 2 vols.
Cambridge, Cambridge University Press, 1915.
73. Wallon, Henri,—*Les Répresentants du Peuple en mission et La Justice Révolutionnaire. Vol. IV.*
Paris, Librairie Hachette et Cie., 1890.
74. Wauvermans, General,—*Napoleon et Carnot,* Episode de l'Histoire militaire d'Anvers.

Bruxelles, Th. Falk, ed., 1888.
75. Wilkinson, Spenser,—*The French Army before Napoleon.* Oxford, The Clarendon Press, 1915.
76. Young, Arthur,—*Travels in France and Italy.* New York, E. P. Dutton & Co., 1915.

VI. PERIODICALS.

1. Arbelet, Paul,—"La Jeunesse de Prieur de la Côte-d'Or," *Revue de Dix-Huitième Siècle,* 5e année, No. 2, 1918, pp. 97-115.
2. Aulard, F. A.—"Les Idées Politiques de Carnot." *La Révolution Française,* XIV, 1888, pp. 640-658.
3. Aulard, F. A.—Review of M. Bonnal's *Carnot D'Après Les Archives Nationales, Le Depot de La Guerre et Les Séances de la Convention,* in *La Révolution Française,* XV, 1888, pp. 567-571.
4. Aulard, F. A.—Review of Charavay, Étienne, *Correspondance de Carnot, I,* in *La Révolution Française,* XXIII, 1892, pp. 190-192.
5. Caron, P.—Review of Arne Ording's *Le Bureau de police du Comité de salut public,* in *La Révolution Française,* LXXXIV, 1931, pp. 84-86.
6. Chapuisat, Edouard,—"Carnot à Geneve," *La Révolution Française,* LIV, 1908, pp. 334-340.
7. Charavay, Étienne,—"Autographes et Documents Révolutionaires," *La Révolution Française,* VI, 1884, pp. 726-732.
8. Charavay, Étienne,—"Lazare Carnot D'Aprés Sa Correspondance," *La Révolution Française,* XIX, 1890, pp. 481-506.
9. Colfavru, J.-C.—"Opinion de Lazare Carnot sur le principe de l'obéissance Passive dans l'armée," *La Révolution Française,* VI, 1884, pp. 992-998.
10. Colfavru, J.-C.—"Opinion de Robespierre sur la necessité et la nature de la Discipline militaire," *La Révolution Française,* VII, 1885, p. 268.
11. Colfavru, J.-C.—Review of Hippolyte Carnot's *La Révolution Française, Résumé Historique,* in *La Revolution Française,* V, 1883, pp. 177-180.
12. Colfavru, J.-C.—"La Statue de Carnot à Nolay," *La Révolution Française,* I, 1881, pp. 81-86.
13. Destrem, Jean,—"Les Mémoires de Larevellière-Lepeaux," *Revue Historique,* X, 1879, pp. 68-91.
14. E. C.,—Review of *Mémoires sur Carnot par son Fils* (School edition of 1893), *La Révolution Française,* XXV, 1893, p. 96.

15. Editorial, *Edinburgh Review, The,* XXIV, Nov., 1814.
16. Farges, Louis,—Review of *Notice Sur M. Hippolyte Carnot,* by M. Ant. Lefevre-Pontalis, *Revue Historique,* XLVII, 1891, pp. 100-101.
17. Farges, Louis,—Review of Charavay, Étienne, *Correspondance Générale de Carnot,* I, *Revue Historique,* L, 1892, pp. 360-361.
18. Gamiers, Arthur de,—"Lazare Carnot, L'Organizateur de la Victoire," *Revue des Questions Historiques,* XXVIII, 1893, pp. 444-483.
19. Girard, René,—"Carnot et l'Éducation Populaire Pendant le cent Jours," *La Révolution Française,* LII, 1907, pp. 424-448.
20. Handelsman, Marcel,—"L'Opinion de Lazare Carnot sur les cent Jours," *La Révolution Française,* LXXVI, 1923, pp. 149-151.
21. *Historische Zeitschrift,* VIII, 1862, p. 461, brief note on *Mémoires sur Carnot par son Fils,* I.
22. Mantouchil, P.—"Carnot et 'L'Union Sacrée' en 1815," *La Révolution Française,* LXVIII, 1915, pp. 444-454.
23. Mathiez, Albert,—"Les Divisions Dans Les Comités du Gouvernement à la Veille du 9 Thermidor," *Revue Historique,* CXVIII, 1915, pp. 70-87.
24. Mathiez, Albert,—"La Fortune de Carnot," *Annales Révolutionnaires,* XI, 1919, pp. 123-124.
25. Mautouchet, P.—Review of Albert Meynier's *Les Coups d'État du Directoire,* in *La Révolution Française,* XCIII, 1930, pp. 79-85.
26. Meynier, Albert,—"La Journée du 18 Fructidor, an V," *La Révolution Française,* LXXX, 1927, pp. 23-45.
27. Meynier, Albert,—"Le Prétendu Complot Royaliste de Fructidor An V," *La Révolution Française,* LXXX, 1937, pp. 236-248.
28. Monod, G.—Review of Charavay, Étienne, *Correspondance Générale de Carnot,* I, in *Revue Historique,* LIV, 1894, pp. 111-112.
29. Notes de Lecture, "Une Lettre de Carnot en 1815," *La Révolution Française,* LXVI, 1914, pp. 160-161.
30. Ording, Arne,—Letter in *La Révolution Française,* LXXXIV, 1931, pp. 352-354, in reply to a letter of Lieut.-Col. Carnot, *Ibid.,* pp. 177-179.
31. Pierre, Victor,—Review of *Notice Sur M. Hippolyte Carnot* by M. Lefevre-Pontalis in *Revue des Questions Historiques,* L, 1891, pp. 696-697.
32. Réimpressions, "Discours prononcé au Tribunat par Carnot

sur la motion relative au Gouvernement Héréditaire, Séance extraordinaire, du 11 Floréal, an XII," *La Révolution Française,* LXXI, 1918, pp. 266-271.
33. Reuss, Rod.,—Review of P. Mautouchet's *Correspondance Générale de Carnot,* IV, *Revue Historique,* C. 1909, pp. 335-336.
34. Schnerb, R.—"Une lettre inédite de Carnot," *Annales Revolutionnaires,* XIV, 1922, pp. 508-509.
35. Schroeder, V.—"Robespierre, homme de lettres," *Revue du Dix-Huitième Siècle,* 3 e Année, No. 2, 1916, pp. 149-162.
36. Sorel, Albert,—"Le Comité de Salut Public et La Question de la Rive Gauche du Rhin en 1795." *Revue Historique,* XVIII, 1882, pp. 273-322.
37. Welvert, Eugène,—"Les Conventionnels Régicides Après La Révolution," *Revue Historique,* LXIV, 1897, pp. 298-326.
38. Welvert, Eugène,—"Les Derniers Conventionnels," *Revue Historique,* LXVIII, 1898, pp. 55-60.

INDEX